Hermann Wilhelm Ebel, William Kirby Sullivan

Celtic Studies from the German

Hermann Wilhelm Ebel, William Kirby Sullivan

Celtic Studies from the German

ISBN/EAN: 9783337296872

Printed in Europe, USA, Canada, Australia, Japan

Cover: Foto ©Thomas Meinert / pixelio.de

More available books at **www.hansebooks.com**

CELTIC STUDIES.

FROM THE GERMAN OF

DR. HERMANN EBEL

WITH AN

INTRODUCTION

ON ROOTS, STEMS, AND DERIVATIVES, AND ON CASE-ENDINGS OF NOUNS IN THE INDO-EUROPEAN LANGUAGES.

BY

WILLIAM K. SULLIVAN, PH.D., M.R.I.A.,

PROFESSOR IN THE CATHOLIC UNIVERSITY OF IRELAND, AND IN THE MUSEUM OF IRISH INDUSTRY.

C574

WILLIAMS AND NORGATE,
14 HENRIETTA STREET, COVENT GARDEN, LONDON;
AND
20 SOUTH FREDERICK STREET, EDINBURGH.
1863

PREFACE.

THE history of the variation of opinion about the Celtic languages would make a curious and instructive chapter of literary history. Their relationships with other languages, like those of the peoples who spoke them with other branches of the human race, depended rather upon the dictates of passion than of reason. There was indeed but little room in most cases for the exercise of the reason, because those who theorized about the Celtic languages were generally wholly ignorant of them, or, at least, knew them very imperfectly, and in their most modern and corrupt forms. The rudest tongue is dear to those whose first thoughts were expressed in it. The pride which the Irish or Welsh take in their language is legitimate, and the exaggerated estimate which they may sometimes form of the beauties and powers of their respective dialects can readily be pardoned. But the same indulgence cannot be extended to writers who contribute to bring science into discredit, and contempt upon the language and literature of a people, and therefore upon the people themselves, by fanciful and baseless speculations. It matters not whether, like Vallancey's, these speculations tended to exalt the Celtic language, or, like Pinkerton's, to degrade it: both are injurious to the growth of true learning. Indeed, the former are the worse, because passages like the following, written by Mr. Pinkerton, could only degrade the author: " The mythology of the Celtæ (which is yet to be discovered!) resembled in all probability that of the Hottentots or others, the rudest savages, as the Celtæ anciently were, and are little better at present, being incapable of any progress in society". I have called up the literary shade of Pinkerton from the oblivion into which he has sunk, not because these old opinions are now of much consequence of themselves, but because they show one of the extremes of opinion once held regarding the affinities of the Celtic language. This kind of literature now very rarely disgraces comparative philology, but, as may be expected in a subject like ethnology, which, as yet, scarcely deserves the name of a science, and in which mere assertion too frequently usurps the place of inductive hypotheses, it still constitutes, if not an important, at least a very popular element.

There is scarcely a language in the world between which and the Celtic some one has not attempted to prove a connection; or, to speak more precisely, its chief existing dialect, the Irish. The disciples of the Pinkerton school were, of course, desirous that its affinities should be with the languages of the inferior races, and accordingly one found a great similarity between it and the tongue of the Jaloffs, on the coast of Africa; another found that it was a distant cousin of that of the Leni Lenappe, a great family of American Indians, who formerly possessed the region of the Susquehannah. Others, again, found its true relations in the Lappish, the Ostyak, the Tungus dialects, and other tongues of North Siberia. On the other hand, the admirers of the Celtic tongue endeavoured to establish what, at one time, was considered the noblest of origins, a Hebrew descent. This Semitic relationship was, no doubt, suggested by the traditions of an eastern origin, which pervade the Irish chronicles. As every ethnological puzzle was attempted to be solved by means of the Ten lost Tribes of Israel, it was of course suggested that the Irish were descended from them; the favourite Semitic ancestors of the Celts of the west were, however, not the Israelites, but their cousin-germans the Phenicians; as p is always represented in the Irish by f, the *bearla fene* was the *lingua punica:* and then was not the *bálltainé* of May-eve a remnant of the worship of Baal? Carthage was founded by the Phenicians; the Carthaginians must, therefore, have been cousins of the Irish, and, consequently, the fragments of their language preserved in the Pænulus of Plautus may be interpreted through the Irish; and so they were. But Sir W. Betham left Vallancey a great way behind, when he found that the affinities between the Irish and the Hebrew were often so close that he could not detect closer between the Irish and Welsh!

There seems to have always existed among writers on languages a belief in the great antiquity of the Celtic tongues,—that they were much more ancient than most other European languages; and under this impression is was suggested that the Greek, Latin, and even the Sanskrit tongues were derived from them, or rather from a primitive Celtic mother-tongue. If even a fourth or fifth cousinship could not be permitted with the Greek or the Gothic, how could it be tolerated that Celtic should be made the progenitor of them all? Accordingly, such pretensions were thus summarily dismissed by a writer who, whatever may have been his pretensions as an Orientalist, seems to have had no claim to be considered a Celtic scholar, except perhaps that of having a Gaedhelic name. "The Celtic, therefore, when divested of all words which have been introduced into it by conquest and religion, is a perfectly original language; but the originalities incontrovertibly prove that neither Greek, Latin, or the Teutonic dialects, nor Arabic, Persian, or Sanskrit were derived from the Celtic, since these languages have not any affinity whatever with that tongue".* The tradition which brought the Milesian Irish through Spain in their journey from the East, suggested an affinity with the Basques and Gascons, which some persons have stated to be so close, that an educated Irish-speaking man would be able to hold a dialogue with a Basque peasant speaking the Escaldunac. There is, of course, not the shadow of a ground for this statement, but Irish and Basque affinities are still confidently spoken of by English writers who know neither the Irish nor the Escaldunac tongue.

The Escaldunac is not the only tongue, the affinities of which are still doubtful or obscure, with which the Celtic languages have been connected by Engish writers; for Armenian, and Albanian, and even Coptic words have been found in them. That some affinity exists between Celtic and the first two is of course probable enough, as they are now beginning to be considered Indo-European; but the grounds upon which such affinities were assumed were as unscientific as those which connected the Irish with Phenician.

It was only through sources like Pinkerton, Vallancey, Betham,

---

* Researches into the origin and affinity of the principal languages of Asia and Europe, by Lieut.-Col. Vans Kennedy. London, 1828, p. 85.

and Kennedy, that thirty years ago the scholars of France, Germany, and other foreign countries could have learned anything of the Celtic language or literature of these Islands; and scarcely anything was known of the Armoric of Bretagne. What wonder then that Malte Brun, F. Schlegel, and others, should have adopted the opinion of Pinkerton, that Irish was a peculiar language unconnected with the other European tongues? The first man who had the merit of investigating the problem of the affinities of the Celtic was the distinguished ethnologist Dr. Prichard, who in 1832 published a supplement to his Researches into the Physical History of Mankind, under the distinct title of *The Eastern Origin of the Celtic Nations*.[b] Before the publication of this work, Bopp had published his Sanskrit Grammar, and J. Grimm his great German Grammar, works which mark an era in the history of comparative philology. Dr. Prichard was consequently able to base his inquiries upon the labours of these great scholars by whom the true foundation of the science has been laid. Although this work is now of very little, if any use, it was, considering the time at which it was written, and that the author appears to have been only able to use chiefly the modern forms of the Welsh, in which the inflexions are to a great extent lost, a very meritorious work, and one which will always be valuable in a historical point of view, as the first in which a true scientific method of investigation was attempted. In this work Dr. Prichard endeavoured to prove that the true affinities of the Celtic languages were with the Sanskrit, Greek, Latin, Gothic, and Slavonian, which were considered to form a family derived from a single primitive tongue, and to which the name Indo-Germanic was given, and furthermore, that it was a member of that family, which should henceforward more appropriately be termed the Indo-European, or, as it seems now destined to be called, the Aryan family.

Soon after the appearance of Dr. Prichard's work, and, no doubt, owing in a measure to it, the Celtic languages began to attract the attention of Continental scholars. Comparative philology had now grown into a great science, and was vigorously cultivated by many ardent labourers. Between 1837 and 1840,

---

[b] A reprint containing much additional matter, but altogether of an ethnological character, by the editor, Dr. Latham, was published in 1857.

three important works on Celtic philology appeared. The first was *De l'Affinité des Langues Celtiques avec le Sanskrit*, by Adolph Pictet (Paris, 1837). The author, who had long devoted his attention to the subject of Irish antiquities, having published, in 1824, his work on *Du Culte des Cabires chez les Anciens Irlandais*, made the Irish the basis of his study. This work still retains its value, and its author is still an ardent and respected labourer in the same field. The second work was *Die Celtischen Sprachen* of Bopp, which was published at Berlin in 1839. This work, which contains several important discoveries, may be looked upon as a supplement to his great work, the *Comparative Grammar*, which did not include the Celtic. The third work was the *Celtica* of Dr. Diefenbach, which was published at Stuttgart in 1839 and 1840. Although this work is rather ethnological than philological, yet, as the first part was the earliest attempt to bring together the numerous Celtic words, or, at least, those which are presumed to be so, that are scattered through the works of Greek and Roman authors, and determine their comparative etymological relationships with different languages, it must always be regarded as one of the classics of Celtic philology.

The honour of having done in a great measure for the Celtic dialects what J. Grimm did for the Germanic ones by his celebrated grammar, and of having thus established the basis by which the Indo-European character of those dialects could be subsequently rigorously established, was however reserved for J. Kaspar Zeuss. After thirteen years of labour, he unexpectedly presented to the world in 1853 his *Grammatica Celtica*, written in Latin, a monument at once of his genius and of his unexampled perseverance. In this great work he has left us the materials by which we may clearly establish that the Celtic languages are pure Indo-European tongues without any admixture of heterogeneous foreign elements, and consequently that they are members of the family in the same sense that Latin or Gothic is. That the labours of his predecessors had not definitely settled the latter point, or at least had not brought conviction to the minds of many English ethnologists, is very evident from the following observation of Dr. Latham: " *A* relationship was mistaken for *the* relation. The previous tongues were (say) second cousins. The Celtic was a fourth or fifth. What was the result? not that a new second cousin was found, but that the family circle was enlarged".—*Man and his Migrations*, p. 87.

It is right to state that the writer in question does not seem to have been influenced in his opinion by the publication of the *Grammatica Celtica*. The passage above quoted was written in 1851. Here is what he says in 1857: " The real condition, however, in which Prichard left the question was this, viz., that if the value of the class called Indo-European was to be raised by any fresh additions, the Keltic group of languages should form either the part or the whole of such additions. More than this I cannot find in his paper; more than this I cannot find in either Bopp's or Pictet's; more than this I cannot find anywhere. By which I mean that I nowhere find evidence upon either of the two following questions: 1st, That the Kelt (or indeed any other language) can be made Indo-European without raising the value of the term. 2nd, That any good is effected by so raising it.

" If the writers in question expressed themselves to the fact that the tongues in question were absolutely Indo-European, or (still more) if they derived them from the East, they left omissions in their argument which, to say the least, were illegitimate".—*Prichard's Celtic Nations, by Latham*, p. 356.

Dr. Latham, to be sure, seems to attach very little importance to the labours of comparative philologists of the German school; for he does not believe in the method of analysis by letter-changes. He says, " Whether the clever manipulation of letter-changes has, by enabling men to go wrong according to system, done as much harm as it is destined to do, is doubtful. It is pretty certain that it has done almost all the good of which it is capable. For all useful purposes, Prichard used it, the results being what we have seen. It is not, then, from this quarter that any advancement of Kelt ethnology is to be expected"—*ibid.*, p. 382. If the instrument of research in comparative philology be not the use of the laws of letter-changes, what is it? Dr. Latham does not tell us, at least he does not do so in the following passage: " An improved logic, and a greater sobriety of idea, combined with a great breadth of view, are the real desiderata, at least for the settlement of the more general questions"—*ibid.*,

p. 382. These are desiderata in all scientific inquiries, but they do not constitute the method of research of a science. Either the changes which the words of any given language undergo when that language branches into dialects or distinct languages, are arbitrary, or follow regular laws. If the former, the relations of languages can only be guessed at from the accidental resemblance which words may offer when placed at random in parallel columns; in this case there can be no *science* of comparative philology. If the latter, the first problem for the philologist is to determine the phonetic laws of each language; and no dependance can be placed upon any conclusions which may be drawn from researches made upon languages, the phonetic laws of which are not accurately known. These laws can only be determined by careful induction from many and varied researches. Even were the phonetic laws of a whole family of languages accurately known, it does not necessarily follow that every one could use them correctly. As in every other branch of science, a true instrument may be wrongly or unskilfully used. No one objects to mathematics as an instrument of investigation in physical science, because, having been wrongly used, it has sometimes led to erroneous results. For the same reason, the mistakes made by Leo about the Malberg glosses upon a copy of the Lex Salica, or Holtzmann's astounding conclusion that the Gauls were Germans and that both were Celts, is no proof against the doctrine that a correct etymology can only be arrived at by means of a study of the letter-changes. In the hands of Bopp and of his school, comparative philology, founded upon a judicious use of letter-changes, has been raised to the rank of an inductive science. But this does not imply that Bopp never made a wrong induction or proposed a false hypothesis. In comparative philology, as in all other sciences, no hypothesis, however logically established, can be wholly true; the proportion of error in it will, among other things, depend on the state of development of the science, and on the greater or lesser generality of the hypothesis itself—that is, on the greater or lesser number of phenomena embraced by it.

This brings me to a more general objection which is raised, not merely to comparative philology, but to all sciences—namely, that its hypotheses are continually changing. To make this objection, or such an one as has been made to letter-changes, of an illegitimate use having been made of its methods, is to mistake the scaffolding, by means of which an edifice is erected, for the permanent structure itself. If a little more attention were bestowed upon the historical development of different branches of science, the mistake would not be so frequently made. We should then learn what a large amount of scaffolding and useless materials are cast aside in the course of a single century's growth—scaffolding and materials which may, perhaps, have formed the sole subject of that century's intellectual strife.

Once the Celtic tongues were proved to be Aryan, the detailed study of their grammar, from a comparative philological point of view, became a necessity in connection with the comparative grammar of the whole family. In 1856 a special journal was established in Germany, called *Beiträge zur vergleichenden Sprachforschung*, devoted to the Aryan, Celtic, and Slavonian languages, edited by Drs. Kuhn and Schleicher, as a kind of supplement to the well-known *Zeitschrift für vergleichende Sprachkunde*, founded by Drs. Th. Aufrecht and Ad. Kuhn, and now edited by Dr. Kuhn alone, the domain of which is the Germanic, Greek, and Latin. Of the Beiträge, a volume consisting of four parts appears every two years; three volumes have already been published. It is eminently entitled to the support of all persons interested in the advancement of Celtic philology, and no public library in Ireland, Scotland, or Wales, at least, should be without a copy. Besides the papers published in this repertory, there is now quite a Celtic philological literature, of which I shall only mention a few of the most important works, namely, the remarkable book of Glück, about the Celtic names which occur in Cæsar (*Die bei C. J. Cæsar vorkommenden keltischen Namen, in ihrer Echteit festgestellt und erläutert* von Cr. W. Glück, Munich, 1857); the *Ethnogénie Gauloise* of the Baron Belloguet, which contains a Gaulish glossary, and a collection of Gaulish inscriptions; the *Monuments des Anciens Idiomes Gaulois*, par H. Monin, Ancien élève de l'Ecole Normale. Paris, 1861; and the *Origines Europœae—Die Alten Völker Europas mit ihren Sippen und Nachbarn: Studien* von Lorenz Diefenbach. Frankfurt a. M., 1861.

Among the Celtic papers which appeared in the Beiträge

were a remarkable series entitled *Celtic Studies*, by Dr. Hermann Ebel, the separate titles of each being:—1. Loss of *p* in Celtic (vol. I., p. 307); 2. Some prepositions (*ibid.*, 311); 3. The pronoun *som, sem* (*ibid.*, 313); 4. Declension (*ibid.*, 155; No. 4 appeared before the others); 5. The so-called prosthetic *n* (vol. II., p. 64); 6. Addenda to Declension (*ibid.*, 67); 7. The gradation (*ibid.*, p. 78); 8. Phonology (*ibid.*, p. 80). Besides these there is a paper entitled Celtic, Greek, Latin, the subject of which is the position of the Celtic languages in the Indo-European family, and a still more important and elaborate one on the same subject entitled the *Position of the Celtic*. Of the Celtic Studies the most important is the paper No. 4, on Declension; it is indeed nearly equal in length to all the others put together. Nos. 5, 6, and 7 may be looked upon as supplements to No. 4. The object of these papers on declension was to determine, according to the principles of the Boppian School, the kinds of stems which belonged to the several series of each order of declension, according to the classification of Zeuss, and attempt from this to determine the case-endings antecedent to the oldest forms known, and thus determine the various changes which they underwent from the primitive or mother-tongue of the family.

I felt that papers of this kind ought to be brought under the notice of Celtic scholars, and especially of Irish scholars, and I accordingly undertook to translate the papers on declension for the ATLANTIS. When the translation was complete, I found that by itself it would be practically unintelligible to the majority of those for whom it was written. Zeuss has the reputation of being very difficult to be understood, and with equal truth the same may be said of Dr. Ebel; for in the first place his papers presuppose a knowledge of the *Grammatica Celtica*, and in the second place because, like the German philologists generally, his style is extremely condensed. There is a third difficulty, which is, however, a local one. Comparative philology is not very much studied in Great Britain or Ireland, and although Bopp's great comparative grammar has been translated, yet scholars are not in these countries very familiar with the method of analysis of the Boppian school. Irish scholars, likewise, with very few exceptions, have not hitherto turned their attention in this direction. Perhaps this is the less to be regretted in the case of those who have heretofore devoted themselves to the study of the ancient language, literature, and historical monuments of Ireland, because, had the object of their labours been the mere abstract study of the Irish language, we should perhaps not have obtained the great results in a national point of view, which those labours have yielded. There is, perhaps, no country in Europe, in which in the same space of time and under a similar amount of difficulty, so much has been done, in about twenty-five or thirty years, for the collection, preservation, and publication of the records of its ancient history, as in Ireland. So, also, it would be difficult to rival in patient and conscientious work and solid learning such men as Petrie, O'Curry, O'Donovan, Todd, and Reeves, to speak only of those who have occupied themselves with the earlier periods of Irish history and archæology. The period has now, however, arrived, when the cultivation of Comparative Philology, besides its own intrinsic worth, would confer important advantages upon Irish literature, and very greatly facilitate the study of the ancient MSS. I thus ran the risk of labouring in vain, and of missing the opportunity of stimulating some of our young scholars to enter, and earn for themselves a name in a field of study which is so peculiarly their own, and for the cultivation of which they possess so many advantages. Under these circumstances, I had no alternative but to prepare an explanatory introduction—to venture in fact upon the hazardous undertaking of becoming, without any special qualification, the interpreter of the German School of comparative philology.

My first idea was to make an introduction of two chapters; the first to contain an explanation of the nature of roots and stems, the formation of stems and their classification, and of derivation and composition as distinguished from stems. In the second chapter I proposed to give a summary of the case-endings of nouns in the several Indo-European languages, in order to afford the student an opportunity of comparing the Irish forms with those of the other members of the family. As the limits which a periodical necessarily imposes were exceeded by the first chapter, which was of course the most important for my purposes, I was unable to add the chapter on the case-endings. For the same reason, as well as on account of pressure of other occupations, I was only able to publish, in No. V. of the ATLANTIS, Nos. 4, 5, and part of 6, of the *Celtic Studies* connected with declension. It has been stated above that Dr. Ebel's papers are based upon the *Grammatica Celtica*. To study them profitably, indeed to do so at all, the reader must have before him the part of that work on declension. As many of those into whose hands the ATLANTIS was likely to have come, may not have had an opportunity of consulting that book, I thought it desirable to add in the form of an appendix, a translation of the part just alluded to; some of the shortest passages in other parts of the book referred to by Dr. Ebel were likewise translated, and placed among the foot notes. As the paper on the *Position of the Celtic* possesses interest for a wider circle of readers than those on declension, I translated it also, and published it in No. VI. of the ATLANTIS.

Some friends having suggested that it would be desirable to have separate copies of these papers printed before the type of the ATLANTIS was distributed, I thought it a favourable opportunity to add the *Studies* omitted through want of space, namely, on the Celtic Dual, on the Degrees of Comparison, and an extremely important one, 9. *Zur Lautlehre*, which had been in the meantime published in the first part of the third volume of the *Beiträge;* I have likewise added the chapter on Case-Endings. I also took advantage of this opportunity to considerably modify the first chapter in several parts, with a view of more clearly distinguishing the different kinds of stems, and marking the difference between stem-formation and derivation. Although Dr. Ebel does not place his paper on the *Position of the Celtic* among his *Celtic Studies*, I thought it more convenient to do so, to avoid the necessity of a long title. I have also put all the papers on Declension together as a chapter divided into sections, the shorter papers forming in every case a distinct section.

As it may add to the value of the paper on the *Position of the Celtic*, to give a brief analysis of the discussion out of which it arose, I will give here the substance of the note with which I prefaced it in the ATLANTIS.

So soon as the Celtic was firmly established as a branch of the Indo-European family of languages, the next question to be determined was its position with respect to the other branches of the family. The general opinion at one time was, that the Celtic branch first separated from the parent stem. To this early separation was attributed its apparent deviation from the family type, above all, the mutilation and partial loss of its inflexions, which is found even in the oldest Irish. In an admirable article, published in the seventh volume of the *Zeitschrift für vergleichende Sprachforschung*, Dr. Lottner endeavoured to show, that no special relationship could be scientifically established between the Hellenic and Italic branches of the Indo-European family, a doctrine which must appear heretical to most classical scholars. In discussing this subject he had formed the opinion that the Celts, Germans, and Lito-Slavonians had lived together as one people, and from them the Celts first separated, and then the Germans. In a short paper, entitled "*Celtisch, Griechisch, Lateinisch*" (Beitr. I. 429), Dr. Ebel discussed the position of the Celtic, and on the whole supported Lottner's view of an intimate relation between the Celtic and German languages. Indeed, he appears to have long entertained such an opinion; for he says, in the paper just alluded to: "I cannot deny that already on my first acquaintance with Zeuss' *Grammatica Celtica*, the Celtic made an impression on me of an intimate connection with the Northern Languages, and that this impression had been continually strengthened during my Celtic studies". In the very same number of the *Beiträge*, and immediately following the paper of Dr. Ebel, there is a paper by the distinguished philologist Prof. Schleicher, entitled, *Die Stellung des Celtischen im Indogermanischen Sprachstamme*, in which he says: " If in those words of Ebel (just quoted) I put Latin, instead of Northern languages, I will accurately describe the impression which the study of the Celtic made on me". As may be anticipated from this, Prof. Schleicher is of opinion, that the Celtic is most nearly connected with the Graeco-Latin branch, standing towards those languages somewhat in the same relation that the German does to the Slavo-Lettish, coming nearer to the Italic (Latin), however, than to the Greek. The object of his paper is to bring forward arguments in support of this Latin relationship, while he left to Ebel the task of discovering the agreements between the Celtic and the Northern Languages. The paper which is here translated is Dr. Ebel's answer to that invitation. Instead, however, of attempting to determine the agreements in question merely, he has taken a wider range, and endeavoured to lay a solid foundation from which the whole problem of the affinities of the Celtic with all the other members of the Indo-European family may hereafter be investigated.

Since the publication of Dr. Ebel's paper, Dr. Lottner has published another under the title of *Celtisch-Italisch* (Beitr., ii. 309), in which, without at all departing from his opinion regarding the absence of special affinities between Latin and Greek, he has slightly modified his views about the position of the Celtic. This change is due to the light which the Gaulish inscriptions have thrown upon the forms of the Old Celtic. These inscriptions reveal to us words which not only do not yield in antiquity of form to those of classic Latin, but even attain, in many respects, that of the archaic language of the Romans. They show, beyond a doubt, that the inflexions which Irish has retained are older than the absence of inflexions in Welsh, and that the wonderful phonetic peculiarities of the modern Celtic, the umlaut, aspirations, the nasals in the Old Celtic, are foreign to it. One interesting result has followed the investigation of these inscriptions, namely, that they give us in part the very forms which were anticipated by Dr. Ebel according to the phonetic laws of the later Celtic. As I cannot give a translation of the whole of this interesting paper, I may, however, state the ethnological deduction which he has made. First, as he had already shown in his paper published in the *Zeitschrift*, the European bough of the Indo-European family, after its separation from the Asiatic one, formed a single people, from which the Hellenes (or perhaps the Helleno-Phrygians) first separated. The remainder subsequently split into two divisions, the South-West and the Northern. The former became subdivided into the Italic and Celtic branches, while the latter became subdivided into Germans and Slavonians, the Slavonians in turn becoming further subdivided into Slaves proper and Letts. Of course, much remains to be done before this ingenious hypothesis can be looked upon as more than a probable explanation, and more than this Dr. Lottner does not claim for it. It has much to recommend it, however; it rationally explains the ethnological problem of the present European races, and this explanation harmonizes with the ancient Irish tradition respecting the Celtic one. Although genealogical traditions of races reaching back into very remote times are not safe materials out of which to frame ethnological theories, neither can they be altogether disregarded; and consequently a hypothesis founded upon strictly scientific deductions, which, at the same time, accords with the popular traditions, may be fairly considered to possess many elements of truth.

It is almost unnecessary to say that an introduction such as that which I have prefixed to Dr. Ebel's papers, could, from its nature and objects, be to a great extent only a compilation from the works of those scholars who are considered to be masters in the science. Indeed, I have avoided, wherever I could, introducing any examples of my own. In the classification of stems, I have, however, ventured to deviate in some degree from that usually followed, whether with advantage or not remains to be seen. In an essay intended to be merely explanatory of a system, and admittedly compiled from the works of those who are authorities upon it, it is not necessary to refer to those authorities in every case in the text; here, however, it may be useful to mention the chief books to which I am indebted for materials. These are: Bopp's *Vergleichende Grammatik* (2nd ed.); Grimm's *Geschichte der Deutschen Sprache;* Curtius, *Die Bildung der Tempora und Modi;* and *Heyse's System der Sprachwissenschaft*, edited by Dr. H. Steinthal.

A great many notes have been added to the papers by Dr. Ebel on Declension, and a considerable number of words added to the lists in his paper on the "Position of the Celtic", especially to that of the Latin loan-words in Old Celtic. For the most of these additions, which are distinguished by being enclosed in [ ], I am indebted to Whitley Stokes, Esq. I also take this opportunity to give my best thanks to that distinguished scholar, Prof. C. Lottner, from whom Celtic philology has so much to expect, for the great pains he took in looking over the proof sheets; and also to my friend, John E. Pigot, Esq., without whose encouragement the task would never have been undertaken.

With the view of rendering the materials contained in the important paper *On the Position of the Celtic* as serviceable as possible in the construction of that great desideratum of Irish literature, a dictionary, I have added full Indices Verborum. This addition has added much to the size of the book, but I hope it will be found to be a practical contribution to Irish lexicographic materials.

In conclusion, I wish to direct the attention of such of my readers as may not be members of the Irish Archæological and Celtic Society to a work published by that body, which contains much that illustrates the subject of the following pages, or that is actually supplementary to them, namely, *Irish Glosses, a mediæval tract on Irish Declension, with examples explained in Irish*, to which is added the *Lorica of Gildas*, with the Glosses thereon, and a selection of Glosses from the Book of Armagh, edited by Whitley Stokes, A.B.

In point of varied learning, skill, and cautious discretion in the grammatical analysis, the work is unquestionably the best contribution to the comparative philology of the Celtic languages which has yet appeared in the English language, and may fully rank with any similar works by German or French scholars. It is at once a valuable and a timely contribution towards the materials for making an Irish dictionary, and as such the Archæological and Celtic Society has well expended its funds in the publication of it.

The most valuable feature of the work in question, so far as regards the Celtic Studies of Dr. Ebel, is the large number of paradigms of the declension of Irish nouns and adjectives which it contains. For the purposes of reference, I think it will be useful to enumerate them all.

Masculine, neuter, and feminine *a*- and *â*-stems: nom. sing. *cenn*, stem *cinna* (masc.), p. 39; nom. sing. *forcetal* (*n*), stem *forcitala* (neut.), p. 51; nom. sing. masc. *mall*, an adjectival stem, p. 97; nom. sing. *rann*, stem *rannâ* (fem. *â*-stem), p. 38; nom. sing. *dia*, a masc. *a*-stem, p. 45.

Masculine and feminine *iâ*-stems: nom. sing. *rannaire*, stem *rannaria* (masc.), p. 37; nom. sing. *caile*, stem *caliâ* (fem.), p. 54; nom. sing. masc. *núe*, an adjectival *ia*-stem, p. 97.

Masculine and neuter *i*-stems; nom. sing. *fáith*, stem *fâthi* (masc.), p. 36; nom. sing. *fiss*, stem *fissi* (neut.), p. 117.

Masculine *u*-stems: nom. sing. *bith*, stem *bithu* (masc.), p. 62.

Masculine *t*-stems: nom. sing. *fili*, stem *fíliat* (masc.), p. 36.

Masculine *g*-stem: nom. sing. *ri*, gen. *ríg*, a masculine *g*-stem, p. 119.

Feminine *n*-stem: nom. sing. *talam*, stem *talaman*, p. 48.

Ant-stems: nom. sing. *cara*, stem *carat*, from *carant* (masc.), p. 65. A paradigm of the declension of *ainm* (*n*), probably originally an *ant*-stem, but which was in Old Irish a neuter *ann*-stem, is also given at p. 116.

Masculine *r*-stem : nom. sing. *athir*, stem *athar*, p. 39.

C-stems : nom. sing. *cathir*. According to Dr. Ebel (see p. 94), *cathir* is an *r*-stem, taking the determinative suffix *c*, but Mr. Stokes considers it to be a *c*-stem, p. 38.

Anomalous nouns : nom. sing. *ben*, all the singular and plural forms of which are given, p. 121.

At p. 45 a paradigm of the declension of the article is also given. What renders these paradigms the more valuable is, that in almost every case the forms of the dual number are also given. As several of the words declined by Zeuss and Dr. Ebel are also declined by Mr. Stokes, the corresponding paradigms of each writer may be instructively compared.

Dr. Ebel's papers are frequently referred to in Mr. Stokes's book; and as each may be said to, in a measure, supplement the other, the almost simultaneous appearance of the following translation of the Celtic Studies, and of the admirably edited book in question, may be deemed a fortunate coincidence. I hope, also, that the introduction which I was obliged to prefix to the papers of Dr. Ebel may likewise enable a larger circle of readers to appreciate the importance of Mr. Stokes's contribution towards our more perfect knowledge of the language of Ancient Erinn.

CONTENTS.

INTRODUCTION.

CHAPTER I.—ON SIMPLE WORD-FORMATION: ROOTS, STEMS, AND DERIVATIVES.

§ 1. *Of Roots and Root-forms.* Nature of a root as a phonetic symbol, p. 3. The permutations or letter changes which take place in the same word in different dialects of the same language, or in different languages of the same family, not arbitrary, p. 3. Example of the law of transposition or provection of sounds (called by Grimm Lautverschiebung), p. 3. The analysis of words which have had a common origin does not give roots, but only root-forms, p. 4. Root-forms of the same root often very dissimilar: examples, p. 4. Objects of modern comparative etymology, p. 4. Modern classification of the kinds of words of which rational speech is composed, p. 4. Corporal and formal, or formational words, p. 5. Corporal and formational roots, p. 5. Of the composition of roots in words: 1. Parathesis; 2. Agglutination; 3. Amalgamation, p. 6. Classification of languages according to their relative degree of composition, p. 6. Bopp's classification somewhat different from that here given, p. 6. The amalgamating languages the most complex; are represented by the Indo-European or Aryan family of languages; such languages contain no uninflected roots in their primitive state; but many naked roots occur in their modern derivatives, pp. 6-7. Roots preserve their identity; exception to this in the process called Root Variation; this process gives rise to affiliated roots, one of which is primary to the others; all large roots are secondary; examples, p. 7.

§ 2. *Of Elementary Word-formation and Inflexion.* Word-formation or Word-building; elementary words must be further modified by inflexion; the process of elementary word-formation and inflexion the same; what those are:—1. internal phonetic change; 2. addition of phonetic material, p. 7-8. Vowel change a predominant process of this kind in the Semitic languages; only appears as *ablaut* in the Indo-European tongues; definition of *ablaut*; chief agent of word-formation in the Teutonic languages, p. 8. Of *umlaut*; it acquires inflexional signification: examples, p. 8-9. Of Breaking or Fracture, p. 9 (note on the German nomenclature employed, *note* 4, page 8). Progressive assimilation in the Finno-Tatarian family, a kind of *umlaut*; the rule "*caol le caol*" in Irish, and the weakening of the root vowel in Latin by the vowel of a prefix, may be considered as progressive assimilation, p. 9-10. Affixes the chief agent of word-formation in Indo-European tongues; the affixes used in word-formation and inflexion, and in composition; some of the affixes used in word-formation and inflexion traceable to independent words;—examples; generalization of this result; word-formation and inflexion were originally synthesis of independent roots;—this view is the basis of the agglutination theory; the theory now generally admitted; some, however, modify it so as to admit two kinds of affixes, p. 10-11.

§ 3. Of the stem, a form intermediate between the root and the word; distinction between roots and stems; stems are of many kinds; hence there are four categories of phonetic forms, p. 11-12. Word-formation consists of stem-formation and derivation; phonetic methods of primary or pure stem-formation.—I. Modification of the root vowel:— by (a) *ablaut* proper; (b) obscuration; (c) strengthening—either (1) by lengthening a short vowel, or (2) by gunation and diphthongation, (note explanatory of those terms). II. Consonantal strengthening of the root by—(a) duplication of final consonant; (b) affixation of a foreign mute consonant; (c) affixation or intercalation of a nasal—by (1) nasalizing an internal vowel, (2) affixation of the nasal in the auslaut, either after vowels or after consonants, or (3) affixation of a whole syllable accompanied by nasalisation; or (d) reduplication;— examples, p. 12-14. Exceptional cases of primary stem formation; *e. g.* an intensive introduced into the root; other classes of true stems; occasional difficulty in distinguishing stems from roots, and simple words from stems, p. 14.

§ 4. *Of noun-formation and secondary stems.* Separation of grammatical categories by the addition of signs to stems; signs by which a stem becomes a verb; sign of noun-formation (to which the present analysis is confined); distinction of gender; nominative sign—masc., fem., and neuter; Bopp's view as to origin of neutral adj., ending-*ata*; relative degree of preservation of the nominative sign *s* in different languages, p. 14-16. Introduction of a vowel between the stem and ending; the declension vowel (note 7 on the Finnish two-syllabled Stems), p. 16. Cases of stems formed by a whole syllable—derivative Stems, p. 16-17. Two-fold classification of stems according to auslaut and relation to the grammatical ending: I. vocalic stems—1. pure stems; 2. middle forms produced by affixing a declension vowel; II. consonantal stems—1. pure stems; 2. middle forms produced by affixing a syllable ending consonantally, p. 16. Table of the classification of true stems, and of derivative stems, p. 16-17.

§ 5. *Of vocalic stems.* [I.] Pure stems; examples: Greek, Latin, Gothic; Gothic nouns properly belong to second class, the Teutonic languages having no pure stems (but see note 12, p. 28, for some probable exceptions), p. 18-19. [II.] Middle forms ending vocally. Division of all vocalic stems into *a*- stems, *i*- stems, and *u*- stems, p. 19. (1) I. Stems. Greek, Latin, Gothic; peculiarities of adjectives derived directly from stems, p. 19-20. (2) *A*- Stems. In Greek and Latin: 1. where the primitive *a* is preserved or changed into *e*,—(α) stems with primitive short *a*, (β) stems with long *a* or *e*; 2. where the primitive *a* is changed into *o* in Greek, and *u* in Latin. *A*- stems with primitive *a* short; (examples). Gothic *a*- stems; (examples); peculiarities of Gothic adjectives—examples, p. 20-22. [III.] *yá*-, or *IA*- stems. Peculiarities in the Gothic, the O. H. German, M. H. German, and N. H. German adjective forms of *ya*- stems—examples from the Latin and Gothic, p. 22-24. [IV.] Consonantal stems changed into vocalic (*a*- and *i*-) stems. Examples from the Latin and the Greek. Apparently irregular Greek stems. Analogy of certain Gothic nouns with the Latin All these probably consonantal *n*- stems, (note 10, expressing a doubt as to the hypothesis in respect to the Greek stems, and giving a different explanation of Ahrens, p. 24). Tables of examples. Gothic feminine nouns ending in *-ei*; probably mutilated *n*- stems; (examples). Declension, in the Germanic (though not in the Latin or Greek) languages, affected by the dropping of the *n*. Examples. Peculiarity of the weak declension, in adding the *n*. The weak adjective declension; (examples). Examples of vowel endings distinguishing genders. The *s* in "sanguis", p. 24-26. [V.] *u*- stems. Greek, Latin, Gothic. Peculiarities of adjectives, p. 26-27

§ 6. *Of consonantal stems.* [I.] Pure stems. (1) *S*- stems; Greek and Latin. (2) Stems with sonant auslauts (semi-vowels: *m, l, n, r, ng*); Greek and Latin. (3) Stems with medial auslauts; Greek and Latin. (4) Stems with tenuis auslauts; Greek and Latin. (5) Stems with aspirated mute auslauts; Greek. Gothic pure stems belong rather to middle forms; examples (note 12 already referred to giving examples of some which are perhaps exceptions), p. 27-28. [II.] Consonantal middle forms. The "thema", distinguished from the true stem form. (1) *S*- stems—Greek and Latin. (2) Stems with sonant auslauts. *L*- stems, *N*- stems, *R*- stems, (Latin, Greek, and Gothic). (3) Stems with medial auslauts. (4) Stems with tenuis auslauts (examples from Greek and Latin). p. 28-31.

§ 7. *Of Derivation.* Affixes: 1. single letters or syllables, not traceable to independent words; 2. syllabic affixes, once independent words, but modified so as to have lost that character. Difficulty of distinguishing stem-formation from derivation. "Derivative Stems" (Greek examples). Examples showing the formation of words by the process of Derivation, pp. 31-33.

§ 8. *Of Composition.* Definition. Peculiar power of composition in the Sanskrit and the Greek; in the Germanic languages. Composition distinguished into: 1. synthetical; and 2. parathetical. Particle composition to be classed as parathetical. Introduction of a copulative vowel in the older languages; Greek and O. H. German; Modern German, and English (examples). Combination sometimes accompanied by phonetic changes in one or both the constituents (examples in the Latin). Relation of the constituents of compound words (examples), pp. 33-34.

CHAPTER II.—ON THE CASE-ENDINGS OF NOUNS IN THE CHIEF INDO-EUROPEAN LANGUAGES.

§ 1. *The Accusative Singular.*—(As to the nominative, refer to Ch. 1., § 4). The sign of the accusative: *m*, in Sanskrit, Zend, Latin; *n*, in Greek, Lithuanian, and Old Prussian. Primitive sign probably *m*. In the Latin: *m* affixed, 1. directly to vocalic stems; 2. with intercalated copulative to consonantal stems. Transformation of Sanskrit *m* into nasal *n*, by "*anusvâra*"; (note on "anusvara"). Observations as to the Lithuanian, Latin, Oscan. Nominatives in modern languages (Italian, Portuguese, Spanish), derived from the mutilated Latin accusative. Greek and Latin declensions compared. The Greek affix *ν*. Exceptions (stems in ω and ευ). In the Gothic the sign of the accusative lost, pp. 34-36.

§ 2. *The Genitive Singular.*—The Sanskrit and Zend, p. 36. The Latin. The genitive in *-ius*, pp. 36-37. The Oscan, p. 37. In the Greek; gen. sing. formed by: (*a*) affixing ς to fem. 1st decl.; (*b*) affixing ς with a copulative *o*; (*c*) where the noun does not form the gen. in ς, pp. 37-38. The Gothic. The Germanic languages, pp. 38-39. The Lithuanian and Slavonian, p. 39.

§ 3. *The Dative, Locative, and Instrumental, Singular.* The Sanskrit and Zend, p. 39. The Latin. The Oscan, p. 40. The Greek, p. 40. The terminations of adjectives (masc. and neut., and fem.), in the Gothic, O. H. German, and M. H. German, compared; (Paradigm), p. 41. The Lithuanian and Slavonian, pp. 41-42.

§ 4. *The Ablative Singular.* Peculiarities in the Sanskrit, Zend, and Latin. Ablative sign recognizable in adverbs, p. 42.

§ 5. *The Dual.* Peculiar forms only found in Sanskrit, Zend, Greek, Slavonian, and Lithuanian. (Note: reference to Ebel's observations on the relics of the Dual in Irish). Traces in Latin, pp. 43-44.

§ 6. *The Nominative and Vocative Plural.* Comparison of the Sanskrit, Zend, Old Latin, and Greek. Endings in *i*. Neuters in *a*. Plural endings in *-as*; opinions of philologists, pp. 44-45. The Gothic:

(Paradigms of the strong and the weak declension). Comparison of the Gothic with the Old and the Middle High German; (Paradigm). Formation of the plural in the modern languages, pp. 45-46. The Lithuanian and Slavonian, p. 46.

§ 7. *The Accusative Plural.* The Sanskrit, Zend, Greek, Oscan, and Latin compared, p. 47. The Gothic and O. H. German, p. 47. The Gothic *-ns.* Examples, p. 48. Parallel in Greek, p. 48.

§ 8. *The Genitive Plural.* The Sanskrit (*-ām*), and Zend (*-anm*), p. 48. The Latin (*-rum*), pp. 48-49. The Greek (*-ων*), p. 49. The Gothic. The M. and N. H. German, p. 49. The Lithuanian and Slavonian, p. 50.

§ 9. *The Dative, Locative, Instrumental, and Ablative Plural.* The Sanskrit and Zend, p. 50. Two forms in the Greek and Latin, pp. 50-51. The Gothic, O. and M. H. German, pp. 51-52. The Lithuanian and Slavonian, p. 52.

Paradigm of all the case-endings of nouns in the chief Indo-European Languages. (The Sanskrit; Zend; Latin; Oscan; Umbrian; Greek; Gothic; O. H. German; Lithuanian; Old Slavonian; Old Prussian). *Folding plate facing p.* 52.

CELTIC STUDIES.

CHAPTER I.—ON DECLENSION AND THE DEGREES OF COMPARISON IN IRISH.

§ 1. *Bopp's View of the Aspirations and Eclipses in Modern Irish, and the modifications which it undergoes through the old Irish forms.* Zeuss' determination of the Old forms of the article; (notes, giving the passages from Zeuss). Bopp's opinions modified as to the *t* and the *h* before vowels. (Note on *dona* from *donabis*, correcting Dr. Ebel's theory regarding the O. Irish dat. plur.), (note on "aspiration"—"Infection", or "mortification"), (note on the *t* in the nom. sing. masc. of the Irish article), pp. 55-56. Bopp's opinion modified as to the nom. plur. masc., p. 57. Discovery of the neuter, and of the accusative cases in Old Irish, p. 57.

§ 2. *Stems which belong to the several orders and series of Zeuss.* Objections to views of Pictet and Bopp as to the distribution of the vocalic stems, pp. 57-58. Consideration of the words and suffixes which belong to the several classes. Examples, pp. 58-59. Examples of forms in cognate languages, pp. 59-60. Adjectives, pp. 60-61. Verbal substantives taking the place of the infinitive; pp. 61-62. Forms of the article, p. 62.

§ 3. *Test afforded by Irish Phonology for determining inductively the Primitive Forms of the Celtic Case-endings.* Two close points of contact between the Irish and the German vocal systems: umlaut of *a* by *i* and *u*, and fracture of *i* and *u* by *a*. Examples, pp. 62-63. The vowel of the ending determinable by the vowel changes in the stem, p. 63. Table of masc. and neut. endings. (I.); (examples), pp. 63-64. (Note: table of hypothetical endings of masc. and neut.), p. 63. Table of endings of fem. *a*-stems; (examples), p. 64. Table of endings of masc. stems (III.); (examples), p. 64. Table comparing auslaut in Old Irish and N. H. German, p. 64. How the Gaedhelic has been harder than the Gothic; (examples), p. 65. Explanation of mutilations of the auslaut, p. 65. Table: (Primitive period,—Pre-historic period,—Historic period), p. 66.

§ 4. *Declension of Consonantal Stems.* Zeuss' five classes. Analysis, p. 66. Table of common endings, p. 67. As to the length in the acc. plur. comparison with the Greek, the Latin, and the Gothic, p. 67. Observations on the several cases. Examples, pp. 67, 69. Table of declension of neutral *n*-stems, (I.), p. 69. Nouns of relationship in *-thar*, (II.), p. 69. Table: (Primitive Period,—Pre-historic Period,—Historic Period), p. 70. Addition of a "determinative suffix"; (but,—note on this theory of Ebel), p. 70. Comparison of Gaedhelic with the Classic languages as to the consonant declension of the *l-*, *n-*, and *r-* stems, p. 71.

§ 5. *Declension of Masc. (and neut.)* A *and* IA- *Stems.* Stems included in the vocalic declension, p. 71. Inflections of masc. *a-* stems; compared with Sanskrit, etc.; (examples), pp. 71-72. Anomaly in the neuters, preparing for disappearance of the neut. in the Gaedhelic, pp. 72-73. As to adjectives, p. 73.

§ 6. *Declension of masc.* I *and* U *Stems.* Consideration of each case, pp. 74-76. Table of declensions (of U stems and I stems), arranged according to periods (Primitive, Pre-historic, Historic), but without the secondary forms, p. 76.

§ 7. *Declension of fem.* A *and* I *stems.* Confusion in their declension; how the primitive stem only now to be recognized; (but,—note on this). Examples, pp. 76-77. Hypothesis of Dr. Ebel, pp. 77-78 (see also for completion, p. 154). Tables of forms of *ia-* stems compared with those actually occurring, p. 79. Other examples of same degeneration of original forms, p. 79. Modern Irish losing its inflexions, like the Kymric. Examples, pp. 79-80.

§ 8. *The distinction of the plural in the Kymric.* No inflexions preserved in Kymric except distinctions of plural, and this very arbitrarily employed. As in the N. H. German: (1) old plural form remaining, and consequently true inflexion; (2) stem-ending preserved, dropped in the sing.; (3) a determinative suffix, wholly foreign in place of the ending, p. 81. To (1) belong: 1. Kymric plur. without endings; (examples), p. 81; 2. plurals in -*i*; (examples), p. 81; 3. plurals in -*au* and -*iau*, p. 82. To (2): especially *n-* stems; (examples), p. 82. To (3): 1. many plur. in -*au* and -*iau* in which the ending is foreign to the words—stem proper; (examples), p. 82. 2. most words in -*ion* or -*on*; (examples); 3. endings -*et*, -*ot*, -*ieit*, -*eit*, and -*ed*, -*yd*, -*oed*; (examples), pp. 82-83.

§ 9. *Note on a-, i-, d-, t-, and nt- stems.* Gen. in -*i* and nom. in -*as*, in *a* stems, found in Ogam inscriptions. Obscuration of *a* to *o* at a remote period, p. 83. The neutral *aill*, p. 83. As to Mr. Stokes' corrections, recognizing stems in -*d*, -*t*, and -*nt*, in Zeuss' Ordo Posterior, ser. 4, pp. 83-84. As to Dr. Ebel's view of the fem. in Zeuss' Prior, Ser. V., p. 84; fusion of *i-* and *á-* stems, p. 86.

§ 10. *On the Celtic Dual.* Answer to Mr. Stokes. Whether the Celtic has a dual; (examples), pp. 85-86. How much of it has been preserved, pp. 86-87. Of undoubted dual-forms only the masc. and acc. of substantives, and the whole of the cases of the numeral Two, pp. 87-88. The *in* of the article, p. 88. Few dual forms of consonantal stems preserved, p. 88.

§ 11. *On the Article in Modern Irish.* Theory as to the article *an*, p. 88. (But—note questioning this theory of Dr. Ebel), p. 89. Observations on certain finer influences of neighbouring languages on one another, p. 89.

§ 12. *On the so-called Prosthetic N.* ["Prosthetic"="Eclipsing". Theory of Mr. Stokes and of Dr. Ebel, p. 90.] Correction of Zeuss' views as to this *n*. Mr. Stokes' examples. Examples of this *n* as a relic of the article, p. 90. Other examples, p. 91. Some spurious prepositions recognized as accusative forms, p. 91. The *n* of *ainm-n*; previous observation of Dr. Ebel corrected in note, p. 91. Supposed three-fold preposition *do-air-in*, p. 92. The *n* after verbal forms; examples, p. 92.

§ 13. *On the degrees of comparison.* As to the -*ns* stems. The -*a* in the more ancient, -*u* in the newer secondary formations, p. 92. Explanation of these formations, pp. 93-94.

CHAPTER II.—ON THE POSITION OF THE CELTIC.

§ 1. *Views regarding the special affinities of the Celtic and words borrowed from the Latin.* Points of contact between the Celtic and the Italic tongues on one side, and the Teutonic on the other, p. 97. Views of Dr. Lottner and Professor Schleicher, p. 97. Celtic closer to Latin than to Greek, p. 97. Points of agreement between the Celtic and the Northern tongues, p. 98. Words in Celtic languages in common with or borrowed from the Latin, p. 98. Method of denoting the Kymric dialects, p. 98. Glossary of Latin loan-words in Old Celtic, pp. 99-107. Words borrowed by the Latin from the Gaulish, and later from the British, p. 107.

§ 2. *Glossarial affinities of the Celtic and Classic languages.* Glossary of words and roots exclusively common to the Celtic and Classic languages, pp. 107-109.

§ 3. *Glossarial affinities of the Celtic, Classic, Teutonic, and Lito-Slavonian languages.* Glossary of words and roots common to the Celtic and Classic languages, but also found in the Teutonic, Slavonian, and Lithuanian, pp. 109-112. Of certain other roots to be added to this list. Examples, pp. 112-113.

§ 4. *Glossarial affinities of the Celtic, Classic, and Teutonic lauguages.* List of words and roots common to the Celtic, Greek, and Teutonic, p. 113. List of those common to the Celtic, Latin (or Italic), and Teutonic, pp. 113-114.

§ 5. *Glossarial affinities of the Celtic, Teutonic, and Lito-Slavonian languages.* Mutual borrowing among the languages. Examples of borrowed words, pp. 114-115. List of words and roots common to the Celtic, Lithuanian, Slavonian, and Teutonic, pp. 115-116.

§ 6. *Glossarial affinities of the Celtic and Teutonic.* List of words and roots common to the Celtic and Teutonic, pp. 116-119.

§ 7. *Glossarial affinities of the Celtic and Lito-Slavonian.* List of words and roots common to the Celtic, Lithuanian, and Slavonian, p. 119. Original words in the Celtic, p. 119. Agreement with the Sanskrit in nomenclature of the cardinal points, p. 119. Summary of results of the foregoing tables, as regards the true relation of the Celtic to other European languages, pp. 119-120.

§ 8. *Phonological affinities:—Vocalismus.* Study of principles on which to judge of an earlier or later separation of tongues yet imperfect. Example: comparison of treatment of the neuters in the Old Gaedhelic and the Hebrew,—the Polish and the Slavonian. Want of a geography of sounds; (note on this subject), pp. 120-121. The elementary developement of the vocalismus only to be followed out with clearness in the Gothic, p. 121. The Gothic short vowels, a, i, u, p. 121. The Latin and Greek, and the Celtic compared, pp. 121-122. Analogous vowel changes in Teutonic, Slavonian, and Celtic roots, p. 122. In the diphthongal system the Celtic nearest to the Teutonic. Examples, p. 122.

§ 9. *Phonological affinities:—Consonantismus.* Celtic analogous to Lithuanian and Slavonian in having no aspirate in its older phonetic stage, p. 122. Celtic in this contrasts with the Greek, p. 123. Deviations from the Teutonic, p. 123. Agreements, p. 123. Changes of secondary aspirates into medials, or medial-aspirates, p. 123. Hardening of medials in the Celtic and Teutonic, p. 123. The Gaedhelic thickening of the n (or nn), p. 123.

§ 10. *Affinities of word-formation.* The suffix -*tion* exclusively Italo-Celtic, p. 123. Other suffixes; (-*li*; -*iá*; -*aire*; -*ire*; -*dóit*;) p. 124. The peculiar suffix-combination: *antat*, (-*atu*, -*etu*), p. 124. Celtic word-formation of a modern character, p. 124. Wider use of K than in the Classic languages; (-*ach*), p. 124.

§ 11. *Affinities of declension.* Only the Pelasgic languages have fem. *a*-stems. Agreement of Celtic with the northern languages, p. 124. Masc. *a*- stems foreign to the Celtic, p. 125. Few fem. *u*- stems in Celtic, p. 125. Celtic approaches the Classic languages in having preserved more pure consonantal stems, but differs from them in treatment of *s-* stems, p. 125. As to the ablative, p. 125. As to the *b* in the dative plural, p. 125. Want of pronominal declension, p. 125. Agreement of gen. sing. and nom. plur. of masc. *a-* stems in the Old Gaedhelic and the Latin, p. 125. Other agreements less exclusive, pp. 125-126.

§ 12. *Affinities of gradation (or comparison).* Peculiar forms of gradation in the Greek, the Latin, the Celtic. Analogy of some Gaedhelic forms, p. 126.

§ 13. *Affinities of the pronouns.* Celtic peculiarity in giving up the nom. sing. of the 1. and 2. person, p. 126. Analogy with the Teutonic in the 3. person, p. 126. Analogy with forms in the Sanskrit, p. 127. The *ta*; the *ana*; p. 127.

§ 14. *Affinities of conjugation.* Peculiar combinations and new formations in conjugation. Examples, p. 127. Remarkable analogy with Teutonic and Slavonian, p. 127. Paradigm of Old Gaedhelic and Lithuanian—ending of the present and preterite, p. 128. The Kymric *-st*, (2. pers. sing. præt.) p. 128. Pictet's view of this *-t*, p. 128. Distinction of the imperfect and perfect in the Slavonian by separate verbs, p. 128. Use of the present as a future, p. 129. Peculiar force, in the Teutonic and Slavonian, of the particle in composition, p. 129. Analogy in the Celtic; (1) the perfect denoted by a special particle; (*ru-*; *ro-*; *ra-*), pp. 129-130. Peculiarity of Celtic in use of this particle, p. 130. (2) The pres. and fut. changed into the perfect future exactum by this particle (*ro-*), p. 130. (3) The present forms (especially the conjunctive pres.) turned into future by it, p. 129. All three uses in the Gothic, p. 131. Gaedhelic particle to tenses of incomplete action, (*nu-*, *no-*), p. 131. Middle position of the Celtic, between the Italic and Greek, and the Teutonic and Lito-Slavonian, p. 131. Other points of contact to be sought in a comparative syntax of these languages, p. 131.

CHAPTER III.—ON PHONOLOGY IN IRISH.

§ 2. *Necessity of establishing an organic orthography; and great importance of a comparison of the modern Irish forms for the purpose.* Schleicher's opinion, p. 135. Want of linguistic materials on the continent, p. 135. Inaccuracy of those published: (examples in Zeuss, O'Donovan, etc.) p. 135. How to attain what is required, p. 135. Comparison wanted between Middle and Modern Irish forms, p. 136. Disfigurement and irregularity of Modern Irish forms; (errors of Pictet and Bopp), p. 136. Examples, pp. 136-138. Necessity of comparison with newer forms nevertheless; (error of Zeuss), p. 138.

§ 2. *Vocalismus.* The chief difficulty of the Irish phonetic system, p. 138. Three kinds of *e* and *o*, p. 138. Suggestion of a mode of distinguishing them in print, p. 138. Examples, p. 139. Of the *a* corrupted from the *o* in Old Irish. Examples, pp. 139-141. Correction of mistake in preceding chapter, (p. 88; § II. *On the article*, etc.) as to the modern form of the article *an*, note, p. 140.

§ 3. *Consonantismus.—Aspiration of mediae after vowels.* Important results of comparison of the newer forms. Examples, p. 141. Influence of the *s*, p. 141. Comparison of the modern forms especially necessary to determine whether the tenuis or media is to be aspirated or not. Examples, pp. 141-142. Aspiration of the simple *m* in Modern Irish. *M.* for *bh.* *Mm* (or *mb*) in Old Irish, deduced from *m* (in inlaut) in Modern Irish. (Note: *mm* in several examples, compared with the *nn* of the article), p. 142. Mediæ after vowels always aspirated in Modern Irish; after consonants not so, except where a vowel dropped out, pp. 142-143. Mediæ assimilated after iquids, p. 143 Observation on the so-called Eclipse, p. 143.

2*

§ 4. *Consonantismus.—Aspiration of tenues after vowels.* Tenues when aspirated, pp. 143-144. Organic Mediæ changed into tenues in Old Irish, in two ways, p. 144. Comparison of Modern Irish, pp. 144-145. Observation as to the so-called eclipse of the tenuis, p. 145. Conclusion : (Examples), p. 146.

§ 5. *Consonantismus.—Cases which afford occasion for aspiration after a preserved or lost vowel:* (I.) *in inlaut ;* (II.) *in anlaut;* (III.) *in syntax.* Inference of aspiration from the presence of a vowel, p. 146. Examples. Three categories.

(I.) In *inlaut*, p. 147. Examples from conjugation. p. 147. Confirmation of Zeuss as to the *l, n, s, d, t, th.* (Observation as to O'Donovan on the Modern Irish Passive and Participles), pp. 147-148. Examples, from declension, p. 148. Derivatives in *-te*, p. 149. Derivation with various suffixes, p. 149.

(II.) In *anlaut.* Of the second member in composition, p. 150. Omission by Zeuss as to the exceptions to the aspiration rule, p. 150. Grimm's observations as to *t* and *d*, in Mod. Irish, remaining unchanged after liquids, not quite correct. ("*Mactire*", explained), p. 150. Examples of other exceptions, p. 150. Explanation of " *Dunpeleder*" in Zeuss, p. 151. No aspiration following O and Mac, in names, p. 151.

(III.) Caution as to use of Mod. Irish in determining laws of anlaut (not developed by Zeuss), p. 151. Phonetic changes, how produced in syntax, p. 152. (1) Original terminations of the article, in the several cases. Examples, p. 152. Phonetic laws after the article, p. 153. Rule as to Eclipse (O'Donovan), apparently inexplicable, p. 153. Explanation, however, by comparison of O'Donovan's examples from Keating, p. 154. Observations as to confusion of case-endings (p. 78 *et seq.*) completed, p. 154. Peculiar use of acc. for nom. in Old Irish, p. 154. Confusion in the spoken language; (examples), p. 154. The true acc. in the so-called dat. sing., p. 154. Comparison with Mod. Greek, as to loss of dat., p. 155. Example (Table of Declension) of the treatment of the *anlaut* after the article, p. 155. Explanation of so-called Eclipse of *s* after *is* (*in*), p. 156. Of the Adjective after the article, p. 156. (2) Influence of auslaut on following *anlaut* between adj. and subst., p. 156. Examples in Zeuss few, p. 156. Examples for the aspiration of the adj., p. 157. Suppression of aspiration in certain cases, p. 157. Transvected nasal, p. 157. Examples for the aspiration of the subst., p. 157. Correspondence with what is known of the Dual : (O'Molloy and O'Donovan), p. 158. Eclipse after numerals, p. 158. (3) Combination between subst. and succeeding genitive much weaker, p. 158. Examples of nasal preserved in acc., p. 158. Other examples, p. 159. (4) Pronouns: (Examples), p. 159. (5) The *anlaut* after prepositions and other particles, p. 160. (6) Action of the verb on the object, p. 161.

§ 6. *Loss of P in Celtic.* Preservation of the guttural in the Gaedhelic (replaced by the labial in the Greek and the Kymric). Examples, p. 161. Primitive *p* replaced even by *c* or *ch*. Examples, p. 161. Aversion to *p* in anlaut. Examples, pp. 161-2. Want in the Celtic languages of the prepositions with *p-* anlaut in the Sanskrit and other cognate languages, p. 162. Assumption by Pictet and Bopp: (examples). "*Frith*". "*Fri*", p. 162. The Sanskrit "*pra*" and "*pari*", p. 163. The prefix "*ro*", "*ire*", pp. 163-4.

§ 7. *Loss of the P in Celtic (continued).* Example of loss of *p* in anlaut in "*én*" (avis), p. 164. Pictet and Pott as to "*are*", p. 164. Prepositions in Old Irish in a double, and even a treble form, p. 164. Examples, p. 165. Fundamental meaning of "*ar*", p. 165.

APPENDIX.

I.—ZEUSS ON THE INFLEXIONS OF NOUNS IN IRISH.

[Translation of the part of Chap. II. of Zeuss' *Grammatica Celtica*, referred to by Dr. Ebel.]

A. *Declension.* Two orders of declension, p. 169.

    FIRST ORDER.—The "Vocalic", p. 169.
      Declension of Nouns, masc. and neut. Paradigm. I. Series; II. Ser.; III. Ser., p. 170.
      Declension of nouns fem. Paradigm. IV. Ser.; V. Ser., p. 170.
      I. SERIES. External Inflexion; nouns in *-e*, p. 170.
        Singular; (examples in all the cases), p. 170. Plural; (examples in all the cases), p. 171.
      II. SERIES. Internal Inflexion, p. 171.
        Singular; (examples), p. 171. Plural; (examples), p. 172.
      III. SERIES. External Inflexion, except dat. sing., p. 172.
        Singular; (examples), p. 173. Plural; (examples), p. 173.
      IV. SERIES. External Inflexion; fem. nouns in *-e* and *-i*, p. 173.
        Singular; (examples), p. 173. Plural; (examples), p. 173.
      V. SERIES. External and Internal Inflexion; fem. nouns, p. 173.
        Singular; (examples), p. 174. Plural; (examples), p. 174.

    SECOND ORDER.—The "consonantal", p. 174.
    Paradigm of five series; the first three liquid, the last two mute, p. 175.
      I. SERIES. Subst. in *-im*, *-in*, taking gen. sing. *-a* or *-e*, etc. Examples, p. 175.
      II. SERIES. Nouns taking in oblique cases *-an*, *-in*, and *-in*, *-en*; (two divisions), p. 175. Examples, p. 176.
      III. SERIES. Nouns of relationship, masc. and fem. in *-ir*, p. 176. Examples, p. 176.
      IV. SERIES. Derivatives in *-id*, declined by variation of internal vowels; (two divisions). Examples, p. 177.
      V. SERIES. Contains fem. nouns in *-r*, to which are added the suffixes, *-ach*, *-ich*, *ig*, p. 177. Examples, p. 178.
    The Dual Number, p. 177.
    Paradigms of the series of the First Order. Examples from the MSS., pp. 178-9.
    Anomalous Substantives. Examples, p. 179.

(B) *Diminutives.* Instances from MSS., p. 180.

(C) *Degrees of Comparison*, p. 180.
      COMPARATIVE. Two Forms. Examples, pp. 180-181.
      SUPERLATIVE. Two endings. (Examples), p. 181.

II. THE CELTIC MSS. UPON WHICH ZEUSS' GRAMMATICA CELTICA WAS FOUNDED; AND THE TABLE OF THE ABBREVIATIONS USED IN REFERRING TO THEM, P. 182.

INDICES VERBORUM TO POSITION OF THE CELTIC.

INDO-EUROPEAN OR PRIMITIVE ARYAN.			*Italic and Romance.*		
			Latin Index	. p.	187
SOUTH ARYAN.			Mediæval Latin Index	.	191
Sanskrit Index	.	p. 185	Picenian	,, . .	,,
Old Persian ,,	.	. ,,	Sabine	,, . .	,,
NORTH-WEST ARYAN.			Oscan	,, . .	,,
Hellenic.			Umbrian	,, . .	,,
Greek Index	.	,,	Romance	,, . .	192

Italian Index		p. 192	*Windic or Lito-Slavonian.*		
Provençal „		„	Old Slavonic	p.	195
French „		„	Polish Index		196
Teutonic.			Servian „		„
Gothic Index		„	Lithuanian Index		„
Old Teutonic „		193	Lettish „		197
Old High German		„	Old Prussian „		„
Middle High German Index		194	*Celtic.*		
New High German „		„	Old Celtic Index		„
Old Saxon „		„	Old Irish „		„
Frisian „		„	Middle Irish „		204
Low German „		„	Modern Irish „		„
Middle Dutch „		„	Welsh „		„
Anglo-Saxon „		„	Kymric „		208
English „		195	Cornish „		„
Old Norse „		„	Armoric „		211

CELTIC INDEX TO PHONOLOGY IN IRISH.

Gaulish and Old Celtic Index	p. 213	Kymric Index	p.	220
Irish Index	213	Cornish „		„
Welsh „	220	Armoric „		„

CHAPTER I.

ON SIMPLE WORD-FORMATION: ROOTS, STEMS, AND DERIVATIVES.

§. 1. *Of Roots and Root-Forms.*

THE method of investigation employed in the modern science of Comparative Etymology may be described as an analytic process, to which the words of cognate languages are subjected; consisting in successively stripping from them certain letters or syllables which have the symbolical power of expressing the qualities, proportions, or relations in space and time, under which the subject contemplates the object—that is, so much of the phonetic whole constituting the word, as fixes or limits the idea intended to be expressed by it, and makes it the symbol of a definite conception. By this stripping process we obtain a residual syllable or nucleus to which the term Root (French, *Racine;* German, *Wurzel*) is given. A large number of different words in the same language, subjected to this kind of analysis, may leave the same syllable or root; hence we may consider the Root of a series of words as a phonetic symbol of an individual but logically indefinite idea, the limitation or logical definition of the idea being given by the sounds or syllables stripped off. The assumption of such mono-syllabic nuclei in words has given rise to the hypothesis that the formative process or growth of languages was a synthesis, the reverse of our analysis; or, in other terms, that the first symbols of ideas in language were Roots, out of which were elaborated the more developed forms and words.

If we compare the different forms which the same word assumes in the several dialects of a language, we shall find that the difference is due to the substitution of certain letters for others. A similar comparative study of all languages, shows us that they may be grouped into families, the members of each of which may be looked upon as dialects in a wider sense, of some more primitive language. Although at first sight, the permutations, or letter changes from one language to another, appear to be quite arbitrary, they nevertheless take place according to definite laws, which are proper to each language. A very good example of these phonetic laws is afforded by the remarkable permutation or alteration in historical times of the mute consonants in the Teutonic languages (*Lautverschiebung*), schematized by J. Grimm, according to which these consonants appear, in passing from the Greek or Latin to the Gothic, and thence to the Old High German, to be shifted forward in the direction in which the sounds are naturally developed—that is, the labial, dental, and palatal medials pass into the corresponding tenues, and the latter into the aspirates—thus the Gr. medial *b* is represented by the Goth. tenuis *p* and by the O.H.G. aspirate *ph* or *f*; the Gr. *p* by Goth. *f* and the O.H.G. *b*, etc.; the Gr. dental medial *d* by the Goth. tenuis *t* and the O.H.G. aspirate *th*; the Gr. medial *g*, by the Goth. tenuis *k*, and the O.H.G. aspirate *ch*, *e.g.*: Gr. πούς, gen. ποδός, Goth. *fótus*, O.H.G. *vuoz*; δάκρυ, Goth. *tagr*, O.H.G. *zahar* (the sibilant *z* for the aspirate *th*); Lat. *gelidus*, Goth. *kalds*, O.H.G. *chalt*, etc.[1]

By the study of the phonetic laws which govern the permutations or letter changes in each member of a family of languages, we may determine the words in each family which have had a common origin. On analysing these words we obtain a series of residual syllables, which, like the words from which they were obtained, differ from each other, and are nevertheless but forms of the same root. The primitive form of the root could only be found in the mother tongue of the family; but as no monument of this language has been handed down to us, we can only discover this root inductively, by a comparative study of all the languages of the family. What we obtain by the analysis of the words of a language, are not, therefore, properly speaking, roots, but only *Root Forms*. The root forms of the same root may often present so great a dissimilarity, that, without a knowledge of the permutations of the letters, and a comparison of all the forms in a family, we would not suspect any relationship between them. Thus the German word *wer* presents at first sight so little resemblance to the Latin one *quis*, that we could not suppose that they were the same word, or even that they contained the same root; and yet this becomes evident enough by comparing the forms of the word in several languages, which give us the intermediate links, *e. g.*: Skr. *kas*; Gr., τις; Lat., *quis*; Goth., *hvas*; O.H.G., *huer*; N.H.G., *wer*. The object of comparative etymology is to determine first, the root forms, and then the roots; but it also includes that of the grammatical terminations which are added to the roots. Comparative Etymology may, consequently, be considered as a species of Palaeography which has for its object the determination, from their mutilated relics, of

---

[1] I do not profess, in this Introduction, to discuss the value of particular laws, my object being merely to explain the nature of Roots, Stems, etc. I have endeavoured to state Grimm's law as simply as possible, but, of course, the form in which I have given it is not wholly unobjectionable; and this the more so, as I am aware that some of the examples do not harmonize with Benary's important law.

the primitive forms of a language,—of that of the parent language of a family of languages,—and, ultimately, of the parent language of all; exactly as the object of Palaeontology is to reconstruct from the bones, shells, etc., the forms which extinct animals had when living.

Leaving out of consideration interjections, we may classify the different kinds of words of which speech is composed according to the following division, which is that usually followed by grammarians:—

CORPORAL WORDS.   FORMATIONAL WORDS.

I. SUBSTANTIVES.

Noun-substantives.   Pronominal substantives (pronouns, *I, thou, he, she, it, who,* etc.)

II. ATTRIBUTIVES.

A. WORDS DEFINING THE SUBJECT—PREDICATE WORDS.

α. *Adjectives.*

a. Qualitative adjectives.   b. 1 Quantitative adjectives (numerals, etc.)
                                              2 Pronominal adjectives (*mine, thine, this,* etc.)
                                              3 Articles.

β. *Verbs.*

a. Concrete verbs (*to love*).   b. Abstract verbs (*to be*).

B. WORDS DEFINING THE PREDICATE—ADVERBS.

a. Qualitative adverbs (derived from adjectives).   b. Adverbs of time, place, number, etc.

III. PARTICLES.

Prepositions.
Conjunctions.

This arrangement renders the distinction between the words which constitute the materials of speech, and those which express the varying relations of space, number, time, etc., very evident. And as the words of each class may be subjected to the process of analysis, we get two kinds of roots, distinguished also as *Corporal*, and *Formal* or *Formational Roots*. As we may get the same root from a noun, an adjective, a verb, or an adverb, a corporal root must be considered to have the embryonic power of a whole sentence; that is, of expressing a whole concrete conception, but without possessing any means of expressing the person, time, etc. Corporal roots may therefore be considered as germs of nouns and verbs, rather than as possessing the explicit power of either.

All languages may be classified into a few classes, according to the manner in which the two kinds of roots are joined to one another. We may, for example, assume three stages of composition: 1, Parathesis, or the mere juxtaposition of roots; 2, Agglutination, or the adhesion of roots; 3, Amalgamation, or the fusion of roots.

Parathesis. A language at this stage would consist of monosyllabic roots simply, the grammatical relations being expressed by juxtaposition with other roots. The same root, according to its position in a sentence, may perform the function of a noun, an adjective, verb, etc. Pott calls such languages, of which the Chinese affords an example, *Isolating languages.*

Agglutination. In this stage the grammatical relations—mood, tense, person, and class of verbs, number, cases, etc., of nouns, are expressed by affixes to monosyllabic roots, which, though invariable in function, are not inseparable from the root, the several relations being expressed by successively added affixes. In some agglutinating languages all the affixes are suffixes; thus, in the Finno-Tatarian languages, where the root-vowel, itself inflexible, modifies the vowels of the suffixes, giving thereby rise to the so-called vowel harmony. Other agglutinating languages have apparently almost exclusively prefixes, as the Kaffir languages of South Africa. The Semitic languages show a higher stage of agglutination by admitting of prefixes as well as suffixes, the cases of nouns being expressed by prefixing prepositions,[2] and still more by employing internal vowel changes as means of inflexion.[3]

Amalgamation. When the corporal and formational elements become so intimately blended that both fuse into an indissoluble unity, the formational elements give rise to true inflexion, which produces a complete logical distinction of the grammatical categories. Languages at this stage are called by Pott, *Amalgamating.*

Bopp's classification is somewhat different. He makes three classes also, the first corresponding to the parathetical; but in the second he includes both agglutinating and amalgamating, and makes of the Semitic languages a third distinct class.

The amalgamating languages are consequently those which have the most perfect organization, and include the Indo-European family of languages, which comprises the Sanskrit, Latin, Greek, Celtic, Slavonian, Gothic, and their modern descendants. In their primitive state such languages cannot contain uninflected roots. In process of time, however, and especially if great per-

---

[2] The Arabic, however, has real case terminations.

[3] Some examples illustrative of the process of agglutination in the Northern Family of languages may be found at pp. 92 and 94, vol. I., of the ATLANTIS, in the first part of my paper "On the influence which the Physical Geography, the Animal and Vegetable Productions, etc., of different regions exert upon the Languages, Mythology, and early Literature of Mankind, etc."

turbations and mixtures of different peoples take place, the grammatical elements affixed to the roots get shortened, mutilated, or drop off wholly, so that the root is laid bare. In modern languages, as, for example, the English, we find several naked roots, which, however, have the value of the words from which they have been obtained by the gradual wearing off of the clothing; thus the word *hand* is in reality a root-form, having now the full signification of a primitive noun, which in Gothic had the form *handus*.

No matter how great the phonetic modifications which a root may undergo in producing a number of root forms, it preserves its identity. Some philologists, however, admit of exceptions to this rule; that is, they consider that certain phonetic modifications of a root may alter its signification so as to produce a new root. The process by which this is believed to be effected is called *Root Variation*, and may be described as a phonetic change that modifies or tempers more or less the concrete value of the root, without the latter ceasing to be a root. The result of this variation is to produce in the same language, or in cognate branches of the same family of languages, two or more affiliated roots with almost synonymous signification, but differing in a slight degree phonetically. These synonymous roots may appear to have been evolved, as it were, parallel to one another, or the one to be primary, and the other secondary. Of two such synonymous roots we may consider the one which has the greatest phonetic dimensions to be the secondary root. This hypothesis has been so far generalized by some philologists that they believe all roots of considerable phonetic dimensions to be secondary roots, even where we can no longer detect the primitive root. Many, on the other hand, do not admit that such a change can at all take place in a root. Assuming, however, that this kind of variation takes place, it must do so either: 1, by simple modification of one or more letters—vowels or consonants—*e.g.* γλαφ, γλυφ; γραφ, *grab;* or 2, by the addition of a sound or sounds— *e. g.* Skr. *bhá*, to shine, which gives the extended root *bhásh*, to speak, Gr. φη (φημί), to speak, extended roots φαυ, to shine, to speak (φά(ϝ)ος, πιφαύσκω), φαν, to shine (φαίνω); Skr. root *ru*, to sound, extended root *rud*, to weep. In the change of the root into a stem, to be described further on, there is no such modification of the root-idea.

§. 2. *Of Elementary Word-formation, and Inflexion.*

Assuming that language was synthetically developed from isolated monosyllabic roots, we have next to consider how words were formed from roots in the Indo-European, or amalgamating languages, to which family the following pages will exclusively refer. The development of words from roots may be called *Word-formation*, but the elementary words thus formed must undergo further modification, in order to express the varying relations of speech. Thus, a Verb must have special contrivances to express time, person, etc.; and the Noun, number and case, etc. This further modification is called *Inflexion*, or *Word-bending*. The processes by which elementary Word-formation and Inflexion are effected are fundamentally the same; they are—

1. Internal phonetic change, which can only affect the root-vowel, as the change of a consonant would necessarily produce a change in the symbolic value of the root.
2. Addition of phonetic material to the root, which may be of two kinds:
    a. Such as springs from the root itself; or Duplication.
    b. Affixes; which may be Prefixes or Suffixes, but especially the latter. These Affixes may be:
        α. Single sounds or syllables, which only are used as formational elements of words, having by themselves no signification in the fully-formed language, and do not consequently occur isolated in it.
        β. Affixes which possess of themselves a distinct meaning, and consequently may occur as isolated words in the language.

In the Semitic languages, vowel-change is a predominant mode of word-formation and word-inflexion. In the Indo-European languages it only appears as *Ablaut*;[4] that is, an interchange in the body of the root of the primitive pure short vowels, *a*, *i*, *u*, but, at a later period, of the newer vowels *e* and *o* also, which were produced by the softening of the primitive vowels. This kind of vocalic change (ablaut) appears to have been a fundamental principle of word-formation in the Teutonic languages.

The vowel change known as *Umlaut* is the change or obscuration of the fundamental root vowels *a*, *o*, *u*, into the impure or obscure vowels, *ä*, *ö*, *ü*, under the regressive assimilating influence of *i* (or *u*) in the syllable immediately following the root. In the Teutonic languages, umlaut by means of *u* only occurs in the Old Norse, in which it has been fully developed; umlaut does

---

[4] Wherever special technical terms are invented in any language to express certain definite ideas, they should be retained in translating from that language, if the laws of euphony of the language into which the translation is made at all admit of it. The words *ablaut, umlaut, vorlaut, nachlaut, anlaut, inlaut,* and *auslaut* are convenient terms, and better than any which could be made out of Greek words. I have consequently used them throughout. Ablaut, umlaut, vorlaut, and nachlaut are fully explained where they first occur. *Anlaut* is the initial sound, and *auslaut* is the final sound of a word.

not at all occur in the Gothic. In the Zend umlaut is produced by both the vowels (*i* and *u*), *a* becoming *ai* under the influence of an *i* following, and *au* under the influence of an *u* following. When the *i* is softened to *e*, the umlaut remains as a rule, and even is retained when the *e* is dropt. Umlaut thus apparently acquires the flexional signification of the ending, by the action of which it was produced, and now acts as its substitute, although originally it was a mere phonetic consequence of it. We have a good example of this in the preterite of the conjunctive mood in the O. H. German; the preterite forms of the strong conjugation, which have conditional or potential signification, are characterized by an *î*, *i*. In the M. and N. H. German, this *i* passes into *e*, but leaves evidence of its existence in the umlaut of the root vowel, which now characterizes the conjunctive: O.H.G. Præt. Ind. sing. first, second, and third persons, *las*, *lâsi*, *las*; præt. conj. *lâsî*, *lâsîs*, *lâsi*; M. H. G., *laese*, *laesest*, *laese*. The following are additional examples of umlaut: O. H. G., *anti* (*enti*), M.H.G., *Ende*; O.H.G., *handi*, *hendi*, N.H.G., *Hände*; O.H.G., *trâki*, N.H.G., *träge*. There is also a phonetic process of regressive assimilation, the reverse of umlaut, and which is called *Breaking*, or *Fracture*, by which *i* is changed into *e*, and *o* into *u*, by the action of an *a* following.

The remarkable law of progressive vocal assimilation already alluded to, and which constitutes so characteristic a feature of the Finno-Tatarian family of languages, may be described as a kind of *progressive umlaut*, which it will be useful to describe, as it will be alluded to hereafter. In the languages of that family the vowels may be divided into three classes: hard, *a*, *o*, *u*, and in some languages, *y*; 2. soft, *ä*, *ö*, *ü*; 3. neutral, *i*, and in some languages, as the Finnish and Samoyede, *e* also. If the root syllable, which is invariable in all the languages of the family, be hard, the vowel of the suffixes cannot be soft; conversely, hard vowels cannot follow soft ones. The vowel *i*, and in Finnish, etc., *e*, also, may be followed either by a hard or soft vowel. The Irish rule of "broad to broad, and slender to slender", may be looked upon as progressive assimilation; the Irish broad vowels being *a*, *o*, *u*, and the slender *e*, *i*. Wherever this rule is followed, a consonant, or consonants, should in every written word lie between either two broad, or two slender vowels; or, in other words, if the vowel of a syllable be broad, the vowel of the next succeeding syllable should be broad; if the vowel be slender, the following one must likewise be slender.

The peculiar weakening of the root vowel which is produced in Latin words by the vowel of a prefix, whether due to composition or reduplication, may likewise be looked upon as a species of progressive assimilation analogous to that which exists in the Irish. The Finno-Tatarian languages having no prefixes, all progressive assimilation must affect not the root but the endings, hence the difference between this phonetic change in the Latin and the languages in question. The following examples will show the character of the change in the Latin: under the influence of *e*, *i*, and also *o*, *a* becomes *ĭ* or *e*, *ĕ* becomes *ĭ*, *œ* passes into *ī*, *au* sometimes into *ū*, *ō* into *ĭ*, *ŭ* into *ĕ*—*tango, tetigi; pars, expers; facio, efficio; placeo, displiceo; jacio, objicio; annus, perennis; fallo, refello; carpo, decerpo; castus, incestus; ars, iners; lego, diligo; rego, corrigo; quœro, inquiro; caedo, cecĭdi; claudo, includo; notus = gnotus, cognitus; juro, pejero,* etc. There are, however, numerous exceptions, and in compound words formed by prefixed particles or prepositions, such as *circum, ante, per,* etc., it does not occur. In *ago, abigo,* we have a change into *i* produced by *a*.

Phonetic change, by means of affixes, is the great agent in word-forming in the Indo-European languages. The first kind of affixes are those employed in word-formation properly so called, and in inflexion. The second kind of affixes—that is, those which possess of themselves a distinct meaning—are used in making compound words. Some of the first kind of affixes may, however, be distinctly traced to independent words: as examples may be mentioned the personal endings of the verbs, the signs of many of the cases, etc. Thus the ending of the first person in the Sanskrit and Greek was *mi*: bha-*mi*, tudâ-*mi*, dâsyâ-*mi*; εἰ-μι, φη-μί, Dor. φα-μί; in the Latin the *i* has been lost, and the ending is now only *m*—*su-m, inqua-m, dicere-m*; this *mi* is the pronominal stem *ma* softened to *mi*, as we actually find it in *mi-hi*. The first person plural ending in the Sanskrit is -*mas*, in the Veda dialect, *masi*, in the Doric dialect of the Greek, μες: Skr., bhâ-*mas*; Dor., φα-μές; in the Latin it was *mus*, and in the O. H. German, *més*. From the Veda form *masi*, Curtius considers the ending to be made up of the pronominal stems of the first and second pronouns: *ma* + *si* (*si* = *ti*); that is, *I* + *thou* = *we*. Again, the Greek endings, -σα and -σω, of the 1 Aorist (ἔγραψα for ἔ-γραφ-σα), and of the future (γφάψω for γράφ-σω), and of the Latin ending of the perfect, -*si* (*scripsi*), are obtained from the verb, in the Greek εἰ-μί, Dor. ἐμμί, Lithuanian *esmi*, root *as*. And lastly, the Latin imperfect, -*bam*, and the future, -*bo*, are derived from the root *fu* (in *fuam, fu-turus, fu-i*). The English suffixes -*ly*, -*hood*, -*ship*, -*some*, are also good examples, meaning originally *like*, *state* (A. Sax. *hâd*), *shape*, *same*. Indeed, the distinction between simple word-formation and composition cannot be always accurately defined; practically, however, it exists in fully formed languages.

If some of the affixes can thus be derived from significant words, it is perfectly reasonable that philologists should endeavour to generalize the fact, and assume as probable that all word-forming and flexional affixes, which possess the symbolic signification of formational words, were originally formed by affixing such words to the word to be grammatically modified. In modern languages where the flexional endings have been worn off, their functions are again performed by words already existing in the language. Such a view naturally leads to the assumption that in the gradual development of languages all word-formation and flexion were synthesis or composition.

The hypothesis that word-formation and flexion were primitively synthesis, and that the phonetic additions by which they are affected were at first independent words, constitutes the basis of what is known as the agglutination theory. This theory is now generally considered to be the correct one. Some philologists seem disposed, however, to modify it so far as to admit two kinds of word-forming and inflexional materials: 1, Simple sounds or syllables, which were never words by themselves, their symbolic power being derived from that which each individual letter is considered inherently to possess; 2, independent words worn out into word-forming and flexional elements.

§. 3. *Of Primary Stem-formation.*

In the foregoing sections three kinds of forms have been mentioned: 1, roots; 2, elementary word-forms; and 3, words clothed with the inflexional elements, which express their relations to each other as members of a sentence. But these do not include every form. The simple word-forms are not as a rule obtained by the direct addition of a grammatical element, derivational or inflexional, to the root. Between the root and the grammatically complete word there lies the *word-stem* (French, *Radical;* German, *Stamm,* and corresponding to the *Crude-form* of some English writers), to which, and not to the root itself, the grammatical elements are added. Stem-formation is, consequently, the first stage of word-formation, a stem is not a root, nor yet a complete word. From the root it is logically distinguished in this, that the unlimited, or, as we might say undulating contents of the root are fixed or solidified, and rendered fit to serve as a symbol of the completely determinate conception represented by the grammatical word. While there are but two classes of Roots, corporal and formational, there may be many kinds of Stems: for example, we may have verbal, nominal, pronominal, and particle Stems—each kind of root branching into many stems, according to the grammatical changes it may undergo. Instead, then, of three categories of phonetic forms, we have, in reality, four: Roots, Stems, being of a two-fold kind, Simple word-forms or derivatives, and Words clothed with inflexional elements.

Word-formation from roots consists, then, of two distinct processes: 1, the formation of stems from roots, or, *Stem-formation*; and 2, the formation of words from stems, or *Derivation* in its simplest form. Both processes are effected by phonetic means to be hereafter described, but here it may be useful to mention that they cannot always be absolutely distinguished,—the same phonetic change or addition being at one time stem-formation, and at another true derivation. There is, however, an essential difference between stems and derivatives, the basis of the true stem is the root, while the derivative always proceeds from the stem. The two processes are, therefore, logically, even when not phonetically, distinct.

The Phonetic methods of primary or Pure Stem-formation may now be described in detail; they are:—

I. *Modification of root-vowel.*

1. Ablaut proper, which is a very frequent change in the Greek; it is rather an accompaniment than a means of stem-formation. It does not often occur in the Latin, but in the Teutonic languages it is very common, and was apparently the primitive means of stem-formation. Examples: root N.H.G. *brach*, stems *brich, bruch;* root βαλ, stems βολ, βελ, verb ἔ-βαλ-ον, nouns βολ-ή, βέλ-ος (*tego, toga*).
2. Obscuration of the root-vowels *a* and *i* to *e*, and of *u* to *o*. The Greek and Latin have no fraction of *u, i* to *o, e*, the change is always the inverse. As an example of the breaking of *a* to *e* may be given: root *lag*, stems λεγ, *leg*, verbs λέγω, *lego;* and of *i* to *e*, the Teutonic root LIB, to remain (=λιπ), Goth. *liban*, to live = O.H.G. *lebên*.
3. Strengthening of the root-vowel, which may take place:
    a. By lengthening the short vowel, as: root λαθ, stems λnθ, λᾱθ, verbs λήθω, Dor. λᾱθω, nouns λήθη, Dor. λάθα.
    b Gunation[5] and Diphthongation—Examples of gunation: root ι, stem ει, verb εἶμι; root φυγ, stem φευγ, verb φεύγω; in Gothic, root *bug*, stem *baug;* root *vit*, stem *vait*. Examples of Diphthongation: root φαν, stem φαιν, verb φαίνω; root ταν, weakened root form τεν, stem τειν, verb τεινω; root δα, stem δαι, verb δαίω. The latter and similar roots ending in a vowel show the true relation of the *i* to the root-

---

[5] The term gunation is applied to the process by which *ê* (*ai*) is produced by prefixing *ă* to *i* or *î*, or *ô* (*au*) by prefixing *ă* to *u* or *û*. Diphthongation and gunation are well expressed by the German terms *nachlaut* and *vorlaut*.

vowel in φαίνω. Curtius has shown that in the latter the form was φαν-ι-ω, a derivational *i* (Sanskrit *ya*), being originally placed after the root, but which by metathesis afterwards entered the root. Gunation, according to some scholars, does not occur in the Latin, and consequently the derivational *i* retains its place outside the root in the verbs in *io* of the third conjugation, as *capio, morior*, etc. This opinion is not, however, strictly correct; for although gunation may be rare, the following examples show that it does sometimes occur: *foedus* for *foidus* (if we may connect πέ-ποιθ-α), root *fid*, πιθ, *bi(n)d; aurum, aurora*, compare *uro, us*-tum, Sanskrit root *ush*. The occurrence of this derivational *i* as an element of stem-formation gives rise to a distinct and important class of stems, which will be fully discussed further on in the section on *ya*- or *ia*-stems.

II. *Consonantal strengthening of the root.*
 1. Duplication or doubling of the final consonant.
  In the Greek λλ, dialectically ρρ and νν; σσ (Bœot.) permutated in the new Attic to ττ, root σπαρ, σπερ, stem σπερρ, verb σπερρω[6]; root κταν, κτεν, stem κτενν, verb κτεννω (Lesbian). In the Latin there is frequent duplication of *l*, root *pal, pel*, stem *pell*, verb *pello*, and in the German of *l* and *m*, root *scal*, O.H.G. *scellan*. In the former case it is the result of the assimilation of a derivational *y* by the final consonant.
 2. Affixation of a mute consonant foreign to the root. In the Greek and Latin a τ is thus affixed frequently, *e.g.*, root βλαβ, stem βλαπτ, verb βλάπτω; root τυπ, stem τυπτ, verb τύπτω; root *pac* or *pec*, stem *pect*, verb *pecto* [the Greek κτείς however suggests that the *ct* of *pecto* may be radical]. In the Teutonic languages this process is not now recognizable.
 3. Affixation or intercalation of a nasal.
  a. Nasalizing an internal vowel. This change is common in the Latin—*e.g.*, root *pag*, stem *pang*, verb *pango*; root *liq*=λιπ, stem *linq*, verb *linquo*; root *frag*, stem *frang*, verb *frango*; it also occurs in the Gothic, root *staþ*, inf. *standan*, Engl. *stand, stood*.
  b. Affixation of the nasal in the auslaut:
   a. After vowels. In the Greek we get from τα, γα, ταν, τεν, γεν. It is sometimes combined with diph-

---

[6] Such would have been the Lesbian form, at least; Attic, σπείρω.

thongation, as in root βa, stem βαιν, verb βαίνω,
In the Gothic we have ga becoming gang.

β. After consonants. Only few examples in the Greek; e.g., root ταμ, τεμ, stem τεμν, verb τέμνω. In the Latin we have sterno, sperno, etc.

c. Affixation of a whole syllable, accompanied by nasalization, of which we can only find examples in the Greek, e. g., νε, να, root δαμ, stem δαμνα, verb δαμνάω; as αν, by which the root-vowel becomes likewise nasalized, root λαθ, stem λανθαν, verb λανθάνω.

4. Reduplication: root, μνα, reduplicated stem μι-μνη, inchoative verb μι-μνή-σκ-ω. Lat. root min, men = Skr. man = μνα? stem me-min, verb memini.

All the more important methods of primary or pure stem-formation are embraced under the preceding categories. There are also a few exceptional cases, such as where an intensive s is introduced into the root, e. g., root μιγ, stem μισγ, verb μίσγω; Latin, misceo (compare Ir. cummasc, commixtio), which must not be confounded with the derivational sc of inchoative verbs. Besides primary or pure stems, there are, however, other classes of stems which are formed by the addition of a vowel, or of a syllable ending with a consonant, and which will be described hereafter. It may be well to observe here, that the circumstance of stems being formed by the addition of a whole syllable, the introduction of an intensive s into the body of the root, etc., shows us how cautious we should be in concluding that stem-forms, which at first sight appear extremely simple, are the roots themselves. For example, φαν and κριν, although apparently forms of very moderate phonetic dimensions, have been, in reality, enlarged from φα and κρι. Then again, it is necessary to be careful to distinguish between the stem and the pure words or stem-words. For example, ἔπος and corpus are true stems, as is shown by attaching flexional elements to them; thus, ἔπεσ-ος contracted to ἔπεος, corpus-is softened to corpor-is. On the other hand, φιλέ(ω), λόγο(ς), fructu(s), are full words, containing the derivational elements, ω, ς, s, respectively.

§. 4. *Of Noun-formation, and Derivative Stems.*

The formation of stems may be considered the first separation of words into grammatical categories, but it does not complete it; for although some stems are essentially verbal, and others nominal, there are many which admit of being made the basis either of verbs or of nouns. The complete separation is only effected when one of the signs which characterize the complete word is affixed to the stem. These grammatical signs are the derivational and inflexional elements.

The characteristic signs by which the stem becomes a verb, are the personal endings µι, σι, τι; *m*, *s*, *t*, etc.: root ι, stem ει, verb εἶμι,—µι being the personal ending for the first person sing. ind.; Skr. root *tud*, stem *tuda*, verb *tuda-si*,—*si* being the ending of the second person sing. ind. As Dr. Ebel's paper does not deal with the verb, I shall confine myself exclusively to nouns. The characteristic signs by which nouns are formed are the gender and case endings. The vocative, from its nature, ought to present us with the pure nominal stem, but in the actual language this is not generally the case; and hence it is found more convenient to assume the nominative as the basis of analysis.

One of the most characteristic distinctions between objects is that which life affords, and accordingly the sign, by the affixation of which to the stem the nominative form of the noun is produced, is a gender sign. For living objects, the sign primitively affixed to noun-stems in the Indo-European languages was *s*. Some scholars hold that neuter nouns were distinguished by *t*, which they consider possesses a certain power of symbolizing lifeless or inert bodies. But the evidence that *t* was ever used, except in pronominal declension, as a sign of the neuter gender, is very doubtful. The Gothic neut. adjective-ending *ata* is, according to Bopp, merely a suffixed pronoun. Mankind has, however, at all times, figuratively endowed certain lifeless objects with life, and abstract conceptions, such as justice, virtue, etc., are expressed by words of masculine or feminine gender, according as our fancy chooses to consider them of the one or other sex; the names which are used to symbolize these objects or abstract conceptions take, accordingly, the sign of living objects.

The nominative sign *s* has, however, been but imperfectly preserved; in the Sanskrit it is usually softened to *h*; the feminine forms, which incline to vocalic auslaut with long vowels, seem to have thrown it off, apparently with the object of marking the distinction of the sexes. This tendency to have vocalic auslaut is well shown in the adjectives having the endings in the Sanskrit, *as*, *â*, *am*; in the Greek, ος, α (η), ον. Even masculine forms often lose the *s*. In the Zend and Lat. it is frequently dropped altogether. In the Gothic it is generally only preserved in masculine substantives with vocalic stems, and in masculine adjectives and pronouns. In the O.H.G. the substantives have altogether lost it, while in adjectives and pronouns it has become *r*.

The neutral *t* of the pronominal forms has to a great extent been lost. In the Greek it does not occur at all; in the Latin it has become *d*: *id, illud, quid*, etc. In the Gothic it occurs in the pronouns *is, si, ita;* English *he, she, it;* Old Irish *é, sí, ed;* Gothic *sa, so, thata*, Anglo-Saxon *se, seó, thät*=Greek ὁ, ἡ, τό for τοτ= Sanskrit *tat*. In the O. H. German it becomes *z*: Gothic third person of the pronoun masc. *is*, neuter *ita*=O. H. German masc. *ir* sometimes *er*, neuter *iz*, sometimes *ez*. In the Gothic *blindata, gódata*, O. H. German *plintaz, guotaz*, M. H. German *blindez, guotez*, the ending *ata*, as above observed, is a suffixed pronoun, and cannot consequently be considered as a proof that *t* was the sign of the neuter, in other than the pronominal declension. In many cases the neutral *t* has been replaced by *m* or *n*, which, however, belonged originally to the accusative singular.

The grammatical signs or endings cannot always be directly affixed to stems; this is especially the case with those beginning with a consonant, and where the stem ends consonantally. If in such cases the ending were affixed directly, the final stem-consonant would be rendered liable to change, and the modification may proceed so far as to render the stem unrecognizable. Therefore a vowel is introduced between the stem and the ending, which originally had a mere phonetic function, and possessed no etymological or grammatical signification. The vowel by itself is always short, and consesequently very changeable. It is often an extremely difficult problem to distinguish between the vowel thus added and a derivational vowel, and therefore between a derivational and stem-form. It is also an important one: for this vowel, though originally having no stem-forming or derivational character, has gradually come to be looked upon as an integral part of the stem-ending, and has even penetrated where it was not absolutely required.[7] It will be useful to call this stem-forming vowel in nominal stems the *Declension Vowel*, in order to distinguish it from a second vowel which is sometimes used as a mere copulative in the oblique cases, and which is never an integral part of the stem-ending. A similar stem-forming vowel is found in verbal stems.

Forms which must be looked upon as true stems are, however,

---

[7] In Finnish nearly all the stems are two-syllabled. The first or root syllable is accentuated, the second has a short vowel auslaut. This short vowel, unlike the root-vowel, which is invariable, sounds differently according as the stem is pronominal or verbal. It is a mere rhythmical addition to the root which sometimes acquires the signification of a derivational suffix, and has consequently a striking analogy to the declension vowel of the Indo-European languages, and makes Finnish stems appear very much like those in the Gothic, which will be described further on as vocalic middle forms. The affixation of this vowel is the only mode of stem-formation in the Finnish; in Hungarian it has been to a great extent obliterated. It would be extremely interesting to trace this rhythmical stem-forming vowel through the whole Finno-Tatarian Family. Here however, it would be out of place to dwell further on the analogy.

sometimes made by the addition of a whole syllable, the consonant forming the auslaut, taking the place of the declension vowel. The forms produced in this way approach nearer to the character of derivatives than those obtained by the mere addition of the declension vowel,—indeed many of them have the character of true derivatives.

In the Greek nouns in της, we have a perfectly analogous class of stems formed by the addition of a syllable ending vocally instead of consonantally; they are, however, in part undoubted derivatives formed by affixing the derivational suffix τη to an already fully formed stem. We may call all such stems, formed by the addition of a syllable to verbal or nominal stems, which thus perform, as it were, the function of roots, *Derivative Stems*, and treat of them as a distinct class of vocalic or consonantal stems, according as the suffix ends in a vowel or a consonant. But as there is a real logical distinction between the true stems which start from the root, and these pseudo-stems which are derivatives of true stems, it will be better not to consider such pseudo-stems under the head of stems, but to refer all of them to the category of derivatives.

We have accordingly three distinct classes of true nominal stems as regards their relations to the grammatical endings:— 1, primary or pure stems, to which the nominative *s* is directly affixed; 2, stems which require a vowel between them and the ending; and 3, stems formed by the addition of a syllable ending in a consonant in place of a vowel. The second and third classes may be called secondary stems or, better still, middle forms, that is, intermediate between pure stems and true derivatives. Of the pure stems some have vocalic and some consonantal auslaut. The middle forms, produced by affixing a declension vowel, may all be looked upon as vocalic ending stems, while the middle forms, which result from affixing a consonantal ending syllable, are consonantal stems.

The following table, to which I have likewise added the derivative stems, will render the classification of stems above given more intelligible:—

I. True Stems formed from the Root.

Vocalic Stems.

1. Pure Stems.
2. Middle Forms produced by:
   a. affixing the declension vowels, *a i, u.*
   b. *ya*-stems, or, *a*-stems, with an intercalated *i* (*y*) before the declension vowel.

Consonantal Stems.

1. Pure Stems.
2. Middle forms or stems produced by affixing a syllable ending consonantally to the root.

II. Pseudo, or Derivative Stems.

3. Stems formed by the addition of a derivational suffix ending in a vowel, to an already fully-formed stem.

3. Stems formed by the addition of a derivational suffix, ending consonantally, to an already fully-formed stem.

§. 5. Of Vocalic Stems.

PURE STEMS. All monosyllabic nouns may, strictly speaking, be considered to be pure stem-words, in which the nominal sign is directly affixed to the stem without any intervening phonetic material. Such nouns occur in the Greek and Latin, though they are not numerous.

GREEK: root κι, stem κῑ, noun κί-ς (masc. gen. κι-ός), γραῦς (γρᾱ-ός); δρῦς, θώς (roots δρυ, θο, stems δρῦ, θω) possess still more of the character of pure stems. Some forms usually included under this category are undoubtedly not primitive pure vocalic stems; for example, βοῦς may perhaps be more properly reckoned among the consonantal stems, as it stands for βοϝ-ς (root *bo*).

LATIN. In the Latin there are extremely few forms which can be considered, strictly speaking, as pure vocalic stems. Perhaps the only form is *grus*, stem *gru*, for it is doubtful whether the *r* in the plural *vî-r-es* of *vîs* (stem *vîr?*),—and in the old form of the genitive *sueris* (*su-er-is*) of *sus*, Sanskrit, *sû-kara*,—be not organic instead of being, as is generally supposed, merely euphonic.

GOTHIC. In the Gothic a number of such monosyllabic words, belonging to what is called the strong declension, is to be found; in the masculine and feminine they have the nominative sign *s*, while in the neuter no suffix can be found, and the stem accordingly occurs in its naked form, *e.g.:* masc. *fisk-s*, *dag-s*, *balg-s;* fem. *anst-s;* and neut. *leik*. These nouns correspond with the Greek nouns derived from consonantal stems: θρίξ, αἴξ, πῦρ, and the Latin nouns *urb-s*, *pon-s*, *mel*. In the nominative case, the analogy is complete; but if we compare them through all their cases, we shall find that in the Greek and Latin the nouns of this kind affix the case-endings to the stem in exactly the same way throughout, namely, its nominative directly, and the others by means of a copulative vowel, which is the same in all the cases, while the Gothic nouns take different vowels in the plural. For example:

Nom. and Voc. . .	fiskô-s	balge-is
Gen. . .	fiskê	balge
Dat. . .	fiska-m	balgi-m
Acc. . .	fiska-ns	balgi-ns.

It would appear from this, that the Gothic nouns under consideration are only relics of more primitive forms, still preserved in the plural, but blotted out in the singular. According to this view, all the nominal stems must have been clothed with a vocalic auslaut, which was either *a* or *i*, and called by Grimm the *Declension Vowels*, a term which I have extended above to the corresponding vowels of the vocalic middle forms in the Greek and Latin. The primitive form of *fisk-s* must therefore have been *fiska-s*, and of *balg-s*, *balgi-s*—forms which approach very close to the Latin, as may be seen by comparing the primitive form of *gast-s*, *gasti-s* = Latin, *hosti-s*. The view just put forward is supported by the circumstance that there exists a class of nouns, in which the clothing or declension vowel of the stem is *u*, that are not syncopated like those with the vowels *a* and *i*. Although at first sight the Teutonic languages appear to contain the largest number of pure stems, the preceding considerations apparently show that there are no pure nominal stems in those languages. On this account I will include the whole of those Gothic nouns under the middle forms with vocalic auslaut.

MIDDLE FORMS ENDING VOCALLY. The term middle form implies that we have passed beyond the stem, but have not yet arrived at a true derivative. The nouns derived from those middle forms have the same analogy to those obtained from pure stems, that the Greek verbs in άω, έω, ίω, etc.—as τιμάω, φιλέω, μεθύω,—have to some of those in μι,—as εἰμί, φημί, etc. The nominal middle forms have, however, much less of a derivational character than the verbs above named; so that, while always bearing their mode of genesis in mind, we may consider them as vocalic stems.

As the primitive vowels were *a, i, u,*—*ĕ* and *o* having been formed later,—the primitive stem-forming vowels must have been also *a, i, u*. To these were added at later language-periods *e* and *o*,—*ĕ* being formed by the softening of *ā*, *e* of *i*, and *o* of *a*. There is also a secondary *u* produced from *a*, which must not be confounded with the primitive *u*. We may consequently include all vocalic stems under *a*-stems, *i*-stems, and *u*-stems.

I-STEMS.—I-stems approach closest to the character of pure stems. In the Latin the *i* often becomes *e;* in the Greek it sometimes becomes in the oblique cases ε.

GREEK.—The masculines and feminines of the third declension in -ις, gen. -ιος, -εως, belong to the *i*-stems; *e.g.*, φύσις (-εος) πόλις. There are no neuter nouns in *i*. The adjectives like ἴδρις, ἴδρι are of this class.

LATIN.—The masculines and feminines of the third declension in *is*, and the feminines in *ēs*, which do not take an augmenting syllable in the genitive, belong to the *i*-stems, as, *hosti-s*, *civi-s*, *aede-s;* the *i* being changed in the latter into the long *e* characteristic of feminines. In neuters the *i* is changed into *ĕ*, but in the plural the *i* again appears: *mar-ĕ, mar-i-s, mar-i-a*. The stems, *brevi, dulci, levi*, of the adjectives, *brevis, dulcis, levis*, belong to this category.

GOTHIC.—Among the Gothic *i*-stems which correspond to the preceding, may be mentioned the primitive forms: masc., *gastis, gardis, balgis*, existing in the Gothic, in the syncopated forms: *gasts, gards, balgs*, but showing traces of the vocalic clothing of the stem in the plural: nom., *gasteis, gardeis, balgeis*; fem., *dêdis, vaurtis*, syncopated in the Gothic to *dêds, vaurts*; nom. plur., *dêdeis, vaurteis*. It will be seen from the preceding, that the feminines also retain the nominative sign *s*, the feminine form appearing to be marked by a gunation of the vowels of the endings in the genitive and dative singular, thus:

	Masc.	Fem.
Nom.	gast-s	ded-s
Gen.	gast-is	ded-ais
Dat.	gast-a	ded-ai

As in the Greek there are no neuters formed from *i*-stems.

In addition to the feminines above discussed, and all of which belong to the strong declension, there is another peculiar class of *i*-stems belonging to feminine nouns of the weak declension, such as *managei*, gen. *manageins*, which will be better understood when I treat of the *a*-stems.

Adjectives derived directly from stems, and not through other forms, although differing essentially from substantives in their flexion, exhibited primitively the same distinction of stems into *a*-, *i*-, and *u*-stems, corresponding to the Greek adjectives in ος, α, ον, and υς, εια, υ; and to the Latin in *us, a, um*, and in *is, e*. But the primitive distinction is very much obscured in the Gothic, in which, with the exception of traces, the *i*-stems have wholly died out, while only a few of the *u*-stems remain; and even these pass in the oblique cases into the *a*-stems, with the addition of a derivational *i* (see the discussion of this subject under the head *a*-stems), so that the primitive character of the stem is only recognizable in the nominative. In the Gothic adjective there are consequently only *a*- and *u*-stems to be distinguished.

A-STEMS.—GREEK AND LATIN.—The *a*-stems in the Greek and Latin admit of being divided into two classes:—

1. Stems in which the primitive *a* has been preserved unchanged, or changed into *ē*, and which may be subdivided into:
    α. Stems with primitive short *a*.
    β. Stems with *ā* or *ē*.

2. Stems in which the primitive *a* has been changed into *o* in the Greek, and into *u* in the Latin.

A-stems with primitive short a. In the Greek the masculines of the first declension in -ας, -ης are referred to this class, e.g., βορέας, Ἑρμείας contracted to Ἑρμῆς; the nominative ς is retained, but the vowel is inorganically lengthened. In the Latin, also, only the masculines of the first declension, which, like the feminines of the same declension, have lost the nominative *s*, belong to this category, as, *scriba, agri-cola*, etc. Pott considers the long vowel as the result of contraction. It is probable that all the words belonging to this form are, in reality, derivatives in the second degree from nominal and verbal stems, that is, they contain, besides the nominative *s*, a second derivational element, which may still be recognized in the Greek nouns in της, as, πολίτης, etc., in which the derivational suffix is the syllable τη, as has been already pointed out in discussing the different classes of stems at p. 17.

A-stems with ā or ē. As was stated above, feminine nouns prefer long vowels and vocalic auslaut; accordingly we find that this class includes the feminines of the first declension in the Greek and Latin, all of which have no nominative *s*. In the Latin the *ā* is invariably shortened, but in the Greek it is partly retained, or changed into η and partly into ă, e.g., χώρᾱ, δίκη, σφῦρᾰ. While the vocative of the *a*-stems, with primitive short *a*, appears as a rule with the organic short *a*, that of the stems with *ā* or *ē* is the same as the nominative, and consequently sometimes has an inorganic short *a* whenever the nominative has one. The primitive long vowel has been preserved in the form *ē*, and likewise the nominative *s*, even in the vocative, in the nouns from stems of this class, which belong to the Latin fifth declension, which is but an older form of the first, e.g., *di-e-s, fid-e-s*. Here also we meet with forms which appear to belong to the class of vocalic stems obtained by means of a derivational syllable-suffix, as described above, the analogy being strongly supported by their admitting of being declined either according to the first or fifth declension, e.g., *materies* or *materia, canities* or *canitia*.

A-stems, in which the primitive a has been changed in the Greek into o, and in the Latin into u. This change occurs in the words of the second declension in ος, ον, and *us, um;* those in ος and *us* are, as a rule, masculine (*as* in the Sanskrit is always masculine); there are some, however, exceptionally feminine, as ἡ τάφρος, *fagus*, etc. The vocative shortens *o, u,* to *ĕ*, has organically no nominative *s*, and in the neuter is the same as in the nominative. To this category belong the Greek adjectives in ος, α (η), ον, and the Latin ones in *us, ă, um*. From this it will be seen that the vowel is shortened in the feminine in the

Latin, but not in the Greek; but, on the other hand, some Greek adjectives of this category do not distinguish the feminine at all.

GOTHIC.—To the Gothic *a*-stems belong the masculine, feminine, and neuter forms corresponding to the Greek forms in *ος, α, ον*, and the Latin ones in *us, a, um*, discussed above, and to the Sanskrit in *as, â, am*. For example: masc. *dags, fisks*, etc., which are syncopated forms from *dagas, fiskas*, etc., as I have already fully described, nom. plur. *dagôs, fiskôs*, etc.; fem. *giba, bida*, etc., nom. plur. *gibôs, bidôs*, etc.; neuter, *vaurd, leik*, etc.; nom. plur. *vaurda*, etc. The masculines have lost the *a* in the singular, but retained it in the form of *o* in the nominative plural, *e* in the genitive, and *a* in the dative and accusative (see declension of *fisks*, pp. 18, 25); the feminines have retained the *a* in the oblique cases as *a* or *o*, but have no nominative *s*. The neuter form has lost the *a* in the singular as well as the neuter nominative sign, if it ever had such:—the full form of the nominative singular of *vaurd*, for instance, should have been *vaurdat*, if we admit *t* to be the neutral sign of nouns, more probably it was *vaurdam*=Latin *verbum;* it has retained it in the plural *vaurda*.

I have already spoken of the Gothic adjectives, and here it is only necessary to add that, although the distinction between the clothing vowels of the stems was earlier obscured, and to a greater extent in the case of the adjectives than in that of the substantives, the signs of the genders have been much better preserved. Indeed, in the latter respect the Gothic adjectives belonging to the *a*-stems have endings of a much more primitive form than either the Greek or the Latin, or even than the Sanskrit.[8] These endings are *s, a, ata*, or, in the primitive form, *s, a, t*, as for example:—

	Masc.	Fem.	Neut.
Primitive organic form . .	blind-a-s	blind-a	blind-a-t
Syncopated Gothic form . .	blind -s	blind-a	blind-a-ta

YA- (YÂ-) OR IA-STEMS.—Besides the primitive *a*-stems, above described, there exists another class of stems, which, as they do not give rise to any essentially peculiar flexion, may be considered as a class of secondary forms of the simple *a*-stems. They are formed by the intercalation of an *i* (*y*) between the stem and the declension-vowel, and may accordingly be distinguished as *ya*- (*yâ*-) stems.[9] In the Gothic the stems of this class are usually considered to be middle-forms, properly so called, the Gothic *a*-stems being reckoned as pure stems. I

---

[8] On the assumption that *t* was the primitive neuter gender sign, which is not, however, generally admitted. Bopp considers the ending *-ata* to be a suffixed pronoun. See § 4, p. 15.

[9] *Ya-* masculine and neuter; *Yâ-* feminine.

think I was justified, however, in classing them along with the middle forms of the Greek and the Latin, and, this being so, in considering that the *ya-* (*yâ-*) stems approached still nearer to true derivational forms than any of those yet mentioned.

The Greek and Latin forms which come under this category, are the substantives and adjectives in ιος, ια, ιον, *ius, ia, ium*—*e. g.*, κύριος, ἴδιος; *filius, medius, media, medium.*

As the only forms of this kind referred to in Dr. Ebel's paper are Gothic, and as the object of this sketch is merely intended to elucidate that paper, I will not further consider the Greek and Latin *ia-*(*iâ-*)stems [*ya-*(*yâ-*)stems], and will accordingly confine myself to a few observations upon the Gothic ones.

In the Gothic the intercalated *y* is firmly retained before the endings through all the cases, *e.g.*: *haryis* instead of *hari-s* (the primitive organic form of which would be *haria-s*); gen. *haryis;* dat. *harya,* etc. In the Old High German the nom. sing. alone retains it. If the stem-syllable be long, or ends in two consonants, *yi* changes into *ei:* Goth. *hairdeis* instead of *hairdi-s* (the primitive form of which would be *hairdia-s*); O. H. G. *hirti,* gen. *hirtes;* M. H. G. *hirte,* gen. *hirtes.* In the Modern High German it passes into the weak declension: *der hirte, des hirten.* Some of the feminines of this category retain the full organic form, such as *vrakya, brakya;* and in some the *i* is even preserved in the Old High German as *y* or *e,* as for example, *suntya;* while other words throw off the *a, e. g.,* Goth.—*bandi, kunthi,* instead of *bandya, kunthya.*

The distinction between the *a* and the *ya*-stems disappears in the masculines and feminines when the *a* and *i* of the Old High German are softened into *e,*—the two forms then coinciding; the existence of such a distinction being only betrayed by the umlaut of the stem-vowel in the *ya* series. The same observation applies to the neuters, one example of which will suffice to show their forms, *e.g.:* Goth. *kuni,* gen. *kunyis,* instead of the full organic form *kunya-t,* or *kunya-m,* or *kuny-a;* O.H.G. *chunn-i,* gen. *chunn-es,* the *i* being dropped, as was already noticed in the case of the masculines, in all the cases except the nom. sing. In the Middle High German the *i* becomes *e* as in the other genders: *künne,* in which the umlaut of the stem-vowel betrays the *ya*-stem. In N.H.G. frequently even the final *e* is dropped, as, Goth. *badi* (from **badya*), O.H.G. *betti,* M.H.G. *bette,* N.H.G. *bett,* Engl. *bed.*

The adjective forms of the *ya*-stems are exactly analogous to the substantives. In the Middle and New High German the character of the stem is betrayed only by the umlaut. The striking analogy between some of the Gothic and Latin adjective forms of the *ya*-stems, is well shown by the following comparison: Lat.—*medius, media, medium* = Goth.—*midis, midya, midyata.*

CONSONANTAL STEMS CHANGED INTO VOCALIC (A- AND I-) STEMS.—Some Latin *n*-stems drop the *n* in the nom. sing., *e.g.*: in *ŏn*,—*homo, ordo, margo,* of which the full forms with the nominative *s* should be, *homon-s, ordon-s, margon-s;* in *ōn*,—*leo, latro, carbo,* the full forms of which should be, *leon-s, latron-s, carbon-s;* the feminine verbal nouns in *io,* which is obviously *ion,* with the *n* dropped—*actio, ratio, statio,* etc., the full forms of which should be, *action-s, ration-s, station-s.* These nouns give us in the inorganic form of their nom. sing. apparent vocalic stems. A comparison between the full organic forms of the verbal nouns, which are undoubted derivatives in the second degree, and those of the other examples given above, affords strong grounds for believing that the latter also are derivational forms of the second degree. Except in not having a final *n* in the nom. sing., these nouns are perfectly analogous, in all the other cases, to the Latin nouns in *in,* especially to those in which the *i* is softened to *e* in the nom. sing., *e. g., pecten,* etc.; and the verbal nouns *flumen, tegmen, lumen, carmen,* etc., and may be compared with the Greek ἀκτίς, gen. ἀκτῖνος; λιμήν, gen. λιμένος; ἀηδών, gen. ἀηδόνος; εἰκών, gen. εἰκόνος; λειμών, gen. λειμῶνος.

There is a class of Greek nouns, chiefly feminine, which at first sight appear to form their stems in ω, and which, as a rule, do not take the nominative *s, e. g.:* ἡ πειθώ, gen. πειθόος, the ω being shortened to ο; ἡ ἠχώ, gen. ἠχόος, etc. Some are, however, formed with the ς, as ἡ αἰδώς, gen. αἰδόος, the ω being shortened; ἥρως, gen. ἥρωος, etc., without the shortening of the ω. According to Curtius, all these forms are the relics of mutilated *n*-stems.[10] There is an obvious difference, however, between them and the Latin forms *homo,* etc., with which, if this hypothesis be correct, they would connect themselves, namely, that the *n* appears regularly in the oblique cases of all the Latin nouns, not only of those ending vocally in the nominative, but even of those which take the nominative *s,* as *sanguis,* which is evidently for *sanguin-s.*

In the Gothic, a class of nouns with vocalic auslaut is also found, which exhibit a remarkable analogy with the Latin nouns just discussed; for example, *guma,* Eng. *g(r)oom,* gen. *gumins,* which may be equated with the Latin *homo,* gen. *hominis; rathyó,* gen. *rathyôns,* with the Latin *ratio,* gen. *rationis; namô,* gen. *namins;*

---

[10] This hypothesis of Curtius, by which ω, ως, ας, αν, are considered to be= αν, is, to say the least, extremely improbable. Ahrens is more likely right in regarding αἰδώς, etc., as original *á*-stems, to which a *y* (*i*) is superadded.

nom. plur. *namna*, with the Latin *nomen*, gen. *nominis;* nom. plur. *nomina*. The reasonable conclusion from this is, that these vocalic forms are in reality consonantal *n*-stems, having more or less of a true derivational character. According to this hypothesis, their full nominative forms should be, *guman-s, rathyôn-s.* This hypothesis receives considerable support from the fact that several of those forms have again taken up *n* in the Modern High German, *e. g.:*

Gothic.	Old High German.	Middle High German.	Modern High German.
	bogo, ...	boge, . . .	bogen.
	grabo, krapo, . .	grabe, . . .	graben.
garda, .	garto, ...	garte, . . .	garten.[11]
namô, . .	namo, ...	name, . . .	{ name and also namen.

Probably all the foregoing examples may be referred to *n*-stems; but there is likewise a class of feminine nouns, which, considering them as vocalic stems, may be classed as *i*-stems, and which in the Gothic end in the diphthong *ei, e. g.: audagei, managei,* gen. *manageins,* etc.; they present the same peculiarities of inflexion as the others above mentioned, as will be shown further on. In this case also we are led to the conclusion that they are *n*-stems which have thrown off the *n*, not only by the analogy of inflexion, but also by the fact that the greater part of this class of nouns take up an *n* in the nominative in the O. H. German; we thus get, along with *manikî, manakin,* while in the N. H. German we have *menge,* unlike the *a*-stems. So also O. H. G. *ôdhîn* and *odi,* N. H. G. *oede,* O. H. G. *sterchín,* N. H. G. *stärke.*

The dropping of the *n* does not, as has been already remarked, affect the declension of the Latin or Greek nouns; but it is not so in the Germanic languages, where a peculiar declension has been developed, known as the weak declension, in contradistinction to the strong or true declension of words like *fisks, dags,* etc. The difference will be better understood by the following comparison:

Strong: Nom. sing. fisks; gen. fiskis; dat. fiska; acc. fisk; plur. nom. fiskôs.
Weak: „   hana; „ hanins; „ hanin; „ hanan; „ hanans.

All the nouns of the class we have been here considering

---

[11] Besides *garda,* there is also in the Gothic the word *gards* (plural *gardeis*)= house, family, etc.; but evidently having the meaning of garden also, as is proved by *veingards*=vineyard; *aurtigards*=orchard. The German *garten*= English *garden,* could not, however, be obtained from it; but, on the other hand, the English *yard* (as in court-yard) is derived from it.

belong to the weak declension, the great peculiarity of which is the addition of an *n* to all the endings of the cases, except the nominative singular and dative plural. It belongs to adjectives as well as to substantives, but while the latter decline exclusively strong or weak, adjectives may be declined according to either declension. The weak adjective declension corresponds with that of the substantive; its chief peculiarity is that of having in the nominative singular vocalic auslaut in all three genders, *e. g.*:

Gothic. { *Masc.*   *fem.*   *neut.*
          blinda,   blindô,   blindô.

The same vowels characterise the genders of the substantive, *e. g.*: masc. *hana;* fem. *tuggô;* neut. *hairto*. In the Old High German the masculine *a* and the feminine *ô* change to *o* and *a*. In Middle and New High German both the *a* and *o* become *e*, so that all genders end alike. This change is not, however, confined to the vowels; for although in the Gothic the case-endings are not affected by the addition of the *n*, the genitive *s* is dropped in Old High German, and *hanins* becomes *hanin*. In the Middle High German, the uniform ending *en* took the place of all the various endings, both singular and plural, with the exception of the nominative singular.

The existence of the *s* in such Latin forms as *sanguis* (for *sanguin-s*), which belong to the same class as *ratio, nomen,* etc., justify, as I think, the additions of that nominative sign, in reconstructing the full organic nominative forms of those and similar nouns. For its addition in the analogous German nouns, I have the great authority of J. Grimm; but Bopp's discovery that the primitive nominative sign in the Indo-European language was *s*, places the matter beyond doubt. It is right, however, to state that some philologists, amongst others Heyse, consider that the full organic forms never had *s*. A full discussion of this point, however important, is incompatible with the limits of our space, and would be in other respects foreign to the specific objects for which this introduction has been written.

U-STEMS.—GREEK. Under this head come the Greek words in ὔς of the third declension, which retain the υ in the oblique cases, *e. g.*: nom. ὁ ἰχθύ-ς, voc. ἰχθύ, gen. ἰχθύ-ος, etc., neut. ἄστυ.

LATIN. The Latin *u*-stems belong exclusively to the words declined according to the fourth declension, such as those in *ŭs:* they are chiefly masculine, but also exceptionally feminine, *e. g.*, *manus, socrus,* etc.; verbal nouns in *tus*, which may be considered to be true derivatives in the second stage, and to which the observations made at p. 17 respecting derivative stems consequently apply, *e.g.*, *ductus;* neuters in *ū*, *e.g.*, *cornu*. The nouns of the second declension, which appear to contain *u*-stems, are *a*-stems, the *a* having been replaced by *u*. This secondary *u* is much more unstable than the primitive *u* of the fourth declension, which is never suppressed by the vowel of the ending, but, on the contrary, absorbs the latter in the genitive singular and nominative and accusative plural, *e. g.*, *fructûs*, instead of *fructuis*, *fructues*. It has not wholly resisted modification, however, having been, in most cases, softened into *i* in the dative and ablative plural, *e.g.*, from the older *fructubus*, has come *fructibus*; in others, however, it has remained unchanged, as in *acubus*, *lacubus*. The whole declension may be considered as a contracted secondary form of the third declension.

GOTHIC. The Gothic words founded on *u*-stems correspond exactly with the Greek words in υς of the third declension, and the Latin ones in *us* and *u* of the fourth. Unlike the Gothic *a*- and *i*-stems, the *u*-stems are not syncopated, and consequently we get them in their primitive organic forms, the masculine and feminine taking the *s* in the nominative singular, *e.g.*: masc. *vulthus*, *sunus*, nom. plur. *sunyus*; fem. *handus*, nom. plur. *handyus*, *vrithus*, etc. The neuter exhibits no trace of a peculiar sign *t* or *m*, *e. g.*, *faihu*. The masculines and neuters preserve the *u* in the singular in the Old High German, but lose the nominative *s*, *e. g.*, *sunu*, *vihu*, etc. In the plural the *u*-stems pass into the *i*-stems; and in the Middle High German they altogether disappear, the masculines and feminines becoming confounded with the *i*-stems, and the neuters with the *a*-stems.

I have already mentioned that the primitive distinction between the *a*-, *i*-, and *u*-stems was very much obscured in the case of adjectives; and that, with the exception of traces, the *i*-stems had wholly died out. The *u*-forms of the adjective, which were not very numerous, took *s* in the nominative of both the masculines and feminines, but the neuters had no sign of gender, *e. g.*: nom. masc. and fem. *hardus*; neut. *hardu*. The *u*-forms died out in the Old High German, leaving for all adjectives only *a*-stems.

§ 6. *Of Consonantal Stems.*

PURE STEMS. S-STEMS.—*GREEK AND LATIN.*—ὁ μῦς, (*mus*.) gen. μυός, which stands for μυσ-ος, =*muris* for *mus-is*. In the forms like οὖς, gen. ὠτ-ός—φώς, gen. φωτ-ός, etc., either the τ has become ς, or the nominative *s* has inorganically affixed itself, in which case the *t* dropped out. In either case these forms belong primitively to dental tenuis-stems, and not to the *s*-stems. *Mus*, *flos*, *mas*, without the nominative sign. Except in *vas*, *vasis*, *s* becomes *r* in Latin in the oblique cases, as it stands between vowels. It sometimes appears duplicated, as in *os, ossis*, but here it stands for *st* (compare ὀστέον).

STEMS WITH SONANT AUSLAUTS. (SEMI-VOWELS, M, L, N, R, NG).
—*GREEK AND LATIN: semi-vowels*—*nix* for *nigv-s*, *bos* for *bov-s*, etc.; *l-stems*—ἅλ-ς, *sal*; *n-stems*—ῥίς for ῥίν-ς, the liquid having dropped out; φρήν, without the nominative sign; *Pan*, without the nominative suffix; *r-stems*—χείρ, θήρ, etc., *fūr*, without the nominative signs.

STEMS WITH MEDIAL AUSLAUTS.—*GREEK AND LATIN: b-stems*— φλέψ for φλέβ-ς, the -ς being the nominative suffix; *urb-s, scob-s; d-stems*—πούς for πόδ-ς; *pes* for *ped-s; vas* for *vad-s*, the dental having dropped out; *g-stems*—φλόξ for φλόγ-ς; *lex* for *leg-s, rex* for *reg-s*.

STEMS WITH TENUIS AUSLAUTS.—*GREEK AND LATIN: p-stems*— γύψ for γύπ-ς; *op-s*, etc.; *t-stems*—φώς for φώτ-ς; *dens* for *dent-s, pons* for *pont-s*, etc.; *k-stems*—λύγξ for λύγκ-ς, σφήξ for σφήκ-ς; *pax* for *pac-s*.

STEMS WITH ASPIRATED MUTE AUSLAUTS. — *GREEK:* θρίξ for τρίχ-ς, βήξ for βήχ-ς.

GOTHIC.—It has been shown in a previous section, that pure consonantal stems, properly so called, do not exist in the Gothic,[12] and that the forms which at first sight might come in here, belong rather to the vocalic middle forms, under which they have accordingly been treated. I shall merely give here a few examples of forms which might otherwise have come under the respective categories above given for the Greek and Latin: *saiv-s, fraiv; bagm-s, hilm; stol-s, mel; stiur, figgr-s; stab-s, lamb; sand-s, land; hug-s, gagg; hup-s, skip; skuft-s, beist; strik-s, leik; munths*, etc.

CONSONANTAL MIDDLE FORMS.—The nominative of some of the forms which come under this head exhibit the complete stem, which in the oblique case may be unrecognizable, owing to letter-changes or the dropping of letters. In most cases, however, the stem can be better determined from the oblique cases, in consequence of the nominative *s*, or the change of the vowel of the affixed syllable so altering the appearance of the stem in the nominative as to render it unrecognizable. The form of the stem to which the case-endings in the oblique cases are affixed is usually called the *Thema*, to distinguish it from the true stem-form, with which it sometimes coincides, but generally not. The neuter form of adjectives is best adapted for determining their stems.

S-STEMS.—In studying the stems of this class, we should be careful to distinguish the *s*-stems proper from words with the auslaut *s*, in some of which the *s* is secondary, being formed by

---

[12] Perhaps *baurgs* (f), a castle, town, gen. sing. nom. plur. *baurgs*; *Guth* (n. m.) gen. *Guths*, and some besides, are exceptions.

the softening of a *t*, etc., and in others it is the nominative *s*, before which the liquid *n* and the mutes *d* and *t* have dropped out.

GREEK.—Neuters of the third declension in ος (= Sanskrit *as*) which show the pure stem in the nominative; in the oblique cases the o becomes ε, and the ς drops out, *e. g.*—γέν-ος, gen. γέν-ε-ος for γέν-εσ-ος, and contracted to γέν-ους. Adjectival substantives in ης, εος = ους, *e. g.*, ἡ τριήρης;—forms of this kind may be considered as true derivatives. Adjectives in ης, ες, *e.g.*: σαφής, σαφές, gen. σαφ-έ-ος for σαφ-εσ-ος, and contracted to σαφοῦς.

LATIN.—To this category belong certain isolated masculine and feminine substantives in *ōs*, such as, *honos*, *arbos*, the *s* of which was afterwards softened to *r*. The adjective *vetus* comes under this head also. The substantives in *is* and *us*—*pulv-is*, *cin-is*, *Ven-ŭs*, *tell-ŭs*, are most probably *r*-stems, in which the *r* has dropped out before the nominative *s*. Neuters of the third declension in *us* (= Greek ος), the affixed syllable *us* being weakened before the oblique case-endings to *ŏr* or *ĕr*, *e. g.*: *corp-us*, gen. *corp-us-is*, weakened to *corp-ŏr-is*, *genus*, gen. *gen-us-is*, weakened to *gen-ĕr-is*.

STEMS WITH SONANT AUSLAUTS.—The stems which come under this category are: in the Greek those in ν, ρ; in the Latin and the Gothic *l*, *n*, *r*. *M* does not occur as the auslaut of a stem in either the Greek or the Latin. The pure stem is preserved in the nominative in the neuter,—the vowel being always short in the Greek. The other genders are distinguished in the Greek either by the nominative *s*, before which the liquid drops out, or especially in the feminines, by lengthening the vowel of the formational or affixed syllable. No such distinction of gender occurs in the Latin, the nominative *s* having given way to the liquid in almost every case, except in a very few instances, *e. g.*, *sanguis* for *sanguin-s*.

L-stems: stem-forming syllable *il*—masc. Latin *pugĭl*, *mugĭl*.

N-stems: stem-forming syllable *ăn*—Greek neuter adjective μέλᾰν; *ān*—masc. παιάν, gen. παιᾶνος; *ĕn*—λιμήν, gen. λιμένος, *ēn*—Ἕλλην, gen. Ἕλληνος; *ĭn* softened to *en* in the nominative in *pectēn*, and in the derivational suffix of verbal nouns, *-men*, gen. *-minis*, *e. g.*—*lumen*, *flumen*, etc.; *ĭn*—ἀκτίν for ἀκτίν-ς; *ŏn*—Greek adjective πέπον, masc. substantives δαίμων, gen. δαίμονος; *ōn*—λειμών, gen. λειμῶνος. To the preceding may be added the nouns with vocalic auslaut, which are considered to have thrown off the *n*, and which I have already discussed, as, *homo*, *Macedo*, *carbo*, etc.

R-stems: stem-forming syllable *ăr*—νέκταρ, Latin *Caesar*, Gothic *Kaisar*, *fadar*; *ār*—*calcăr*, gen. *calcāris*; *ĕr*—ὁ ἀήρ gen.

ἀέρος, Latin *anser;* ēr—κρατήρ—in this and similar words the stem-forming syllable may be considered to be τηρ, and to be a derivational one for verbal nouns; ŏr—ῥήτωρ, gen. ῥήτορος— here the stem-forming suffix is τορ, which may be compared with the Latin ones in *tor* and *sor, e.g., lector, cursor;—marmor* is produced, however, by duplication and not by suffix; *ŭr—* masc. *augur,* gen. *auguris,* in which the *u* remains unchanged in the genitive case; *turtur* is a stem also formed by duplication; neuters which retain the *u* in the oblique cases—*sulfur* and the duplicated stem, *murmur;* neuters which soften the *ŭ* to *ŏ—femur,* gen. *femoris,* etc.

STEMS WITH MEDIAL AUSLAUTS.—Stem-forming syllables: *ib—* adjective *caelebs,* gen. *caelibis; ŭb—*ὁ χάλυψ, for χάλυβς, gen. χάλυβος; *ăd—*λαμπάς, gen. λαμπάδος, *lampas,* gen. *lampădis; ēd—mercēs,* gen. *mercedis; ĭd—*ἐλπίς, gen. ἐλπίδος, *cuspis,* gen. *cuspidis, praeses,* gen. *praesĭdis: ĭd—*κρηπίς, gen. κρηπῖδος*; ŏd— custos,* gen. *custodis; ūd—palus,* gen. *paludis. Ag* is not found either in the Greek or Latin; *ĕg—lelex,* gen. *lelĕgis; ig—remex,* gen. *remĭgis; ŭg—*πτέρυξ for πτέρυγ-ς (in the Greek the nominative *s* fuses with the labial mute *b* and in the Greek and Latin with the palatals), gen. πτέρυγος.

STEMS WITH TENUIS AUSLAUTS.—Stem-forming syllables: *ăp* —ἡ λαῖλαψ for λαῖλαπ-ς, gen. λαίλαπος*; ĭp—adeps,* gen. *adĭpis. Princeps* and similar words do not come here, as they are true compound words in which one of the constituent stems is the pure stem *ceps.   Op* and *ōp* occur only in stems forming constituents of compound words, *e. g.,* κύκλωψ, gen. κύκλωπος, etc. *At*—a great number of the Greek forms in *ăt* throw off the *t* in the nominative, and are, therefore, somewhat analogous to the Latin *n*-stems *homo, ordo,* etc., which throw off the *n, e.g.,* σῶμα, στόμα, δρᾶμα, πρᾶγμα, etc., which form their genitive in τος. Sometimes τ is replaced in the nominative by ρ or ς, *e.g.,* ἧπαρ, gen. ἥπατος; κρέας, gen. κρέατος.   To the same category belong such forms in *ĭt,* as μέλι, gen. μελίτος.   The Latin forms which may be referred to stems in *ăt, āt, ĕt,* and *ēt,* drop the *t* in the nominative, but retain the *s, e. g., anas, libertas, teges* (the *e* becomes long after a vowel, as in *abiēs*), *quies.*   So likewise the Greek forms in *ēt* and *it,* such as: ἐσθής, gen. ἐσθῆτος; χάρις, etc.   The Latin forms in *ĭt* have the *ĭ* softened to *e, e.g., miles,* gen. *milĭtis.*   The following forms also occur: *ĭt—Samnis,* plur. *Samnītes; ōt—*ἔρως, gen. ἔρωτος; *nepōs,* gen. *nepōtis; ūt—salus,* gen. *salūtis.*

To this category belong also the Greek forms in κ and the Latin in *c,* of which it will only be necessary to mention a very few.   Stem-forming syllables: ακ, *ac—*πίναξ for πίνακ-ς (we may also add here the forms in -ακτ, as ἄναξ, gen. ἄνακτος); *ăk, ăc*—θώραξ; *fornax*, and the adjectives having the derivational suffix *ac*, such as *audax, capax*, which inorganically retain the nominative *s* in the neuter; εκ, *ĕc*—ἀλώπηξ, gen., ἀλώπεκος, the neuter *halec*, or, fused with the nominative *s*, masc., *halex*; ικ, *ĭc* and *īc*—φοῖνιξ, *salix*, gen., *salīcis, radix*, gen., *radīcis*; *ŏc*—*Cappadox*; *ōc, ferox*; υκ, *ūc*—κῆρυξ, gen., κήρυκος, *Pollūx*.

There are also in the Greek stems in ντ, νθ but not in νδ; in the Gothic there are also stems in *n*, (*t*), and *nd*, but as my object is rather to show what stems are, than to give a detailed account of all their forms, I will not dwell further upon this part of the subject.

§. 7. *Of Derivation.*

Having so often spoken of derivation as distinguished from middle forms, and *ya*-stems, I think it will not be out of place if I say a few additional words upon the subject here. Derivatives are words formed by the addition of affixes to verbal, nominal, and other stems. The affixes employed for this purpose are of two kinds: 1. Affixes consisting of single letters or syllables, which in their present state are not only not independent words, but cannot even be traced up with certainty to independent words, though having a definite symbolical signification which modifies the meaning of the stem. 2. Syllabic affixes which afford evidence of their having been once independent words, but which in process of time have been modified and have lost that character.

I have already remarked that Stem-formation cannot always be absolutely distinguished from Derivation; this is especially true in the case of the stems called middle forms, and derivatives formed by the derivational affixes of the first kind, which often consist of only a single letter. In discussing the different kinds of stems, I have pointed out some examples of this difficulty in the case of the Greek nouns in της, the verbal nouns in τορ, τηρ, *tor, sor*, and *men*, for which I proposed the term *Derivative Stems*, that is pseudo-stems formed upon already-existing stems, and not starting from roots, as all true stems do. The derivatives formed by the second kind of affixes are much less liable to be confounded with true stems; they often have, indeed, almost the character of compound words, that is, of words formed by the union of two or more stems. The proper distinction between Stem-formation and Derivation will, however, be best understood from a few examples of the different kinds of words which are formed by the latter process. From one kind of verbal form we may derive several others, thus, by the addition of the suffixes (Gr.)

σκ, (Lat.) *sc*, we get inchoative verbs, as, βόσκω from βόω, *cresco* from *creo*; by the suffixes (Lat.) *it*, etc. (N.H.G.) *er*, etc., we get frequentatives, as, *cogito* from *cogo*, *klappern* from *klappen*; by the suffixes (Lat.) *ill*, *ul*, etc. (N.H.G.) *el*, we obtain diminutives, as, *scribillo* from *scribo*, *ustulo* from *uro*, *ustum*, *säuseln* from *sausen*; by the (Lat.) suffix *ess* we get intensives, as, *capessere* from *capere*; by the (Lat) suffix *uri*, we get desideratives, as, *esurio* from *edo*, *esum*. Or we may derive verbs from nouns by the addition of such suffixes as (Gr.) α, ευ, αιν, etc. (Lat.) *are*, *ere*, *ire*, etc., *e. g.*, λιπάω from λίπας, κολακεύω from κόλαξ, λευκαίνω from λευκός, *nominare* from *nomen*, *lucere* from *lux*, *finire* from *finis*. We may in turn derive nouns from verbs, thus by the addition of the suffixes (Gr.) ευς, της, τωρ, μος, etc. (Lat.) *tor*, *tio* or *ti-on*, etc. (N.H.G.) *el*, *ung*, *ing*, *t*, *d*, etc., we get substantives such as γραφεύς from γράφω, ποιητής from ποιέω, 'Ρήτωρ from ῥέω, δυσμός from δύω; *victor* from *vinco*, *actio* from *ago*; *Hebel* from *heben*, *Reibung* from *reiben*, *Findling* from *finden*, *Macht* from *mögen*, *Jagd* from *jagen*; and by the addition of the suffixes (Lat.) *ac*, *bilis*, *ilis*, etc., we get adjectives, as *loquax* (for *loquac-s*) from *loquor*, *placabilis* from *placo*, *facilis* from *facio*. So in like manner we may get different kinds of substantives from one kind, such as diminutives, feminines, etc.; adjectives from substantives, and the converse; adverbs from adjectives, etc., of which, however, we need not give examples.

The greater number of the affixes mentioned in the preceding examples belong to the first kind. Those of the second class, being, on the other hand, of greater phonetic dimensions, have been less intimately fused with the stem, and consequently their historical development out of independent words can be more clearly traced. This kind of derivation was originally without doubt simple composition of the same kind as that by which compound words are still formed in living languages. It is the first stage of amalgamation from the mere agglutination which takes place in the formation of such words, as, *penknife*, *moonshine*, etc. Its transitional character is made still more evident by the circumstance that the affixes of this class are prefixes as well as suffixes, and that the former differs from particle composition in this only, that in the latter, two independent words still existing in the language, combine together, while in the former, an independent stem combines with a letter or stem not now independent.

In the Greek and Latin the derivatives of the second class are neither so well marked nor so numerous as in the Germanic languages. The suffixes -ειδης, -φορος, *-fex*, *-dicus*, etc., are really stems, and consequently we may consider words ending in them to be compound words, rather than derivatives, *e. g.*, θεοειδής, κανηφόρος, *artifex, mendicus,* etc. In the English we have a number of well marked derivational suffixes of this class; *e. g.*, *-hood*=N.H.G. *-heit,* Goth. *haidus,* way, condition, as for instance, *girlhood; -ship*=N. H. G. *-schaft,* O. H. G. *scaf,* shape, property, etc., as *partnership; -dom*=N.H.G. *-thum,* Goth. *dóm,* primitively, judgment, tribunal, dignity or condition of a person in general, as, for instance, *dukedom; -some,* a stem which signifies similarity, and, hence, Goth. *sama,* Eng. *same, e. g., handsome; -ly*=N.H.G. *-lich,* Goth. *leiks,* O.H.G. *lich,* Eng. *like,* similar, equal. Compare in the Romance languages the Italian suffix *-mente,* Fr. *-ment* (*e. g., sainement, purement*), from the Lat. *mens.*

§ 8. *Of Composition.*

Composition is the union of two or more stems, or even words with grammatical endings, so as to form one word, and may be looked upon as the highest stage of word-formation. Some languages possess the power of forming compound words with great facility, especially the Greek and Sanskrit. Among modern languages, German possesses it to some extent. Two kinds of Composition may be distinguished, the Synthetical and Parathetical. The first kind is where the first word loses its inflection, that is, occurs as a stem, and the last alone is inflected; the second kind consists of mere juxtaposition, each element of the compound retaining its inflexion. The parathetical may be considered to be the first stage of composition. Particle composition, such as that by which compound verbs are formed by prefixing prepositions, comes under the category of parathetical composition In the older language-periods a copulative vowel was frequently introduced between the constituent words — a phenomenon which offers a remarkable analogy to the stem copulative vowel. In the Greek, this vowel was generally *o,* seldomer ι, or ε; in the Latin *i,* and exceptionally *o,* or *u;* in the Old High German it was generally *a,* afterwards *e;* and in the Modern German, as in the English, it has dropped out,[13] or an *s,* and in the former language an *en,* which are flexional endings, have taken its place, *e. g.,* ἡμερ(ο)δρόμος, *carn(i)fex, nacht(i)gall, Hülf(s)buch, Tasch(en)buch, doom(s)day.* It is worthy of remark that the English word *night(in)gale* presents a kind of transition between the simple copulative *i* and the more usual Modern German *en.* The copulative vowel belonged, in the older languages, only to noun forms, and not to those obtained by the union of verbs and particles. Combination is sometimes accompanied by phonetic changes in one or both of the constituents; such, for example, as that which takes place in the stem-vowel in the Latin

---

[13] It is, however, sometimes retained in N. H. G., as in *Tage-buch.*

verbs, *legere, colligere*, and which has been already noticed when discussing the subject of progressive assimilation, etc.

One of the constituents of a compound word represents the fundamental idea or basis of the conception; the other, the secondary idea by which the former is determined, modified, or limited. The former may be compared to the root of a word, and the latter to the grammatical affixes; with this difference, however, that the latter are chiefly suffixes, while in compound words the fundamental word is usually the last member; the qualifying word is consequently prefixed, *e.g.*, *bride-groom, glass-window*, and *window-glass*. In some Greek verbal nouns the reverse position of the constituent members is apparent, *e.g.*, φιλόλογος, etc. It was probably the oldest form of composition, but has almost wholly disappeared from written language, even from the Sanskrit. Curiously enough, it exists both in the spoken English, French, and German, *e.g., breakfast, tire-botte, taugenichts*. This circumstance is interesting as to the question of the origin of affixes.

CHAPTER II.
ON THE CASE-ENDINGS OF NOUNS IN THE CHIEF INDO-EUROPEAN LANGUAGES.

§ 1. *The Accusative Singular.*

As the classification of stems discussed in the foregoing chapter is based upon the manner in which they become nouns by affixing the nominative sign, I was obliged so far to anticipate the subject of flexional endings, as to describe in section 4 of the preceding chapter the character of the nominative ending. I need not, therefore, say anything further on that point here, and will accordingly pass on to the oblique cases, and first to the Accusative Singular.

The sign of the Accusative in Sanskrit, Zend, and Latin, is *m*; in Greek *ν*, Lithuanian and Old Prussian *n*. It is probable that in the primitive Indo-European language it was likewise *m*.

LATIN. The *m* was affixed: 1. directly to vocalic stems of the masculine and feminine forms of substantives and adjectives—*via-m, fide-m, cive-m, manu-m;* 2. with an intercalated copulative to all consonantal stems—*reg-e-m, arbor-e-m.*

The consonantal stems which have passed over into apparent vocalic stems, alluded to at p. 24, follow the rule of consonantal stems in the oblique cases, that is, require a copulative: *ratione-m, carbon-e-m.* According to some philologists, the *i-* (*e-*) stems also take the copulative vowel like consonantal stems, the declension vowel, or stem vowel, giving way before the flexional copulative. According to this view, *civem* would be *civ-e-m*, not *cive-m* with the *i* of the stem changed to *e* as was assumed above. The first view is the simpler and more rational.

The Sanskrit *m* is usually transformed by *anusvâra*[14] into the nasal *ṅ*. The Lithuanian *n* is also similarly weakened. In the Latin the *m* was generally disregarded in prosody, and suffered elision before vowel anlauts. It was dropped altogether in the most ancient Roman inscriptions, as, for example, in the epitaph of L. Cornelius Scipio, who was consul A.U.C. 494: *Hec cépit Córsicá' Aleriá'que úrbe*[15] for *Corsicam Aleriamque urbem*. It is curious that in the modern romance languages the nominative singular has been frequently formed from such mutilated accusative forms: Italian—*buono, imperatóre, leone,=bonum, imperatorem, leonem*. The Portuguese on the other hand retains in many instances the *m—homem, virgem, som,=hominem virginem, sonum*. The Italian forms its nominative plural from the corresponding Latin case—*pórte, sérvi,=portæ, servi;* the Spanish, on the contrary, forms it from the accusative plural—*ricos hombres, los servos, los caballeros*. The Oscan has preserved the accusative *m* in all declensions.

GREEK. The Latin declensions are richer and more varied than those of the Greek. In the former there are five, which, however, may be reduced to three; the fourth may be included under the third, and the fifth under the first, by which we can assimilate them to the Greek.[16] The fuller endings of the Latin, as, for example, the plural ones (*-rum, -bus*, etc.), may perhaps be attributed to the absence of the article, which gives such lucidity to the Greek declension, while it helps to weaken it, by rendering the endings less indispensible, and perhaps also to the frequent use of prepositions in the place of a greater number of cases. The ν may be found directly affixed to the vocalic stems as in the Latin: γραῦ-ν, πῆχυ-ν. The stems in ω and ευ are, however, an exception, as they do not form their accusative in ν: ἠχώ, ἠχύ-α; βασιλεύς, βασιλέ-α. Attention has been already drawn to the anomalous character of the stems in ω (p. 24), which Curtius believed to be relics of *n*-stems. According to the hypothesis of Heyse regarding *civem*, mentioned above, these stems would be considered to take a copulative, before which the declension vowel ω gave way, and that afterwards the ν was

---

[14] 'Anu-svâra,' or "after sound", is the term used by Sanskrit grammarians for the marks . (*ṅ*) that is, a weakening of a nasal auslaut.
[15] Bunsen—Beschreibung der Stadt Rom. III., 616, sqq.
[16] A system which has been very successfully followed by Dr. Donaldson in his Latin Grammar.

dropped; so that the primitive form of ἠχό-α would have been ἠχό-αν. Many other explanations may also be given: it does not, however, come within the objects of this introduction to discuss them.

GOTHIC. The accusative sign has been wholly lost in the Gothic, except in the masculines of the adjectives, so that the accusative form of substantives presents us with the naked stem. The *n* in the accusative forms belonging to the weak declension, such as *hanan*, *tuggôn*, etc., belongs to the stem, but was dropped in the nominative, by which a class of apparent vocalic stems was produced, to which allusion was made at p. 24. In the masculines of adjectives, we find the accusative sign preserved in the form *na*, the *a* being merely an inorganic addition, which was dropped in O. H. German, while the *n* has been preserved in N. H. German: Goth. *blinda-na*, N. H. G. *blinde-n*.

§. 2. *The Genitive Singular.*

SANSKRIT AND ZEND. The genitive singular endings in the Sanskrit are: masc. and neut., *sya*; masc. and fem. *s*; masc., fem., and neut., *as* and fem. *âs*. In masc. and fem. the endings *s* or *as* may be considered to be practically the same, the former being affixed to vocalic stems, and the latter to consonantal; especially as the stem vowels in the *i*- and *u*-stems are always gunated in the genitive: e.g., *kavi-s*, *sûnu-s*, gen. *kavê-s = kavai-s*, *sûnôs = sun-au-s*. With these endings the feminine ending *âs* of vocalic stems naturally connects itself, because if the stem vowel be short, the genitive may be formed by *s* alone with a gunation of the stem vowel, as well as with the ending *âs: e.g., prit-ês = prit-ai-s*, or *prit-y-âs*. In the latter the stem vowel has been changed into *y*; when the stem vowel is long, the *î û* are invariably changed to *y*, *v*, and after *â*-stems a *y* is added, so that the endings are in reality -*yâs*, *vâs*. The genitive singular endings in Zend are: *hê* (also *hyâ*) = Skr. *sya*; *âo* = Skr. *âs*; *s* = Skr. *s*; and *ô* = Skr. *as*.

LATIN. The whole of the *a*-stems, that is those declined according to the first, second, and fifth declensions, no longer form their genitives singular in *s*. The word *paterfamilias = paterfamiliæ* has, however, preserved the true ancient form of the *a*-stems of the first declension, which corresponded with those of the same declension in the Greek. And, again, on old monuments we still find *suaes provinciaes = suæ provinciæ*. The genitive ending of the first declension has thus become *æ* by the loss of the *s* after the diphthongation of the stem vowel. In the second and fifth declensions the genitive ending has been replaced by an affixed *i*, which had probably originally a locative signification; in the second declension the flexional *i* absorbs the stem vowel—*scamn-i;* in the fifth declension the stem vowel is not absorbed, and except that after a consonant it is shortened, it is not further affected—*diē-i, fidĕ-i.*

Stems with consonantal auslaut and pure vocalic stems, that is, all nouns of the third declension, with the exception of the middle forms in *i* (*e*), affix *s* with a copulative *i*, corresponding to Skr. *a*, Gr. o (ος=Lat. *is*): *gru-is, urb-is.* The observation made respecting the *i*-stems, when discussing the accusative ending, explains the reason why the *i*-stems are excepted; some philologists believing that they take a copulative in the genitive also. The *u*-stems of the fourth declension belong likewise to this category; we have the old forms *fructu-is, senatu-is,* afterwards the *s* dropped off and the *ui* contracted to *u* or *i*, as in the dative: *senatu.* According to the oldest inscriptions, as for example the Senatus Consultum de Bacchanalibus, it would appear that the copulative of the genitive was not *i*, but *o* or *u*, as in the words *nomin-us, senatu-os, domu-os,* and later *domu-us.*

Bopp traces the genitive ending *ius* of some pronouns and adjectives to the Sanskrit genitive ending *sya.* He supposes *jus* to be obtained by displacement from *sya* or *sja: hu-jus, cu-jus, illi-us* for *illi-jus,* etc. Donaldson, on the other hand, looks upon the Latin *jus* as a weakened form of the ending *yâs.* May not this latter form represent in fact the first modification, which, according to Bopp's view, *sya* must have undergone? In connection with the latter view it may be mentioned that Steinthal has made the ingenious suggestion that the primitive genitive suffix was *sya*, which he considers to be made up of the nominative *s* and the relative pronoun stem *ya* (fem. *yâ*), so that we might have two forms, a masc. *sya* and a fem. *syâ;* the latter of which would give exactly the fem. suffix *yâs*, while the Latin *jus* might have come from the masc. *sya.*

In the Oscan the genitive singular ending was *as*, for the first declension, and *eis* for the second and third: *Djúv-eis*=Lat. *Jov-is.* Here the Oscan forms are fuller and richer than those of the Latin, for besides preserving the *s* in all cases, we have traces both of the stem and the copulative vowels in the second and third declensions, while the former has been absorbed in the Latin second declension. In the Umbrian the genitive ended in *s.* or *r.*[17]

GREEK. The genitive singular is formed in the Greek by:

(*a*) Affixing ς to the feminines of the first declension in *a, η,* the inorganically shortened *a* of the nominative becoming *ā* or *η*, corresponding to the Sanskrit feminine vocalic stems which

---

[17] See the paradigms of the Umbrian declension quoted from Aufrecht u. Kirchoff's, Sprachdenkmäler, p. 115 *sqq.* in Donaldson's Varronianus.

take the ending ᾱs—Μοῦσα, πεῖρα, gen. Μούση-ς, πειρᾱ-ς. The Attic ending ως of the *i*-stems is considered by some as the complete representative of this Sanskrit *âs*, by which πόλεως = πόλγος is compared with the Skr. *prityâs*. But, as Ebel points out (p. 83), the Homeric πόληος leads rather to πόλεγος. The ending ως is not confined to the feminines, for we have the masculine βασιλέ-ως.

(*b*) By affixing ς with a copulative *o* (Skr. *a*) to stems with consonantal auslaut, pure vocalic stems and vocalic middle forms in ι, υ, ω, ευ: χειρ-ός, σῶματ-ος, κι-ός, ἀληθέ-ος, ἰχθύ-ος ἠχό-ος.

(*c*) Many nouns do not form their genitive in ς, as for example the *a* stems of the first declension in ης, ᾱς, and those of the second declension in which the primitive *a* has passed into *o*; in the Attic these nouns have ου in the genitive. The Attic ου of the first declension was obtained like the Ionic εω and the Doric ᾱ, from the Homeric *ao* (βορέαο, Αἰνείαο) which was obtained from *a-ιο*, and this from *a-σιο* = Skr. *sya*, by dropping σ. Bopp likewise explains the ου of the second declension from *sya*; in the stems in ă, and in the pronouns of the third person, *â-sya* becomes *o-σιο*, the σ then dropped out by which the Epic *o-ιο* was formed, and then *oo* contracted to ου; thus λόγοιο, λύκοιο, and the Old Epic τοῖο must have been obtained from the older forms: λογό-σιο; λυκό-σιο = Skr. *vṛika-sya*; τό-σιο = Skr. *ta-sya*.

GOTHIC. The Gothic *i*-stems which exist in the syncopated form in the nominative, affix the genitive *s* to the full form, the stem vowel *i* of the feminines being gunated: masc. nom. syncopated from *gast-s* (full organic form *gasti-s*), gen. *gasti-s*; fem. nom. syncopated form *ded-s* (for *dedi-s*), gen. *dedai-s*, nom. syncopated form *anst-s* (for *ansti-s*), gen. *anstai-s*. A similar gunation occurs in both masc. and fem. of *u*-stems, which likewise directly affix *s* to the gunated stem: mas. *sunu-s*, gen. *sunau-s*; fem. *handu-s*, gen. *handau-s*. The mas. and neut. of the *a*- and *ya*-stems affix the gen. *s* to the stem by a copulative, *i*, which replaces the declension vowel *a*, or, in other words, they have passed over to the *i*-declension: *fisk-s*, *dag-s*, *vaurd*, gen. *fiski-s*, *dagi-s*, *vaurdi-s*; nom. and gen. *haryis*, *hairdeis*. The masculines of *ya*-stems which decline according to the strong declension, are therefore the same in the genitive as in the nominative The feminine *a*-stems, on the other hand, have preserved the declension *a* in the oblique cases — in the genitive as *o*, but strengthened however before the genitive *s*: *giba*, *gibô-s*, a form which may be compared with the Skr. genitives in *âs*.

The masculine and neuter substantives and adjectives of the weak declension affix the genitive *s* directly to the *n*, which is the universal ending of the bases belonging to the weak declension: masc. *hana, hanin-s;* neut. *hairtô, hairtin-s;* fem. *tuggô, tuggôn-s;* fem. *managei, managein-s.*

In the Germanic languages the genitive *s* has been preserved in all the strong masc. and neut.; but the fem. already lost it in the O. H. G.; and in the N.H.G. they have lost all the flexional endings in the singular. The copulative vowel *i* of the masc. and neut. *a* and *i*-stems, becomes throughout *e* in the O.H.G: Goth., masc *fiskis,* O.H.G., *visces;* Goth., neut. *vaurdis,* O.H.G. *wortes;* Goth., masc. *gastis,* O.H.G. *gastes.* The fem. of the *a*-stems lose the *s* in the O.H.G., but retain the long vowel, which, however, becomes short in the M. H. G.: Goth., *giba, gibôs;* O.H.G., *kepa, kepâ (ô);* M.H.G., nom. and gen. *gebe.* The fem. of the *i*-stems likewise lose the *s* in the O.H.G.: *ansts, anstais;* O.H.G., *anst, ensti.* The declension vowel of the masc. *u*-stems likewise becomes *e*—Goth., *sunus, sunaus;* O.H.G., *sunu, sunes;* but the feminines appear to pass into the *i*-declension, with the loss of the genitive *s*—Goth., *handus, handaus;* O.H.G., *hant, henti.* In the weak declension, the genitive *s* is lost in the O.H.G.: Goth., masc. *hana, hanins;* O. H.G., *hano, hanin;* M.H.G., *hase, hasen;* neuter Goth., *hairtô, hairtins;* O.H.G., *herza, herzin;* M.H.G., *herze, herzen.*

LITHUANIAN AND SLAVONIAN. In Lithuanian the genitive singular ending is *s*. The masc. *a*-stems have lost the *s* and end in *ō;* according to Bopp this *ō* is merely the lengthened stem-vowel which replaces the suppressed case-ending. Schleicher on the other hand explains this *ō* as a contraction from *aya* which arose from *a-sya.* The Lettish has also lost the ending in the corresponding stems, while the Old Prussian has preserved it: Skr. *déva-sya* = Lith. *déwō,* Lett. *deewa,* O. Pr. *deiwa-s.* In *i*- and *u*-stems the stem vowel is gunated as in Gothic, and the Lithuanian has preserved the guna in the masc. as well as in the fem. *i*-stems; as in Sanskrit the *ai* is, however, contracted to *ē*: Lith. *awê-s* = Skr. *avê-s.* The genitive *s* has been lost in Old Slavonic; consonantal stems end in *e,* *o*-stems have the primitive *a* of the stem, *u*-stems *u,* and *i*-stems the naked thema. The Sanskrit ending *sya* is, however, represented by the pronominal ending *go*: Sl. *to-go* = Skr. *ta-sya.*

§ 3. *The Dative, Locative, and Instrumental, Singular.*

SANSKRIT AND ZEND. The singular dative endings in the Sanskrit are: mas., fem., and neut., *ê;* fem., *ai;* masc. and neut. *a*-stems, *âya.* In Zend the endings are also *ê,* and *ai.* In the Greek and the Latin it was perhaps *ĭ* in all declensions. The dative ending in the Gothic was perhaps *a (ê).* The singular locative endings in the Sanskrit are: masc., fem., and neut., *i;*

fem. *âm*. The masc. *u*- and *i*-stems, and sometimes the fem. also, have a peculiar locative in *au*, before which the stem-vowel is dropped, or becomes *y*. Bopp supposes that it was obtained from *âs*, and that it is, therefore, a genitive form used in a locative sense. The singular instrumental endings in the Sanskrit are: masc., fem., and neut., *â*, (*yâ*); masc. and neut. *a*-stems, *a*, with an intercalated *n*: e. g., *çivê-n-a*. The Sanskrit locative endings *i* and *âm* are represented in Zend by -*i*, and -*a?* and the instrumental by *a*.

LATIN.—In the *a*-stems of the first declension, the dative *i*, instead of producing *ai*, fuses with the stem vowel into *æ*. The *ō* of the second declension, like the corresponding Greek ω, has arisen from *oi*, as is proved by the old datives, *popoloi Romanoi*. It is worthy of remark, that while the locative *i* suppresses the thema vowel in the genitive, the latter, in most cases, absorbs the former in the dative. In the third, fourth, and fifth declensions, the *i* is affixed as an independent sound, and often even inorganically lengthened: *su-i*, *urb-i*, *fructu-i*. In some forms of the fourth and fifth declension, the *i* is suppressed by the thema vowel, *u*, *e*: *tactu* (Plautus), *usu* (Lucretius), *facie* (Lucilius). The genitive ending having been replaced by a locative *i* in the fifth declension, the genitive and dative coincide in that declension.

In the Oscan, the dative of the first declension was formed in *ai*, like the locative, which had also *æ;* in the second declension the dative ending was *úi*, the locative being in *ei*, and in the third declension the dative ending was *ei*, corresponding to the Umbrian in *e* for all declensions, which, unlike the ablative, was probably (at least originally), long, although the *morte* in the epitaph of Plautus—*Postquam morte datu' st Plautus Comœdia luget*, if it be an Umbrian dative = *morti*, is short. The Oscan and Umbrian dative endings *ai*, *ei*, and *e*, obviously lead to the characteristic dative endings *aî*, *ê*, in the Sanskrit. This would seem to show that the Latin dative *i* may not have had originally a locative signification, but is a true descendant of a primitive dative.

GREEK.—The Greek dative *ῐ* fuses with the thema vowels, *a*, *ē*, *o*, into a false diphthong in the *a*-stems, that is in the first and second declensions: ἡμέρᾳ, νίκῃ, οἴκῳ, for which we have also the form οἴκοι. With the vowels ε, ο, a true diphthong is produced: πόλει, ἠχοῖ. The stems declining according to the third declension affix the dative *i* directly to the stem, without modification. The Epic form, φι, of the dative ending, will be noticed in the section on the dative plural. The dative suffix in the Greek, and perhaps also in the Latin, appears to have had originally a locative signification, and which several words still show: *e. g*, Σαλαμῖνι, Μαραθῶνι.

GOTHIC. The mas. and neut. substantives of the *a-*, *ya-*, and *i*-stems belonging to the strong declension, form their datives in *a;* in the *a-* and *ya*-stems the ending coincides with the stem vowel, and in the *i*-stems replaces it: *fiska, harya, hairdya, gasta.* In the O.H.G. the dative of these forms is also *a*, which in M. and N.H.G. becomes *e*. The feminine *a-* and *i-* stems form their dative in *i*, which is however gunated as in the genitive: *giba, gibai; deds, dedai*. We might explain *gibai* with Bopp to be for *gibai-a*, with diphthongation of the stem vowel, the dative sign having fallen off. In the same way the O.H.G. dative of *geba, gebô* (*û*) would likewise be an extension of the stem vowel without a dative sign. In the case of the fem. *i*-stems, we must suppose upon Bopp's view that the stem vowel was gunated: *dedai* for *dedai-a*. The dative of the *u*-stems may be explained in the same way; there is no proper dative ending, but instead of it *au*, produced by a gunation of the stem-*u*, as in the genitive: *sun-au, hand-au*, for *sun-av-a, hand-av-a*. In the O.H.G. the gunating *a* is replaced by an *i*. The consonantal middle forms have lost their dative sign: *fiyand* for *fiyanda; brothr* for *brothra*. The nouns of the weak declension have no dative suffix; in the masc. and neut. they all end in *in;* and in the fem. in *ôn* and *ein;* these endings become masc. *in*, fem. *ûn* and *în* in the O.H.G., and *en* in all genders in the N.H.G.

According to Bopp the dative sign *a* was originally the suffix of the instrumental = Skr. *a*. The masc. and neut. *a-* and *i*-stems of the O.H.G. substantives, and adjectives, belonging to the strong declension show an instrumental in *u: tagu, gastu, wortu*, which Bopp believes to have arisen from *a*. The original instrumental has thus assumed a dative meaning, while a phonetically different form has been developed out of it to express the instrumental. In the Gothic the adjectives have in their strong declension a special dative ending for the masc. and neut.; the feminines on the other hand correspond with substantives; in the O. and M.H.G., however, the feminines have likewise a peculiar ending. These endings are pronoun endings which have passed over to the adjectives. The following paradigm will render this passage obvious:

	Masc. and Neut.		Fem.	
	Adject.	Pron.	Adject.	Pron.
Goth.	blind-amma	th-amma	blind-ai	thiz-ai
O.H.G.	plint-emu (emo)	d-emu	plint-êru	d-eru
M.H.G.	blind-em	d-em	blind-er	d-er

LITHUANIAN AND SLAVONIAN. The dative ending in Lithuanian is *i* (in fem. *i*-stems *ei*). In Old Slavonian consonantal and *u*-stems end in *i*. This *i*, according to Bopp, corresponds to the

Sanskrit dative ending $\acute{e}=ai$. masc. and neut. o-stems end in u; fem. a-stems in $\acute{e}$; and Masc. and fem. i-stems in i. In Lithuanian the locative ends in e and je. Although this e is short, Bopp thinks it has arisen from ai produced by the stem-vowel and the locative i. In O. Slavonian the locative ending is i in consonantal and u-stems, and is therefore apparently identical with the dative; in masc. and neut. o-stems, and fem. a-stems it is $\acute{e}$. The locative i has been lost in Lettish, the stem-vowel is however lengthened in a-stems. The instrumental ending in Lithuanian is mi, which is evidently connected with the plural instrumental ending $mis =$ Skr. $bhis$, Zd. bis. Masc. and fem. a-stems do not, however, take the ending, the former end in u, and the latter coincide with the nominative.

§. 4. *The Ablative Singular.*

The Sanskrit, Zend, and Latin, have an ablative singular, but in the dual and plural they express the ablative signification by the dative, as other languages do by the genitive. In the Sanskrit the ablative endings are: masc. and neut. a-stems t; masc., fem., and neut. of the other declensions as, which resembles the genitive. But, as Bopp has concluded from the analogy of the first and second personal pronouns, *mat*, *tvat*, and from the Zend ablatives, the primitive ablative form was t. This is further confirmed by the ablative suffix in the oldest Latin, and in the Oscan, being d, and therefore quite distinct from the dative. Thus we have on the Columna Rostrata: *præsented sumod Dictatored olorom in altod marid pucgnad vicet*.[18] The d was however frequently apokoped: *e. g. mari* for *marid*, *senatu* for *senatud*, etc. In the Umbrian the ablative ends in a vowel which is sometimes a, i, and u, as well as e, and therefore does not always correspond to the dative. In the Sanskrit the ablative has the signification of *whence* in the sense of space; in the Latin it has, however, a wider application, because, in addition to the proper ablative meaning, it often combines in its application a locative and instrumental signification.

The ablative sign may also be recognized in adverbs, as in *bened*, *facillumed*, which are evidently the old ablatives, *bonod*, or *bonud*, *facillumod* or *facillumud*; and in prepositions *suprād*, *entrād*. According to Bopp, the ablative sign is also found in the enclitic pronoun *met* ($=$ Skr. *mat* from *me*), which occurs in the compounds *egomet*, *memet*, and in the conjunction *sed*, anciently written *set*. The suffix *tus* ($=$ Skr. *tas*) in *cœlitus*, and the *de* in *inde*, *unde*, are perhaps likewise related to it.

---

[18] Donaldson's Varronianus, 2nd Ed., p. 229. The Oscan form *praesentid* occurs on the Bantine Table, l. 21.

§. 5. *The Dual.*

Peculiar dual forms of substantives are only to be found in the Sanskrit, Zend, Greek, Slavonian, and Lithuanian.[19] In the Sanskrit the dual endings are: nom., acc., and voc. masc. and fem. *au* (in the Veda dialect *â*, and in the Zend *â*); neut. *î* (which fuses to *ê* with the stem *a*); dative, instrumental, and ablative *bhyâm* in all genders; genitive *ôs*, *yôs* in all genders; and locative *ôs*, which coincides, therefore, with the genitive. The Greek has only two dual forms: 1. that of the nominative, accusative, and vocative; and, 2. that of the genitive and dative. The nom. acc. and voc. dual sign, in all three genders of the third declension in the Greek, is ε; in the first and second declensions the ending is suppressed and the stem vowels *a*, *o*, lengthened to *ā*, ω; the same thing takes place in the masc. and feminine of the *i*- and *u*-stems in the Sanskrit. The dative (also genitive) dual suffix in the Greek is ιν, which in the first and second declension is affixed after the stem vowel, which fuses with the ι into a diphthong; in the third declension the affix is οιν instead of ιν.

The Old Slavonian has preserved the dual ending more completely than the Lithuanian. Masc. *a*-stems end in the nom. acc. and voc. in *a*; fem. and neut. *a*-stems in *ê* (*ye*); masc. and fem. *i*-stems in -*i*; and *u*-stems in *ü* (generally = Skr. *û*), or they pass into the *a* declension; consonantal stems in *i* (sometimes in *ê*). The genitive and locative end in Old Slavonian in all genders in *u*, and the dative and instrumental in *ma*. In Lithuanian masc. *a*-stems end in the nom. acc. and voc. in *u*, which Bopp explains to have arisen from the Veda ending *â*. In the *i*- and *u*-stems the ending is suppressed, as in the Sanskrit, but the stem vowel is not, however, lengthened, as in that language. The Lithuanian genitive dual ending *û*, is borrowed from the plural; Bopp now however thinks that this *û* is a true dual ending, and, like the corresponding O. Slavonian *u*, connected with the Sanskrit genitive dual ending *ôs:* Lith. *dwëj-û* = Skr. *dvay-ôs* duorum, duarum (see Dr. Ebel's opposite opinion, p. 84). The locative is lost in Lithuanian. The dative and instrumental dual in Lithuanian is *m*.

If we compare the dative dual suffix in the Sanskrit *bhyâm*, which is also that of the instrumental and ablative, with the plural suffix for the dative and ablative *bhyas* = Lat. *bus*, the *y* being ejected, we see that *bhya* is common to both, and may therefore be considered as the proper dative suffix, while the proper dual sign may be assumed to be *m*, and that of the

---

[19] See "On the Celtic Dual", §. 10. p. 85, for Ebel's observations on the relics of dual forms in Irish.

plural *s*. The dual sign *m* has been lost in the Zend, and the dative accordingly ends in *bya*. Respecting the Greek dative dual suffix there are two hypotheses. Bopp believes ιν to be nothing more than a crippled form of *bhyâm*. Düntzer, on the other hand, believes that the dual sign ν = μ is simply affixed to the singular dative form in ι.

The only traces of special dual forms in the Latin are *duo* and *ambo;* and in the Gothic and Old High German they are only to be met with in the personal pronouns.

§. 6. *The Nominative and Vocative Plural.*

The nominative and vocative are alike in all Indo-European languages. In the Sanskrit the masc. and fem. ended in *ás;* the neuters ended in *i*, which was affixed to the stem with an euphonical *n* between the stem vowel, which was lengthened, and the *i*. In the Zend the masc. and fem. ended in *ó*, which represents the Sanskrit *as*, and the nom. and acc. plur. of neuter nouns in *a*, which was also the ending in the majority of the old languages of the family. Bopp considers the Sanskrit *i* as merely a weakened form of such an *a*. In the Oscan the first declension ended in *as*, and the second in *ús;* and in the Umbrian, besides *as* and *us*, the endings *ar*, *or*, also occur, the *r* being obviously formed from *s*. In a fragment of Pomponius, which is found in Nonius Marcellus, we meet with the nom. plur. *laetitias insperatas*. These forms perfectly represent the Sanskrit *as*. The Greek ες and the Latin *ēs* of the third declension likewise represent the Sanskrit ending. In the fourth declension in the Latin the ending is *ūs*, the *ū* being formed by the fusion and contraction of the stem vowel with the *e* (*a*) of the ending. In the fifth Latin declension the ending *ēs* results from a similar contraction of *e-es* into *ēs*. We may explain, in the same manner, the long *ē* of the ending of the *i*-stems of the third declension, in which it is organic, as a contraction of *i-es*. In the other forms of the third declension the *ē* is inorganically long. The duplicated form *ás-as*, which occurs in the Vedas, and which appears to have been intended to mark in a very material manner the plural number, has been suggested as an explanation of this inorganic long *ē* in the Latin; but the simplest explanation is to suppose an invasion of the form of the *i*-stems. This tendency in the Latin to give *i*-forms to nouns of the third declension, which had not them originally, is illustrated by such words as *navis* from ναῦς, *civis* from the Oscan *cevs*, etc.

All the masc. and fem. *a*-stems of the first and second declensions in the Greek and Latin end in *i*. In the Greek the ι combines with the stem vowels *a*, *o* into αι, οι; in the Latin *a*- forms of the first declension, the stem vowel and ending combine to *ai*, which, as in the genitive, passes into *æ*. We have evidence of this passage in the Senatus Consultum de Bacchanalibus, where we find *tabelai datai* for *tabellæ datæ*. The *i* of the case-ending has absorbed the *u* of the *a*-stems of the second Latin declension in *us*—*populi, domini;* but in Old Latin it was *poplæ*, from *poplo-i*, etc. On old inscriptions we find, instead of *i*, the anomalous nom. plur. ending *eis* = *īs: hisce magistreis*.

Neuter nouns form their nom. and acc. plural in *a*, which in the *a*- stems of the second declension in the Greek and Latin is affixed in place of the stem vowel *o, u*, which is dropped—δῶρ-α, *dona;* in the third declension the *a* is affixed without dropping the declension vowel—ἴδρι-α, *mari-a;* this is also the case in the fourth Latin declension—*cornu-a*.

According to Bopp the plural ending *as* is merely "an extension of the singular nominative sign *s*, so that there lies in the extension of the case suffix a symbolical indication of plurality". This seems to imply that the *a* of the ending is in reality the plural sign. This affords a simple explanation of the circumstance that, the nom. acc. and voc. plur. of neuter nouns are formed by dropping the nominative *s*, which has a certain positive gender character. Grimm and other philologists believe the true sign of the plural to be *s*. Many forcible reasons may be given in support of this view, which, however, cannot find a place here. The plural ending *i* may be looked upon as the pronominal ending, Skr. *ê* = a primitive *ai*, Lith. and Goth. *ai*, Gr. οι, Slav. *i*, which invaded the substantives.

GOTHIC. All masculines and feminines both of the weak and strong declensions end in *s* in the Gothic. The masc. and fem. *a*-stems of the strong declension end in *ôs*, which represents the Sanskrit *âs*, the long vowel of the Gothic being the result of a contraction of the stem and case-ending vowels. The *i*-stems end in *eis;* the *u*-stems in *yus* (for *ius*). The ending of the masc. and fem. of the weak declension is *ns*, which is directly affixed to the stem; the *n* is the characteristic sign of the weak declension, and, as has been pointed out at p. 25, is added to all the cases except the nom. sing. and dat. plur. All the neuters end in *a;* those of the weak declension having the characteristic *n* before the *a*. The following paradigm will illustrate these rules:—

Strong declension.

	A-STEMS.		I-STEMS.		U-STEMS.	
	Sing.	Plur.	Sing.	Plur.	Sing.	Plur.
Masc.	fisks	fiskôs	balgs	balgeis	sunus	sunyus
Fem.	giba	gibôs	ansts	ansteis	handus	handyus
Neut.	vaurd	vaurda	—	—	faíhu	—

Weak declension.

Masc. hana . . hanans
Fem. tuggô . . tuggôns mauagei . manageins
Neut. hairtô . . hairtóna

In the O.H.G. the *s* dropped off in every case; in the strong declension the long vowel remains: *visc, viscâ; pelk, pelkî; sunu, sunî*. In the weak declension the stem-forming *a, ô* of the Gothic has been obscured to *u*, and the ending is accordingly *ûn*: *zunga, zungûn*. All the neuters drop the *a*, so that those belonging to the strong declension have no ending, while those belonging to the weak end, like the masc. and fem., in *un*: *daz wort, diu wort; herza, herzun*.

In the M. and N.H.G. all the different vowels of the ending become *e* in the masculines and feminines, so that the strong nominative plurals all end in *e*, and the weak in *en*. This *e* has likewise invaded the neuters in the N.H.G., which as a rule take *e*: *Worte*. Sometimes instead of *e*, they take up *er*. This suffix is not a flexional ending, and does not exist in the Gothic; it first made its appearance, according to J. Grimm, in the O.H.G. as *ir* attached to neuters. In the N.H.G. it has however invaded the masculines also, in which, as well as in the neuters, the root vowel is frequently diphthongated: neut. *wörter*; masc. *männer, geister*. The neuters of the weak declension end in M.H.G. like the weak masculines in *en*: *herze, herzen*.

The plural forms of adjectives declining according to the weak declension in the Gothic, Old and Middle High German, are like those of the substantives. In the strong declension, on the other hand, they have, with the exception of the Gothic neuters, forms, which like those of the dative singular, appear to have passed over from the pronouns. The following paradigm will illustrate this invasion of the pronominal endings:

	Masculine.		Feminine.		Neuter.	
	Adject.	*Pron.*	*Adject.*	*Pron.*	*Adject.*	*Pron.*
Goth.	blind-ai	th-ai	blind-ôs	th-ôs	blind-a	th-ô
O.H.G.	plint-ê	di-ê	plint-ô	di-ô	plint-u	di-u
M.H.G.	blind-e	di-e	blind-e	di-e	blind-iu	d-iu

It is worthy of remark that the modern languages,—Spanish, Portuguese, French, and, with few exceptions, English,—form the plural of all nouns in *s*.

LITHUANIAN AND SLAVONIAN. The *s* of the Sanskrit ending *as* has been preserved in the Lithuanian; the masc. *a*-stems have, however, taken the pronominal ending, which in substantives is the diphthong *ai*, and in adjectives *i*. The *s* of the ending *as* has been lost in O. Slavonian, but the vowel has been preserved as *e*. The crippling of the diphthong *ai* to *i*, which occurs in Lithuanian adjectives, extends to substantives and pronouns in O. Slavonian: *vlŭki* lupi, for *vlŭkoi*, *ti*=hi, *oni*=illi. The Lithuanian, on the other hand, contracts *ai* to *ē* in the pronominal declension: Lith. *tė̃*=Lat. *hi*, Skr. *tē*, Goth. *thai*, Gr. τοί. In Old Prussian, substantives, pronouns, and even adjectives of masc. *a*-stems have *ai*, or occasionally for it *ei* and *oi*. In Lithuanian the stem-vowel is lengthened in *i*- and *u*-stems; in Sanskrit the stem-vowel is gunated in the corresponding stems: Lith. *ãwys-* =Skr. *avay-as;* Lith. *sŭ́nū-s*=Skr. *sûnav-as*. In Gothic evidence of a similar gunation is found in the endings of the *i*- and *u*-stems (p. 45); the gunating vowel has been preserved as *i*, which in *i*-stems fuses with the stem-vowel to *ī* (*ei*), and in *u*-stems becomes *y* before *u: gastei-s, sunyu-s* for *suniu-s*.

§. 7. *The Accusative Plural.*

The accusative plural endings in the Sanskrit are—masc. and fem. *s*, *as;* masc. *n;* neut. *i*. In the Zend these endings are: *ó* (=Skr. *as*) for masc. and fem. consonantal, *i*-, and *u*-stems which is affixed with or without guna; *o* (Skr. *s*) fem. *a*-stems; *s* (=Skr. *s*) fem. *i*-, and *u*-stems; and the peculiar ending *eus* of masc. and fem. nouns in *r*, which Bopp explains from *ańs*, the *ń* becoming vocalized, and the *a* changed to *e*. In the Oscan, the first declension had *ass*, and the second *úss*. The masc. and fem. *a*-stems of the first declension in the Greek and Latin ended in *ās*—Μούσᾱς, *mensās;* those of the second declension in ους in the Greek, and *ōs* in the Latin. The *i*-stems, and the stems with consonantal auslaut of the third declension in the Greek, have the ending ᾰς, which, in the case of the latter, is affixed to the pure stem or thema: πόδα, πόδας. The *u*-stems, which retain the *u* in their thema, end in Greek in ῡς: nom. plur. ἰχθύες, acc. ἰχθῦς. The *a*-stems of the fifth declension, the *i*-stems, and those with consonantal auslaut of the third, and the *u*-stems of the fourth declension in the Latin, coincide with the nominative plural, as do the accusative plural of all neuter nouns in the Greek, Latin, etc. In the older Latin, however, the accusative plural of *i*-stems and also of consonantal stems, ended in *eis* or *īs*. In the Umbrian the accusative plural ended in *f* in all declensions.

The accusative plural ending of all masculine nouns, and of the feminine forms of the *u*- and *i*-stems in the Gothic, is *ns*, which is directly affixed to the full stem form: *fiska-ns, balgi-ns, sunu-ns*. The accusative plural of the feminine *a*-stems has not *n*, and therefore coincides with the nom. plur.: *gibôs, bidôs*, etc.

In the Old High German, the accusative plural coincides throughout with the nominative.

The universality of the *ns* in the Gothic accusative plural, and the circumstance that *m* (*n*) is the sign of the accusative, suggests a very simple explanation of the plural suffix. Grimm, in fact, regards it as the accusative singular + the plural *s*: the primitive form would accordingly be -*ms* (-*ns*). The sign of the accusative has therefore been wholly lost in the plural in the Greek and Latin, and, except in the masc. *a*-stems, in the Sanskrit also; the Greek and Latin have preserved the plural *s*, while the Sanskrit forms which have preserved the *n* have lost the plural *s*. The Greek and Latin accusative plural endings must, therefore, have dropped an *n*, so that *āç* and *ās* stand for *avç* and *ams*; *ouç* for *ovç*, and *ōs* for *ums*, *oms*.

Some examples of this complete accusative ending have been preserved in the Greek dialects, *e.g.* τόν-ς = τούς. It has likewise been preserved in Old Prussian in the same form as in the Gothic, both the masc. and fem. having the masc. ending *ns*; the Lithuanian, on the other hand, has only preserved the *s*: Skr. *dêvâ-n*, O. Pr. *deiwa-ns* deos, Lith. *dêwu-s*. In Lithuanian the stem-vowel of fem. *a*-stems, masc. and fem. *i*-stems, and masc. *u*-stems is short, while in the nom. it is long. The *a* of masc. *a*-stems has been weakened to *u*. In Old Slavonian the accusative ending has been lost in all masc. and fem. stems; stems in *n* or *r*, however, add an *i*, which must probably be explained by a transition into *i*-stems.

§. 8. *The Genitive Plural.*

SANSKRIT AND ZEND. The usual ending of the genitive plural of substantives and adjectives in the Sanskrit is *âm*, which is affixed directly to consonantal stems, and to vocalic stems by means of an euphonic *n* between the stem vowel and that of the ending: *pad-âm; çivâ-n-âm, priti-n-âm*. This *âm* was probably primitive *sâm*, a form which in fact we find in the pronouns which preserve the primitive forms longer and completer than the nouns, *e. g.* in the demonstrative *tê-shâm*, (*horum*), *tâsâm*, (*harum*). The *s* is the sign of the genitive singular, so that *am* is, properly speaking, the genitive plural sign. The genitive plural in Zend is *anm;* in the *a*- and *â*-stems this ending takes a euphonic *n*, as in the Sanskrit.

LATIN. The *a*-stems of the first, second, and fifth declensions, form their genitive plural in *rum*. This *rum* represents the Sanskrit *sâm*, and must have been anciently *sum*, which in turn leads to an earlier *sôm* = Skr. *sâm*. The Oscan genitive plural suffix *zum* appears to confirm this view. The *i*-stems, and the consonantal stems of the third declension, and the *u*-stems, form their genitive plural usually in *um* = Skr. *âm: mari-um*, *lapid-um, fructu-um.* The *i-um* of the *i-stems* has penetrated into many forms among consonantal stems, such as *urbium, serpentium,* etc. On the other hand, many *i*-stems drop the stem-forming *-i* in the genitive plural: *can-um, vat-um.* In some antique forms belonging to consonantal stems of the third declension preserved in Varro and Charisius, the full form *rum* is affixed to the stem by means of a copulative *ĕ: lapid-ĕ-rum* instead of *lapid-um, bov-ĕ-rum* instead of *bo-um.* We may also, however, consider them as formed from the genitive singular by the addition of *um: bover-um = bovis-um; lapidĕr-um = lapidis-um.* While, on the one hand, the full form *rum = sâm* was sometimes found in nouns of the third declension, many *a*-stems of the first and second formed their genitive plural in *um: agricol-um, vir-um.*

GREEK. The genitive plural ends in the Greek in ων = Skr. *am.* The ending of the first declension has a circumflex, which points to an original form ά-ων: Μουσῶν, old form Μουσάων. This ά-ων probably represents a fuller form σων = Skr. *sâm* = Oscan *zum* = Lat. *rum,* so that Μουσάων would represent a still more complete form Μουσά-σων = Lat. *Musarum.* In the second declension the copulative *o* dropped out before the ending: λόγ-ων. In the third declension the suffix attaches itself directly to the thema in consonantal and vocalic stems: ποδ-ῶν, ἰχθύ-ων, πήχε-ων, βασιλέ-ων. In the stems formed by the stem-forming suffixes ος and ες, in which the σ drops out, and the thema vowel is ε, the latter is however contracted with the ending: τριηρῶν for τριηρέ-ων; σαφῶν for σαφέ-ων.

GOTHIC. In the masc. and neut. forms belonging both to the strong and weak declension of the *a*-stems, the genitive plural ends in *é;* that of the feminine *a*-stems ends in *ó;* and of the masculine and feminine *i* and *u*-stems likewise in *é.* In the O.H.G. all the *a*-stems form their genitive plural in *ó,* and the *i* and *u*-stems in *i, o,* the usual *n* being intercalated in the weak declension before the ending. The strong feminine *a*-stems likewise introduce an euphonic *n* between the stem and the ending, as in the Sanskrit: Goth. fem. *gib-ó,* O.H.G. *kepó-n-ó* (*cf.* Skr. *çivá-n-ám*).

In the Middle and New High German, all the strong forms end in *e,* and the weak forms lose the vowel-ending, so that the genitive is always the same as the nominative.

The *é, ó* of the Gothic is derived from *á,* so that the *s* and *m* of the primitive ending have been wholly lost, and the vowel only preserved. The *s* has however been preserved as *z* in the Gothic in the adjectives and pronouns declined strongly; in the adjectives the stem vowel is diphthongated. The Gothic *z* becomes *r* in the M. and N.H.G.

LITHUANIAN AND SLAVONIAN. The Lithuanian genitive plural ends in *ŭ*. The Old Prussian has lost the vowel, and preserved the consonant of the ending *am* as *n*. It has also preserved the full form = Skr. *sâm*, in its pronominal genitive plural ending *son*. The Old Slavonian has *ŭ*; in the pronominal declension it has, however, the ending *chŭ*, which Bopp explains as = Skr. *sâm*, O. Pr. *son*.

§. 9. *The Dative, Locative, Instrumental, and Ablative Plural.*

The dative and ablative endings in the Sanskrit for all genders is *bhyas;* for the instrumental the ending for all genders is *bhis*, but the masculine *a*-stems form an instrumental in *is*. The locative plural for all genders is *su (shu)*. In the Zend the dative and ablative end in *byô*, which fully represents the Sanskrit *bhyas;* the instrumental ending is *bis;* and the locative *hva* (= Skr. *su*), *sva* (= Skr. *shu*).

There are two forms of the dative plural ending in the Greek and Latin, one of which is considered to be more ancient than the other. The older form in the Greek is σι, σιν, and in the Latin *bus;* the newer form, which is alike in both, is *is*. The latter occurs in the first and second declension in the Greek and Latin; in the former language the stem vowel combines to a diphthong with that of the ending; in the latter the stem vowel fuses and contracts to *îs*—*mensis* for *mensa-is*. The Oscan dative and ablative plural endings *a-is* (first declension), *ú-is*, *o-is* (second decl.), present us with similar uncontracted forms. The suffix *is* may be looked upon with considerable probability as the locative singular joined with the plural sign *s*.

The old Greek form σι, σιν, which is found in the third declension, originally occurred likewise in the first and second declensions, as is proved by the old datives μούσαισι, λόγοισι, a circumstance which shows that the ending *is* is of later origin. In the Old Greek we find the fuller form σσι—πάντ-ε-σσι, κύν-ε-σσι; this form occurs not only in Homer, but also in the Eolic, and to some extent in the Doric dialects. Aufrecht, Benfey, and others consider this suffix σσι to have arisen from σϝι = Zd. *sva*. The *a* and *o* of the stems in the first and second declension must have changed into αι and οι under the influence of the final ι; this lengthening of the vowel in its turn reacted upon the ending, and one σ dropped out.

The Latin dative and ablative plural ending *bus*, which corresponds to the Sanskrit *bhyas,* may be explained from the dative ending *bi* in *tibi* (= *tu-bi*) *sibi*, and *mihi*, the *b* being softened to *h* in the latter. This *bi* or *bhi* corresponds to the Sanskrit *bhyam, hyam: tu-bhyam* = *tibi; mahyam* mutilated from *mabhyam* =

mihi. It had evidently a primitive locative signification. Bopp compares it with the Sanskrit preposition *abhi*, with which the German *bei* (English *by* in the locative sense) is to be connected. We may also connect *ibi*, which is the locative of the pronominal stem *i-s*, and the analogous form *ubi*. Aufrecht has shown that the basis of the endings *bi* in *ibi* and *ubi*, and *im* in *illim, istim* is a *jim*, which may be recognized in the Umbrian locative plural suffix *fem*, which drops the *m*, and sometimes is weakened to *f*.[20] And further that the Old Epic φι, φιν is the same case suffix. From all this it is evident that *bhyas*=*bus* is simply a singular locative dative *bhi*, combined with the plural suffix *as*. Again, the plural ending of the Sanskrit instrumental is *bhis*=Zd. *bis*=Lat. suffix in *nobis, vobis*. Here too we have evidently a compound suffix composed of a singular *bhi*=Lat. *bi*, and a plural *s*. This Latin suffix fully represents the Greek φιν (in δακρυό-φιν, ὄρεσ-φιν, etc.), which must have been originally φις=*bhis*, for φις bears the same relation to φιν, that the first person plural suffix μες among the verbal endings, does to the other form μεν. This original φις was composed of a singular φι and the plural ς; this φι is now used along with the plural form φιν without distinction for singular or plural, at one time φιν and at another φι; the latter was, however, originally singular and the former plural. In the Old Latin *bus* was used in the first declension also, and at a later period to distinguish the genders—*deabus, filiabus;* and seldomer in the second declension—*filibus, amicibus*. Bopp thinks that the newer *is* of these declensions has come from *abus, obus*, which, in the first place, became *ibis* and then *is*, by dropping the *b*. Aufrecht, on the other hand, believes the *is* to have arisen from *iris*.

GOTHIC. The sign of the dative plural in the Gothic and O. H. G. was *m* for all nouns. In the M. H. G. the *m* is replaced by *n*. The ending *m* was attached directly to the thema in the strong declension. In the Goth. and M.H.G. the *m* of the case ending took the place of the characteristic *n* in the weak declension. In the strong adjectives the thema vowel *a* becomes *ai* in the Goth., and *é* in the O. H. G.; in the masc. nouns it is obscured, and in the fem. it becomes *ô*. The Gothic dative plural *m* is connected with the Sanskrit and Latin endings, *bhyas, bhis*, and *bus, bis*, by the corresponding Lithuanian case suffix *mus* in *mumus*=*nobis, yumus*=*vobis*, which appears in all other words in the syncopated form *ms*. The Gothic has accordingly softened *b* to *m*, and dropped the plural *s: fiskam* for *fiskams*=*piscibus*.

---

[20] The locative in the Umbrian appears to be formed by the addition of *em* to the accusative singular and plural, thus: acc. sing. *tutam* loc. sing. *tutam-em;* acc. plur. *tutaf.* loc. plur. *tutaf-em.*

A trace of the original *ms* remains in the Old Norse forms *tveimr, thrimr* = Lat. *duobus, tribus.*

LITHUANIAN AND SLAVONIAN. In Lithuanian the dative plural is formed by the addition of the pronominal ending *mus* or *ms* above-mentioned; masc. *a*-stems end, however, in *is*. In Old Slavonian the ending is *mŭ*, which is evidently a weakened and crippled form of *mus*. The Lithuanian instrumental plural ending is *mis*, which is apparently the singular ending, to which the plural *s* is added. In the Old Slavonian we have also this ending in the crippled form *mi*—the final consonant being generally lost in that language. Stems in *o* form their instrumental in *ŭ*, in which Bopp recognizes the Sanskrit *â-is*, Zd. *â-is* (in which the *b* has been lost), Lith. *a-is;* according to this, the *s* was lost and the *i* produced umlaut of the stem-vowel. Masc. and neut. *yo-* (*ya-*) stems form their instrumental in *i*. The locative plural is formed in Lithuanian by the endings *sa, su,* or *se,* or, as in the Lettish, more frequently by *s* only. In Old Slavonic the locative plural is formed by the pronominal genitive ending *chŭ*.

The annexed paradigm, which contains all the case-endings mentioned in the preceding pages, may be found useful in comparing the relative state of preservation of each case-ending in the different languages of the family.

PARADIGM OF THE CASE-ENDINGS OF NOUNS IN THE CHIEF INDO-EUROPEAN LANGUAGES.

	Sanskrit.	Zend.	Latin.	Oscan.	Umbrian.	Greek.	Gothic.	O. H. German.
				SINGULAR.				
Nom. and Voc.	-s, m, -f . . .	(-s), -m, f	-s, -m, -d . . .	-s, (-m), -d . .	-s, (-m) . .	-ς, -ν . . .	-s, -ta . . .	Lost (-s, -z) . . .
Accusative	-m	-m, -ĕm, -ĕm	-m	-m	-m, . . .	-ν, -α . . .	Lost except in masc. adj., where it is -na	Lost except in masc. adj., where it is -n
Genitive	-sya, -s, -as, -ās	-he, ahya, ās (-s), -ō . .	-is, -us, -i, -ēs . .	-as, -eís . .	-s, -r . . .	-ς, -ος, -ου . .	-s	s, when last -i, -i, -a
Dative	-ĕ, -ai, -āya . . .	-ĕ, ai . .	-i (fused in ō) -ō (for ai), -ai, -ē	a-i, ei-í, e-í . .	-ĕ	: (sometimes fused into η, η, ψ) . . .	-a, -ai, -au	-a, -i, -iu, -in, -iu, -in
Locative	-i, -ām, ī, āu . .	-a? i . . .	—	a-i, e-e, e-í .	-mem . . .	—	—	—
Instrumental	-ā (-yā), n-a	-a	—	—	—	—	—	—
Ablative	-t, -ās	-ãt, -avāt . .	-d (when last one stone as the def., except that -d is represented by e.)	a-d, ū-d, i-d,	-a, -e, -ī, -u .	—	—	—
				DUAL.				
Nom. Acc. and Voc.	-āu (in the Vedas -ā) -i	-āo, -ā, -ī .	—	—	—	-ε, -ī, ō . . .	—	—
Genitive and Locative	-os, yōs . . .	-ā	—	—	—	-ιν . . .	—	—
Dative Instrumental Ablative	-bhyām . . .	-bya . . .	—	—	—	—	—	—
				PLURAL.				
Nominative and Vocative	-as	-ā, -m . .	(-es), -ēs, -í -ēs, -ús, ūs	-ns, -ūs . .	-s, -r, -s, .	-ες αι, αι,	-ōs, -eis, -jus, -es, -os, -us	-ōs, -i, -iu
Accusative	-ās, -ns, n . . .	-ās, -īs, -ens	-ās, -ūs (and other forms like the nom.)	-ass, -ūsss ? -ess	sf, -n . . .	-ας, -ος, -ους -ῡς	-as, -ōs . .	Same as nom.
Genitive	-ām	-ąm ąm . .	-rum, -um	-rum, -um -ōm, -im ?	-rum, -um,	-ων, ὤν . .	-ē, -ō . .	-ō, -o n-ō, n-o
Dative	-bhyas . . .	-byō .ã	-bus, -is	-ois, -aís, -oís ieis ?	-es . . .	-ις, -σι, -σιν	-m	-im
Ablative	-bhyas							
Instrumental	-bhis, -is	-bīs, -īs .	—	—	—	—	—	—
Locative	-su (shu) . . .	-hvā, -syō .	—	√īn	—	—	—	—

ON DECLENSION

AND THE

DEGREES OF COMPARISON IN IRISH.

§. 1. *Bopp's view of the aspirations and eclipses in Modern Irish, and the modifications which it undergoes through the Old Irish forms.*

BOPP'S sagacity has never been, perhaps, so brilliantly proved, as in the discovery that the whole of the aspirations and eclipses, by which the Modern Irish declension is apparently disfigured, are nothing else than the relics and results of the after-action of the old case-endings.[21] Zeuss' determination of the old forms of the article has confirmed this supposition in the most complete manner, as regards the *n* and the consonant aspirations; the *t* and *h* before vowels are, however, to be somewhat differently explained. After what Zeuss remarks (pp. 59 and 63),[22] we cannot help regarding the *h* as, in the beginning, a useless and arbitrary

---

[21] Die Celtischen Sprachen, etc. S. '22, *et seq.*

[22] (*a*) [The passages in Zeuss are as follows :—

P. 59 : "H is not found as a radical in the Irish ; and if in ancient MSS., besides the combinations *ph, th, ch*, the *h* is also seen alone, which only happens at the commencement of words, it is nothing more than a breathing prefixed to the initial vowel, as in the ancient Gaulish names: Hercynia, Helvii. This *h*, neither a radical nor a necessary letter, occurs, without any fixed rule, in one place, and is not found in another; as: *uile, huile* (all), Wb. fq.; *éula* (wise), Wb., *heulas* (wisdom), Sg. 209^a; *aui, háui* (descendants), Sg. 28^a 30^b; and so on. The ancient language knows nothing of that regular usage according to which the modern dialects, Irish and Gaelic, prefix the *h* in a hiatus to the initial vowel of a substantive following the forms of the article *na* (gen. sing. fem., and nom. and dat. plur.) or preposition ending in a vowel. We find, indeed, for example, *inna hírise* (of the faith), Sg. 209^b, but also *inna idbairte* (of the offering), *inna indocbale* (of the glory), *inna anme* (of the soul), *na œcilse* (of the Church), Wb. 22^c 22^b 25^c 27^a; *na uccobra* (the desires), Wb. 20^c; *la Atacu* (with the men of Attica), Sg. 147^a; *a oentu* (from unity), Wb. 26^b *a albain* (from Scotland), Marian. Scot. ap. Pertz. 7, 481".

P. 63. " The *s* drops out by 'infection' in the ancient language.* The more recent language, indeed, which expresses the aspirate in its primary state as a strong *s*, almost as *ss*, pronounces the same letter when mortified or 'infected' as *h*, but I think this *h* is of still more recent origin than the *h* in a hiatus between the article or a preposition and the initial vowel of a substantive following, of which *supra*. For the ancient Irish MSS. either mark the mortified *s*, like the *f*, by a dot [the *punctum delens*, used commonly in mediæval MSS. to mark a letter written by mistake, and to be omitted], or else omit it altogether".]

* ["Infection", or "mortification", as it is called by some grammarians. Dr. O'Donovan calls it "Aspiration"; which he defines thus: "Aspiration, a grammatical accident, the general use of which distinguishes the Irish, Gaelic, and other cognate dialects of the Celtic, from all other modern languages, may be defined as the changing of the radical sounds of the consonants from being stops of the breath to a sibilance, or, from a stronger to a weaker sibilance".—O'D., Gram., p. 39-40.

addition before vowel anlauts, which, at a later period, permanently fixed itself after vowel auslauts; for the passage of *s* into *h* appears to be foreign to the Gaedhelic branch of the Celtic; in the dative plural, where *h* likewise appears before vowels, it is not *s*, but *b*, which has dropped off; for from *donabis*[23] the Modern Irish *dona* has been first developed through the Old Irish *donaib* or *donab*. On the other hand, we also frequently find the *t* (Zeuss, 55, 231, etc.)[24] after *n* in Old Irish, where otherwise *d* should stand, before eclipsed *s*. Hence, we cannot look upon the *t* in the nominative of the article as a substitute for *s*, but must assume that it had been prefixed to the *s* in the more ancient forms of the nominative, and afterwards remained when *s* dropped off. The Old Umbrian appears to afford a parallel to this: it never shows an *ns*, except instead of *nns* in *Palsans*, but either *nz* or *z* (*enze*=*onse*) or *s* (*neiṙhabas*). Accordingly, in the modern form of the language, this *t* is to be found wherever a vowel has dropped out from between *n* and *s*, equally whether the *s* belongs to the article (as in masc. *an tiasg*, the fish, instead of (*an*(*t*)*s iasg*), or the noun substantive (as in fem. *an tslat*, the rod,[25] instead of *an*(*t*) *slat*).[26] It is absent when *s* or another con-

---

[23] [i. Read **dunnabo* (from **du-sannabo*). Ebel's hypothetical *donabis* is due to his theory that the O. Ir. dat. plur. sprang from an instrumental (Sansk. -*bhis*). But this theory is destroyed by the Gaulish inscription of Nismes (*Revue Archéologique*, 1858, p. 44), in which Dr. Siegfried has recognized two datives plur.— viz., *mátrebo namausikábo* (matribus nemausicis), which are genuine descendants of the Indo-European datives plur. in -*bhias*, Sanskr. -*bhyas*, the *i* (*y*) being ejected as in Lat. -*bus*. In *donaib* the stem-vowel *a* has been weakened into *ai*.]

[24] (*b*) [The passages in Zeuss are as follows :—

P. 55. "The form NT, also, occurs in forms of pronouns coalescing with the preposition *in*, but only when the preposition governs the accusative case: *inte* (= in eam, fem.) Sg. b[a]; *intesi* (gl. in ipsam) Sg. 199[a], 209[b]; *intiu* (in eos) Sg. 7[a], Ml. 21[a]. 28[a]. Thence we might expect for the other persons the forms: *intium* (= in me), *intiunn* (= in nos), *intit* (= in te), *intib* (= in vos), *intis* (= in eum), which I have not met with in MSS. The harder form, *int*, of the article prevails before vowels in the sing. nom. of the masc. gender, in which, after the usual form of the article, *in*, the hard form of the consonants is retained. Therefore the harder form *nt* seems to contain in itself the signification of action (motion, in the preposition), of hardness of form and of the masculine gender; the softer *nd* that of the passive (rest, in the preposition) of softening [of the letter] and of the feminine gender. It is to be observed in addition, that the form of the article *int* prevails almost always (the form *ind* is very rarely found) before the softened, or, as it is called, the 'mortified' *s* in all the cases of the three genders in which *ind* occurs before vowels (*e.g.* in the Article); this is, however, to be compared with the fact, that even the particle *ind* in composition (in the ancient Gaulish *ande-*) becomes *int* before a softened or mortified *s* in the following word.]

P. 231. [Gen. sing. of the article, IN]. "IN, aspirating, before tenues and medials; IND before liquids, mortified consonants, and vowels. * * * * * Instead of the regular IND the form INT also prevails before the mortified *s*, as before at p. 55 [extract, *supra*, note ([24])], and here: *intsechtaigtha* (gloss: "simuationis"), Ml. 31[a]; *fomam intsommai* (under a rich man's yoke), Ml. 27[d].]

[25] The difference between *an tiasg* and *an tslat* is only graphic, as it is pro-

sonant has dropped off; consequently, in the gen. and nom. plur. fem. *na slaite*, instead of *nás slaite*, in the nom. sing. masc. *an sruth*, the scholar, instead of *an(t)s sruth;* in the gen. plur. of both genders *na sruth, na slat*, instead of *nán sruth, nán slat;* in the dat. plur., *dona srothabh, dona slataibh*.

A third point in which Bopp's view undergoes a modification through the Old Irish forms, is the explanation of the nom. plur. masc., which in the Modern Irish is formed as in the fem. in *na* with *h* before vowels, and without alteration of the following consonants. Bopp thence concludes that in the Celtic the article, like the substantive, in the masc. plur. originally ended in *ás;* consequently, that *na* has been deformed out of *anás;* but the Old Irish *ind*, or *in* with an aspiration following, together with the fem. masc., *inna* or *na*, show us that here also the masc. originally ended in a vowel as in almost all the Indo-European languages; consequently, that the modern *na* owes its existence to an inorganic extension of the accusative form, or fem. plur. form, which we already find in the Old Irish neutral plural *inna*, which leaves the consonants following unaffected.[27]

With the exception of these three points, the old forms confirm throughout Bopp's discovery, according to which the nomin. sing. masc., the gen. sing., and the nom. pl. fem., from their very origin ended in *s;* the gen. plur. in *n;* the gen. and dat. masc., and nom. and dat. fem. sing., in vowels.

The finding of the neuter, which has disappeared without leaving a trace in the New Celtic (*an* or *a* in the nominative and accusative singular, and the plural like the genitive), and of the accusative (replaced in the Modern Irish by the nominative), in the Old Irish forms *inn* (before consonants *in*) in the masculine and feminine singular, *inna* or *na* in the plural of all three genders,— and in which we can still plainly recognize the original ending *-n* in the singular, and *-s* in the plural,—is an important enrichment of Celtic grammar.

I hazard no supposition as to the relation of the old forms with *i*, followed by *nt, nd, nn*, to the new with *a* and simple *n;* the vowels of the endings can only be determined through a comparison of the substantive-declension, to which we shall now proceed.

§. 2. *Stems which belong to the several orders and series of Zeuss.*

The philologist recognizes at first sight, in the first order

---

nounced *an tlat*, as in accurate writing even in the Old Irish *s* is provided with a dot or left out, not only in this case but also after vowels.—*Zeuss*, 63.

[26] [ii. The *t* in the nom. sing. masc. of the Irish article has been since shown to be due to the law, pursuant to which, in Old Irish, *d* becomes *t* before aspirated *s*, *an tinsg*, in O. Ir. *intiasc*=an Old Celtic *san(d)as+éscas*, subsequently *indshêsc=intiasc*.]

[27] [See *infra*, §. 11. On the Article in Modern Irish, p. 88.]

(*Ordo Prior*) of Zeuss (App. I., p. 169), a vocali c(or a consonantal changed into a vocalic) declension, in the second order (*Ordo Posterior*), consonantal stems; among the latter, the masculine and the feminine *n*-stems and nouns of relationship in -*thir* (=Sanskrit -*tar*) being especially evident, as had been already recognized and put forward by Pictet and Bopp. On the other hand, I cannot, from external and internal grounds, agree with both these masters in the distribution of the vocalic-stems.

Namely, if we compare the first paradigm or table of Zeuss with the second, his remark, that the first is external, and the second internal inflexion, is at once seen to be incorrect. We have only to take, instead of *ball*, a word with *e*—as, for example, *fer*, man—in order to at once see that the declension of *céle* (companion) does not at all differ in the main from that of *fer*, except that in the former a vowel preceded the dropped off ending, in the latter a consonant. The vowel of the original penultimate undergoes in both the same changes: nom. and acc. sing. and gen. plur. *céle*, like *fer*, gen. and voc. sing. and nom. plur. *céli*, as *fir*, dat. sing. *céliu* as *fiur*, acc. plur. *céliu* as *firu:* it is only in the dative plural that a slight difference occurs between *célib* and *feraib*. In short, I. is only a variety of II., and both are related to one another, like the Gothic *haryis* or *hairdeis* to *fisks*. Let us, therefore, assume for a moment that I. contains *ya*-stems, II., *a*-stems; there remain for III. *u* and *i*-stems. But a similar relation to that between I. and II. also occurs in the feminine between IV. and V., and the differences in the paradigm between *tuare* and *rainne* in the genitive singular, *tuari* and *ranna* in the nom. and acc. plur., are compensated by the secondary forms of the fifth, which we find under the examples gen. sing. -*a* and -*o*, nom. and acc. plur. -*e* and -*i*. We could here also assume in the fourth *yá*-stems, in the fifth *á*-stems, and have only to determine then what has become of the *i* or *î*-stems, in order to remove the objection which could be raised upon external grounds against such a division; for, if feminine *u*-stems are wanting, there is nothing remarkable in the circumstance. We shall again find the feminine *i*-stems under V.; the *î*-stems have, however, either become *ya* or *i*-stems. We find many stems, originally consonantal, changed into III. (exactly as in Latin in the *i*-declension): *e.g.*, *áis, óis* (aetas) = Sanskrit *áyus*, gen. *aisso, óesa*.[28] The feminine *nem*[29] (cælum) = Sanskrit *nabhas*, gen. *nime*,

---

[28] [iii. It is impossible to equate *áis* with *áyus*, final *s* being never retained in Irish, not even in the *ns*-stems.]

[29] [iv. *Nem* (also *nim*) was an *i*-stem—not an *á*-stem—as we see from the Old Irish gen. plur. *nime* in *Oingus Céle Dé*:—

Sén á Christ mo labrad "Bless, O Christ, my utterance,
a choimdiu secht *nime*. O Lord of seven heavens!"]

according to V., reminds us of the Slavic forms mentioned in the Zeitschrift für vergleichende Sprachforschung, iv. 342: *voda*= Sanskrit *udan*, *gora* = ὄρος, *tĭma* = Sanskrit *tamas*. If, accordingly, we designate the five series set up by Zeuss as: I. *b.* masculine and neutral *ya*-stems; I. *a.* masculine and neutral *a*-stems; II. masculine and neutral *i* and *u*-stems; III. *b.* feminine *yâ*-stems; III. *a.* feminine *â* and *i*-stems, we shall find that this classification will receive an external confirmation by a consideration of the words and suffixes which belong to the several classes.

First, most loan-words harmonize, in the most strikingly accurate manner, with their types in the declension. Compare, for example, the *a*-stems—*felsub* = philosophus, *ór* = aurum,[30] *angel* = angelus, *apstal* = apostolus, *epscop* = episcopus, *fial* = velum, *idol* m. = idolum, *ifurnn* = infernum, *salm* = psalmus, *tempul* = templum, together with the genitive *digaim* = digammi, *metir* = metri; the *â*-stems—(*almsin?*[31] = eleemosyna, *epistil ?* = epistola) *persan* = persona, *riagol riagul* = regula, *pian* = pœna, *fedb* = vidua (no doubt borrowed?) *liter* = litera, *sillab* = syllaba; those in *ia* and *iâ*—the masculine *notaire*, *rectaire*, *tablaire*, the feminine *fellsube* = philosophia; those in *i*—the masculine *fáith* = vates; in *u* — the masculine *fers* = versus, *sens* = sensus, *spirut* (gen. *spirito*, *spiruto*) = spiritus. Proper names follow the same rule, such as *róm*, fem. = Roma, *román*, mas. = Romanus, *tit* = titus, *tiamthe* = Timotheus, *grec* = Græcus, although I. *a.* has here encroached rather more, as the dat. *aeneus*, gen. *adim*, *Socrait*, *Aristotil*, show.

The forms of the cognate languages afford a further confirmation, and so do now and then also traditional Gaulish words. *Fer* (stem *fira*) corresponds to the Sanskrit *vira* still more accurately than the Latin *vir* and Gothic *vair* (instead of *vir* stem *vira*);[32] the adjective *fír* to the Latin *verus* (compare *ríg*[33] = Latin *rex*); *óin óen* to the Latin *unus; marb* to the Latin *mortuus* ($b=tv$);[34] *fescor fescar*, masc. to the Lithuanian *vakaras*, Latin *vesper; bran*, raven, to the Slavonian *vranŭ*, Lithuanian *varnas* (Sanskrit *varna*); *rún* fem. to the Gothic *runa; dia* masc., the anomaly of which is only apparent, to the Latin *Deus* (instead of Dêus = Sanskrit *dêva*); *ferc* fem. probably to the Greek ὀργή; *tuath* fem. to the Oscan *tovto*, Umbrian *toto; anim*, fem., from

---

[30] [v. *ór* is even found with the *n* of the neuter termination in the nom. sing. *ór nglan* (pure gold), where *ór n̄* is exactly the Greek αὖρον.]

[31] [vi. Rectè *almsan : epistil* is right—the *i* in the last syllable being due to progressive assimilation—a phenomenon which Irish exhibits in common with Finnish and Magyar.]

[32] The Lithuanian form *wyras*, and the rarity of the Latin *i*, instead of *a*, before *r*, speaks more in favour of *vira* than of *vara*.

[33] [vii. Rectè *rí*=Gaulish *rix*, a *g*-stem.]

[34] [viii. The *b* in *marb*, now *marbh*, is a v. *marb*=*marva, Welsh, *marw*.]

which several cases are formed according to III. *a*. (Zeitschrift f. vergl. Sp. vi. 213), and which corresponds in these to the Latin *anima; lán* to the Latin *plenus* (see *supra*); *colum* to the Latin *columba;*[35] *ardd*, probably, to the Latin *arduus; nú*[36] to the Latin *novus* = Sanskrit *nava*, on the other hand, *nue* is related to the Gothic *niujis* = Sanskrit *navya; aile* to the Latin *alius;* consequently we may refer *uile* to Gothic *alls* by assimilation from *lj*: the neuter *cride* represents exactly the Sanskrit *hṛdaya* (less accurately the Greek καρδία), *tréde* neut. (the Trinity) the Sanskrit *tritaya; muir* shows itself by the Gaulish *mori-* to be an *i*-stem, which, notwithstanding small deviations, the Latin *mare*, Slav. *more*, Gothic *marei*, confirm; *mug* (servus) appears to be identical with the Gothic *magus* (puer), and consequently an *u*-stem; *fid* neut. (arbor) resembles the Old Saxon *widu*, Anglo-Saxon *wudu*, Old High German *witu* (Old Norse masc. *viðr*), and besides is shown by the Gaulish *vidu* to be a *u*-stem, like *cath* (pugna), *bith* (mundus) by the Gaulish *catu-, bitu-*; the fem. *sét* (dat. *séit*, pl. *seúit*) *via* = Gothic *sinþs*, like *dét* (dat. *déit* = Lat. *dens*), fluctuates between *i-* and a consonantal declension; finally the double forms *ben* and *ban* (mulier) may be explained either from * *gvina*[37] (= Gothic *qvinô*) and **gvano* (= Greek γυνή, Bœot. βάνα) or from **gvani* (= Sanskrit *jani*) and **gvana* (exactly as the Slav. *žena* can have been formed from *žana* or *žina*).

But even if we considered these agreements as merely accidental, much more would the identity of the suffixes come out. The adjectives come almost without exception under the classes I. *a*. and *b*. in masc. and neut. III. *a*. and *b*. in femin., consequently to *a*- and *yâ*-stems, which in all the Indo-European languages are the most numerous. The superlatives end in *-em*, of which I have found no inflexions in Zeuss, and are probably derived from *ima*, or *am*, certainly from *-ama*, which is inflected according to I. *a*. Of the adjectives the fem. abstracts in *-e* are very generally formed according to III. *b*., which corresponds to the Sanskrit *yâ*, Lat. *-ia*, Greek *-ια*, Old High Germ. *-î*, Middle High German *-e*, *e.g.*, *amprome* (improbitas) from *amprom*, *sulbaire* (eloquentia) from *sulber*, *dóire* (miseria) from *dóir*, *soire* (nobilitas) from *sóir*, *fírinne* (justitia) from *fírian*, *luinde*, bitterness, from *lond*, *nóibe* (sanctitas) from *nóib*, etc. Among the masc. in *-e* (I. *b*.) the words in *-ire* or *-aire*, corresponding to the Slav. *-aṛi*, as *echire*, *echaire* (mulio), and many loan-words (from the Lat.

---

[35] [ix. *Colum* (rectè *colomb*), gen. *coluimb*, is a masc. *a*-stem, not fem. like *columba*.]

[36] [x. Rectè *núa*. The nom. plur. of *sét* (see below) has the masc. article in Zeuss, p. 237.]

[37] [All words to which an asterisk is prefixed are hypothetical.]

-arius) distinguish themselves; among the adjectives those in *-de* = Sanskrit *-tya*, only of larger use, *e.g. nemde* (coelestis), *talmande* (terrestris), *colnide* (carnalis), etc.; the Sanskrit *-taya* occurs in the numeral adjectives *déde, tréde* corresponding also in gender to the Sanskrit *tritaya, catushṭaya*. We must, therefore, accordingly compare the modern fem. in *-mhuin*, as produced from the older *-maine*, not with the Sanskrit neuter in *-man*, but with the Latin fem. in *-monia* (*seachmuin = sechtmaine*, consequently not accurately corresponding to the Lat. *septimana*), especially as even the Old Irish already sometimes exhibits retrenchment, as *testemin, festimin* stands by the side of the Lat. *testimonium*, the neut. *aill* by that of the mas. *aile = alius*.

The verbal substantives, which take the place of the infinitive, are particularly interesting. Those of them that apparently contain the naked root, as *cumang* (posse, potentia), *fulang* (tolerare), may be recognized by their declension according to I. *a.*, as *a*-stems, to which the Sanskrit gerund in *-am*, and the locative in *-é*, by which the Indian grammarians frequently explain the roots, are parallel. Pictet (De l'affinité des Langues Celtiques avec le Sanskrit, p. 161) compares the infinitive in *t, th, d, dh*, with the Sanskrit *-tum;* Bopp (p. 56) rather with the Slavonic *-ti*, especially because of the form *tinn;* we find among the suffixes in Pictet, the Irish *adh* compared with the Sanskrit *-athu*. We shall become acquainted with *tinn* further on under consonantal declension; about the other forms the Old Irish supplies us with information. There *-ad* and *-ud* follow the second mode of inflexion, *-t* the third; we are consequently the more entitled to presuppose in the former two suffixes *u*-stems (like the Lat. *-tus*, from which the supine, Sanskrit *-tu*, from which the infinitive and gerund *-tum, -tvá*), as, according to the latest statements of Schleicher (Beiträge, I. 27), even the Slavonic infinitive in *-ti* belongs to this formation; on the other hand, the feminine forms in *-t* (according to III. *a.*) are not to be separated from the feminine abstracts in Sanskrit *-ti*, Greek *-τί* (σί), Lat. *-ti* (*si*), Gothic *-ti*, *þi, di*. The feminines in *-ál* (III. *a.*) remind us of the peculiar Slavonic participles in *-lŭ;* but it would be difficult to decide whether *-á* or *-i* has dropped off in them. The feminine in *-em* are *a*-stems, which correspond to the Greek verbal-nouns in *-μη;* the masculine in *-am, -om, -um*, remain obscure to me. Finally, *-ent, -end*, according to I. *a.*, I consider to be borrowed, a supposition to which the forms *legend, scribend*, already point. The masculines in *-id*, gen. *-ada*, in which Zeuss, p. 766, suspected an original *-at*, still deserve to be mentioned; the proper stem-ending is *-ati*, absolutely like the Sanskrit *-ti*, Greek τι (in μάντις), only differently employed, as it appears in the Irish, as a taddhita suffix.[38] The part. perf. pass. appears to be the only exception to this regular correspondence with the cognate languages: they do not end in -*th* or -*d*, according to I. *a.*, as the analogy with the Sanskrit, Greek, Latin, and Gothic would lead to, but in -*the*, according to I. *b.*; but the original form still lies before us in the preterite passive of the impersonal conjugation (sing. -*d*, plur. -*tha*); we have consequently to recognize in the ordinary form an addition (-*ya* or -*aya*) similar to that in the Old Welsh -*etic*. On the other hand, the part. fut. pass. -*thi*, properly -*thí*, accurately links itself to the Sanskrit -*tavya*, Greek -τέος (Lat. -*tivus*).

If, finally, we compare the forms of the article, which, according to Bopp's view, also belong to an *a*-stem, and exactly agree with the stems in I. *a* in the distinguishing cases, gen. sing. and nom. pl. masc., there will be found sufficient external grounds to justify our division. We shall now pass to the inner characteristics which exist in the Irish phonetic relations, in order to develope and explain, as far as possible, the individual forms.

§. 3. *Test afforded by Irish Phonology for determining inductively the Primitive Forms of the Celtic Case-Endings.*

The Irish vocal system exhibits two very close points of contact with the German, the umlaut or obscuring of an *a* by *i* and *u*, and the fracture of an *i* and *u* by *a*. In reference to the first, it is particularly remarkable that the three kinds of assimilation of the *a* before *i* and *u*, which we generally find separated in different languages and language-periods (complete assimilation as in the Sanskrit *giri* and *guru*, diphthongation as in the Zend, *pairi* and *pauru*, umlaut proper as in the Old Norse *hendi* and *hönd*), appear here side by side; thus the well-known particle *ar*- is written *air*-, *ir*-, *er*- [and *aur*-]; the accusative plural of *ball*, at one time *bullu*, at another *baullu*; *rolaumur* (audeo) also *rolomur*. As umlauts of *a* there consequently occur:—1, *ai* or *i*, more rarely *e*; 2, *au* or *u*, more rarely *o*; inversely *i* changes into *e*, *o* into *u*, under the influence of an *a* following, as in the Old High German; thus, for example, in the gen. *feda, moga* from *fid, mug*. We may see how far the last law has extended itself, from the fact that it has even invaded foreign names, as *etal* = Italia; but when Zeuss ascribes the same influence to a succeeding *o* and *u*, it should be considered that *o* and *a* often interchange, as in the gen. *etha* or *etho* from *ith*, where the *e* owes its origin rather to the *a* than to the *o*; but, on the other hand, *o* and *e* arise from simple weakening—namely, before double consonants,

---

[38] [So the Indian grammarians call the secondary suffixes.]

so probably also in *felsub* = philosophus.³⁹ We can just as little recognize an umlaut of the *e* into *i*, for where we have reason to consider *e* as primitive, there is produced by a succeeding *i* or *u*, not *i* or *iu*, but *ei* or *eu*, for example, in the plural *geinti* (gentes) in the dat. *neurt*, from *nert* (virtus, valor).⁴⁰ Zeuss has proceeded in a one-sided manner, inasmuch as he has everywhere taken the vowel which appears in the nominative as the primitive one; while, in cases like *nime*, *giun*, it is rather the *i* changed into *e* by *a* that again appears. On the other hand, it must be admitted that umlaut is sometimes produced by an *e* not derived from *i*, as in gen. *rainne* from *rann* (pars). According to this, the rule for the Old Irish (we pass over here the vowel changes in the Modern Irish, and slight deviations, such as *oi* for *ai*, *ea*, *eo*, for *ao*) may be expressed somewhat as follows: under the influence of a succeeding *a*, *i* changes itself into *e*, *u* into *o*; under that of a succeeding *i* (exceptionally also an *e*), *a* into *i* or *ai* (or *e*), *e* into *ei*, *u* into *ui*, *o* into *oi*; finally, under that of a succeeding *u*, *a* into *u* or *au* (or *o*), *i* into *iu*, *e* into *eu*. It is unnecessary to observe that the factor very often disappears, and the fact remains, so that, just as in German, we can determine by the vowel-changes in the stem the vowel of the ending, a circumstance of so much the more importance, because it will soon appear that the Irish, even in its oldest form, is much more weakened in the auslauts than, for instance, the Gothic.

If we apply the rule just given to determine the vowels of these endings, we obtain, in the first instance, for the masculine and neuter, according to I., the following endings:—

Sing. Nom. -(*a*)s, -(*a*)n	. .	Plur. -*i*, -*â*
Acc. -(*a*)n	. .	-*û*, -*â*
Gen. -*i*	. .	-*an*
Dat. -*u*	. .	-*abis*⁴¹

Examples: *ball* (membrum) *ball*, *baill*, *baull* or *bull*, *baill ballaib* or *ballib*; *fer* (vir), *fer*, *fir*, *fiur*, *fir*, *firu*, *fer*, *feraib*;

³⁹ [xi. Here (at least as to the breaking of *i* into *e* by *o*) Zeuss seems right and Ebel wrong. Thus:

Bretan=Brito (Book of Armagh); lenomnaib (lituris), Zeuss, 739, compare Lat. *lino*; lebor from liber (Zeuss, 744); senod (Cormac), from synodus (y=i) cen*e*l=ceneth(*o*)l=Old Welsh cenitol.]

⁴⁰ [xii. *E* seems changed into *i* by a succeeding *i* in the following instances:— Aristot*i*l (gen. sing.), Zeuss, 887, magist*i*r, nom. pl. of magist*e*r, Zeuss, 1057, herit*i*c (=haeretici) Zeuss, 1055.]

⁴¹ [xiii. Regarding the remarks in notes 23 and 39, the hypothetical endings for the masc. and neut. may be set down as follows:

Sing. nom. . . .	*os*, *on*	Plur. *i*, *â*
acc. . . .	*on*	*ûs*, *â*
dat. . . .	*u*	*âbo* (*abo* ?)
gen. . . .	*i*	*an*

and these agree with the Gaulish endings of the *a*-declension, so far as they have been established.]

neuter, *imned* (tribulatio), pl. *imnetha imneda*. We recognize here distinctly the *a*-stem *balla*, *fera* instead of *fira*, *imnetha* instead of *imnitha*; *fira* harmonizes in a remarkably beautiful manner with the Gothic and Latin stem *vira* (for *vair* indicates a previous short *i*) in opposition to the Sanskrit *vîra*. The feminine *a*-stems lead back to:—

	Sing.	Nom.	-a			Plur.	-ás
		Acc.	-an				-ás
		Gen.	-é(s) or -(á)s				-an
		Dat.	-i or e				-abis

Examples: *nem* (heaven), *nem, nime, nim* (stem *nimâ*, hence the nom. *nim* is still found singly); *delb* (effigies), *delb, delbe, deilb*, plur. *delbæ* (instead of *delba*), gen. *delb*, dat. *delbaib*, with primitive *e*, therefore it is in the dative not *dilb*, but *deilb*. The masculine stems, according to III., exhibit, in the immediately preceding stage approximately the following forms:—

	Sing.	Nom.	(-is or -us)			Plur.	-á(s), -é(s), i(s)
		Acc.	(-in or -un)				-û -i
		Gen.	á(s) or ó(s)				-é(n)
		Dat.	u? or -i?				-ibis (-abis?)

Examples: nom. *dénmid* (doer) instead of *dénmadis*, gen. *denmada*; nom. *bith* (world), dat. *biuth* instead of *bithu*; *gnim* (action) acc. plur. *gnimu*; *aitribthid* (possessor), gen. *aitrebthado*, nom. acc. plur. *aitribthidi*.

It is easily seen that the forms which are attainable by immediate conclusion, do not admit, in any way, of a direct comparison with the primitive forms, as the Gothic, to a certain extent, do, but still require an intermediate stage to connect them. A *baill ballû*, or *ballui*, must necessarily have preceded *balli, ballu*, assumed from *baill, baull*, a *nimâ* the *nima*, deduced from *nem*, a *firûs* (or *firûn*?) the *firû* changed into *firu*, a *firân*, the hypothetical *firan* in the gen. pl. In short, the oldest historical forms of the Irish, in regard to the conservation of the auslaut, stand, at most, and even scarcely, upon a level with the New High German,[42] as the simple comparison of the Irish and the German *ball* may show:—

Sing.	{Irish,	. . Nom.	ball,	Acc.	ball,	Gen.	baill,	Dat.	baull.
	{German,	.	„ ball,	„	ball,	„	ball(e)s,	„	ball(e).
Plur.	{Irish,	. .	„ baill,	„	baullu,	„	ball,	„	ballaib.
	{German,	.	„ bälle,	„	bülle,	„	bälle,	„	bällen.

We find that long vowels have disappeared in the auslaut often even with succeeding consonants; equally so, short vowels, with succeeding *s*; only long vowels before *s* have preserved

---

[42] [xiv. Ebel would not now say this. See, *infra*, "On the so-called prosthetic *n*", §. 12, p. 90.]

themselves in a shortened form: (forms such as *céle* (socius), consequently presuppose either a *célias*, *céleas*, with a fallen off endsyllable, or a *célés* with a shortening of the vowel before the fallen off *s;* we shall more correctly explain *firu* from *firús* than from *firún*, as we everywhere [except in the article and *teora ñ*] see that the long vowel in the genitive plural has disappeared along with the *n*). We could not, in view of such mutilation of the original endings, venture to think of anything like a satisfactory development of the case-endings, were it not that fortunately the above-mentioned law for the vocalism, and the changing of the consonants between the article and substantive, puts into our hands a test.

The end-consonants, except *m* and *r*, have evidently all disappeared; *m* is changed, according to rule, into *n*, only traces of which have, still, been preserved;[43] *s* no longer occurs at the end; *t*, which appears in its place in the Old Irish as *int*, and in the Modern Irish *an t*, shows us that it has only disappeared in the immediately preceding period, only after the dropping out of the short vowel. *The Gaedhelic has, consequently, been harder than the Gothic, in so far that, besides* s *and* r, *it also suffered an* n *in its auslaut, probably derived, however, from* m, *not a primitive* n.[44] Of these three consonants, *s* was the first which dropped off, for it does not appear in any declension or conjugation-ending; not even in the article, where, however, its former existence is betrayed by the *t* in the nom. INT *ant*, and by the conservation of the original anlaut after the form INNA *na;* the second that dropped off was the *n* derived from *m*, which is still visible at least in the article in the acc. INN, and in gen. plur. INNAN *nan* (besides here and there also, *e.g.* in *teora ngutte*, Zeuss. 310); *r* has preserved itself to the present day in the nominative ATHIR *athair* (pater).

The mutilations of the auslaut appear to have taken place in this wise; in the first place the short vowels in the auslaut and before consonants were dropped, the long ones in the auslaut shortened, then (or also contemporaneously, a supposition to which the Lat. -*um*, instead of -*ûm*, would lead us) the long vowels before *n* were shortened, hereupon *s* dropped, finally the long vowel was again shortened, and the short vowel together with *n* dropped. From the primitive Gaedhelic to the Gaedhelic of the oldest monuments, we would have, consequently, to presuppose three or four periods, which may be represented by an example, somewhat in the following manner:—

---

[43] [xiv. See the last mentioned paper.]
[44] [See on this passage the author's paper referred to in the last two notes.]

	Primitive period.	Pre-historic period.	Historic period.
Sing. Nom. . . .	ballas,	balls,	ball.
Acc.	ballan,	balln,	ball.
Gen.	ballî,	balli,	baill.
Dat.	ballui, (ballû?)	ballu,	baull.
Plur. Nom. . . .	ballî,	balli,	baill.
Acc.	ballûs,	ballû,	baullu.
Gen.	ballân,	ballan,	ball.
Dat.	ballabis,	ball(a)bis,	ball(a)ib.

Still later weakenings of the auslaut sometimes occur, as the Old Gaedhelic shows in neut. *aill* from *aile* (similar to the Old Latin *alid*); the Old Kymric especially distinguishes itself from the Gaedhelic by greater weakenings, *e. g.* as *all* (alius) and *oll* (omnis), instead of the Gaedhelic *aile* and *uile*. The adjective in the Welsh exhibits an interesting difference, inasmuch as here the change of *i* and *u* into *e* and *o* first takes place in the feminine, hence a fem. *gwen, cron* is opposed to the mas. *gwyn* (albus) *crwn* (rotundus). We may consequently presume that in the Welsh the fracture was only introduced when the short end-vowels were thrown off, consequently *crunnas crunná* were already become *crunn(s) crunna*, whilst, in the Gaedhelic, the falling off only followed the introduction of the fracture.

§. 4. *Declension of consonantal stems.*

Now only are we in a position to attempt an explanation of the endings; but, in consequence of the extremely difficult *i*- and *u*-stems, we shall begin with the declension of the consonantal stems. We find in Zeuss five classes (not exactly in the most convenient order), of which I. and II. contain *n*-stems, III. and V. *r*-stems, IV. *d*-stems;[45] of these *d* appears to have arisen out of *t*. The inflexion is most regular in the masculine-feminine *n*-stems (II.), and in the masculine *d*-stems (IV.). Both subdivide themselves according to the vowel of the genitive into two divisions, in which we recognize, according to the phonetic laws of the Irish, stems with *a* and with *i;* those in -*man* may be compared with the Sanskrit -*man*, -*iman*, -*van*, and with the Greek -μον (compare *brithem* judge and ἡγεμών); those in -*tin* or -*sin* are, in a similar way, as in the Umbrian and Oscan, shortened from -*tian*, which again appears in the nom. -*tiu*, and consequently express the Lat. -*tio*, -*tionis*, with which they also agree in gender; the infinitive use of these abstracts (comp. Zeuss, 462) explains the infinitives in

---

[45] [xv. Zeuss' series V. contains *c*-stems (in some instances *i*-stems, which, in the oblique cases, go over to the *c*-declension), and under his fourth series he has put *d*-stems, *t*-stems, and *ant*-stems. Among his irregular nouns he gives *ri*, gen. *ríg*, the sole example of an Irish *g*-stem. *Mí:* (a month) gen. *mís*, is a *ns*-stem. So were the comparatives in *iu*, Sanskrit *iyâns*, though undeclined in the oldest Irish.]

-*tinn*, -*sinn* of the present language, which consequently are not at all directly connected with those in -*t* and -*dh*; probably a similar contraction of the stem lies at the basis of those in -*id*, because in the nominative along with *ogi* (hospes), *fili* (poëta), *tene* (ignis), the fuller form *cóimdiu* (dominus) shows itself. Analysis yields the common endings:—

Sing. Nom. (long vowel)	.	.	.	Plur. -*is*
Ac. -*in* (-*en*)	.	.	.	-*ás*
Gen. -*as*	.	.	.	-*án* (-*an*)
Dat. -*i*	.	.	.	-*abis*

Which explain themselves without difficulty. The length in the accusative plural is remarkable; it is proved by *anmana* (animas), *fileda* (poëtas). As a change into the vowel-declension (like in the Latin -*és*, -*eis*, -*is*) in consequence of the *a*, in opposition to the -*u* or -*i*, which alone occurs in masc. vocalic stems, is not to be thought of, this -*á* must be either an inorganic lengthening, or -*ás* has been produced from -*ans*, which has been already surmised to be the original ending of the accusative plural (Zeitschrift f. v. Sprachforschung I. 291, V. 63); the latter is probably the true explanation. Among the other endings, -*as* is remarkable by the peculiar tincture of the Gaedhelic vocalismus. For while the Greek, Latin, and Gothic agree in the weakening of the *a* in the genitive -ος, -*us*, -*is*, -*is*, in contrast with this in the Gothic even the nom. plur. -*as* remains pure, the Gaedhelic, on the other hand, in direct antithesis to the Gothic, has retained the genitive pure,—hence *menman, noiden, druad, coimded*, instead of *menmanas, noidinas, druadas, coimdidas*, and has weakened the nom. plur. to -*is* (or -*es* like Greek -ες?) consequently forming *anmin, aisndisin, druid, filid*. The accusative singular with its -*in* or (-*en*) may be compared with the Lat. -*em*,—in the Zend, even with *a*-stems, *ĕm*,—hence *menmain* (for which also *menmuin* and *menmin*), *airitin, torbataid* or -*tid, coimdid*. The genitive plural has, of course, first shortened its -*án* to *an*, and then dropped it; the dative singular may, probably, be referred as in the Greek and Gothic to the original locative. By the dropping off of the endings and the influence of the end-vowels, the gen. sing. and plur. on the one side, and the acc. and dat. sing. and nom. plur. on the other, of necessity became alike in sound. The dat. plur. took up a copulative vowel, as in the Latin and Gothic, an *a*, which by the influence of the dropped *i* has become *ai* or *i*; before this -*aib*, -*ib*, syncope frequently occurred as before the -*a* of the accusative plural, *e. g.* in *traigthib* (pedibus), always as it appears in the feminines in -*tiu*, the *i* of which, however, has acted upon the succeeding vowel; hence dat. -*tnib*, acc. -*tnea* or *tne*. Zeuss' supposition of an accusative plural *druida, for which

we might expect *druada*, appears to be erroneous.[46] We meet
with various forms in the nom. sing. of *an*-stems, *e. g.*: masc.
menme (mens), masc. *brithem* (judex) fem. *anim* (anima), fem.
talam (terra); of the feminine *in*-stems passing into *iu*, sometimes
weakened into -*u;* of the masc. *ad*-stems as a rule weakened to
-*u*, and in *tenge* (lingua) to *e;* of -*id* generally -*i*, also, however,
-*iu* in *coimdiu* (Dominus), -*u* in *dinu* (agna), and the adjective
bibdu (guilty), -*e* in *tene* (ignis), gen. *tened*, stem *tenid* (instead
of *tanid* as the Kymric *tan* shows); no ending in *traig* (pes).
The form *druith* (druida),[47] from the stem *druad*, appears to
depend upon the same transition into the *i*- declension as Lat.
canis, juvenis, from the stem *can, juven;* for *druith* points back
to *druadis*. According to the analogy of the Sanskrit, the *an*-
stems should have formed the nom. -*á*, which first was weakened
to *a*, then fell off; *brithem*, *anim*, are, consequently, forms perfectly in accordance with rule. The preservation of the vowel
in *menme*, weakened, however, to *e*, appears to have been caused
by the double consonants (as, perhaps, also in the gen. pl. *athre*,
from *athir*, see further on). The -*iu* of the *in*-stems has arisen
from the primitive -*iá* (by passing through -*ia* or *iû;* the Lat.
-*io*, Umbrian -*iu* speaks in favour of the latter), the *u* having
been retained probably by means of the preceding vowel as in
the dative *céliu*, as opposed to *baull*. The *d*- or *t*-stems probably took originally, as in the Lat. and Greek, an *s*, lengthened
the vowel before it as compensation for the *t*, and retained the
shortened vowel after the dropping off of the *s; e. g.* *domnats*
(*domnâs*) *domnûs*, *domnû*, *domnu* (profunditas). Or -*ad* was
originally long, as shortening often takes place in the Gaedhelic,
for example, in the adjectives in ·*ach*= Kymric AUC, *awc* (i. e.
âc)? In *coimdid*, together with *coimdiu*, shortening of the base
of the stem may be assumed as the Welsh masc. in -*iat* (-*iad*, pl.
-*ieid*), given by Zeuss (p. 806) come very near. *Guiliat* (qui
videt) especially appears nearly to correspond to the Gaedhelic
filid,[48] the nom. *fili* would, consequently, be contracted from *filiu*,
for which the dative *duini* together with *duiniu* affords an analogy.[49] *Traig* shows itself to be a *t*-stem by Welsh *troet*, pl.

---

[46] [xvi. *Druide* is the acc. pl. in the Liber Hymnorum. This may perhaps
have arisen, by progressive umlaut, from *druadi*, if *drui* (like *bráthair*) have
passed over to the *i*-declension. The acc. pl. *bráithre* occurs in the epilogue to
the Félire (609).]

[47] [xvii. Ebel has here been misled by Zeuss: *druith* is the nom. *dual*, not the
nom. *singular*, which must have been *drui* (=*drua(d)-s*).]

[48] [See "Note on *a*-, *i*-, *d*-, *t*- and *nt*- stems", §. 9, p. 83.]

[49] Zeuss, 755, considers the *d* as primitive, and compares the Kymric -*ed*, -*id*, p.
803; but, in my opinion, the masculine in -*id* ought rather to be compared with
the Gaedhelic in ·*id*, -*aid*, gen. -*ada*, and the Kymric -*d* (now -*dd*); although

traet; Cornish *troys,* pl. *troyes, treys;* Armoric *troad,* pl. *treid;* but the nom. sing. *traig* and accus. plur. *traigid* are difficult to explain: the best way is, perhaps, by the assumption of a neuter (Zeuss, 274), by which the want of the ending would be justified; but the *i* in *traigid* is remarkable: we should have expected **traigidá,* **traigeda, traiged.* Other deviations will be treated of hereafter; as regards *cú* (canis), whereof only the comp. *banchu* (bitch), and the derivative *conde* (caninus), occur in Zeuss, we may ascribe to the Old Irish the forms: acc. *cuin,* gen. *con,* dat. *cuin;* plur. nom. *cuin,* ac. *cona,* gen. *con,* dat. *conaib.*[50] The neutral *n*-stems (I.) all derived with the suffix *-man* deviate from the expected form:—

Sing. Nom. and Acc. *-m*	.	. Plur. *-man* (from *-maná, mana*)
Gen. **-man* .	.	*-man*
Dat. **-main* .	.	*-manaib*

Putting aside slight fluctuations between *a* and *e* (*e.g.* nom. plur. *ingramman,* gen. *ingremmen*) in the gen. and dat. sing., the dative exhibits an exceptional *m* instead of *n*: *anmim, anmaim* (nomini), which appears to have arisen from assimilation; the gen. *anma, anmae, anme,* has dropped the *n*. The remaining forms are made in a perfectly normal manner, but the nom. sing. appears to have weakened the *a* of the original end *-ma* to *i*, before it fell off, because of the continual occurrence of umlauts: *ainm* (nomen), *béim* (plaga), *ingreim* (persecutio), *teidm* (pestis), *togairm* (vocatio), *senim* (sonitus).

The nouns of relationship in *-thar* (III.) contain the original *á* of the nom. sing. weakened to *i*, either by the influence of the liquids (Bopp, p. 7), or, as appears to me more probable, because the *á* weakened to *a* should have dropped out in the third period (as in *ballán, ballan, ball);* but this could not take place, in consequence of the unpronounceable double consonant (*thr*) thence resulting, and so at least the lightest vowel was chosen. The same reason caused, no doubt, the retention of the vowel in the gen. and dat. sing., the syncope of which was to be expected according to the analogy of other languages and of the plural cases (although a formation *atharas, athars, athar, athari, athir,* would not be impossible), and in the gen. plur. the retention of the ending-vowel in its weakened form *e*,[51] at least, there is no reason to assume for the Old Irish a transition into the *i*-declension, which

---

ancient, it is not primitive (compare Lat. *lapid,* Greek ἐλπίδ, κορυθ, Zeitschr. f. v. Sp. iv., 325, 332).

[50] [xviii. Rather thus: acc. *coin ṅ,* gen. *con,* dat. *coin;* plur. nom. *coin,* acc. *cona,* gen. *con ṅ,* dat. *conaib.*]

[51] [xix. This gen. plur. in *e* only occurs in *athre, bráithre,* and is certainly due to a passage over to the *i*-declension. *Máthair* forms its gen. plur. regularly— thus: *máthar ṅ.*]

to be sure would easily explain the form *athre*, but which even the Latin *patrum* spurned. In the dative plural, *a*, and not *i*, is also used as a copulative vowel, as *athraib* shows,[52] and if *braithrib* occurs beside it, we must either view it as an invasion of the secondary *i*, or an indication of the early introduction into Irish of orthographical confusion. The nom. plur. is not supported by evidence; we cannot put it down otherwise than as *athir*, as Zeuss does. On the other hand, there is no evidence to entitle us to assume with Zeuss an ending *-u* for the masc., as we have no where detected, except in the nom. *druith*, a transition into the vocalic declension. We accordingly assume the following genetic development:—

		Primitive period	Pre-historic period.	Historic period.
Sing. Nom.	.	athâr	athar	athir
Acc.	. . .	atharin	athirn	athir
Gen.	. . .	athras	athars	athar
Dat.	. . .	athri	athir	athir
Plur. Nom.	. .	atharis	athirs	*athir
Acc.	. . .	athrâs	athrâ	*athra
Gen.	. . .	athrân	athran	athre
Dat.	. . .	athrabis	athraibs	athraib

The addition of a determinative suffix already shows itself in the Old Irish in some *r*-stems (V.); in the Modern Irish its action has been felt over a much wider circuit, and has even penetrated the nouns of relationship.[53] Unfortunately, too few forms of this class have been preserved to us to give a complete idea of the declension, nevertheless we see from the existing ones of *cathir* (oppidum):—

    Sing. . . . cathir, cathraig, cathrach, cathir.
    Plur. . . . cathraig.

—at least so much clearly, that these words, to which *nathir* (natrix) likewise belongs, even when assuming this suffix, followed a consonantal declension. Bopp's conjecture, adopted by Kuhn also, in his review (observation 15), that this *ch* (*g*) represents an original *k*, is now completely justified by the Irish phonetic law, according to which the tenuis between vowels changes into the aspirata (fluctuating into media); but to his comparison of the Gothic *brôthrahans* and the Sanskrit *-aka* may be added

---

[52] [xx. In Gaulish *ĕ* was used as a copulative vowel, as is shown by *mâtrĕbo* (matribus), cited *suprà*. Note 23, p. 56.]

[53] [xxi. This "determinative suffix" is a dream. The Old Irish nouns to which Ebel alludes (though *i*-stems in the nom. sing.), have, like γυνή, passed over to the *c*-declension in the oblique cases. There are, of course, *c*-stems in all cases. Thus *tethra*, gen. *tethrach* (a scald-crow), is the Greek τέτραξ, gen. τέτρακος. The gen., dat., and acc. pl. of *cathair* may be set down with certainty as *cathrach h*, *cathrachaib*, *cathracha*, respectively; *for huasalathrach* (patriarcharum) occurs in St. Patrick's hymn (*Liber Hymnorum*), and *huasalathrachaib* (patriarchis) in Zeuss, p. 827 (the nom. sing. is *huasalathair*, cf. Ang.-Sax. *heahfædher*), and *coercha* (sheep, acc. pl.) for *cáeracha*, in St. Brogan's hymn, v. 33.]

the still more apt one of the Greek -κ in γυνή γυναικός, like the opposite employment of the *c* in Latin, *senex, senectus*, along with *senis* (compare the essay of Curtius on individualizing suffixes in Zeit. f. v. Sp. Bd. iv.) The dative *cathir*, no doubt, likewise rests upon a similar mutilation, as is frequently found among the *n*-stems, and should not have been placed by Zeuss in the paradigm; the normal form would be *cathrich* or *cathraich*, in the plur. acc. *cathracha*, gen. *cathrach*, dat. *cathrachaib* may be expected.

In its most ancient stage the Gaedhelic, consequently, harmonizes with the classic languages by the conservation of the consonant declension of the *t*-, *n*-, and *r*-stems; it even exceeds the Latin in the conservation of the purity of the nom. acc. and gen. plur.; on the other hand it associates itself to the Gothic by the passage of the *s*-stems into the vocalic declension, which takes place as in the Slavonic languages in two ways: by an addition in *áis*, *áisa*, contrasting with the Sanskrit *áyus;* by a loss in *nem* (*nima*) in contrast to the Sanskrit *nabhas*, with a change of gender, as in the Slavonic *tĭma*, against the Sanskrit *tamas*.

§. 5. *Declension of masc. (and neut.)* A- *and* IA-*stems.*

According to what has been said above, the vocalic declension includes masculine and neutral *a*-, *i*-, and *u*-stems, feminine *á*- and *i*- (*î*-) stems; feminine *u*-stems are wanting, as in the Lithuanian.

We have already carried back the inflexions of the masculine *a*-stems to the oldest attainable Celtic forms. Most of them scarcely require an observation. The nom. sing. -*as*, -*a*, -*an*, instead of -*am*, gen. plur. -*ân* instead of -*âm*, agree exactly with the Sanskrit; the dative plural -*abis* presupposes a more ancient phonetic condition than we find preserved either in the Sanskrit instrumental -*âis* or in the dative -*ébhyas*, and which is easiest explained from the instrumental (primitive form -*abhis*), for the dative form -*abhyas* would have led (through -*abias* -*abeas*, or through -*abîs* -*abî*, through -*abês* -*abê*) to -*abe* or -*aibi*.[51] (The -*ai* in -*aib* is not a diphthong, but umlaut, as the secondary form -*ib* shows; it is, consequently, not comparable with the Sanskrit -*é* in -*ébhyas*). The dat. sing. -*ui* (or *û?* undoubtedly formed out of -*ui*) and the acc. plur. -*us* agree with the Lithuanian and Slavonian, being in the former -*ui* and -*us*, and in the latter -*u* and -*y;* the gen. sing. and nom. plur. -*i* agree with the Latin (besides the dat., Latin -*ô* from -*oi* = Oscan -*ui*). In the nominative plural the pronominal ending (Sanskrit-*é* = primitive -*ai*, Lithuanian -*ai*, Gothic -*ai*, Greek *oi*, Latin *î*, older form -*ei*, Slavonian -*i*), has,

---

[51] [xxii. See note 23, p. 56.]

consequently, penetrated into the substantive declension in the Celtic also, as it does every where except in the Sanskrit, Gothic, Umbrian, and Oscan, and *indfîr* (pronounced *indir*) from *innî firî* corresponds exactly with *illi viri;* this *î* has, consequently, been formed out of *-ai* or *-ei*. On the other hand, in the genitive singular, the most difficult form, the *-î* corresponds to the Latin *-î*, which, as is well known, is written not *-ei*, but *-i* in Lucilius, and in the Sen. Cons. de Bacc., an important circumstance for the correct explanation of the Latin form; as for the rest, the explanation is easier in the Irish than in the Latin. Of the primitive ending = Sanskrit *asya*, not only *y*, which has everywhere fallen away, but also a vowel-flanked *s* must have disappeared in the Irish (Zeuss, 60, 63); thus arose *-ií* (as in *íth* = Kymric, *iot*, *ícc* = Kymric *iacc*) which of course coalesced immediately into *î;* it only remains doubtful whether this *-â* also belongs to the Kymric or exclusively to the Gaedhelic.[52] The agreement of both forms with the Latin is, no doubt, the chief reason why the words borrowed from the Latin have mostly preserved, in so strikingly faithful a manner, the declension-type, and that transitions into this declension have only taken place from the third Latin one;—a change which the gen. *-is* induced, as, for example: *socráit*, in consequence of *socratis* (even in the nom. *preceptóir*, plur. *preceptori*, in consequence of *preceptoris*), not the reverse, except where it was necessary to join a word to a known ending, as in *peccad* masc., gen. *pectha pectho* from *peccatum*, in consequence of the many words in *-ad* having similar meaning. The words in *-e*, sometimes written *-a*, and *ya-* (*ia-* and *aia-*) stems form a subdivision of the *a*-stems; in them either *-i* before *-a* was changed into *-e*, or *-ia* was contracted into *-ê*, *-ii* into *-î*,—these long vowels being naturally shortened in the auslaut; all forms admit of being explained in both these ways in the most perfectly satisfactory manner. The *-u* in the dat. sing. remained here in the combination *-iu* in the auslaut, for which, however, *-u* and *-i* also occur; in the dat. plur. a slight shortening took place, as *iíb* did not give *-íb*, but *-ib*.[53]

The neuters exhibit a curious anomaly, inasmuch as the primitive *-â* of the nom. and acc. plur., shortened to *-a* in the second period, should have dropped off in the third; if we connect with *-a* of this case an analogous singular phenomenon, namely, that the *inna, na*, of the article, as in the feminine, does not affect the suc-

---

[52] [xxiii. In the Old Irish, as in the Latin, the gen. sing. of masc. and neut. *a*-stems was originally the locative sing., and has nothing whatever to do with *asya*. Ebel is now inclined to admit this. See, *infra*, On the Position of the Celtic, §. 11, p. 125.

[53] Zeuss erroneously remarks, page 248: quae *-ib* dativi non inficiens ex *-ab* defecisse videtur. The observation would have been in place at p. 253.

ceeding consonants, we shall be able to assume, with great probability, that in the Gaedhelic the disappearance of the neuter, which in the Kymric can be no longer detected, had even then already been prepared in the plural, by the invasion of the feminine form, for the *inna* of the article does not admit of being explained otherwise than from *innás*. The Irish *na cenéla* (nationes) consequently admits of being compared with the Italian *le arme* instead of *illa arma*. Even the accusative plural masculine *inna, na*, appears to rest upon an inorganic invasion of the feminine form, because the substantive forms lead us to expect rather *innu, *nu [conversely *-iu*, (*-u*) = Lat. *eos*, occurs suffixed to the prepositions, even as feminine]; this form has also penetrated in the Modern Irish, from the accusative even into the nominative, so that a difference of genders is nowhere to be found in the plural. The *-ia* stems form the plur. nom. regularly in *-e*, as in the singular.

The adjectives mostly follow the rule of the substantives, only that the *ia*-stems readily shorten the acc. plur. mas. into *-i*, and the nom. plur. neuter often shows *-i* instead of the more normal *-e*. The *-i*, which the *a*-stems often exhibit in the neuter plural, is more remarkable, and is hitherto inexplicable to me.[54] A stem *sáinia*, instead of *sánia*, may probably be assumed for *sáin* (diversus), in consequence of the *ai*. This has maintained itself in the form of the nom. plur.; in the others it has shortened itself like *aile* into *aill*. But how are we to explain *isli, dilsi, comaicsi?* Of the pronominal *a*-stems, a form has, however, been preserved, in spite of the frightful ravages here occasioned by the phonetic laws, which sets aside the only reason which could probably be still put forward (except the accidental similarity with the stem-auslaut *a* in the Sanskrit) in favour of explaining the gen. *-a* of the following class by the Sanskrit *-asya*. Of the stem *a*, there have been preserved: gen. sing. masc. and neut. *á*, with affection of the succeeding consonants, consequently primitively a vowel-ending stem; gen. fem. *á* without affection, consequently for *ás*; gen. pl. *an, a*, consequently produced from *án* instead of *ám*. Bopp therefore believed himself able to explain the masc. *á* by *asya*, and the fem. *á* (instead of *ás*) by *asyâs*. But now *ái* appears as the most ancient form of the gen. sing. masc. and neut. (in Zeuss, 334, 345), besides *ae, e* (evidently *é*) also (Zeuss 347); consequently *asya* modified itself in the first instance into *ái*, and from thence issued the Gaedhelic forms *á* and *é* like the

---

[54] [xxiv. Adjectival *a*-stems *never* exhibit *i* in the nom. pl. But (as was to be expected) this is done by adjectival *i*-stems, such as *sáin, isil, dilis, comacuis*, whence *sáini, isli, dilsi, comaicsi*. The adjectival *i*-declension exists at the present day. See the paradigm (*geanamhail*), O'Donovan's Grammar, p. 112.]

Kymric *y, e*. Thus even this form, which in consequence of its shortness must have sounded fuller, differs very little from the usual genitive of the *a*-stems. The neuter of the article *an*, which has weakened itself even to *a*, rests no doubt on a primitive form *anat*,[55] which from the outset must have become *ana, an*, because *anan* (instead of *anam*) must have always retained an *n*; the fundamental *-at* also explains the more violent shortening in the neut. *aill*, as compared with the masc. and fem. *aile*.[56]

§. 6. *Declension of masc. ɪ- and v-stems.*

The explanation of the case-endings is much more difficult in the following classes, where the separation of the masculine *u*- and *i*-, and the feminine *â*- and *i*-, stems, is already difficult.

The *i*- and *u*-stems sound in the nom. and acc. sing. perfectly alike, for *-is, -in, -i* must drop off like *-us, -un, -u*; even the vowel of the stem does not always give us information, although *dénmid* (factor), for example, proves itself by the genitive *denmada* to have been altered from *dénmad, muir* (mare) announces itself by its *ui* as an *i*-stem; we must, therefore, endeavour to ascertain the stem from other sources, as, for instance, in *bith* (mundus), from the Gaulish *bitu;* in *fid* (arbor), from the Gaulish *vidu* and the Saxon *widu;* in the verbals in *-ad*, from the analogy of the Latin in *-tus*, etc. The only case which shows the stem clearly, the accusative plural,[57] the *-ûs* and *-îs* of which have changed into *-u* and *-i*, is unfortunately only very weakly represented, so that, in many cases, no certainty can be attained. In the dative singular *-ui* and *-î* are certainly to be assumed; these should become *-u* and *-i*, and leave behind umlaut, but most words take no umlaut (no doubt, in consequence of the primitive length of the stem-vowel). Among the whole of the examples in Zeuss, *biuth* alone shows umlaut, which he accordingly has placed in the paradigm. It would appear as if the endings *-a, -o, -e* established a difference in the genitive singular; but this is by no means the case, as *aithrebthado*, from the nom. *aithribthid* (possessor), for example, shows a decided *i*-stem; we must look upon *-o* rather as an obscuring of the *-a, e*, exactly as *-ea* and *-eo* are the result of the subsequent action of a preceding sound, or of one which had preceded. The explanation apparently

---

[55] [xxv. More probably the neut. article *an* (*a* before a noun beginning with a tenuis) stands for *sa-n*—the *n* being the neut. ending, and the *sa* the well-known pronominal stem. The *s* appears in composition with non-aspirating prepositions.]

[56] [For confirmation of this hypothesis see, *infra*, "On the so-called prosthetic *n*", §. 12, p. 90.]

[57] [xxvi. The nom. and acc. plur. (-*i*) and dat. plur. (-*ib*) of *i*-stems show the stem clearly enough. But Ebel here, as elsewhere, suffers from the incompleteness of Zeuss's collection of examples.]

nearest at hand, that *-o* is derived from *-aus* (= Sanskrit *-ôs*), is, consequently, to be rejected, and we are to assume either that *-aus*, as well as *-ais*, has become *-a*, or, to start from the fundamental form, *-avas* and *-ajas*, which must likewise become *-âs*, *-a;* as the dative cannot be explained from- *avi*, *-aji*, the first hypothesis is, probably, to be preferred.[58] According to the analogy of the consonantal declension (compare also Gothic *-yus* and *-eis*), a fundamental form *-avis* and *-ajis* is to be laid down for the nom. plur.; *-ais* must arise from *-avis*, and this, on the dropping of the *s*, could be contracted to *-â*, *-ê*, or *-î; -ajis*, in consequence of the preponderance of the *i*-sound, passed, as it appears, exclusively into *-î*, certainly at least in the masculine in *-ati* (nom. *-id*, gen. *-ada*); the auslauts were, as everywhere, subsequently shortened, so that, along with *-ai*, *-ae*, *-a*, *-e*, and *-i*, also occur, e.g.: *gnímai, gnímae, gnína, gníme, gními*, from the stem *gnímu* (action). The form *mogi*, from the stem *mugu*, along with *mogae*, is interesting, as their common origin from *mogui* is betrayed by their *o*. The ending *-e* of the gen. plur. is remarkable; it appears to announce itself in *moge* as a degeneration of *moga;* on the other hand, it has produced umlaut in *forcitlaide* (præceptorum); either there existed formerly a difference here, as in the nominative plural, so that *-avan* contracted itself into *-ân*, *-ajan* into *-iun*, *-ên*, or, the umlaut in *forcitlaide* is inorganic, and *-e* is in both cases degeneration of *-a*, from *-ân* = *-avân* and *ajân*, which forms we take as a starting point according to the analogy of the Gothic *-ivê* and *-ê* instead of *-iyê*. The dative plural shows a remarkable anomaly, the normal *-ib* of the *i*-stem indeed appears in it, but not the *-ub* or *-uib* to be expected in the *u*-stem, but, instead of it, *-aib* (compare *aitrebthidib, mogaib*); either interchange has here taken place between *ui* and *ai*, a circumstance otherwise without example (*ui* for *ai* is frequent), or the generality of the ending *-aib* introduced it inorganically here also, in the same manner as in the Greek πόλεσι, πήχεσι the ε appears to have penetrated by means of the false analogy of the other cases. The neuter plur. in the nom. and acc. *rind* (constellations) *mind* (insignia), *fess* (scita), appears, at first sight, to be altogether anomalous without an ending, which is the more striking as even the *a*-stems show an ending where one ought not to expect it; if,

---

[58] [xxvii. Surely it is easier to assume that the *i*-stems (with one or two exceptions, such as *tír, tire*) passed over in the gen. sing. to the *u*-declension. Hence the *-o* (*-a*) = *-ôs, -aus*. The fem. *á*-stems likewise, in the gen. sing.— with five exceptions (*inna, óena, mnda, cacha, nacha*)—have passed over to the *i*-declension, and consequently exhibit the ending *e* = *ês*, of which the *e* was probably produced, by a very ancient contraction, from *a-i* (cf. Goth. *anstais*). Here, of course, as also in the Sanskrit and Lithuanian *ávés, awés*, "ewe's", the stem-vowel has been gunated.]

however, we start from a fundamental form -*vá*, -*ja*, in which the *v* and *j* were dropped, a development -*á*, -*a*, may also be conceived (perhaps we should even take *á*=*ava*, *aja* for a starting point, with inorganic gunation, in which case *rind* would bear the same relation to *gnima*, as ταχέα does to ταχέες). In spite of much obscurity in details, it is at least clear from the preceding, that the *i*- and *u*-stems by no means so fully coincided from their origin, as would appear from the representation of Zeuss. For the sake of greater clearness, we shall here also attempt to give an idea of the declension arranged according to the different periods, without the secondary forms however:—

U-STEMS.

			Primitive period.	Pre-historic period.	Historic period.
Masc. Sing.	Nom.	.	bithus	biths	bith
	Acc.	.	bithun	bithu	bith
	Gen.	.	(bithavas) bithâs?	bethâ	betha
	Dat.	.	bithui	bithu	biuth
Plur.	Nom.	.	(bithavis) bithais	bethai	betha
	Acc.	.	(bithuns) bithûs	bithû	bithu
	Gen.	.	(bithavân) bithavan	bethân	* betha
	Dat.	.	bithubis	bithuibs	* bithuib
Neut. Sing.		. . .	fidu	fid	fid
Plur.		. . .	(fidvâ) fidâ	feda	fed

I-STEMS.

Masc. Sing.	Nom.	.	dénmadis	dénmids	dénmid
	Acc.	.	dénmadin	dénmidn	denmid
	Gen.	.	(dénmadajas) dénmadâs?	dénmadâ	dénmada
	Dat.	.	dénmadâ	dénmadi	dénmid
Plur.	Nom.	.	(dénmadajis) dénmadîs?	dénmidî?	denm
	Acc.	.	(denmadins) dénmadîs	dénmidî	dénmidi
	Gen.	.	(dénmadajân) dénmadajan	dénmadân	* denmada
	Dat.	.	dénmadibis	dénmidibs	dénmidib
Neut. Sing.		. . .	fissi	fiss	fiss
Pl.		. . . .	(fissjâ) fissâ	fessa	fess

According to this view, it is only the dative plural of the *u*-stem *mogaib* that appears to be distinctly inorganic; the gen. plur. *moge* shows a weakening of the *a* into *e*, which we shall presently find again in the feminine.

§. 7. *Declension of fem. a- and i-stems.*

The feminine *á* and *i*-stems have suffered still greater confusion in their declension, so that the primitive stem can now only be recognized from the vocalization of the nom. sing. and by comparison with other languages.[59] Thus the following show them-

---

[59] [xxviii. It is true that in the Old Irish the fem. *á*-stems have in the gen. (but see note 58), dat. and acc. *sing*. gone over to the *i*-declension; and in the dat. this was the case in Gaulish, as we learn from *Belesami* (nom. *Belesama*) in the inscription of Vaison. But in the Old Irish the fem. *i*-stems are (with very few exceptions*) still clearly distinguishable from the fem. â-stems.

* *Gabáil* and its compounds are declined in the plur. like *á*-stems. so *idbairt*, *epert*.

selves by *e* and *o* to be *á*-stems: *ess, iress* (fides), *nem* (cœlum), *tol*[60] (voluntas), *breth* (judicium), *croch* (crux), *ingen* (filia), *aimser* (tempus), and the words in *-em*, such as *moídem* (laus), *cretem* (fides); by *ia* instead of *é—grian* (sol), *briathar* (verbum), *bliadan* (annus); by comparison — *rún* (mysterium) = Gothic *runa, ferc* (ira) = ὀργή, the words in *-acht* and *-echt*, which presuppose a Sanskrit *-akatá* and *-ikatá*, and which are not consequently derived directly from the stem-substantive, but through a hypothetical adjective in *-ach* or *-ech* (= Sanskrit *-aka*, *-ika*), as for example, *déacht* (divinitas), which is not obtained directly from *dia*, but through *déach* (divinus). We must consider as *i*-stems especially the verbal-nouns in *-t*, such as *epert* (locutio), *tabart, tabairt* (datio), and also *iarfigid* (inquisitio, quæstio); the secondary forms, as *muing*, f. = *mung*, m. (a mane), quoted by Pictet, (*Op. cit.* p. 123), appear to be *i*-stems (whose nominative *-î, -i, 2*, cannot be distinguished in its actual state from *-is, 2s, 2*). No certain distinctions can be at all recognized in the case-endings, and nothing can be based upon the secondary forms. The genitive singular shows, for instance, along with the dominant *-e*, also *-a* and *-o;* but if we would assign the *-a* to the *á*-stems, and the *-e* to the *i*-stems, we find our proposition contradicted by the circumstance that *-e* is the commonest ending, and appears just in those words the vowels of which point to *-â*, as in *nime, irisse, ingine,* and that *-a* occurs frequently in characteristic *i*-stems, as in *eperta;* if, on the other hand, we would assign *-a* to the *i*-stems, from the analogy of the masculine, and *-e* to the *a*-stems from the analogy of the Latin *-æ*, the feminine of the adjectives like *cacha, nacha,* (and even *óena,* along with *aine*), will remain unconsidered; consequently *-a* is clearly the oldest form in both classes, it weakened itself into *-o* and *-e*, even in the same words; *e. g., dúile* and *dúlo*, from *dúl* (mundus, res, creatura), and the umlaut before *e*, in spite of its universality, is inorganic; the fundamental forms *-ás* and *-ajas* had also to follow the same course: *-ás, -á, -a,* or if we prefer starting from *-ais* in-

---

In addition to the circumstance that the *á*-stems in general have their gen. sing. in *-e*, whereas the *i*-stems make it in *-o* (*a*), the nom. and acc. pl. of fem. *i*-stems end in *-i*, but those of the *á*-stems in *-a*. Next, the gen pl. of fem. *i*-stems ends in *ae, -e;* that of fem. *á*-stems has no ending. Thus *nime, dule, caille, rígne, infinite, bliadne, fochraice, fochide,* are the Old Irish genitives plur. respectively of *nem, nim* (heaven), *dúil* (a thing), *caill* (a wood), *rígain* (a queen), *infinit* (an infinitive), *bliadain* (a year), (not *bliadan* as Ebel wrongly gives it); *fochricc* (a reward), *fochaid* (tribulation). Thirdly, the dat. pl. of fem. *i*-stems ends in *-ib*, that of *á*-stems in *-aib* (*áirmib*, Zeuss, p. 670, probably comes from *áirim:* cf. Welsh *rhif*).]

60 In the Lord's Prayer, as given by O'Donovan, there is, however, *bid do toil* (thy will be done), which indicates an *i*-stem.*

* [xxix. *Toil* here is the accusative sing., according to the regular Old Irish syntax (Zeuss, p. 894): the nom. sing. is *tol*, which was anciently a fem. *á*-stem.]

stead of *-ajas*, we have *-ais, -ai, -a*. The *i*-stems could form the dat. sing. in *-î, -i* (or *-aji, î, -i*, which is less probable), the *a*-stems either in (*-ái*), *-é, e*, or (*-ai*), *-î, i-*, as in the nominative plural of the masculine; both of them consequently agree, as may be expected, in the umlaut. An *-îs, -î, -i* might have been expected in the nominative plural, as in the masculine, from the fundamental form *-ajis;* but an *ais, -ai, -a*, was equally possible; and if the examples give *-a, -e*, and *-i*, an *-ai, -î, -i* is not impossible, even in the case of *a*-stems (compare Greek *-αι*, Latin *-ae*): consequently a separation of both classes, according to the ending, is neither *a priori* necessary, nor in the actual state possible (see the examples in Zeuss, 262, 263); although, no doubt, the assumption of a primitive difference between *-a* (from *-âs*) and *-i* (from *-ajis*) would have much in its favour. What is most striking is, that no ending whatever is found, not only in *persin* from *persan* (persona), which is treated in Modern Irish altogether as an *n*-stem (nom. *pearsa*), but also in *aimsir;* and only in the vowel is there an indication of *-i*. Zeuss considers the *e* and *i* as secondary forms, which have resulted from assimilation: *litre, epistli*, appear to speak in favour of this view, but not *bliadni;* for an *a* has been here dropped. The following hypothesis appears to me to offer most advantages: the feminines in *-i* formed like the masculines the nominative plural in *-i* (see above), those in *-â*, contracted *-ái* (as in the Greek and Latin), into *é* or *í*, which, in consequence of its genesis from *-ái*, yielded somewhat more resistance to retrenchment than the *-i* of the masculine resulting from *-ai*, and which therefore maintained itself, in part, in the weakening *-e, -i*, and in part actually dropped off; but the form *-a* rests (as in Slav. *-y, -e*), on an interchange with the accusative, which already in some instances took place in the old language, but which has deformed the whole declension in the modern. This hypothesis is supported by the nominative plural of the *iá*-stems, which never contain *-e*, but everywhere *-i;* a circumstance which points to an earlier *-î* generated from *-ie* or *-ii*. The class-distinctions are completely obliterated in the gen. plur. (without ending), dat. (*-aib* and *-ib* without distinction), and acc. plur.,[61] which often terminates in *-a* even in undoubted *i*-stems, e. g., *idbarta* (oblationes), seldom in *-i*, as *dúli* (res), *epistli* (epistolas).

If almost everywhere here, an invasion occurred of the most numerous *â*-stems, the reverse appears to have taken place in the accusative sing., which exhibits, almost without exception, umlaut or a primitive *i;* only *delb* (imaginem) and *nem* (cælum) point to an ending *-an* (*ân*). Even if we were to assume that *-an*

---

[61] [See Note 59, p. 76.]

was changed, as in the Zend, into *-en* (in the consonantal declension we were led to an accusative *-in* or *-en*), the cause why this degeneration did befall the primitive *-án* of the feminine rather than the *-an* of the masculine, would still remain unexplained. The *iá*-stems partake of the above mentioned deformities in the accusative singular, which terminates in *-i* instead of *-e*, and in the accusative plural, which likewise ends in *-i*, on the other hand the gen. sing. *-e* leads us back to the primitive *-a* of this case; the nominative plural *-i* appears to be formed according to rule, except that all the end syllables are shortened. Accordingly, instead of the forms to be expected,—which are somewhat as follows:

Sing. Nom.	-á	-a	—	-is	ꝛ s	ꝛ
Acc.	-án	-an	—	-in	ꝛ n	ꝛ
Gen.	-ás	-á	-a	-ás	-á	-a
Dat.	-i	-i	ꝛ	-i	-i	ꝛ
Plur. Nom.	-i	-i	ꝛ (?)	-is	-i	-i
Acc.	-ás	-á	-a	-is	-i	-i
Gen.	-án	-an	—	-aján	-án	-a
Dat.	-ábis	-aibs	-aib	-ibis	-ibs	-ib

—we find the following actually occurring:

Singular . . —, ꝛ	Plural . -a (-i, ꝛ)
ꝛ (—)	-a (-i)
ꝛ e (-a, o)	—
ꝛ	-aib (-ib)

in which ꝛ represents the after-action of the retrenched *i*. The same degeneration of the original forms occurs, as may be expected, in the Modern Irish, where *an cholam* (columba) fluctuates in the gen. sing. and nom. plur. between *na colaime* and *colama*, and even in the dat. sing. between *do'n cholam* and *cholaime;* it is still further increased by the circumstance that the genitive has also frequently thrown off the inflexion vowel, e. g. *na hoigh* from *an oigh* (virgo). In general, however, the *á*-stems appear to have assumed the ending *-e;* the *i*-stems on the other hand *-a*, e. g.: *slat* (rod), gen. sing. and nom. plur. *slaite; sgiath* (wings), gen. *sgeithe; neamh* (heaven), gen. *neimhe;* but *feoil* (flesh), has however, gen. sing. and nom. plur. *feola;* and *oigh*, although in the gen. sing., it has *hoigh*, in the plural it is *na hogha*. The fluctuation has even passed over to the masculine, for *iasg* (fish) forms gen. *éisc*, plur. *éisc* or *iasca;* and *sruth* (scholar), in both cases *sruith* or *srotha*. Already in the Old Irish, the vocative has been replaced throughout in the plural by the accusative; in the singular there are only some forms of the *a*- and *á*-stems preserved, *e.g. fir* from *fire*, as in other languages; *duini* from *duinie;* and among consonantal stems the single one *ath(a)ir* in the Lord's prayer. We have already found in the Old Irish beginnings of a permutation of the accusative and nominative. The consonantal *n*- and *t*-stems suffer likewise a peculiar mutilation in the Old Irish. The secondary forms of *anim* (anima); gen. *anme*, dat. and acc. *anim*, admit of being explained from a vocalic base: not so the anomaly, which not unfrequently occurs, that the nominative directly supplants the dative and accusative. Examples: *do foditiu* (ad tolerationem), *do aurlatu* (ad obedientiam), acc. *aurlatu* (obedientia); compare also Pictet's observations (Beiträge zur vergleichenden Sprachforschung, I. 82 *sq.*), where the reverse is likewise proved. The circumstance that, in the Modern Irish, there is mostly (except in the anlaut) no difference to be found between the nominative and dative singular, agrees with the foregoing; it consequently appears that the accusative first was identified with the nominative, and then the dative. The language is, therefore, in a fair way to lose all its inflexions like the Kymric dialects, and first of all the genitive plural, which now is already mostly like the nom. sing.;—properly speaking, only the gen. sing. and plur. and dat. plur. are yet retained: nay, even the latter has been already deprived of its ending in the article, in the same way as the adjectives have lost all their inflexions. The decision as to the origin of the modern forms of the consonantal stems is rendered more difficult by this phenomenon. Only few still correspond to the old form, thus *breitheamh* (judex), gen. *breitheamhan*, nom. plur. *breitheamhuin*, with BRITHEM, gen. BRITHEMAN, nom. plur. BRITHEMAIN. *Daileamh* (butler), for example, deviates already in the gen. *daileamhuin*, from *dálem* (caupo), gen. *dáleman*. The majority have affixed -*e* or -*a* either in the nom. plur. or in both cases, and it is difficult to decide whether we are to look upon this as a simple transition into the vocalic declension (as in New High German *brunnen*, instead of *brunn*), or whether the nom. in -*a* is not really an accusative; perhaps the accusative form first passed into the nominative, and then the genitive singular followed the analogy of the nominative plural now appearing vocalic. A striking example of this mixture of forms is afforded by *cu* (canis); gen. *con* (perfectly normal), or *cuin* (*a*- stem); dat. *coin* (normal); nom. plur. *cona* (accusative form), or *con* (spurious formation), or *coin* (normal); gen. *cu* (mutilated), or *con* (normal); dat. *conaibh*. The nominative plural *athara* from *athair* (father), has assumed the accusative form, and thereby got the external appearance of a vocalic stem, an example in which it was followed by the gen. sing. *athara* (in use besides the primitive *athar*); side by side with them forms with -*ach* have been introduced; e. g.: *aithreach* (as in Old Irish CATHIR).[62] The applica-

---

[62] [XXX. *Aithreach* is simply due to a passage over to the *c*-declension. So

tion of the suffix -*adh* (compare *dénmid*, *dénmada*, or *tenga*, *tengad*), as an inflexion-copulative, is new; e. g., in the plural *bogadha* (for *bogha*, bows), considered also by Pictet (*Op. cit.* 128) to be a new formation; but, perhaps, it may help us to an explanation of the Kymric plural forms.

§. 8. *The distinction of the plural in Kymric.*

The Kymric, on which we must in conclusion cast a glance, has preserved nothing more of its whole inflexions, even in the oldest documents, than the distinction of the plural, but this it employs very arbitrarily: compare *trimeib* (tres filii) with *meibion*, *meibon*, and *tyreu* (turres) with *tyroed*. Obviously, as in the New High German, this is of three kinds: either the old plural form remains, consequently true inflexions, as *brüder*, *gäste*, *fische*, from the Gothic *bróthrjus*, *gasteis*, *fiskós;* or the ending of the stem, dropped in the singular, behind which the grammatical ending has disappeared, as in *mannen*, where the -*an* of the Gothic *manna* (stem *mannan*), which has vanished in the singular, has been preserved, while the proper ending, the *s* of *mannans*, has been dropped; or a suffix (determinative), wholly foreign to the stem, like the German -*er* in *eier*, to which true inflexion-endings were, at an earlier period (Anglo-Saxon *ägru*), attached, but which, after their loss (as in the Old High German nom. *eigir*), exactly occupies the place of the ending, like German *länder* instead of *lande*, except in the dative plural.

To the first kind belong: 1, the Kymric plurals without endings, and with umlaut, such as Welsh *llygeit* = Cornish *legeit* (oculi); Welsh *seint* = Armoric *sent* (sancti); Welsh *chwaer* (sorores), from *chwior;* *traet* = Cornish *treys*, Armoric *treid* (pedes), from *troet*, Cornish *troys*, Armoric *troad*,—or without umlaut, as *tridyn* (tres homines), *teir morwyn* (tres puellæ). · All these forms have lost an -*i*, probably a primitive -*î* or -*is* (-*is?*), and consequently may be compared to the Gaedhelic forms such as *maicc* (filii), to which the Welsh *meib*, or *traigid*, the Kymric *traet*, *treys*, *treid* correspond; for instance, the masculine verbals in -*iat*, -*iad*, pl. -*ieid*, such as *guiliat*, are parallel to the Gaedhelic in -*i*, pl. -*id (filid)* (see above). 2. The plurals in *i*, such as *meini* (lapides), from *maen*, Corn. *esely* (membra) = Armoric *ysily*, from *esel*, appear to correspond to the Gaedhelic -*i* (in *ia*- and feminine stems); but interchanges occur, however, such as Cornish *meyn*, Armoric *mein*, alongside of Welsh *meini*, and this even in the same dialect, e. g.: Cornish *tell*, and also *tylly* (foramina), from *tol*, which do not allow a strict

in Early Middle Irish we have *mainistir* (from *monasterium*), making its gen. sing. *manestrech*. Zeuss, xxviii. so *altóir*, from *altare*, gen. *altórach*.]

separation to be effected. As further instances may also be adduced *llestri*, Cornish, and Armoric, *listri*, which represent Gaedhelic *lestir, while on the other hand *dyn* is the Gaedhelic *dóini*. 3. Finally, the plurals in *-au* and *-iau* with their different formations (Zeuss, 290, 122), also belong originally to this category; *e. g. tyreu* (turres), Cornish *dethyow* = Armoric *diziou* (dies); *-au* appears to have belonged originally to the *u*-stems, the verbals in *-at (-iat)*, *-ad*, pl. *-adau* also correspond to the Gaedhelic abstracts (infinitive) in *-ad*, *-ud*, which take *-a* in plural, so that *-au* may be very well explained from the Sanskrit *-avas*. Pictet's (*Op. cit.*, p. 135) comparison with the Sanskrit *-as*, which changes into *-ó* before sonants, although adopted by Bopp and Kuhn also, is certainly erroneous. But afterwards confusion came in here likewise, so that we see *-au* exactly like the Slavonian *-ov* and the Greek *-ευ* and other determinatives applied to other stems also, and hence even arose *-iau*. Besides, all three suffixes occur in both genders, so that perhaps the *-i* of the feminine may confirm the above assumed Gaedhelic fundamental form of the nominative plural.

The second kind embraces especially *n*-stems, such as the apparently anomalous *ki* (canis), the plural of which is in Welsh, CUN, *cwn*, Cornish KEN, and which corresponds exactly with the Gaedhelic *cú*, plur. *cuin* (the Gaedhelic *ú* is the Kymric *i*); and *ych* = ox, plur. *ychain* (ancient, *ychen*) = oxen;—further, Welsh *brawt*, which has lost its final *r*, plur. *brodyr*, (Cornish *braud* and *broder*, while in the Armoric sing. *breur*, *breer*, the *d* has yielded, plur. *breuder*).

Kuhn (p. 595) wished also to include under the third category the *-an* of gen. *cluasan* (the ears), but in this word it belongs undoubtedly to the third, as *cluas* is evidently the old stem, which, in the beginning, was treated in the declension like *áis*.

To the third kind belong the following: 1. Many plurals in *-au*, *-iau*, in which the ending is foreign to the word-stem proper, such as *penneu* (capita), stem *pinna* (or *pinda*) = Gaedhelic *cinna*, from which nom. *cenn*, dat. *ciunn*, or *breicheu* (brachia), stem *breich*, instead of *brechi*; 2, most words in *-ion* (or *-on*), *e.g.—deneon*, *dynyon* (homines), from the stem *dini* (instead of *dinia*, as the Gaedhelic *dúine* shows), or *meibion* (filii), along with which appear likewise after numerals the forms *meib*, *dyn*, and all Welsh plural adjectives, *e.g. meirwon*, along with *meirw*, from *marw* (mortuus) = Gaedhelic *marb*, plural *mairb* (*moírb*). The *-n* consequently takes exactly the same place here as in the German adjectives and many feminines. 3. The endings *-et*, *-ot*, *-ieit*, *-eit*, and *-ed*, *yd*, *oed*, which otherwise occur as derivatives, and in this respect have been already compared above with the Gaedhelic *-ad*, *-id*, likewise join many stems as determinatives, in which respect they are parallel with the -*ad*, in Irish *bogadha*, already compared, if I am not mistaken, by Kuhn. (Both forms are related to one another, as χαριτ is to ἐλπιδ in the Greek.) Compare the following words in -*t*: *merchet* (filiæ), from *merch* (is this identical with Lithuanian, *merga?* cf. p.), Cornish *denys* (homines), Armoric *bretonet* (Britanni) with those in -*ed*: Welsh, *bydoed* (mundi) from *byt* = Irish *bith*, Cornish *eleth* = Armoric *aelez* (angeli). On the other hand, the favourite suffix of the Gaedhelic -*adh* is not employed as a determinative in Kymric.

In the representation of my results, I have altogether followed the same analytical way which I had gone in the investigation itself, in order to render the verification easier to the reader. Some points will require completion and correction. On the whole, I hope that the results obtained will be found correct.

§. 9. *Note on A-, I-, D-, T-, and NT- Stems.*

According to a communication of Mr. Stokes, that has reached me through Professor Kuhn,[63] the *a*-stems show in the Old Ogam inscriptions not only the gen. in *i*—MAQVI[64] (a form which explains by its *qv* not only the Kymric *map*, but also the Gaedhelic *macc* without aspiration),—but also the nominative in -*as* (CORPIMAQVAS—Cormac). This highly interesting form may accordingly be placed by the side of μάρκαν, Pausanias, x. 19, 11, in which we are now justified in recognizing the true Gaulish accusative of *marcas** (= gen. *marc*, w. 3, *march*, plur. *meirch*). The Ogam secondary forms in -*os*, show us at what a remote period the obscuration of the *a* to *o* was already common. I would not, with Stokes,[65] deduce the length of the dat. plur. from the single form *scéláib*, as even feminine *á*-stems fluctuate between -*ab*, -*ib*, *aib*, which indicates a short vowel; and the *iá*-stems invariably show -*ib*, instead of the -*íb* to be expected.

That the neutral *aill* rests on a vocalic fundamental form, the *t* or *d* being dropped (like Greek ἄλλο), as was already suspected (p. 90), is confirmed by the mortification of the *s* in *alaill sain*, Z. 364.

According to an observation kindly communicated to me, Mr. Stokes now recognizes in Zeuss' Ordo Posterior Ser. 4., three kinds of stems, in -*d*, -*t*, and -*nt*. The latter, to which *dínu*, *fiadu*, *cara*, *náma* (*námae*), belong, correspond accurately with the participles in -*ant*,[66] as, for instance, *cara* (from *cairim*, amo), *fiadu* (= *vêdant*,—Stokes); *dínu* appears to be connected with the

---

[63] [Published in the Beiträge z. v. Sp. i. 448.]
[64] [Given in Mr. Stokes' paper, "Bemerkungen über die irischen declinationen"—Beitr. z. v. Sp. i. 333.]
[65] [Idem, 336.]   [66] Also, Stokes' view, Beitr. i. 457.

Sanskrit root *dhê* ("suckling"); *cara* and *náma* likewise occur in the nom. in Zeuss, who has mistaken the true relation, and led me astray: *imcara fá aescare* (sive amicus, sive inimicus), 674, 831, and *bannamae* (inimica), together with the acc. *bannamít* (hostem), 820, the acc. *carit*, 1055, 1062, *escarit*, 1056. These stems appear to be of the common gender like the Latin participles. On the other hand, the *-it* in *nebcongabthetit* stands no doubt erroneously for *-ith* (as generally in all abstracts). That *traig* is a neuter appears to be confirmed by *traig cethargarait*, 1018 (Gl. proceleusmaticum, consequently an acc.); it looks like a participle (=τρέχον), but inflects the dat. plur. *traigthib*, acc. plur. *traigid; traigthech* (pedes, pedester), and *traichtechdae*, instead of *triagthechdae* (pedester), are derivations; the neuters have, therefore, perhaps thrown out the *n*, and taken a weak form (*traigthib* = *tragitábis*). The Kymric *troet*, plur. *traet*, appears to rest on stem-extension,—compare Welsh, 2. *cilid*, 3. *cilyd*, with Gaedhelic *céle;* at least, a Kymric *car, tan,* stands parallel with the Gaedhelic *cara, tene,* so that we have to recognize in the Kymric forms rather the nominative, than, as in the Romance languages, the accusative (see further on). The comparison made in the article on declension (page 68) between the Kymric *guiliat* and the Gaedhelic *filed* falls to the ground with the explanation of Zeuss; see the corrections to pages 149 and 806, at the end of the *Grammatica Celtica*.

I cannot as yet make up my mind to give up my former view respecting the feminines in the Ordo Prior, Ser. 5 of Zeuss, namely, that an almost complete fusion of the *i-* and *á-*stems took place, and that only few relics of a stricter separation of the forms have been preserved. Along with the acc. plur. in *-i*, to which *súli* Z. 339, likewise belongs, there occur, however, forms with *-a* from undoubted *i*-stems, as *gabála;* along with the dative in *-aib*, forms occur in *ib* from *á-*stems, as *airmib* from *áram*, *slébib* from *sliab;* so that *nimib* also does not prove a stem *nami* (the nom. *nim* along with *nem*, acc. *nem*, the adjective *nemde* = *nimatya* seems to point to *nimâ*, as also the Kymric *nef*, which perfectly corresponds to the feminine of the adjective in the Welsh, while *i, u*, disappear without umlaut in the Kymric; further, that *nem-* never occurs before the endings with *e, i*, but always *nim-;* the gen. plur. *nime* is however remarkable). But I cannot adopt Mr. Stokes' view about the gen. sing. in *-e, -a;* for, in the first place we should not start from Sanskrit *-ês*, but from the fundamental form *-ais* (or *ayas?*), out of which *-a* (*o*), and *-e* could be developed in the masculine stems; but *-yâs* is a special Sanskrit form, which does not again occur in any European language (for that πόλεως is not to be explained from it, but from *πόλεγος, is proved by the Homeric πόληος, the unjustly attacked masc. μάντηος, and the neuter ἄστεως, which, although questioned, is a well-attested form with the Tragic Poets); secondly, because umlaut is as little known before *a* (*o*) among *i*-stems as *a*-stems: compare *flatha*, *flatho*, or even *focheda*, *fochodo*; *a* occurs even before -*e* in *ergabale*; we could not consequently lay down as a basis any such form as -*yas*, and must, as I believe, assume that the umlaut in both classes has only been introduced inorganically with the change of the *a* into *e*.[67] The analogy of the gen. plur., especially the invaluable *nandula*,[68] appears even to speak in favour of our starting, both here and in the masculine of Ser. III., from -*ajas* (not from -*ais*).

As regards the *i*-stems, it appears to me more and more probable, that they have almost throughout passed, as in the Greek, into the *ia*-class (πότνια = *patnî*, etc.)

I have found the umlaut in the dative of the *u*-stems, in *immognǫm*, Z. 984.

§. 10. On the Celtic Dual.

Agreeably to the wish of Mr. Stokes, I here give my views about the Celtic Dual. It appears to me that the answering of two preliminary questions is in the first place needful: 1. has the Celtic a dual to show? 2. how much of it is preserved?

As regards the first question, there can be no doubt that the declension of the numeral *two* presents us with true dual-forms; for the nom. and acc. masc. *da* (as it stands written in all examples, more correctly however *dá*, compare *dáu*, Zeuss 369, and Welsh 1. 2. *dou*, 3. *deu*, now *dau*) exactly represents the Sanskrit *dváu*, Latin *duo*, Greek δύο for the older δύω (δϝώ in δώδεκα), and the primitive vocalic ending is proved by *eter da son*. Z. 197. The nom. and acc. fem *di* = Welsh 2. *dui*, 3. *dwy*, also agrees exactly with the Sanskrit *dvé*, Slavonic *dŭvě*, Lithuanian *dvi*; the dative *deib ndillib* evidently points back, according to the correct observations of Stokes, to a *dvábhim* weakened from *dvábhyám* (or rather *dvabhim*, cf. δυοῖν instead of δυόφιν). We have consequently also to refer the genitive *dá* to *dvaaus* = Skr. *dvayôs*, at all events the aspiration in *dá charpat* is erroneous;[69] the *n* in the nom. and acc. neut. is however difficult to explain. But that dual-forms are likewise preserved in the declension of substantives, is proved by the peculiarity of the Kymric

---

[67] [See notes 58, 59, pp. 75, 76.]

[68] [XXXIV. *Dúla* is, unfortunately, only found in a Middle Irish MS.: in Old Irish MSS. it is always either *dúle* or *dúile*.]

[69] [It is possible that the aspiration after the genitive dual is correct, as this case ends only in Sanskrit in *s*, but in a vowel in Zend, Lithuanian, Slavonic.]

dialects to put, after the numeral 2, the same forms as in the singular. The Welsh *uab* instead of *mab* in (W. 3) *deu uab*,— the Gaedhelic *macc* in *da macc*, is evidently as little a true singular form as the Gaedh. *fer* after *cét* and *míle* is a true nom. sing.; but the form of the nom. sing comes just as well where it distinguishes itself from the only conceivable genitive plural, as here, where the greatest similarity exists between the genitive plural and the nominative singular; in *deu uab* = *da macc* a true dual has consequently been preserved (as the primitive form of substantives has generally been preserved in the Kymric after numerals, *e.g. trimeib* = Gaedh. *trí maicc*, that it is **trís maqvi*, instead of the usual *meibion*), and the agreement of the nom. dual with the nom. sing. in most cases, caused by the Celtic phonetic laws, has led in other cases to an unwarranted extension of the singular form. The Celtic with its dual in the nom. of substantives stands therefore in an interesting contrast to the Teutonic languages, which had already lost the dual in the substantive in its earliest stage, but have preserved it in the Gothic verb.

But the detection of the nom. dual leaves the second question still unanswered. Even in the Greek the genitive-locative is lost, and replaced by the form of the instrumental-dative-ablative; *duo* and *ambo* in the Latin have not remained in undisturbed possession of the accusative, indeed the nom. is replaced in the feminine by *duae;* nay even the Lithuanian, notwithstanding its close affinity to the Slavonian (the only European language which has completely preserved the dual in all forms), has undoubtedly lost the locative, and very probably replaced the genitive by the genitive plural (in spite of Bopp's opposite view, compare Gram. I. 2 Ed. 442; Schleicher, Lith. Gram. 171;— according to Schleicher Beiträge, I. 115, *s* is not dropped in Lithuanian). It need not therefore at all surprise us, if all the dual cases have not been preserved in Irish, and the less so, as the Gaedhelic, like the Kymric adjective, always appears in the plural: Gaedh. *da druith aegeptacdi, da ṅgruad corcra, da ṅainm cosmaili;* W. (3) *deu was ieueinc.* In fact it may be proved, that even the substantives of the *ordo prior* (see Appendix I.) series 2 and 5, consequently *a*-stems and feminines, and all consonant stems (*ordo posterior*), have lost the genitive dual, and replaced it by the genitive plural. The primitive ending of this case *-aus* = Skr. *-ôs*, could scarcely ever (if the phonetic laws laid down in Gram. Celt. I., 165 *sqq.* are correct; and that they are, the almost transparent clearness in which the greater part of the case-endings appear according to them, is a guarantee) so wholly disappear as that, in Old Irish at least, an *-a* as a contraction of *-â* or *-au* would not have remained; but as we find not alone from consonantal stems *da arad*, but also from *a*-stems *da-tarb, dá macc, dá charpat* (instead of *carpat*), *da lethcend* (no doubt more correctly *lethchend*, as a vowel (*i*) has dropped out in the composition, stem *lethi*=Lat. *lătus*, Gr. πλάτος, *lethchenn* is ἡμίκραιρα), *da carachtar*, nay even from *â*-stems (*indarann*) without endings, we must look upon them as genitive plurals, which, as in the Lithuanian, have taken the place of the genitive dual. (To the preceding examples may be further added *a dasyl*. Z. 369, that is *a dá sillab*, with a wrong mortification point; I am in doubt about the stem of *da og*, whether it is *ogi* or *oga?*) The form of the article *in*, also, which even as arising from *innan* is very strange, does not admit of being at all explained from *innás* (*innaus*). The *dd* in *inddá aimserda* is probably only a sign that *dá* should not be aspirated. In the same way we shall consequently have also to explain the forms of the *ia*-stems—*dagutae, indá gutae* fem.; *i*-stems—*inda leithesin* (*n*. or *m*.); *u*-stems—*inddá aimserda, da lino*, which might admit of being explained perhaps otherwise also as real dual forms. It is evidently an accident that we should find just here a form in -*o* among *u*-stems, while the genitive plural otherwise generally ends in -*e*, and only once in -*a* (Stokes, Beitr. I. 346); and least of all should it have misled Zeuss to place even in series 1 and 2 the form of the genitive singular in the paradigma. The dative remains doubtful, as the whole of the forms may be explained as well from -*bin* as from -*bis*, and the Greek and Lithuanian have just preserved this case: *indibmaigib, dib cetaib* Z. 311, 313, *deib ndíllib, dondib dligedib remeperthib, dib rannaib, dib consonaib* 194, *indib nuarib deac, dimutaib, deib traigthib;* I would, however, almost prefer, here also, the explanation as dative plural, because the Celtic has retained so very much less of the dual than the Greek and Lithuanian, no verbal and no adjectival forms.

Of undoubted dual-forms we accordingly have only the nom. and acc. of substantives, and the whole of the cases of the numeral two. The masculine *a*-stems, with the exception of the one-syllabled *dá, da*, have thrown off the ending -*a*, shortened from -*â*, (=Ved. Slav. -*â*, Gr. -ω, Lat. ŏ) or -*au* (=Skr. -*âu*), hence nom. *da macc, da mod, da son*, acc. *indamér* (?), *inda articul, eter da son*, Z. 197; the *ar* II. *canoin* (pro duobus canonicis) kindly communicated by Mr. Stokes, is consequently to be completed *dá canoinech* (more correctly *chanoinech*.). The neuters, in deviating from the Sanskrit and Slavonian, connect themselves with the Greek and Latin, inasmuch as they likewise presuppose an ending -*a*, older -*â* (or -*au*)—*da ngruad corcra, adánimechtar, da cenél;* hence from *ia*-stems—*danorpe, da llae, indagné*, acc. masc.

8

or neut. *da sale* (dat. sig. *dit sailiu* Incant. Sg. in Zeuss). A neuter *da g* (two *g's*) also appears, 710. The feminine *á*-stems agree on the other hand with the Skr. *-ê*, Slav. *-ě*, Lith. *-i*, for they show the after-action of *-i*, *-î* (still preserved in *dí* = *dvé*, Welsh *dui*): nom. *di flisc* (sing. *flesc.* = *flisca), *di huáir*, acc. *di rainn*, *di árim*, *di persin*, *indibrethirso*; from *iá*-stems nom. *digutai*, *díguttai*, *di míli*, Z. 315, acc. *indiguthaighthi airdixi*, 966. The *i-* and *u-* stems appear to have simply lengthened the end-vowel. This was of course followed by a subsequent shortening, and then a dropping of the lengthened vowel: hence nom. masc. *da preceptóir* from *-óri*, *-ôri*, *da atarcud* from *-idu*, *-idû* (gen. sing. *attaircedo*, nom. *attárcud* like *spirut*, gen. *spirito*, *spirto*, *spiruto*), acc. masc. *danóg*, *dánog* from *nógû, masc. or neut. *indarecht* from *rechtû, acc. neut. *indá errend* from *-randi*?

The *in* of the article consequently arises in the nom. and acc. masc. and neut. from *inna, *innâ; in the fem. from *inni, *innî. It appears to have penetrated in the other cases in the same way that in the Greek *-οιν* has done in the genitive, or τώ in feminines; the frequent interchange, in the Irish, of the dat. and acc. after prepositions, is also to be taken into account, as well as the dying out of the cases which has been observed in Modern Irish (p. 80). The *in* cannot be well explained, organically, at least, in the gen., in the dative not at all.

Very few dual forms of consonantal stems have been unfortunately preserved. Of these the nom. *da druith*, and acc. *da sligid*, agree best with the Greek *-ε*, for a Sanskrit *-âu*, or a Vedic *-â*, would have led rather to *druad* and *sliged*. Nom. *dá thene*, acc. *da are*, nom. acc. *dá ainm*, *da nainm* appears to be decidedly inorganic. The frequent coincidence of the form with that of the nom. sing. has here, no doubt, brought about the invasion of the singular forms.

In conclusion, it should not be forgotten, that in the Kymric not only are the commencing consonants in the substantives softened in the dual, but likewise in the following adjective, which is a proof that here also the nom. and acc. dual ended primitively in a vowel.

§. 11. *On the Article in Modern Irish.*

In the modern Irish article *an*, about the relation of which to the old *int*, *ind*, I could not hitherto come to a satisfactory conclusion, I now recognize, with certainty, an intrusion of the neutral form, as the most colourless and weakest, precisely as the Middle High German had formed to its neuter *daz* a masculine and feminine *der*, *diu*, and the Lithuanian and Slavonian (to *to*) its *tas*, *ta*, *tŭ*, *ta*. The English use of *that* (pronoun) and *the* (article) for all genders is especially important in this respect.[70]

It is a fact worthy of attention, but one hitherto scarcely noticed, that, besides the coarser, I may say the material, action of languages upon one another, which shows itself in the evident borrowing of words and forms, a finer, a more spiritual influence is exerted. Thus, certain words, without being borrowed, are preserved living and active, by the neighbourhood of other languages, and some forms of thought and sound, words, expressions, conversational phrases, are so to say, indigenous in the soil. A comparative syntax would bring many examples of this kind to light, especially in the languages which have grown up on Celtic ground, and might determine how much may be ascribed to accident, and how much to intellectual influences. In the Phonology, for example, the Kymric *ui*, *oi*, representing the Gaedhelic *é* (even in loan-words like *cera*, W. 2. *kuyr*, 3. *kwyr*, Cornish V. *coir*, Armoric *coar*) is parallel with the French *oi*, representing the Latin *ê* (avoir = habere); again, the Celtic action of the final sound on the following word has a parallel in the transporting of the final *s* to the next word in *les amis*, etc. Among the words and word-forms which have been preserved on Celtic ground, we may mention: English, *witness* = Gaedhelic *fiadnisse* (testimonium), and the English names in *-ton*, along with the Gaulish in *-dûnum*. Of importance in Syntax are: the French intercalation of the pronoun in *je t'aime, je ne t'aime pas*, as in both branches of the Celtic; the French *c'est moi* and the English *it is me* = Gaedhelic *ismé*; the English leaving out of the relative in, *the man (whom) I saw*, as in the Gaedhelic.[71] Now, in this respect the English *that*, *the*, for all genders, are not without importance for the Celtic also, and permit us to conclude, that in the Modern Irish *an fear* for the Old Irish *in fer*, an analogous process has taken place.—The relative *an* (*a, no, n*) appears to belong to the same stem; we may compare the fluctuation between the relative and the demonstrative in the Homeric language, the peculiar use of the Old Persian *hya*, which Bopp also,[72] as I myself did,[73] now looks upon as an article, and the German antiquated relative *so*.

---

[70] [xxxi. This is an ingenious error. The neut. article is quite lost in Middle Irish, and the Modern Irish article *an* (*an t* before a vocalic anlaut), bears the same relation to the Old Irish *in (int)* that the Modern Irish preposition *an* (written *a n-*) does to the Old Irish *in*; or the Modern Irish interrogative particle *an* does to the same particle in the Old Irish, viz., *in*. But here, as elsewhere, more is to be gained from Ebel's mistakes than from many another man's truths. The relative *an*, *a*, is doubtless identical in form with the neut. article =*sa-n*. Ebel has since corrected this error. See, *infra*, On Phonology in Irish, §. 2. p. 138.]

[71] [But the two last named constructions are found also in the Scandinavian languages, where no Celtic influence is possible.]

[72] Vergl. Gram. I. 473. 2nd Ed.   [73] Zeitschrift f. Vergl. Sp. v. 305.

§. 12. On the So-called Prosthetic n.

[The term Prosthetic *n*, used by Zeuss, is what Irish grammarians erroneously call an eclipsing *n*. Mr. Stokes in the papers above quoted, and Dr. Ebel here show that this *n*, in the majority of cases, belonged to the word immediately preceding that to which it seems prefixed.]

Mr. Stokes, in his valuable observations on the Irish declension, has agreed with my remark, that the *n* of the inflexion has been preserved in TEORA ṄGUTTAE, and here and there also besides the *n* of the article, and has communicated several examples. Zeuss, curiously enough, has altogether misunderstood this *n*,[74] and everywhere looked upon it either as a superfluous addition or as a shorter form of the article, *e. g.*, before AILE, although there it appears only in the nom. neut. and acc. sing. and gen. plur. of all of the three genders,—often in combinations where no article is possible. As a relic of the article I have met with this *n*, only in very few places, and then as the remains of the shortest forms: AN (A-N-) in TRESṄGNÉ, Z. 611, where the E of TRES still indicates an A dropped out, and NI EPUR NÍSIN (non dico hoc, instead of ANÍSIN) 352; IN (acc. dual) in ETARNDIRAINN 278, 614, probably as gen. dual in CECHTARNÁI, NECHNARNÁI 369 (compare the plur. INNAN ÁI). The *n* in LASIN ṄGUTAI (instead of LASINN GUTAI) 619, 1017. The most of the other examples are clear enough. I shall give here some proofs, which may easily be increased. Nom. and acc. neut. FOLAD *n*AILL, OLCC *n*AILL, DES. (*i. e.*, DESIMRECHT) *n*AILL, PRONOMEN *n*AILL 363, IMBÉLRE *n*AILL 580, MÓR *n*AMRI 596, 889, GRAD *n*EPSCUIP 1048, AM. NÁCH ANNSE *ṅ*DUIB (ut non difficile vobis) 703, HUARE ISDILMAIN *ṅ*DOCHECHTAR 369, ANDÉDE *n*ÍSIU 319, 704, ANUATHATH *n*ÍSIU 353, ANDLÍGED *n*ÍSIU 353, MÓOR *n*IMNITH 21, MÓR *n*UILE 609, 889, DLIGETH *n*IMMOGNAMA 984, CACH *m*BELRE 489, FRI CACH*n*AE 319, MIND *n*ABSTALACTE 229, RAD *ṅ*DÉ 55, ÁTA DECHOR *n*AIMSIRE 1037, ÁTA DECHOR *n*ETARRU 374, ISSAIN CACH*n*AE (previously, ILSENMAN) 367, DERED *m*BETHO 985, IS-FUATH *ṅ*EPERTA 985, SAINRETH *n*ANMMAE 1025, ARACUMACTTE *n*ANGID NÍ ÁRMISOM ARCHUMACTTE ([nam] potestatem nequam non numerat ipse pro potestate) 247, NÍFAIL NACH *n*AICCIDIT (non est ullum accidens) 1016, NICUMSCAICHTHI CUMACHTÆ *n*AIRI (non mutanda potestas propterea) 1015, NÍ FITIR IMORRO OLC *n*ETIR (nescit autem malum omnino) 1003, LAA *m*BRÁTHA 479, ALLAITHE *n*DEDENACHDIUD [no doubt ALLAITHEN DÉDENACH DIUD = die extremo (acc. temp.) in fine] 316, ISNOICHTECH RÉ *n*IUIL (est undetricenale spatium Julii) 1075, ISGNÁTH GÁO ET FÍR *n*AND 359. So also—arindí atreba toxal *n*AND 359? Acc. masc. CO RÍG

---

[74] [xxxii. Not so. See Zeuss G. C., page 263, where he conjectures that the very form cited here by Ebel, *teora ṅ*, may stand for *teoran*.]

n ILAINGLECH Colman's hymn—Lib. Hymn. 10 (to the many angel'd king), according to a friendly communication of Mr. Stokes, COFER *n*AILE Z. 884, MARUDBAITSIUS NACH*n*AILE 434, INBITH *n*UILE 366, TRESINNÓEDÉCDE *n*UILE 1074, FOCHOSMUILIUS *n*ADARCÆ 481, INFOGUR *n*ÍSIN 1014; without the article, BESTATID*n*ISIN 611, ÁES *n*ESCI 1074 (three times), NIFAIL CHUMSCUGUD *n*HUIRDD AND 369, TAR RECHT *n*AICNID 613 RECHT *n*IMBIDI 229, LETH *n*GOTHO 1013 (consequently LETH is also masc. like RECHT), CONROIGSET DIA *n*AIRIUIBSI 1076, AIRTHECH. CACHGUTÆ AGUTH *n*INDI 966, TODDIUSGAT GUTH *n*INTIU 1017, CEN RIAN *n*ETROM 616. So also no doubt: NACH *n*AILE 368, TÓINIUD *n*IRESSACH 229, NERT *n*AINMNEDO 975, ATTLUGUD *m*BUIDE 1048 (the acc. instead of the dat.?), CACH*n*OEN CRANN 999? I am not quite certain of the gender in, FRI CUMTACH *n*ECOLSO 260, CUMTACH *n*IRISSE 1045, ECOSC *n*ABSTAL 585, TAIBRITH ATÉICHTE *n*DOIB (no doubt neuter) 56. Acc. fem. FRICACH *n*AIMSIR 367, CECH *n*AIDCHE (instead of AIDCHI) 888, ISARNACH *n*INDOCBÁIL MÓIR 262, HI CACH *n*DEILB 7 HI CACH TARMORCENN 367 (translated by Zeuss as the dat.), I PERSIN *n*AILI 363, FRIRAINN *n*AILI 608, CEN GUTAI *n*ETARRU 1017; also doubtless, ROSCARSAM FRIB DENUS *m*BEICC 310, HIRES *n*ABARCHE 229, SERC *n*DEE 55 (just as NEM, DELB occur in the acc.), CEN ALPAI *n*ETARRU 616,[75] FRIALPAI *n*DESIU 595. Gen. plur. masc. INNAMBALL *n*AILE 229; fem. NA LITER *n*AILE 1012, LITER *n*AILE 1012; neut. ANMAN *n*ADIECHT 433.

Some spurious prepositions, it would appear, may be recognized as accusative forms by the *n*, most distinctly TARÉSI in—U. TARHESI *n*I (U for I) 1012, OLCC TARÉSI *n*UILCC 617, but INDEGAID also in—INDEGAID *n*DÉ 619, INDEGAID *n*GUTTÆ 1013, and DOCHUM in—DOCHUM *n*DÉE 620, DOCHUM *n*IRISSE 461 (bis).

The *n* of AINM-N belongs to the stem in—AINM *n*AFSTIL 229, AINM *n*HETHA 255, AINM *n*GNÚSO 975, AINM *n*DILES 1025, DOBERR AINM *n*DOIB 457.[76] According to this my observation (p. 65), "probably derived, however, from *m*, and not a primitive *n*", must consequently be cancelled, and the single example with an aspiration AINM THRÍUIN Z. 249, considered as an irregularity.[77] As yet I have failed in finding for the masculine and feminine *n*-stems an example of the aspiration, or of a mortified *s*, *f*; I have also, however, nowhere found an N; it conse-

---

[75] According to Stokes (Beiträge zur vergleichenden Sprachforschung I. 468) the *n* of ALPAI-N and INRINDIDE-N belongs to the stem.
[76] See last note.
[77] [xxxiii. The *n* in ainm napstil does not belong to the stem, but (as in pronomen naill cited by Dr. Ebel himself, *supra*) is simply an example of the natural tendency to prefix after *all* neuters in the nom. and acc. sing. an *n* (*m* before *b*) to the following adjective, if this begin with a vowel or a medial.]

quently appears as if the neuter only preserved the N as in the Latin and Slavic,—*ANMEN like NOMEN and IMĘ, while the masculine and feminine dropped it,—*BRITHEMÁ like HOMO and KAMY.

The *n* is much less clear in CECHTARNÁI, NECHTARNÁI Z. 369 (which I consider to be a relic of the gen. dual of the article IN, on account of DOCHECHTAR ṄHÁI, evidently the dative, and of the genitive plural INNAN ÁI), SLIAB ṄOSSA 888 (perhaps acc.?), SIRID INRINDIDE ṄUILE (see note 75) 366, 586, ARBERTAR AS NÓEN TARMOIRCIUNN 592, FAR NÓENDEILB 670, AM. INLOCHAIRNN ṄAFFRACDAI 676, where it appears to be in part actually erroneous; COTÍR NEREND 74, appears to indicate a change of gender (comp. RECHT, LETH, NERT); even there, however, Zeuss also gives FIR NEREND (viri Hiberniæ) with an enigmatical *n*.

There is perhaps a threefold preposition DO-AIR-IN contained in TAIRNGIRE, DURAIRNGERT, DORAINGRED Z. 56, 868; in the same way that CON became mutilated in FRECṄDIRC ÉCNDIRC.

But, very strange, the *n* appears very often after verbal forms; mostly, perhaps exclusively, in dependent sentences, frequently after the so-called relative—AS*n*ÓINDAE INSPIRUT 360, AS*n*ED 675, AM. AS*n*É ASSPLENDOR 333, AS*n*IRESS 456, AS*n*OIPRED 476, AM. AS*n*INDEDUR 580, ÓRE AS*n*DIUL 703, CÉIN BAS*m*BÉO INFER 230, 675, HÓRE AS*n*AMAIRESSACH 705, LASSE BAS *n*UÁIN (NUÁIR?) DO 229, AS*n*DIRRUIDIG[THE] ANAINMSIN 265, AMMI *n*EULIG 252, CONSECHAT *n*ULCU 457, ATA *n*AṄMAN SIDI 894, NI CUMCAT CAMAIPH ILLE 7 ISTE BETA *n*AITHFOILSIGTHECHA DONDÍ AS IPSE 667, INTAIN BES *n*INUN ACCOBOR LENN 603.[78]

Notwithstanding that several examples still remain unexplained, the vast majority show quite clearly, nevertheless, that the *n* is prosthetic, if at all, only in exceedingly few cases; especially the forms assumed by Zeuss, NAILL, NAILE, NAILI, NÍSIN, NÍSIU, and NAND for AND decidedly fall to the ground.

13. §. *On the Degrees of Comparison.*

Among the consonantal stems we have not mentioned the interesting *-ns* stems, the comparative, because no declensional forms of them are any longer to be recognized, with the exception of adverbial dative forms, which offer nothing peculiar (*immou*, magis, *indoa*, minus *indlaigiu*, minus, *intserbu* amarius, *indluindia* commotius). As in the accusative plural, the primitive *-ans* has split itself into *-a* (consonantal stems, feminines, and the article) and *-u* (masc. *a*-stems), so here also we find both forms, the *-a* in the more ancient, the *-u* in the newer secondary formations. Of the former *máa* with its parallel forms,

---

[78] May it be, that as in Greek, an ν ἐφελκυστικόν existed? Stokes also compares *ammi-ṅ* with ἐσμέν.

corresponds to the Lat. *major*, Goth. *mais, maiza;* the Kymric form, W. *mwy*, Corn. *moy*, Armor. *muy*, which deviates somewhat in the vowel, has still preserved the *j, i*, and like all similar forms, has thrown off the final vowel, together with the *s*. *Oa* (minor) appears to have been formed after the superlative *oam =* Skr. *avama*, instead of Skr. *avara*, therefore properly: inferior, deterior; *nessa =* W. *nes* has been already several times compared with the Gothic *néhv néhvis*, its superlative with the Osc. Umbr. *nesimo*, and the dropping of a guttural surmised; *tressa* (fortior)—cf. W. *traha* (audax, fortis)—exhibits the (in Sanskrit) regular throwing off of the suffix before the comparative ending, in opposition to *trén*, instead of *tresn?* (just as *máo* along with *már*); *messa* (pejor) appears to find its positive in the prefix *mi-* (Z. 833) = Goth. *missa*, although the latter aspirates the following consonants; in this respect, however, it has a companion in *du-*, which certainly represents the Skr. *dus-*, Gr. δυς-. The *ss* of the last examples appears to have arisen from *sj*, just as *rr* in *ferr* (melior) = Kymr. *guell, gwell*, whose Oscan and Teutonic affinities are compared in the Zeitschr. f. v. Sp. VI. 421, does from *rj*, (compare also Skr. *variyas*, Gr. ἀρείων?). *Lia* (plus) has been elsewhere compared[79] with the Greek πλείων, and *ire* shown to be a comparative.[80] The only comparative of that kind, which has joined itself to the second formation in the Gaedhelic, *laigiu* or *lugu* (minor)—W. *llei*, has remained true to the first—places itself alongside the Skr. *laghíyas* = Lat. *levior* but Gr. ἐλάσσων; the substantive *lagait* (parvitas) is derived from this adjective. In the same manner the Gaedh. *siniu =* Lat. *senior*, and the Welsh *hyn*, deviate from one another. Among the Kymric forms *hwy* (longior), *is* (humilior), *uch* (altior), *ieu* (junior) = Skr. *yavíyas* which exhibit the rejection of the suffixes of *hir* = Gaedh. *sir, isel, uchel* = Gaedh. *úasal*, are particularly interesting.

The second form *u-* is evidently only a contraction from *-iu*, in the same way as *daltu* occurs in the dative of the *ia*-stems instead of *daltiu, maccidóndu* in the acc. plur. of the same stems instead of *maccidóndiu*, and *ditu, tichtu, epeltu* in the nom. sing. of the *tin*-stems instead of *dítiu, tichtiu, epeltiu;* for the same reason *laigiu* and *lugu, uilliu* and *oillu* (plus), *toisigiu* and *tóisechu* (prior) appear side by side. The majority of stems follow this formation, namely all derivative ones, hence *ísliu, húaisliu* instead of the Welch *is, uch*. In the Kymric *-ach* corresponds to it (with retention of the *s* as *ch*), while the Gaedhelic *-a* has fallen off in the Kymric. The superlative in the Gaedhelic

---

[79] [See his paper, *infra*, "On the Loss of *p* in Celtic", p. 161.]
[80] [See the paper referred to in note 79.]

separated into -*am* and -*em*, does not distinguish itself in the Kymric -*am*. How are these different forms to be explained?

In the first place let us recollect the double formation in the Teutonic and Slavonic, which have been already compared with one another in the Zeitschr. f. v. Sp. v. 309 *sqq.*; as Goth. -*iza*. Church-Slav. -*ii*, so does the Gaedh. -*a* belong almost exclusively to the defective comparatives, as the Goth. -*ôza*, Ch.-Slav. -*êi*, so does the Gaedh. -*iu* attach itself to all secondary formations. We know further that *j* disappears in every position in the Gaedhelic and at least in the middle in the Kymric, except where it is preserved as the vowel *i*. Finally, we found (p. 54), that the ending -*e* (dat. -*iu*) not only represented the Skr. -*ya*, but also frequently -*aya*, an origin which is still sometimes marked by the writing -*ae* (gen. -*ai*). Now as the Kymric forms (and also the single Gaedh. form *ferr*), as well as the analogy of the Teutonic and Slavonic, compel us to assume a shorter form than the Gaedh. -*iu* as the basis of the Gaedh. -*a*, the following hypothesis may best recommend itself:—The Celtic formed two kinds of comparatives, an older one in -*jans*, a newer one in -*ajans* (-*aijans?-âjans?*); the -*ns* fell off in both in the Gaedhelic, as in the acc. plur., and left behind a long vowel, which was afterwards shortened; the *j* dropped out in the first form, but left behind some traces in Gaedh. *messa, tressa, ferr* (?), in W. *mwy, llei, hwy* (?); in the second, -*aja* contracted itself to -*a* in the Kymric, and -*aj* to -*ê*, *i* in the Gaedhelic; in the Kymric, the *s* remained as *ch* after the (primitively long?) *a*, as in *chwech* six = Gaedhelic *sé*, but fell off with the vowel in the shorter form. If this hypothesis be correct, the *e* (*i*) of the Gaedhelic superlative (stem -*ima*, nom. -*em*, gen. -*im*) must have been shortened from *ê* or *í*.

In Modern Irish, -*iu* has become *e* (passing through *i?*) as in the nominatives of the *n*-stems, *e. g. laige* from *laigiu*, like *naoidhe*, from *nóidiu* (compare Pictet, Beiträge I. 83).[81]

[81] [The following is the passage referred to. "*Eriu*, as it appears, is a still more ancient form of the nominative and accusative. It is so in two quotations by O'Connor from Eochaid's poems (belonging to the ninth century—Proleg. II., 40, 42).

H Eriu oll ordnitt Gaedil,—Hiberniam totam ordinavit Gadelius; *H Eriu con huail con idnaib*,—Hibernia cum gloria, cum armis (probably the accusative which cannot be determined, as the continuation is wanting). For this ending *iu* instead of the later *e*, compare in Zeuss (Gram. Celt., 268), *nóidiu*, infans, *frescsiu*, spes, *deicsiu*, visio, *ermitiu*, reverentia, etc. (later and now *naoidhe*, *fresce, deicse, airmidhe*), all of them having *n, nn* in the oblique case, where however the *u* has disappeared, *noiden, infantis, deicsen*, visionis, etc., as in *Erenn, Eireann*. The proper name *Fridriu* or *Frigriu* (Ordnance Survey of Ireland), poem of Aileach, l. 40, 43), whose genitive is *Fridrenn* (39), *Frigrinn* (1), *Frigrind* (2, 53) is another example".]

ON THE POSITION OF THE CELTIC.

§. 1. *Views regarding the special affinities of the Celtic, and words borrowed from the Latin.*

THE European members of the Aryan family of languages form a chain, both ends of which reach over into Asia. The Greek undoubtedly shows the most numerous points of contact with the Asiatic tongues. On the other hand, however, the Slavonian exhibits the greatest number of special agreements with the Iranian.[82] So in like manner the neighbouring links, within the chain itself, are universally acknowledged to be the most closely connected with one another, Greek and Italian, Slavonian and Lithuanian, Lito-Slavonian and Teutonic. Very naturally, therefore, in the Celtic also, which lies nearly in the middle between the others, most points of contact will be found with the Italic on the one side and the Teutonic on the other, and through both with the other already established branches of the European division. It is, of course, very difficult to decide to which of the two it stands nearest, perhaps even impossible at present, when, as regards the question of the separation of languages, so much is still debateable, and when a comparative syntax is still quite wanting.

Lottner has pronounced in favour of the "Northern"; Schleicher for the Pelasgian languages; both, notwithstanding the divergence of their views in other respects, agree in placing the Latin nearer to the Celtic than to the Greek. I look upon so much only as proved, that the Celtic stands closer to the Latin than to the Greek. The circumstance that feminines in -*os*, -*us*, only occur in the Classic languages appears to me to prove conclusively a nearer connection of those languages with each other than with any other. In other respects also I have not adopted Lottner's view in so wholly unconditional a way as Schleicher appears to assume; but, on the contrary, I have often expressly

---

[82] To this category belongs, besides many other points that Schleicher has brought forward, also the frequent occurrence of the suffix -*ka* where it is foreign to other tongues, *e. g.*, Slav. *sladŭkŭ* (dulcis) = Lith. *saldùs*, like Old Persian *vazarka* (magnus) = Skr. *vr̥hat*.

indicated, in general as well as in particular, the points of contact of the Celtic with the Classic languages. This shall not, however, deter me from exposing the points of agreement of the Celtic with the northern tongues, in accordance with his request. Only I shall take the liberty of beginning with a point which Schleicher designedly left aside, namely, with the vocabulary of the Celtic, partly in consequence of the accidental direction of my studies, partly in order to at once meet a foregone conclusion, that many (although certainly not Schleicher) might draw from this very source in favour of a closer relationship with the Latin.

Indeed, it appears at first sight as if thé Celtic languages had an especially large number of words in common with the Latin. If, however, one looks closer, by far the greatest number (even in Old Gaedhelic, but still more in the Kymric dialects) are seen to be foreign or loan-words, often so deceptively assimilated, that when one is about to take off the mask, he involuntarily draws back his hand. So says, for example, Zeuss (p. 80): Non tanguntur certe tenues in vocibus peregrinis receptis. But words like *accidit* ($t=nt$), *ethemlagas* ($th=t$) which yet, unquestionably do not belong to the earliest loans, show what little claim this rule can have to general validity. At most, we can only judge thereby of the greater or lesser perfection of the appropriation and mastery of the foreign material, and in this respect the Kymric surpasses almost the Gaedhelic.

I have constructed two glossaries from the *Grammatica Celtica*, of which the Old Gaedhelic one may be considered to be pretty complete; the Kymric one may, however, undergo considerable enlargement. From these I give the following lists, as the foundation of further glossarial researches. In order to supply in some degree at least the want of an organic orthography, I have retained here also the method of denoting the Kymric dialects which I adopted on a former occasion;[63] unmarked words are Old Gaedhelic. I did not like to pass over the Kymric, because the peculiar phonetic relations of the two branches of the Celtic family necessitate a mutual supplementing and explanation; besides, loan-words are often accidentally wanting in the old documents of the one or other dialect in Zeuss. In the case of the loan-words, a peculiar difficulty occurs in the Kymric dialects, as it is often scarcely possible to decide whether a word has been introduced directly from the Latin, or through the French, Anglo-Norman, or even the English. The decision

---

[63] Beitr., I. 427. [See APPENDIX II., p. 184, for an explanation of the abbreviations used in the following lists.]

is the more difficult because the Kymric vowel-changes mostly agree with the French (especially in the treatment of *ē*); and because in the case of the dialects with regard to which the idea of such a medium would first arise, Cornish and Armoric, our sources are too modern to help us to answer the question from the chronological side. In order to avoid, as much as possible, mistakes in this respect, I have only indicated the medium where it appeared to me certain. The Old Gaedhelic, especially, contains a great number of Latin words (or of Greek ones borrowed through the Latin) from the domain of the Church and of science; but others also are not wanting.

LATIN LOAN-WORDS IN OLD CELTIC.

abbas=[*ab*], V. *abat*, W. 2. pl. *abbadeu*.
[abecedarium, *aibgiter*, W. *egwyddor*.]
abstinentia=*abstanit*.
accentus=*aiccent aiccend*, d. *aicciund*; [W. 3 *acen*.]
accidens=*accidit aiccidit* n.
[acer, *aicher*, W. 3 *egr*.]
acetum : *áctegim* (aceo).
[actualis, *achtail*.]
acutus=*acuit*; *noacuitigfide* (acuenda esset).
adjectivum=*adiect, adiecht*.
adorare : *adras* (qui adorat), *adrorsat* (adoraverunt), *adrad* (adoratio).
adulter-ium=*adaltr-as*.
[adversarius Mid. Ir. *aibherseóir*.]
altare=*altóir* f., V. *altor*; [W. 3. *allor*.]
altum=W. 2 *alt allt all*, 3. *allt* (collis, acclivitas, scopulus), V. *als* (litus).
anachoreta=V. *ancar*.
ancora=*ingor*, V. *ancar*, [W. 3. *angor*], (the *i* as in *ind*-(ἀντι) and *imb*-(ἀμφι) and *g* like *d* in *ind*-(Gaul. *ande*-) make the borrowing a little doubtful; the borrowing of the same word in other European languages (compare for instance Lith. *inkaras*), and of other naval expressions in the Celtic, speak however for it).
angelus=*angel aingel*, V. *ail*, P. *eyll el*, Arm. *ael el hel*.
animal=W. 3. *aniueil*, pl. W. 2. *anyueilyeit*, 3. *anniueileit aniueileit anniueilet*, Arm. *aneualet*.
apostolus=*apstal*, V. Arm. *apostol*, P. pl. *abestely*.
applicare : Arm. *em em applicquet*. (applicate vos).
[aratrum, *arathar* W. 3. *aradr*.]
argentum=[*airget, argat*], W. 2. *ariant*,

3. *aryant*, V. *argans*, P. *arghans*, Arm. *argant*. (External evidence of the borrowing is no doubt wanting, the evident borrowing of the name of gold, as well as physico-geographical reasons, speak however in its favour). [? cf. Gaulish *Argentoratum*.]
(?) arma=*arm, arma*, d. *isind-airmm* (in armatura), W. 2. 3. *arueu arfeu*, P. *arvow*.
armilla=W. 1. *armel*.
[ars, *art*.]
articulus=*articol*, gen. sing.=n. pl. *articuil*, d. *artucol*.
asinus=[*asan*], W. 3. *assen*, V. P. *asen* (The grounds for the borrowing are elsewhere given).
atomum=*atom*, in the phrase 7 *unga* 7 *atom* (et uncia et atomum), not recognized by Zeuss, 312, 1076.
auctoritas=*augtortús*.
[Augusti (mensis), *augaist*, W. *awst*.]
aurum=*ór* (gen. *óir*), W. 2. 3. V. *eur*, P. *owr*, Arm. *aour*. (The *r* undoubtedly indicates borrowing, cf. Sabin. *ausum* and Lith. *auksas*. Grimm consequently errs in his Geschichte d. d. Sprache 1027).
[baculum, *bachall*, W. 3. *bagl*.]
[balbus, *balb*.]
[baptista, *bauptaist*.]
baptizo=*baitsim*; acc. *baithis*, dat. *baithius*, W. 3. *bedyd* m., Arm. *badez* (baptisma).
barba=W. 3. *baraf, baryf*; V. *barf baref*. (The borrowing is no doubt remarkable, I cannot however explain otherwise *f* in contradistinction to Lith. *barzdà*, Slav. *brada*, O.H.G. *bart*.)
[barca, *barc*, W. 3. *barg*.]

M. Lat. baro=W. 3. barwn.
[basilica, baislic.]
[basium, bay, P.]
battuere : V. bat (numisma), W. 2. V. bathor (numularius, trapezita), P. batales (proeliari).
[beatus=Mid. Ir. biat.]
benedico: bendachæ (benedicis), nobbendachat (salutant vos), indatbendachub (benedicam te); bendacht, W. 3. bendith, Arm. bennoez (benedictio); W. 2. bendicetic, P. benegis, Arm. ben(n)iguet (benedictus).
bestia=W. 3. bwyst-uil (appears to be compounded with mil like the German Maulthier, etc.), O. Gaedh. béisti f. pl.
blasphemare (Fr. blâmer)=P. blamye.
[Med. Lat. brace, braich, W. 3. and V. brag.]
[brachium, bracc, V. brech, W. 3. breich.]
brassica=braisech.
brevis (syllaba)=breib.
broccus brocchus (see Diez), Fr. broche =V. broche (spinther). [Mid. Ir. proiste.]
[bulla, boll, W. bwl.]
buxus=V. box.
calamus=[W. 1. calamennou]. W. 3. keleu-yn m. (singulative); V. kalagueli (stramentum).
M. Lat. caldaria=W. 1. callaur, V. caltor. [Arm. kaoter.]
[callidus, callaid.]
calix=[cailech], V. kelegel.
[camisia, caimse.]
[cancella, caingel.]
cancellarius=W. 2. kaghellaur, kyghellaur.
cancer=W. 1., V. cancher.
candela=V. cantuil, W. 3. cannwyll: candelarius=caindlóir, Z. 744; candelabrum : V. cantul-bren.
canon=acc. canóin.
[capellanus, Mid. Ir. cabellanacht.]
capistrum=W. 1. cepister, 2. kebyster, pl. kebystreu kebesteryeu.
[capitulus, caiptel.]
[captus, cacht, W. 3. caeth.]
[caput, caut.]
carbunculus=carmocol Z. 1168. [W. 3. carbwncl.]
carcer=carcar (gen. pl. carcre, dat carcáir); W. 3. karchar.
(?) caritas (cf. charité)=K. * cardaut (beneficium) in W. 3. cardotta (mendicare). The ending -taut (=tât) occurs especially in loan-words.
car(o)enum instead of car(o)enaria

=V. ceroin (cupa), [W. 1. ceroenhou, gl. dolea.] W. 3. kerwyn (lacus, lebes).
[carpentum, carpat.]
caseus=[cáise], W. 2. kaus, 3. caws, V. caws cos.
castellum=[caisel], pl. W. 2. cestill, 2. cestyll.
[castus, cast; castitas, castoit.]
catena=W. 3. cadwcyn.
cathedra=W. 3. cadeir (sella), Arm. cador.
[catholicus, cathlac.]
[Med. Lat. cattus=V. kat, W. 3. cath.]
[caucus, cuach, W. 3. cawg.]
caules=V. caul (olera).
causa=dat. cóis.
[cedria, cedir.]
[cella, cell, V. tal-gel gl. cellarium.]
census=cis (census, fiscus, vectigal).
cera=[ceír], W. 2. kuyr, 3. kwyr, V. coir, Arm. coar.
[cervical, cérchaill.]
[cervisia, ceirbsire, "brewer".]
character=carachtar n. (littera).
chorda=P. pl. kerdyn (funes), V. corden (fidis).
christianus=[cresen], W. 3. cristawn, Arm. christen.
[chrisma, crismal.]
[cilicium, cilic.]
circare (see Diez)=W. 3. kyrchu, Arm. querchat. querchit (quærere, pergere, intrare).
[circinus, cercenn, W. 1. circhinn.]
circulus=acc. cercol.
circumflexus=circumflex.
civitas=W. 3. kiwtawt; kiwtawtcyr (cives).
clarus=P. clear, Arm. scler (with prefixed s).
[classis, clais.]
[claustrum, V. cluuster, cloister.]
clericus = [clérech], V. cloireg, Arm. cloarec.
[clima, climata, pl.]
M. Lat. clocca=[clocc,], V. cloch; clechir (tintinnabulum), clechti (cloccarium), clochmuer (campana).
coccus: W. 3. coch (ruber). pl. cochyon.
coloni = W. 3. kalaned pl. (habitatores).
(?) columba=colum, V. colom, Arm. coulm, (cf. Slav. golǫbĭ in Schleicher, 106).
columna=W. 2. kolouen (i.e. columina, with an intercalated vowel), O. Gaedh. [colomna, n. pl.], columnat (columella).

*cominitiare, Fr. commencer; Arm. comancc (initium), m=mm.
commatres=Arm. coma(e)zreset.
commodum=comad-as; comadasogod (accommodatio).
[communio, Mid. Ir. command, W. 3. cymun.]
[Med. Lat., companium, companacht.]
[compar, W. 3. cymhar.]
comparativus=comparit, pl. -iti, gen. -ite.
compatres=Arm. compizrien.
concedere: Arm. concedis (consensi).
confessio=[coibse], Arm. coffes.
confligere: conflechtaigthi (congrediendum).
confortare=P. comfortye; dyscomfortys (debilitatus, turbatus).
[consecratio, coisecrad; consecravit, cusecar.]
consilium=[cuisil], Arm., V. cusul, P. cussyl cusyll cusill.
consona = conson, gen. cousine. [W. cyson.]
[conucula (Med. Lat.), cuigel, V. kigel, W. cogail.]
conventus=W. 3. koveint m. (monasterium, fr. couvent).
[coquina, cuicenn.]
coquus=[coic], W. 1. coc (pistor), V. kog (coquus); coquina=W. 3. kegin, V. keghin (the k proves the borrowing, the true Kymric forms have p: V. popei (pistrinum), peber (pistor), W. 2. popuryes, pophuryes, f.).
corona=[Mid. Ir., coróin],V. curun; W. 3. coronawc (coronatus).
corrigia=W. 1. corruui, 3. carrei.
(?)corylus=coll; W. 2. coll (coryletum); col ennf.=V.col-viden(corylus).
craticula=W. 1. gratell.
creator = V. creador, Arm. croeer crouer; creatura=V. croadur(?), Arm. croeadur.—W. 1. creaticaul (genialis).
[credulus, credal.]
[crepusculum, crepscuil.]
[creta, críad.]
[cribrum, ribar.]
crudelis=Arm. cruel (French, or directly ?).
crux=croch, V. crois, P. crows.
crystallus [Mid. Ir., crisdal], transformed in W. 3. krissant m.
(?)cucullus (first in Martial and Juvenal)=[cochull],V. cugol.—According to Diefenbach (n. Jahrb. f. Phil. u. Päd. lxxvii. p. 756); the Latin word had been already borrowed from the Celtic.

[culcita, colcaid.]
cultellus=W. 1. cultel (" artuum"), celeell (" culter"), 3. cyllell, pl. cylleill kylleil (sica); V. collell (" cultellus"), kellillic (" artavus").
culter=W. 1. cultir, [W. 3. cwlltor], V. colter.
cuprum=V. cober.
[cymbalum, cimbal.]
[cypressus, cupris.]
daemon=gen. demuin, gen. pl. demne.
damnare=P. dampnye, Arm. daffny; P. dampnys, Arm. dafnet, daffnet (damnatus).
[debilis, diblide, gl. senium.]
decedere=Arm. decedy.
decima=W. 2. decum, degum.
defendere=Arm. difen; [W. 3. diffenu], V. diffennor (" excusator").
denarius=dinair, Arm. diner.
[deprecatio, diprecoit.]
descendere=W. 3. disgyanu, P. dyskynna, Arm. disquennet.
desiderabat=P. deserga.
despectus=P. dyspyth, Arm. despez.
diabolus=diabul, Arm. diaoul, P. pl. dywolow dewolow.
diaconus= V. diagon; O. Gaedh. pl. bandechuin (diaconissae).
dictator=dictatóir.
[dies Jovis, deyow, P.]
[dies solis, dew sull, P.]
digamma=digaim.
dignus=Arm. din (French or directly ?).
[diluvium, diliu.]
discere=P. dysky, Arm. disquif; W. 2. desko (didicerit); P. dyskas (doctrina).
discipulus=descipul, V. discebel, Arm. desquebel, pl. P. dyscyplys dyscyblon, Arm. disguiblion.
[discretus, discreit.]
discus = [tesc], W. 3. dyscyl disgyl (discus, lanx). [W. 1. discl.]
divinator=Arm. diuiner.
doctus=W. 3. doeth (prudens), pl. 2. doythion (sapientes), 3. doethon (docti). Also Arm. doetaf(fallo)?
dolor=W. 3. dolur.
[dominica (dies), domnach.]
draco=[drac], W. 3. dreic, pl. dreigeu.
dubitare=Arm. douetaf; douet (dubius); doetanc (dubitantia).
(?) durus=[dúr], W. 1. dur (dirus), 3. dyrys (durus).
ecclesia=dat. abl. aeclis, gen. ecolso ecilse, etc.; W. 3. eccluis, 3. eglwys, V.P. eglos, Arm. ylis.
eleemosyna=almsan., acc. almsin (erro-

neously given as a nominative at p. 59).
elephantus=W. 3. *eliffeint*, V. *oliphans*.
emendare: W. 2. *emendassant* (emendarunt).
episcopus=*epscop*, V. *escop*, pl. W. 2. *epscip*, 3. *escyb*; archiepiscopus=V. *archescop*, Arm. *archescob*, pl. W. 3. *archescyb*.
epistola=*epistil*.
eremita=V. *ermit*.
esculus: *escal-chaill* (esculetum).
(?) esox=[*iach*], W. 3. *ehawc*, V. *ehoc*; the Latin was perhaps borrowed from the Celtic).
French. *estonner*, étonner=Arm. *estonaff*.
etymolog-ia=*ethemlag-as*.
excommunicatus=W. 2. *yskumunetic*, according to Z. also=*eskemun*; 3. *ysgymunn* (maledictus).
evangelium=V. *geaweil*, Arm. *auiel?*
faba=*seib*, (cf. frenum, flagellum).
facies, Engl. face=P. *feth fyth*.
fagus=W. 3. *ffa, ffa-wyd*. [O. Ir. *fagde*, faginus, Z. 765.]
[falco=V. *falhun*, Arm. *falc'houn*.]
fallere: P. *fall* (defectus), *fyll* (deest), *fallens* (deficiunt, peccant), Arm. *fall* (malus), V. *guin fellet* (acetum, i. e. vinum corruptum).
favere (faustus): V. *fodic* (felix).
femininum=*femin*.
fenestra=V. *fenester*. [Mid. Ir. *sinistir*.]
fibula=W. 1. *fual*.
ficus=V. *fic-bren*; O. Gaedh. *ficuldae* (ficulnus).
fides=P. *feth fyth*, Arm. *fez feiz*.
figura=*ind-figor* (figuratio).
finis=W. 2. *fin*, P. *fin-weth*, Arm. *fin-uez*; finire=Arm. *finissaf* (Romance, finisco).
firmamentum=[M. I. *firmamint*.], V. *firmament*.
flagellum=*srogell*, W. 3. *ffrowyll*.
flamma=W. 3. *fflam* f., V. *flam*.
[flecto, *slechtaim*.]
foeniculum = V. *fenochel*. [W. 3. *ffenigl*.]
M. Lat. follis (cf. Diez-Wörterbuch, where, however, the perfectly analogous German *Windbeutel* is forgotten)=W. 3. *ffol*, V. *fol*, P. *fol foll*, Arm. *foll* (stultus).
M. Lat. fontana=W. 2. *finnaun* f., 3. *ffynnawn*; V. *funten*; P. *fynten fynteon*; Arm. *feunteun feunten*, pl. *feuntenyou*.
M. Lat. forestis foresta=W. 3. *fforest* m., Arm. *forest*.
forma=V. *furf*. [W. 3. *ffurf*.]

fossa=W. 2. Arm. *fos, foss*.
fragrare (with dissimilation): V. *flair* (odor), Arm. *flerius* (foetidus).
frenum=*srían*, W. 1. *fruinn*, 2. *fruyn*, 3. *ffrwyn*.
fructus=Arm. *fruez*; W. 3. *diffrwyth* (sine fructu).
fugere=W. 3. *ffo*; P. *fo* (fuga).—V. *fadic* (profugus).
fulgur, French foudre=Arm. *foultr*.
funis=W. 1. pl. *funiou* (vittae), 2. pl. *funenneu* (ligamenta).
fur=V. *fur* (sollers, prudens), Arm. *fur* (sapiens).
furca=W. 3. *fforch*.
furnus=V. *forn* (clibanus). [O. Ir. *surnn*.]
fustis=W. 3. *ffust* (flagellum); *ffustawd* (pulsavit). [*suist*.]
geminantur=*emnatar*.
gentes=*genti geinti* (m. as in French); *gentlide* (gentilis); gen. f. *geintlecte* (gentilitatis) 1059.
genitivus=*genitiu* f.
[gens, pl. *geinti*; gentilis, *geintlide*.]
gerundium=*gerind*.
[glossa, *gluais*.]
[gradale, Mid. Ir., *gredáil*.]
gradus=*grád* n. (gen. *gráid*), V. *grat*.
γράφω: W. 2. *gref* (liber, chirographum), W. 1. *grefiat* (notarius).
gratia=P. *gras*.
[gratias agimus, *grazacham*.]
gravari=P. *grevye*.
gravis (accentus)=*graif*.
M. Lat. gridare (quiritare)=W. 3. *gryd* (clamor), *grydiaw* (**vociferari**), *griduan* (vociferatio).
[habilis, W. 3. *abl*.]
haeresis = acc. *innerese*; haeretici= *heritic* pl.
[Med. Lat. hanapus=V. *hanaf*.]
(Fr. haster, hâter=Arm. *hastomp*, festinemus).
[hastula, *asdul*.]
[historia, Mid. Ir. *sdair*.]
[honor, *onóir*.]
(? hora=*uar*, P. or, W. *awr*?)
hospes=W. 3. pl. *ysp*.
humilis=[*umal*], V. *huuel*; humilitas= (*h*)*umaldóit* (*h*)*omaldóit*, V. *huueldot*.
[hymnus, *ymun*.]
idolum=*idol* m.
[idus, *id*.]
[imago, V. *auain*.]
(impedicare?) Fr. empêcher = Arm. *ampeig* (impedimentum).
imperator=W. 3. *amherawdyr*, f. *amherodres*; V. *emperur*, f. *emperiz*; W. 3. *amherodraeth* f. (imperium).

incensum (cf. Fr. encens)=V. *encois* (thus), *incoislester* (thuribulum).
infamis=Arm. *ifam.*
infernum=*ifurnn,* gen. *ifirnn;* W. 2. *ufern,* 3. *uffern,* P. *yffurn yffbrn.*
infinitivus=*infinit.*
[initium, *init,* W. *ynyd,* "Shrovetide".]
[instrumentum, Mid. Ir. *instrumint.*]
[interjectio, *interiecht.*]
interrare=Arm. *enterraf.*
[? jejunium, *aine.*]
judex: *iüg-suide* (tribunal).
[jusculum=V. *iskel.*]
justitia=Arm. *iustice.*
[kalendar, *calann.*]
laicus=[*laech*],V.*leic,* pl. W. 2. *lleycyon.* [W. 1. *leeces,* gl. maritae.]
[latex=V. *lad.*]
latro=V. *lader;* P. *lader ladar,* pl. *ladron laddron;* W. 3. *lleidr lleidyr.*
[lector, *legtoir.*]
[lectus, *lecht.*]
legalitas=Arm. *lealtet.*
legere=*legend; airlech* (recita), *inroleg* (num legit?) etc.
legio : W. 3. *kaer-llion* (castra legionum).
leo=W. 3. *llew,* V. *leu.*
liber=*libur lebor,* V. *liuer;* pl. P. *luffrow,* Arm. *leiffrion.*
[ligo, W. 1., pl. *liuou.*]
lilium=V. *lilie.*
(?) linum=*lin* (rete), K. *lin* (linum).
liquida=*lechdach.*
littera (not litera)=*liter;* W. 3. *llythyr-en,* V. *lither-en* (singulative).
loculus=V. *logel.*
locus=*loc,* Arm. *lech,* W. 3. *lle* (in no case primitively related, as the O. Lat. *stlocus* shows).
[locusta=V. *legest,* W. 3. *llegest* 'lobster'.]
longa (syllaba)=*loing.*
(navis) longa=W. 3 *llong* f. (navis), pl. 2. *loggeu loggou,* 3. *llongeu;* W. 3. *llyghes llynghes* (classis); O. Gaedh. [*long*], *forlongis*(navigatione),Z.1129.
[lorica, *lüirech.*]
lucerna = *lúacharnn,* V. *lugarn.* [W. *llygorn.*]
lunaris=*lúnáir.*
magister=nom. pl. *magistir,* acc. pl. *magistru;* V. *maister,* P. Arm. *mester.*
(?) major=[*máer, mór-máer*],W. 1. 2. V. *mair,* W. 3. *maer.*
maledicis = *maldachae;* maledictio = *maldacht;* maledic = Arm. *millic;* maledictus=W. 2. *melldicetic.*
malitia : Arm. *dimalice, dinalice.*
[malva=V. *malou.*]

[mancus=V. *mans* (leg. manc?), Arm. *manc.*]
manere ; Arm. *manen* (manebam).
[manna, *mainn.*]
[mantellum=*matal,* V. *mantel.*]
[manus, *man.*]
margaritae=W. 3. *mererit.*
martulus (martellus)=W. 1. *morthol* (seta), 3. *myrthw* (malleus).
martyrium=*martre* f. pl. *martri;* Arm. *martir.*
masculinum=*mascul.*
medicus=V. *medhec,* W. 3. *medic;* W. 2. *medheeynyaet* f.=V. *medhecnaid* (medicina); W. 3. *medeginyaethu* (mederi).
membra=*membur,* pl.
memoria=*mebuir.*
mendicus : *mindechu mindchichthiu* (tenuior, properly mendicior), *mindchigitir* (emendicant).
mensa=[*mias*], V. *muis,* W. 3. *muys* (?) cf. Goth. *mes,* O.H.G. *mias.*
mensura=Arm. *musnr,*(cf.W. 1. *dognomisuram?* Z. 1076).
meretrix—*mertrech, meirddrech.*
metrum : gen. *metair metir.*—W. 3. *metrut* (cogitabas).
miles = *mil,* W. 3. *miluor;* militia *mille.*
(?)mille=*mile* f., K. *mil* (from *milia?*).
[millefolium, V. *minfel.*]
ministrare: Arm. *ministren* (ministrem), V. *menistror* (pincerna).
(minus facere Diez) Fr. mesfaire, méfaire : Arm. *mesfectouryen* (malefactores).
M. Lat. mirare: Arm. *mir* (serva), *miro* (videbit), *miret*=P. *meras* (servare, videre).
mirus: P. *marth* (miraculum); Arm. *maruaill* (mirabile)=Fr. merveille.
modus=*mod* (gen. *muid,* dat. *mud*).
(?)molina=*mulenn* (pistrinum), K. *melin,* pl. W. 3. *melinen.*
monachus=[Old Ir. and] V. *manach,* pl. W. 2. *menich;* f. W. 3. *manaches,* V. *manaes.*
monasterium=gen. pl. *monistre.*
moralis : dat. *moral-us* (praecepto).
[morticinium, *muirtchenn.*]
morus=V. *moyr-bren.*
[Med. Lat. multo=*molt* V. *mols.*]
(?)mulus=acc. pl. *mulu.*
murus=[*múr*], W. 3. *mur,* pl. *muroed.*
muta=*múṫ;* mutus=W. 3. *mut.*
myrias=W. 3. *myrd.*
myrtus = *mirt-chaill* (myrtetum).
natalicia=W. 2. *nodolyc,* 3. *nadolic* (nativitas). [O. Ir., *notlaic.*]

[nates, nát.]
natio=Arm. *nation.*
negotium=W. 3. *neges* f.
neutrum=*neutor, neutrálde.*
[nimbus, *nimb.*]
nota=*not* pl. 1011, *nota,* 1016; notarius=*notaire notire,* Arm. *noter.*
[novellus, W. 1. *nouel.*]
numerus=W. 1. *nimer,* W. 3. Arm. *niuer nifer,* P. *nevor.*
(? nuptiæ: W. 3. *neithawr*?).
obediens=Arm. *obediant.*
[oblatio, *oblann.*]
offerre: W. 2. *ofrum,* Arm. *oferen,* pl. *offerennou* (oblatio). [*oiffrenn.*]
olea: *ola-chrann* (oliva), *ola-chaill* (olivetum); V. *oleu-bren* (oliva),—oleum =W. 1. V. *oleu.*
[operarius, V. *oberor.*]
optativus=*optait optit.*
opus [opera?]=*obar*? (*saibes inobar,* gl. inanem fallaciam Z. 1040) usually *oipred,* gen. *oipretho*; P. *ober*; Arm. *ober auber,* pl. *obercu euffrou*; P. *oberor* (operarius); V. *drochoberor* (maleficus).
oraculum: [*airecal*], *oirclech* (flamen=oraculicus).
[orate, *orait,* W. 1. *araut.*]
[oratio, acc. s. *orthain.*]
ordo=*ord ordd ort urt,* Arm. *urz*; ordino=*oirdnimm*; Arm. *ordren* (ordinatio), *ordrenhat* (ordinare).
[ostiarius, *oistreoir.*]
ostreum=V. *estren.* [W. 3. *histr,* Arm. *histren.*]
[paganus, *pagán.*]
pagus=P. *pow,* O. Armoric (of the year 833) *pou.* [W. *pau.*]
[pallium, *caille,* W. 3. *pall.*]
[palma=V. W. 3. *palf.*]
palus=W. 3. *pawl,* pl. *polyon.*
(palus) M. Lat. padulis (?)=W. 2. *pull* (fossa, lacana), V. *pol* (puteus); W. 3. *pyllawc* (lacunosus, paluster).
[panis, *páin.*]
papa=*papa,* W. 2. *pap,* pl. *papeu.*
papilio=*pupall,* W. 3. *pebyll* (tentorium, Fr. pavillon).
[papyrus, *paiper.*]
paradisus = [*partus*], Arm. *paradis, paradoes.*
parare=W. 3. *peri* (facere, jubere)?
paries=V. *poruit* (*ui*=*é* instead of *ĕ* as in the French paroi).
[parochia, *pairche,* Mid. Ir. *fairche.*]
pars=W. 1. *part parth pard* f., P. *parth,* Armoric *parz perz.* [Irish *pairt.*]
pascha=W. 2. 3. *pasc,* O. Gaedh. acc. *caisc.* f.

[passio, *pais.*]
patella=[W. 1. *patel,*] W. 2. *padell* f., V. *padel-hoern* ("sartago") i. e. patella ferrea.
pauper=Arm. pl. *peoryen.*
pausa (?)=W. 1. Arm. *poues* (quies), P. *powesough* (quescite); but W. 2. *poguis-ma,* etc. (a place of rest).
pavo=W. 3. *pawin,* V. *paun.*
pax=Arm. *peuch.*
peccatum=*peccad* m., W. 3. *pechaut,* Arm. *pechet,* pl. *pechedou.*
pedester=W. 3. *pedestyr* (pedes).
[πέλεκυς, W. 1. *pelechi* gl. *clavae.*]
[pelliceus, *pellec.*]
pensus (Romance *pêso*)=[*píss*], W. 3. *pwys,* P. *poys* (gravis, ponderosus).
[pentecoste, *cingcidis.*]
penultima=*peneult.*
peregrinus = V. *pirgirin.* [W. 3. *pererin.*]
perfectus, Fr. parfait: Arm. *parfetaff* (perficere).
[pergaminum, V. *parchemin.*]
persona=*persan,* W. 3. *person.*
petere=P. *pesy,* Arm. *pidif pidiff*; Arm. *peden,* pl. *pedennou* (oratio precatio); P. pl. *pesadow*—appetere, =Arm. *appetaff.*
phiala=W. 3. *ffiol,* V. *fiol.*
philosophus=*felsub*; philosophia=*fellsube.*
pethedic (minutus) W. 3. appears to be from the same stem as French petit; its *th* points back to *tt* or *ct.* [Ir. *pit,* W. *peth.*]
[pinnaculum, *penakyll,* P.]
pinus=V. *pin-bren.*
piper: [*scipar.*], W. 3. *pebreid, pybreid* (piperosus).
pirus=V. *per-bren.*
[piscis=V. *pisc,* W. 3. *pysg.*]
[piscator=V. *piscadur,* W. 3. *pysgadwr.*]
[plaga, *plag.*]
plangere (properly planctare) = P. *plentye* (accusare).
plenus: Arm. *plen* (omnino).
plebs=O. Arm. (year 862) *ploi plue, plueu*; Sp. *ploe ploue,* pl. *ploueou*; V. *plui* (vicus, parochia); Arm. *plocys* (plebani).
(?) plicare=W. 3. *plycca*; Arm. *pligadur* (voluntas, beneplacitum).
pluma=[*clúm*], V. *pluuen* (penna); W. 1. *plumauc,* V. *plufoc* (pulvinar)
poena=*pén pían*; Arm. *poan* (angustia), pl. *poanyou*; P. *peynys* (dolores).—Arm. *penedour* (afflictione gravatus), W. 3. *penydyaw* (poenitere), O. Gaedh. *pennit* (poenitentia).

pommaille (Fr.)=Arm. *pomell.*
pondo=W. 1. *punt* m.
pons=W. 2. *pont*, V. *pons.*
populus=*popul*,V.*popel, pobel*,P.*pobyll.*
(?) porcellus=W. 3. *parchell*, V. *porchel.* [Ir. *orc=porcus.*]
porta, portus=*port* m. (domus), Beitr. I. 334; W. P. *porth* m. pl. W. 3. *pyrth*, P. *porthow* (porta).
portare=W. 3. *porthi* (perferre), *porthes*; P. *porthas* (nutrivit); Arm. 2. *porz* (quaere, adjuva), *porzit* (subvenite, sublevate); W. 3.*porthant* (provisio, nutritio), *porthmon* (hospes, caupo).
positivus=*posit.*
postilena=W. 1. *postoloin.*
postis=W. 2. *post* (columna).
praebendarius=V. *prounder.* [pl. *pronteryon* P.]
praeceptum=*precept* f.; *praeceptor=preceptóir.*
praedico = *predchim, predach, predag*; Arm. *prezec* (praedicare).
praelatus=[*prelait*], Arm. *prelat.*
praeservare: Arm. *preservo* (praeservet).
praestare: Arm. *prestis* (praestitit).
prandium=*proind* (prandere).
[presbyter, *cruimther*?]
pretiare: P. *praysys* (celebratus).
primus=*prim*, W. 3. *prif-.*
princeps=P. *prins, pryns*, pl. *princis.*
[prior, Mid. Ir., ban-*prioir.*]
prison (French): Arm. *diprisonet* (excarceratus).
probus: *amprom* (improbus), *amprome* (improbitas), *rondpromsom* (q. id probavit ipse), *promfidir* (probabitur); Arm. *proffe, prouffe* (probaret); P. *previs, prefis* (probatus).
[prologus, *proluch.*]
pronomen=*pronomen* n.
[propositus, *propost.*]
propheta=V. *profuit*, pl. P. *profusy.*
prudens=W. 3. *prud.*
psalmus=*salm*, pl. *sailm*, acc. *salmu*; psalterium=dat.*saltir*, Arm.*psaulter.*
[psalterium, *saltair*, gen. *saltrach.*]
[purgatorium, *purgatoir.*]
purpura=*corcur*, W. 2. *porffor.*
purus=[*púr*], W. 3.*pur, purdu, purgoch, purwynn.*
putana (Rom.)=W. 3. *putein.*
(?) puteus=*cute*, Beitr.I. 334 (strikingly reminds us of the Low German *kaute*, *kute*, a pit).
[quadragesima, *corgais*, W. *grawys.*]
[questio, *ceist.*]
[quinquagesima, *cingices.*]
[rastrum, *rastal*, W. 1. *rascl.*]

recommendare(Fr.)=Arm. *recommant.*
? regnare=Arm. *renaff*—but compare Arm. *roen* (rex)—?
regula=*riagul, riagol*; Arm. *reol.*
[reliquiae, *reilic.*]
remus=*rám* (cf. Fr. rame), V. *ruif.*
rendere for reddere (Rom.): Arm. *rento* (reddet).
rete=V.*ruid*, Arm. *roed.* [W. 3. *rhwyd.*]
rosa: *ros-chaill, ros-tán* (rosetum), *rostae* (rosarium).
[ruta, V. *rute.*]
[sabbatum, *saboit*, pl. *saputi.*]
sacerdos=*sacardd.*
[sacrificium, *sacorbaic.*]
sacrilegium=Arm. *sacrileig.*
saccus=[*sacc*], V. *sach.*
[sacculum, *saigul.*]
[saliva, W. *haliw*, O. Ir. *saile.*]
[salicastrum, *sailestar*, W. *elestr.*]
saltus=*salt*, gen. *salto* (astronom.).
salutare=Arm. *saludomp* (salutemus).
salvare. Fr. sauver (with the old diphthongal Norman pronunciation, see Diez. Rom. Gramm. I^2, 425)=P. *saw* (salva), *sawye* (salvabat), *sawye* (salvatus).
sanctus=[*sancht*], W. Arm. *sant*, pl. W. 2. 3. *seint*, Arm. *sent.*
[Med. Lat., *sappetus*, V. *sibuit.*]
scabellum=V. *scauel.*
scala=W. 3. *yscawl*, pl. *ysgolyon.*
(?) scandere=W. 3. *yscynnu*; W. 2. *eskenho, eskynho* (scanderit).
schola=[*scol*, gen. *scule*], V. *scol*; V. scolheic=W. 3. *yscolheic* (scholasticus), pl. W. 2. *escoleycyon*, pl. *yscoleigyon*; W. 2. *escolectaut* (status scholaris).
sciens: V. *skientoc*; P. *skentyll, skyntyll* (sapiens); Arm. *squient* (spiritus, intelligentia); V. *diskient* (insipiens), *guan ascient* ("energuminus").
scribere=*scríbend*; V. *scriuit, scrinen* (scriptura), *scriuiniat* (scriptor); P. *screfe* (scribere).
scrinium=*scrín* m.
scripulus=W. 1. *scribl*; O. Gaedh. *lethscripul* (dimidio scripulo).
scutella=V. *scudel*, P. *scudell* (discus, lanx).
[sebum, V. *suif*, W. 3. *swyf*, Arm. *soav.*]
securus=P. *sur.*
senator=*senatóir.*
[senior, *seinser.*]
sensus=*sens*, dat. pl. *siansib.*
sepelire=Arm. *sebeliaf.* [sepultura, *sabaltair.*]
(? septimana = *sechtmaine*). [V. *seithum.*]

[septuaginta, *septien.*]
sermonarius=Arm. *sarmoner.*
[serus, W. *hwyr.*]
sextarius=W. 1. *hestaur*, pl. *hestoriou*, 3. *hestawr* f., (the *h* in the loan word is remarkable).
[Med. Lat. sicera, V. *sicer.*]
signum=[*sén*], Arm. *sin.*
[situla, [Mid. Ir. *sitheal.*]
solarium=[Mid. Ir. *soiler*,] V. *soler.*
solitarius=Arm. *soliter.*
[Med. Lat. solta, V.*sols*, W. *swllt*, Fr. *sou.*]
(somniari) Fr. *songer*=Arm. *soingéf* (credo).
[sophista, Mid. Ir. *soifist.*]
(sors) Fr. sorte=Arm. *sceurt*, i.e. *sört* (modus).
soutenir (Fr.)=Arm. *soutenet* (sustentatus).
spatium=W. 3. *yspeit.*
sperare: Arm. *esper* (spes).
[spina, Mid. Ir. *spín.*]
[spiraculum, *spiracul.*]
spiritus=*spirut*, V. *spirit*, Arm. *speret.*
spoliare=W. 3. *yspeilaw; dispeilaw* (denudare, gladium).
[spongia, *songe.*]
[sponsa, Mid. Ir. *písta*, W. *pwys, yspwys.*]
stabulum=[W. 1. *stebill*, pl.], W. 3. *ystabyl.*—V. *steuel*, W. 2. *estauell*, 3. *ystauell* f. (triclinium, cubiculum) appears to belong also to this place; but compare also Fr. *estaminet.*
stagnum=*stán.*
[stannum, Mid. Ir. *stanamhail.*]
status=Arm. *stat.*
stendardo (Romance), W. 3. *ystondard* f.
stimulus=W. 1. *sumpl.*
stola=V. *stol.*
stragulum=V. *strail* (tapeta), *strail elester* (matta).
strata=W. 2. *strat istrat*, 3. *ystrat* (vallis aperta, planities).
stratura (M. Lat)=[*srathar*], W. 1. *strotur.* (stravi=W. 1. *strouis?*).
strigilis=V. *streil.*
superlativus = *superlait superlit*, pl. *superlati.*
syllaba=*sillab.*
synodus=[Mid. Ir. *senadh*], V. *sened.*
tabellarius=*tablaire.*
[taberna, Mid. Ir. *taibherne.*]
[tabes, *tám.*]
talentum=*talland* (facultas, ingenium, Fr. talent).
tardare=Arm. *tardomp* (tardemus), *tardet* (tardate).
[tellus, *telluir*, gen. *tellrach.*]

tempero=W. 1. *temperam* (condio).
templum=*tempul*, Arm. P. *tempel.* [W. 3. *teml.*]
temptare=P. *temptye.*
(?) tendere=W. 3. *tynnu*; Arm. *emtennet* (se recipere), *teniff* (pergam); P. *tensons* (tetenderunt).
terminus=P. *termyn* (terminus, tempus).
[tertia (hora), *teirt.*]
testis=*test*, V. *tist*, Arm. *test*, pl. W. 2. *testion*; testimonium=*testimin*, V. *tistuin*, P. *tustunny*; W. 2. *testu* (testari).
[theca, *tíach.*]
[theoria, *teoir.*]
[thesis, *teis.*]
thronus=Arm. *tron.*
thus: *tus-lestar* (turibulum).
[Titan, Mid. Ir. *tital.*]
titulus=*titul titol*, acc. pl. *titlu.*
[Fr. tonneau, V. *tonnel.*]
torneamentum (M. Lat.)=W. 3. *turneimeint.*
torques=*muin-torc*, W. 3. *torch.*
torta=[*tort*], W. 1. 3. *torth* (panis).
tractus=[*tracht*], W. 3 *traeth* (sabulum maris), V. *trait* (arena).
[totus, *tot-mael* gl. Totus Calvus.]
traditio (Fr. trahison)=P. *treason.*
tribunus: *trebun-suide* (tribunal).
trinitas=*trudóit*, [W. 1. *trintaut*], Arm. *trindet.*
[tripus, W. 3. *tribedd*, V. *tribet.*]
tristis: [W. 1. *trist*, P. *trest*], W. 3. *tristit tristyt tristwch* (tristitia), *tristau* (tristem esse).
tructa=V. *trud.*
[truncus, W. 3. *truch*, V. *trech.*]
(?) tuba=gen. *tuib.*
[tunica, *tuinech.*]
(?) turba=W. 3. *twryf twrwf.*
turris=[*tuir*], W. *twr.* m., pl. 3. *tyreu*, *tyroed*, V. *tur.*
[tympanum, *timpan.*]
ultima=*ult*, acc. *uilt.*
uncia = *ungae unga* (see above: *atomum*).
unguere, unctare=P. *untye.*
[unicornis V. *uncorn.*]
ursus=V. *ors.*
(?) vagina=[*faigen*], W. 3. *gwain*, V. *guein*, P. *goyn.*
velum=*fial* (velamen), [V. *guil.*]
venenum=W. 3. *gwennwyn; gwenwynic* (venenosus), V. *guenoinreiat* (veneficus).
[versatile? Mid. Ir. *fersaid*, W. 3. *gwerthyd.*]
versus=*fers*, gen. *fersa ferso.*
? verus=*fír*, V. Arm. *guir*, W. 3. *gwir*, P. *gwyr.-?*

vetus: *fetar-laice fetarlíce fetarlícce* (vetustas).
[? vidua = *fedb*, V. *guedeu*, W. 3. *gweddw*.]
[vigil, *figil*.]
villani=W. 2. pl. *byleynyeyt*.
[vinea, *fine*.]
vinum=*fín fínn*, K. *guin*.

viperae=W. 3. pl. *gwiberot*.
virtus=P. *vertu*; O. Gaedh. gen. *ferto ferte*, nom. pl. *ferte*, acc. *firtu* (virtus, prodigium).
[visio, *fis*.]
vitium=Arm. *vicc*, (Fr. vice).
[vocula, *focul*.]

To these are to be added a number of French words in the Armoric. Even from this list, which would, of course, be greatly enlarged if we were to include the more modern words, and in which, no doubt, many old loan-words are certainly only accidentally wanting, we can see what numerous borrowings took place already in ancient times, from the Latin, Middle Latin, and Romance. And even though the borrowing be doubtful in the case of some words (certainly not many), nevertheless the majority of the apparently exclusive correspondences of Celtic and Latin have been thereby removed.

The Latin has taken other words from the Gaulish, partly already in the classical period; and later also from the British (as *covinus*); in any case, however, their number is not very great; in regard to some of them there exist, too, doubts, which at present we are unable to solve. Those are especially important, which, although taken at a late period, have nevertheless passed into the Romance languages (as *vertragus*=It., *veltro*, etc., from this again V. *guilter*, molossus); but for our present object we may here fitly pass over these.

§. 2. *Glossarial affinities of the Celtic and Classic languages.*

The Celtic has about the following words and roots, in common exclusively with one or both of the classical languages (or at all events, with such peculiarities of form or meaning as only recur in them).

WORDS AND ROOTS EXCLUSIVELY COMMON TO THE CELTIC AND CLASSIC LANGUAGES.

aér díar m., W. 3. *awyr*=ἀήρ, aura (or derived from *aër* perhaps itself borrowed?)

ag (root): *atomaig* (impellit me)=Lat. *adigit*;—ἄγω, ago.

ailïgim (muto)=ἀλλάσσω.

ainm, W. 3. enw, P. (h)anow, Arm. *hanu*=ὄνομα (in the form).

[*alt*=Lat. artus.]
W. 3. *alarch* m., V. *elerhc*=Lat. olor?

anim, V. Arm. *enef* = Lat. anima (Zeitschr. VI. 213).

[*arba* (read *arva*), W. 3. *erw*, V. *erv*, *ereu*=Lat. arvum.]

ardd=Lat. arduus (Gr. ὀρθός appears to have been Fορθός), not a loan-word as the Gaulish *Arduenna* ("heights", *Cebenna* "ridges") shows.

as (*a*, *es*)=ἐξ, ex.

V. *auhel*, Arm. *auel* (aura), W. 3. *awel* (flatus).—V. *anauhel* (procella), =ἄελλα?

V. W. 3. *auon* f. (flumen), pl. W. 3. *auonyd*=Lat. amnis?

[*ball*=φαλλός.]

V. *ber*, W. 3. *bereu* (veru)—O. Gaedh. *berach*, *birdae* ("verutus")—=Lat. veru (Umbr. berva, berus?).

? *bethe* ("buxus"), [W. *bedeu*], V. *bedeven* ("populus") = *betula betulla*? (according to Pliny, Gaulish).
*bou; O. Gaedh. *bóchaill*, V. *bugel* (bubulcus, pastor), W. 1. *boutig* (stabulum); also W. 1 and 2. V. *buch* (vacca)?=βοῦς, *bos* (in the form; the other languages preserve the guttural).
V. Arm. *brech*, W. 3. *breich*=*brachium*, βραχίων.
[*buide* 'yellow'=*badius*, Fr. *bai* bay.]
can (root): W. 3. *kanu*, P. *cane* (canere), W. 3. *datkanu* (recitare, revelare), O. Gaedh. *forchun forcanim forchanim* (praecipio), *foircthe* (eruditus), *forcital forcetal* (doctrina), *forcitl*(*a*)*id forcetlid* (praeceptor), *tercital* (vaticinium), *doaurchanaim* (sagio), *cétlaid* (cantor), also *cél* (augurium)[84] and gen. *ciuil* (instrumenti musici)?; —V. *cheniat* (cantor), *canores* (cantrix),—Lat. *cano*.
W. *cann*, V. *can* (albus)=Lat. *candidus* (cf. the loan-words under candela).
car (root) (widely ramified in both languages, no doubt also the source of the, so far as I know, exclusively French form *chérir*)—Lat. *carus*? W. 3. *karw*, V. *caruu*=Lat. *cervus* (if it be not borrowed?—the O.H.G. *hiruz* shows another suffix).
cathir (civitas), K. *cair caer* (oppidum) =Lat. *castrum*?[85] (compare as to the phonetic relations *sethar siur*, W. 3. *chwior*=Goth. *svistar*).
claideb, W. 2. *cledif*, 3. *cledyf*, Arm. *clezef*, P. *clethe* (fundamental form *cladibas)=Lat. *gladius*.
clói, W. 2. *cloeu* pl.=Lat. *clavi*. [a loan-word?]
cnám (os)=κνήμη?
corp, K. *corf*=Lat. *corpus*. [a loan-word?]
cos (pes)=Lat. *coxa*? [*costa*?]
cretim (rel. *cretes crettes creites*, pl. *cretite*), W. 3. *cret* (fides), Arm. *cridif* =Lat. *credo*, (see Stokes Beitr. I. 458). [loan word.]
[*cruitr* W. 1. V.], V. *croider* (perhaps also O. Gaedh. *criathar*, gl. cerebrum?)=Lat. *cribrum*.
W. 3. *cwydaw*, P. *cothe*=Lat. *cadere*? (in the form rather=*cédere*).
cúl (tergum)=Lat. *culus*.

di, W. 1. Arm. *di*, P. *the*, W. 3. *y*= Lat. *de*.
du- (*do*-)=δυς-, Skr. *dus*-.
[W. 3. *ffer*=σφυρόν.]
[*fí*=Lat. virus, ἰός, Skr. *visha*.]
V. *gurah*, W. 3. *gwrach* (anus)—γραῦς?
[*ibim*, Lat. *bibo*, Vedic *pibámi*.]
inis gen. *inse*, W. 2. *inis*, 3. *ynys* f., Arm. *enes*=Lat. *insula*? (if perhaps this be a diminutive formation, not as Pott would make it=εἴναλος).
itir etir etar, P. *intre yntre*, Arm. *entre* (foreign to the Welsh)=Lat. *inter*. [Skr. *antar*.]
ith gen. *etha* (frumentum), V. *yd* seges); Lat. *ador* (interchange between *d* and *t* in *ithim* likewise).
V. *yorch* (caprea)= ζόρξ, δόρξ?
W. 3. *keissaw* (instead of *kessiaw, *kassiau) scarcely=Lat. *quaerere*? (Gaulish λαγκία Diod. Sic. V. 30. probably an erroneous supposition, otherwise=*lancea*, λόγχη).
[*lacht*], V. *lait* (*lac*), W. 1. *laidver* ("lacocula"), W. 2. *laethauc* (lac praebens)=Lat. *lac*.
*leïc (sine), *leïcci* (sinit); general, but in the form exactly=*linquit*.
liac, W. 3. *llech* f.; *lapis*, λίθος, λάιγξ?
lobur [W. *llwfr*] (infirmus); Lat. *labor*, *labo*, *labes*?
loth gen. *loithe* (palus, coenum), W. 3. *lludedic* (coenosus); Gaul. *Luteva*, *Lutetia*—Lat. *lutum*.
matin, V. *metin*, W. 3. *yr meitin* (mane) —Lat. *matutinus* (borrowed?).
[*mil*], V. *mel*=*mel*, μέλι.
midiur-sa (puto), W. 3. *medwl medol* (cogitatio), *medylyaw* (cogitare)— μέδομαι, meditor.
W. 3. *mynyd*, V. *menit*, P. *meneth*= Lat. *mons*; emineo?
naue (gen.), *noe*=*navis*, ναῦς. [Skr. *náv*, *náu*.]
nezaff Arm. (*z*=*dh*)=νήθειν, νέειν, *nere*?
nert, K. *nerth* (virtus); ἀνήρ, Osc. Umbr. *ner*, Sab. Lat. *nerio*, *Nero*.
W. 2. 3. *oet*. (aetas), 3. *hoedel hoedyl* (vita), *oetawc oedawc* (aetate provectus)=Lat. *aetas*? (*v* could have dropped out as well in Celtic as in Latin, but compare also the still unexplained *ui*, *oe* in the verbal substantives).
[*saiget*], W. 3 *saeth*, P. *seth*=Lat. *sagitta* [borrowed?]

---

[84] [Compare with this rather Old Norse *heill*, omen.]
[85] [*Castrum* is probably for *cad-trum*, and cannot be connected with *cathair*, gen. *cathrach*=an Old Celtic *catarax, cfr. *cataracton*.]

sái=Lat. sagum.
*saillim=ἄλλομαι, salio (Goth. salta a different form).
samail samal (similitudo)=*samali; amail amal (=dat. loc. *samali) W. 2. mal, P. avel, Arm. euel (ut); cosmail cosmuil cosmil (=*consumali), W. 3. kyffelyp kyffelyb (consimilis)—Lat. similis.
W. 3. sarff=Skr. sarpa, Lat. serpens (ἑρπετόν).
sciath (O. Arm. scoit-, scoet-)=Lat. scutum? (the vowel is different).
sech (praeter, extra, supra), K. hep heb (sine)=secus, ἑκάς.
W. 2. helic, V. heligen=Lat. salix.

su- [W. he-]=Skr. su-, Gr. εὐ.
tar, W. 2. trus, 3. dros, P. dris drys (Arm. dreist)=Lat. trans, Umbr. tráf.
W. 1. tarater, 2. taradyr=τέρετρον, terebra.
tarvos (Gaulish), O. Gaedh. tarb, W. 2. taru, P. tarow=taurus, ταῦρος(consequently to be separated from Slav. turŭ, O. Norse þior, Goth. stiur).
tir, K. tir (terra) nearest affinity=Osc. tecrúm (possibly Lat. terra).
[uan, W. 3. oen, V. oin=agnus, for avignus, "ewe-born"?]
úrde, W. 3. gwyrd, V. guirt = Lat. viridis.
fáith=Lat. vates (borrowed?).

§. 3. *Glossarial affinities of the Celtic, Classic, Teutonic, and Lito-Slavonian languages.*

Others may no doubt be placed side by side with Latin ones, but are not the less Teutonic, Slavonian, and Lithuanian. The following occur more or less generally, for instance:—

WORDS AND ROOTS COMMON TO THE CELTIC AND CLASSIC LANGUAGES, BUT ALSO FOUND IN THE TEUTONIC, SLAVONIAN, AND LITHUANIAN.

accus ocus (vicinus), comacus (vicinus), comaicsiu f. (vicinia), W. 3. agos, P. ogas (vicinus), W. 2. kauzcus, 3. kyfagos (propinquitas, vicinitas), V. carogos (affinis, consanguineus)—first in the Greek ἐγγύς, ἄγχι, but also Lat. angustus, O.H.G. angi; Slav. ązа jązа, ązŭ vązŭ (vinculum), Lith. anksztas ankszta (N.H.G. enge). The conjunction acus ocus ocuis (et) appears to be a dat. loc., as it has the power of aspirating. From the same root comes octe ochte (necessitudo), compare Lat. angor, angustia, Slav. jęzа (morbus). Interchange between cc and ng occurs elsewhere likewise, e. g. in cumacc, cumang, cumacht.
aile, K. all=alius, ἄλλος, Goth. alis alja- (O.H.G. ali- in some few words, among which may be mentioned elithiotic, as was already observed by Graff = W. 2. alldut, pl. alltudion); in this form (with l) it is wanting in the Slav. and Lith.
ainm (see supra)=Goth. namô, Slav. imę, Prussian emnes.
áis óis, Gen. áisa aisso, óissa óesa (aetas), W. 1. ois (seculum), 3. oes (vita), V. huis (seculum), P. oys (aetas); nearest affinity=Skr. áyus, but then also αἰών, aevum, Goth. aivs, O.H.G. êwa; is wanting in the Slav. and Lith.

ar (root) (arare); general in all European languages.
athir (K. tat, like Gr. τέττα)=pater, πατήρ, Goth. fadar; is wanting in the Slav. and Lith., which again differ from each other.
ben, ban (mulier), V. benen (sponsa), benenrid (femina), benenuat (matrona), P. benyn (mulier), pl benynas=γυνή, Bœot. βάνα, Slav. żena, Goth. qvêns qvinô, O.H G. chona; is wanting in the Latin and Lithuanian (however there is Prus. *ganna).
bar, ber (root), (ferre) general.
bráthair bráthir, W. 1. braut, 3. brawt pl. brodyr, V. braud broder, Arm. pl. breuder = frater, φρητήρ (Zeitschr. VII. 436), Goth. brôþar, Slav. bratrŭ bratŭ, Lith. brôlis.
bou (see supra) = O.H.G. chuo, Slav. goveedo, Lettish gôws.
biu béo (vivus), bethu beothu (vita), beod (vivus), biad (victus, esca), beoigidu (vivificat); W. 3. byw, Arm. beo, P. beu (vivus), V. biu (vita), W. 3. bywyt m., Arm. buez buhez, P. bewnas bennans (vita), Arm. beuaf (vivam), P. bewe (vivere); vivus, βίος, Goth. qvius, Lith. gývas, Slav. zivŭ, etc.
cride n. =καρδία, cor, Goth. hairto, Lith. szirdis, Slav. srŭdĭce.
camm (curvus, obliquus), dat. pl. cammaib, cammderc (strabo), camthuisil

(casus obliqui), W. 2. 3. Arm. V. *cam.* (curvus), V. *camhinsic* (injustus), Gaul. *Camba, Cambodunum,* Μορικάμβη; Gr. κάμπτω, Lith. *kàmpas* a corner, *kùmpas* crooked. [*cnu*, Lat. *nux* for *cnux, hnot*, Eng. *nut.*]
cruim f., V. *prif*, W. 3. *pryf* (vermis)= *vermis*, Goth. *vaurms*, Lith. (*kìrmis*), *kìrmėlė', kìrminas*, Slav. *czrŭvĭ,czrĭvĭ* (but *czrŭmĭnŭ*),—Gr. ἕλμινς?).
cú, K. *ci*=κύων, *canis*, Goth. *hunds*, Lith. *szů* (Slav. *suka, sobaka*).
W. 3. *cudyaw* (abscondere, celare), P. *cuthe*, Arm. *cuzet* (occultare)=κεύθω, further Lat. *cutis*, O.H.G. *hút* f., *hutta* f.
W. 3. *keffyl* (equus vilis)=Lat. *caballus* (καβάλλης probably borrowed), Slav. *kobyla, kobylica, konĭ*, Lith. *kumėlė, kumelùkas*, (*kuìnas*, probably borrowed).
[*dér*], W. 1. *dacr-lon* (uvidus), pl. W. 3. *dagreu*, P. *dagrow* (lacrimae)=δάκρυ, *lacr-ima*, Goth. *tagr*, Lith. *aszarà*; is wanting in Slav.
daur (quercus), *daurauch* (quercetum), *daurde dairde* (quernus), *derucc* (glans), W. 3. V. *dar*, pl. *deri*, Sg. W. 3. *derwen*[86] (quercus); δόρυ, δρῦς, Goth. *triu*, Slav. *drěvo* (arbor), *drŭva* (ligna), Lith. *derva*; is wanting in the Latin. [? Dr. Siegfried compares *laurus* from *daurus*, as *lingua* from *dingua, lacrima* from *dacrima*, etc.]
dam (root) (in the Celtic, with a peculiar application of meaning): *fodaimim-se* (patior, tolero), W. 1. *guodeimisauch* (sustulistis), P. *gotheff gothevell*, Arm. *gouzaf gouzaff* (tolerare) =*domo*, δαμάζω, Goth. *timan, tamjan*.
det, K. *dant* m. (V. *dans*, pl. W. 3. *danned*)=*dens*, ὀδούς, Goth. *tunþus*, O. Norse *tönn*, O.H.G. *zand zan*, Lith. *dantìs*; is wanting in Slav.
dess, W. 2. *dehou*, 3. *deheu*, P. *dyghow*= δεξιός, *dexter*, Goth. *taihsvs*, Slav. *desĭnŭ*; Lith. *deszinė* (dextra).
dia (dies), W. 2. *diu dihu*, 3. *dyw* along with *dyd*, V. *det*, P. *dyth deth*, pl. *dethiow*, Arm. *deiz*, pl. *diziou*=Lat. *dies*, Slav. *dĭnĭ*, Lith. *dėnà*; it is wanting with this meaning in German and Greek.
dia (deus), W. 2. *diu dyu dyuu dyhu duhu duo*, 3. *duw*, V. *dug*, Arm. *doe* —W. 2. *duyuaul* (divinus)=*deus*, θεός (?), Lith. *dėvas*, Lettish *dews*;

is wanting in German and Slavonian. [But cf. O.N. *tivar* "gods".]
dorus, W. 1. [*drus*], *dor*, pl. 3. *doreu*, W. 3. *drws*, V. *darat*=θύρα, *fores*, Goth. *daur daurô*, Lith. *dùrys*, pl. Slav. *dvĭrĭ*.
ech, K. *ep*=*equus*, ἵππος, O. Sax. *ehu*, O. Norse. *iôr*; Lith. *ászva* (equa); is wanting in Slavonian.
W. 3. V. Arm. *elin*, (ulna)=Goth. *aleina*, ὠλένη, Lat. *ulna*; in the Lith. Slav. there is another suffix, where it is not wholly different.
gaim-red, W. 1. *gaem*, 2. 3. *gayaf*, V. *goyf*, Arm. *gouaff*—W. 3. *kynnhaeaf*, V. *kyniaf* (auctumnus, i.e. forewinter) =*hiems*, χιών χειμών, Lith. *žěmà*, Slav. *zima*; is wanting in German.
1, gen (root Skr. *jan*)—in *gigno* (*g*)*nascor*, γίγνομαι, γεννάω, Goth. *kuni*, N.H.G. *kind*, Slav. *zentĭ* (gener), Lith. *gimtì*; appears in Celtic partly with *q: nogigned* (nascebatur), *rogen(a)ir* (natus est), *dogéntar gentar génthir* (fiet), *dogníu* (facio), *foġní* (servit), *gním* (factum), *fognám* (servitus), *congnam* (contributio), *gnéthid* (operarius), *gein* (ortus) Z. 466, gen. *geine* Z. 1043, *geinddae* (genitalis), W. 3. Arm. *ganet*, P. *genys* (natus), W. 2. *guneyr* (fit), 3. *gwnaf*(facio, faciam)=P.*gwraff,graf*, Arm. *groaff graf gruif griff*, etc. ; partly with *c*: *cenél* (natio, gens, genus), *cenélae* (genus), *cenélach* (generalis), *cenaélugud* (generatio)= W. 1. *cenitol* (generatio), *cenitolaidou* (natales), 2. *kenedel*, 3. *kenedl kenedyl* (genus), V. *kinethel* (generatio)= γένεθλον.
2 gen. (root—Skr. *jnâ*)—in γιγνώσκω, (*g*)*nosco*, Goth. *kan*, Lith. *zinàu*, Slav. *znają*; O. Gaedh. *adgén-sa adgeuin* (cognosco), *etargeiuin* (noscit), *gné* (ratio), *aithgne* (sapiens, n. cognitio), *irgnae, etargne, etarcne* (cognitio), *itargninim* (sapio prudentia), *nometargnigedar* (me commemorat).
ithim (mando), *estar* (edit), W. 3. *ryt yssu* (comesum esse); the primitive *d* in W. 2. *keuedac* (comessatio, epulae); the root *ad* is general. (The derivational *ith* (puls), W. 1. *iot* "pulsum" appears to correspond to the Greek εἶδαρ).
W. 3. *ieuanc*, pl. *ieueinc*, V. *iouenc jouonc*, P. *yonk*, sup. W. 2.3. *ieuhaf*, O. Gaedh. *óclachdi* (juvenilia),

---

[86] Erroneously explained in Zeitschr. VII. 211;—*en* is singulativ.

ócmil (tiro) = *juvenis* (juvencus), Goth. *juggs* compar. *juhiza*, Lith. *jáunas*, Slav. *junŭ* (Servian *junak* hero), (Gr. *ἥβη*?).

W. 1. *iou*, V. *ieu*=*jugum*, *ζυγός*, Goth. *juk*, Slav. *igo* (i. e.- *jĭgo* instead of *jŭgo*), Lith. *jungas*.

lagait (parvitas), *laigiu lugu* (minor), *lugimem* (minimam), W. 3. *llei* (minor) —*ἐλάσσων*; Lat. *levis*, Slav. *lĭgŭkŭ*, Lith. *lengvas*, Goth. *leihts*.

lán, W. 3. *llawn*, P. Arm. *len leun* (plenus), O. Gaedh. *láne láine* (impletio), *lanmair* (impleti), *linmaire* (plenitudo) =*plenus*, Slav. *plŭnŭ*, Lith. *pĭlnas*, Goth. *fulls* (i. e. *fulns*), the Greek has only the root, not the same derivatives; Goth. (*fulljan*) and Celtic have verbs derived from it: W. 3. *llanw* (implere), O. Gaedh. *forlán* (abundavit), *rolín* (implevit), *comalnadar* (implet), *línad* (explere).

il, compar. *lia*, etc. See Beitr., I. 340.

leth led (latus, dimidium), = *latus*, *πλάτος*, O.H.G. *blat plat*.

lethan, W. 1. *litan* (latus)—*πλατύς*, Lith. *platùs*, Goth. *braids*.[87]

ligim (lingo)=*λείχω*, *lingo*, Goth. *laigô*, Lith. *laižau*, Slav. *liżą*.

malg (root); Mod. Irish *meilg* milk, old gloss *do omalgg* mulxi, Z. 71; everywhere.

man (root): *rommunus rommúnus* (scio, didici), *domuinur-sa domoiniur domḗnar-sa* (puto, spero), *admuinur* (volo), *ni cuman lim* (nescio) and many derivatives; W. 2. *menoent* (voluerint), 3. *mynych mynnych* (vis, voles), *mynnir*, (placet), P. *mynny* (vis), Arm. *menaf mennaf minif* (volo, posco, cogito), W. 3. *gofyn*, P. *govynny* (interrogare); *memini*, *μέμονα*, Goth. *man*, Slav. *pamęti* (memoria) &c.

mar (root): *marb* (mortuus), W. 2. Arm. *maru* (mori); general (German and Greek only in derivatives).

máthir, suppressed in Kymric by the endearing word *mam* (=*mamma), preserved however in V. *modereb*, W. 1. pl. *modreped* (matertera),=*mater*, *μήτηρ*, O.H.G. *muotar*, Slav. *mati*; Lith. *motė'* (mulier).

medón, W. 2. *meun*, 3. *mywn* (medius, medium): cognate words everywhere even though nowhere with this suffix.

melim (molo), *damil-si* (edis); general (Gr. *μύλη* along with *ἀλέω*).

mí (Beitr. I. 461), [*mistae* menstruus], W. 2. *mis*, 3. *mys*, V. *mis*=*μήν*, Ion. *μείς*, *mensis*, Lith. *mėnŭ* (instead of *ménes*), Slav. *mėsęcĭ*; deviating somewhat Goth. *ména* (luna), *mênôps* (mensis).

muir, K. *mor* (mare); general (Gr. *πλημμυρίς*).

masc (root—otherwise *misc*): *cummasc* gen. *cummisc* (commutatio), *commescatar* (miscentur), V. *commisc*, W. 3. *cymysc* (mixtio), P. *kemeskis*, *kemyskis* (commixtio), Arm. *kemmeski* (misceo); O. Gaedh. *cumsciget* (mutant), *rochumscigther* (immutatum est), *nicumscaichthi* (non mutandum est), do not appear to belong to this root, because of *conosciget* (mutant), *conroscuigissiu* (summevisti), *conoscaige-siu* (admoveto); *misceo*, *μίσγω*, Lith. *maiszýti*, Slav. *mėsiti*, O.H.G. *miscjan*.

in niulu (in nubibus) = *νεφέλη*, *nebula*, O.H.G. *nibul*; Slav. Lith. another suffix, and partly another signification.

noct; O. Gaedh. *innoc(h)t* (hac nocte), [W. 1. *henoid*], K. *nos* (nox); general.

nú, [recte *nua*] *nue nuae*, *núide* (novus, novicius); general in forms which partly correspond to the Skr. *nava*, and partly *navya*.

V. *oin*=Lat. *agnus*, Ch. Slav. *agnica*, *agnĭcĭ jagnĭcĭ*, *agnę jagnę*.

óin óen, K. *un*=Lat. *unus* (O. Lat. *oenos*), Goth. *ains*, Lith. *vėnas*, Lett. *wēns*. [Prus. *ains*.]

V. *palf* f.=*palma*, *παλάμη*, Ang. Sax. O.H.G. *folma*.

W. 3. V. *rud* (ruber); general.

roth=Lat. *rota*, O.H.G. *rad*, Lith. *rátas*.

salann, V. *haloin halein* (sal)=*sal*, *ἄλς*, Slav. *solĭ*; Goth. *salt*.

[*suan*], W. 3. V. Arm. *hun*=*somnus*, *ὕπνος*, Slav. *sŭnŭ* (Lith. *sápnas*, Lett. *sapnis* a dream), O. Norse *svefn*.

sruth (rivus, fluvius, torrens), W. 2. *frut* f., 3. *frwt.*, V. *frot*=Skr. *srótas*; Gr. *ὀέω* (*σρέω*), Slav. *struja struga*, O.H.G. *stroum*, Thracian *Στρύμων*, Lith. *sraumė*.

V. *hveger* (socrus), *hvigeren* (socer)= *ἑκυρός ἑκυρά*, *socer socrus*, Slav. *svekrŭ, svekry svekrŭvĭ*, Goth. *svaihra*, *svaihrô*.

W. 3. *sych* = *siccus* (O.H.G. *biseh*, *bisihan* Graff VI, 133?), Gr. *σαυκός*

---

[87] [Much nearer is Old Norse *flatr*=English *flat*.]

(σαυχμός, σαυσαρός, but also αὐχμός, αὐχμηρός), Lith. *saúsas*, Ch. Slav. *suchŭ*.

sethar siur (also *siar*, *fiar* according to Stokes), W. 3. *chwior*, pl. *chwaer chwioryd*, V. *piur* [*rectè huir*] = Goth. *svistar*, Slav. *sestra*, Lith. *sesŭ'*, Lat. *soror*; it is wanting in Greek, unless perhaps ἔταρος ἑταῖρος belongs to it.

1 *sak* (root—to follow): *sechem* (sequi), *saigim* (adeo), *doseich* (persequitur), *saichdetu* (consequentia), *sechimtid* (sectator)=*sequor*, ἕπομαι, Goth. *sakan*, *sôkjan*, Lith. *sekù*.

2 *sak* (root—to say): *saigid* (loqui, disputare), *saiged* (dicit), *dosaig* (dicit), *saiges* (g. dicit), *insce* (sermo), W. 3. *heb* (inquit)=*insece*, ἔννεπε, Lith. *sakaú*, O.H.G. *sagên*.

sad (root—to sit): *insádaim* (jacio), *dorósat*, *doforsat* (condidit, constituit), *adsaitis* (resideant), *sosad sossad* (turris, positio), *suide* (sessio), *suidiguth suidigud* (positio); W. 3. *gor-sed-ua* (sedes sublimis), P. *set-va* (sedes), *settyas* (posuit)=ἵζω, *sedeo*, Goth. *sitan*, Slav. *sěsti*, Lith. *sė'sti*. W. 3. *heul*, V. *heuul*, P. *houl* (sol); perhaps, also, O. Gaedh. *soillse* f. (lumen)?=Goth. *sauil*, Lith. *sáulė*, Lat. *sôl* (doubtful Gr. ἤλιος=ἀϝέλιος, it would be much better to consider it with Curtius=*ausil?*); Slav. *slŭnĭce* (deviates).

[Gaulish *Seno*-magus], *sen*, K. *hen*=Lat. *sen-ex* (Gr. ἔνη), Lith. *sénas* old, *sènis* an old man, Goth. *sin-eigs sinista*, O.H.G. *siniscalc*; it is wanting in Slavonian.

teg tech (domus), gen. *idul-taigæ* (fani), dat. *taig* (the fundamental form is, consequently, **tagi*), W. 3. *ty*, pl. *tei*, Arm. *ti ty*, V. *ti*—from which *tigerne*, dat. *tigerni* (dominus), W. 1. *tigern*; cf. Lat. *tug-urium*; Gr. τέγος, O. Norse *þak*, O.H.G. *dach*, Lith. *stógas* (roof). [Ir. *a-staig*.]

temel m. (obscuritas), W. 3. *tywyll* (obscurus, obscuritas), V. *tivulgou*, P. *tevolgow* (tenebrae)=Slav. *tĭma*, Lith. *tamsà*, Lat. *tenebrae, temere* (blindly), O.H.G. *demar* (crepusculum); it is wanting in Greek.

[*tana*], W. 3. *teneu* (tenuis), P. *tenewen* (látus); *tenuis*, ταναός ταυυ-, O.H.G. *dunni*, Slav. *tĭnĭkŭ*.

túath, K. *tut* (populus)=Lith. Lett. Prus. *tauta*, Osc. *túvtú*, Umbr. *toto*, Goth. *þiuda*; it is wanting in Slav. and Gr. (as in Lat.).

og, V. *uy*, W. 2. pl. *uyeu*=*ovum*, ᾠόν, O.H.G. *ei*, Pol. *jaje*, Ch. Slav. *ai-ce jaice*; it is wanting in Lithuanian.[68]

fich (municipium, pagus)=*vicus*, οἶκος, Goth. *veihs vêhs*, Slav. *vĭsĭ* (praedium), Lith. *vẽsz-pats* lord, *vėse'ti* to be a guest.

fer, V. *gur*, W. 3. *gwr* (ground form **vira*)=Lat. *vir*, Goth. *vair*, O.H.G. *wĕr* (*wĕralt* hominum aetas, seculum, generatio), Lith. *výras*, Lett. *wirs*; it is wanting in Slav. and Gr.

fedb, V. *guedeu*=Goth. *viduvô*, Sl. *vĭdova*, Prus. *widdewú*, Lat. *vidua*; it is wanting in Greek; ἠίθεος is scarcely connected.

fescor, W. 3. *ucher*, V. *gurthuper*, P. *gwesper*, Arm. *gousper*=*vesper*, ἕσπερος, Lith. *vákaras*, Slav. *veczerŭ*; it is wanting in German.

W. 1. *gulan*, V. *gluan*, Arm. *gloan*= Goth. *vulla*, Lith. *vìlna*, Slav. *vlŭna*, Lat. *lana?*; Gr. ἔριον is another form.

To these are to be added the generally recurring roots Skr. *as*, *bhû*, *dhâ* (O. Gaedh *dénim* (facio), Arm. *doen doan*, P. *doyn* (facere), and in the British compounds W. 3. *bydaf*, P. *bethaff*, Arm. *bezaff*, *bizif*), *vid*, *çru* (in all European tongues *klu*) and the numerals below 1000. If some of them are wanting in individual languages, it does not signify much for our present object, as here also we find everywhere agreements between the north and south. For example, *daru* [?] and the root *sru* are wanting in the Latin, *vaskara*, *ghaima* in the Teutonic,

---

[68] [The Teutonic words are scarcely connected with the Greek and Latin: O.H.G. *ei*, O.N. *egg*, A. Sax. *ägg*; Crimean Gothic *ada*, point to original ADDIA, compare Skr. *aṇḍa*, egg.]

svastar, tamas, vidhavâ in the Greek, *árja* in the Lithuanian, *akva, dacru, dant, sāna,* and the root *sak* in the Slavonian. Even the absence of words from two languages (*e.g.* Lat. and Lith. *ganâ,* Teut. and Gr. *diva,* Slav. and Gr. *sáuala, tautâ, vîra, aina,* Teut. and Slav. *daiva*) becomes for us of higher signification, only when these are the two nearest related languages,' say Latin and Greek, or Slavonian and Lithuanian.

§. 4. *Glossarial affinities of the Celtic, Classic, and Teutonic languages.*

Of words which are wanting in the Lithuanian and Slavonian, the Celtic has the following in common with the two Classic languages and Teutonic: *aile, athir, elin, palf, níule* (?) With the Greek and Teutonic it has, for example:

WORDS AND ROOTS COMMON TO CELTIC, GREEK, AND TEUTONIC.

dark (root—Skr. *dṛç*): Arm. *derch* (aspectus), O. Gaedh. *airdirce erdirc irdirce,* pl. *erdarcai* (conspicuus= περιδερκής?), *erdaircigidir* (concelebrat)=όέρκω, O.H.G. *zorht zoraht, zorft.*

* K. *garan*=γέρανος, O.H.G. *chran-uh* (in the form) in opposition to L t. *grus,* Lith. *gervė* f., Slav. *žeravlĭ* (* *gerarjas*) m.

lang (root): *loingtech* (acceptus, gratus), *julang* (tolerare), *immefolngai immefolngai immolngai* (efficit). *immeforling imforling* (efficit)—this form shows the composition, contrary to Zeuss 756, notwithstanding *arafulsam* (toleremus)—*indlung* (findo), *indlach* (disceptatio), *cuimlengaithi* (congrediendum); cf. λαγχάνω? O. H. G. *galingan.*

trag (root): Gaul. *ver-tragus* ; O. Gaedh. *traig,* K. *troit* (pes); τρέχω, Goth. *þragja.*

ban ben (root): *dofuibnimm* (succido), *etirdibnet* (perimunt), *imdibenar* (absciditur), *immerundbed* (circumcisus est), *bémen* pl. (vulnera, plagae), [P. *bom,bum*], *tōbe* (decisio), *nebthōbe nephthōbe* (praeputium), *imdibe* (circumcisio), *etardibe* (interritus), *bás* (mors), *bathach* (moribundus); secondary root *bal* in : *epil* (interit), *atbela* (morietur) =φεν in φόνος, πέφνον, πεφήσομαι, όcnνήφατος, Goth. *banja* a wound, O.H.G. *bana* f. (homicidium), *bano* m.(occisor),*banón* (quatere, exercere), O. Norse *bana* to kill, *bani* m. (occisor, homicidium).

(?) *borg* (borce, borggde), P. *burges* (burgensis)=Goth. *baurgs,* also Gr. πύργος (φούρκος)? — (may have been borrowed from the German).

gen, dat. *giun* (os, oris)—compare χαίνω, O.H.G. *ginén ginón*? ; the Latin *hiare* has different forms.

[*scath*], V. *scod* (umbra)=Goth. *skadus,* Gr. σκότος?

sid, W. 3. *hedwch* (pax)=Goth. *sidus,* Gr. ἔθος, ἤθος?

The following are Celtic, Latin (or Italic), Teutonic:

WORDS AND ROOTS COMMON TO CELTIC, LATIN (OR ITALIC), AND TEUTONIC.

ad- O. Gaedh. only in combinations, as already in Gaulish, Kymric *ad-* and *at* (difficult to be distinguished from *aith*=* *ati,* see Beitr. I. 312)=Lat. *ad,* Goth. *at.* [But also Lith. *at.*]

asil, K. *esel* (membrum)=Lat. *ala,* axilla, O.H.G. *ahsala* ?

al (root): *notail* (qui te alit), *altram* (nutritio)—Lat. *alo,* Goth. *alan, aljan,* O. Norse *ala.*

[*caech*], V. *cuic* (luscus, monophthalmus)=Goth. *haihs*; Lat. *caecus.*

W. 3. *crych* (Gaul. *Crixus*?), O. Gaedh. *crichaib* (sulcis), W. 1. *criched* (ruga) =Lat. *crispus*; O.H.G. *krûs.*

Gaulish, κάρνον τὴν σάλπιγγα, Hesych.

(κάρνυξ, Schol. Il. σ, 219), Kym. *corn*
=Lat. *cornu*, Goth. *haurn*.
gabor (caper), W. 2. V. *gauar*, W. 3.
gafar (capra) = Lat. *caper, capra*,
O. N. *hafr*, Ang. Sax. *häfer*.
gab (root), Kymr. *cav* (i. e. *cabh*)=
Lat. *capio*, Goth. *hafja*.
lí, W. 3. *lliw*, P. *lyw* (splendor, color, gloria)—V. *liuor* (pictor), *disliu* (deformis)—Lat. *liveo livor lividus*, O.H.G. *pli pliwes* lead (Stokes).
nathir, V. *nader*=Lat. *natrix*, Goth. *nadr*, O.H.G. *natra natara*. (The O. Gaedh. with its declension, stands as it were midway between Teutonic and Latin).
nessa, superl. *nesam*=Osc. Umbr. *nesimo*, Goth. *néhv-*, already alluded to.
[*niae*], V. *noi*=Lat. *nepos*, O.H.G. *nefo*, A. Sax. *nefa*, and
necht, V. *noit*=Lat. *neptis*, O.N., A. Sax., O.H.G. *nift*, O.H.G. *niftila*.
[*nid*], V. *neid*=Lat. *nidus*, A. Sax., O.H.G., *nest*. (The Slav. *gnězdo* is obscure.)
V. *pisc*=Lat. *piscis*, Goth. *fisks*.
[*rí*, gen.] *ríg*, V. *ruy*=Lat. *rex*, Goth. *reiks* (O.H.G. *richi*).

W. 1. *taguel*, 2. *tawel* (silens), W. 3. *tewi* (tacere), W. 3. P. *taw* (tace)= Lat. *tacere*, Goth. *þahan*?
rect recht (lex), W. 2. *reith reyth reis* (lex), Arm. *reiz rez* (rectus, justus) =Lat. *rectus*, Goth. *raihts*, O.H.G., O. Sax. *reht* n.
tenge, gen. sing. pl. *tengad*=Goth. *tuggô*, Lat. *lingua (dingua)*, although with a different suffix in each language.
drog droch, W. 3. *drwc*, P. *drok* (malus), W. 3. *drycket* (malitia), O. Gaedh. *drochgnim*, acc. pl. *drochgnimu* (malefactum), V. *drocger* (infamia), *drocgeriit* (infamis), *drochoberor* (maleficus)—cf. Lat. *trux*, O. H. G. *triugan* — Skr. root *druh*. [cf. τρύχω?]
V. *guins*, P. *gwyns*, Arm. *guent* (i.e. Kymr. **guint*)=Lat. *ventus*, Goth. *vinds*. [Skr. *váta*.]
caille (velamen)—cf. Lat. *occulo, celo*, O.H.G. *helan, heli* f. (amictus, velamentum), Goth. *huljan*, O.H.G. *hulla* (hülle); [*caille* is probably borrowed from *pallium*.]

§. 5. *Glossarial affinities of the Celtic, Teutonic, and Lito-Slavonian languages.*

Among the words the Celtic has in common with the Teutonic, Lithuanian, and Slavonian, besides those above quoted, which recur in Latin or Greek, we must no doubt remove many more which have come into all or several of these languages in the same way, by borrowing from the Latin, as for example: *angelus* = Lith. *ángëlas*, Ch. Slav. *anĭgelŭ*, O.H.G. *angil, engil* (Got. *aggilus* from the Greek), O. Gaedh. *angel aingel;* or *apostolus* = Lith. *apásztalas*, Ch. Slav. *apostolŭ* (Goth. *apaustaulus*), O.H.G. *postul*, Arm., Corn. *apostol*, O. Gaedh. *apstal.* Mutual borrowing among the other languages did not take place to anything like the same extent, and we run much less risk of mistaking the apparent relationships due to borrowing for primitive relationships, in this case, than in the comparison of the Celtic and Latin. The Cornish has borrowed the most from the Teutonic languages (especially from the English), like the Armoric from the Romance (French), next to them the Welsh; the mutual influence between Gaedhelic and the Teutonic tongues may be considered as evenly balanced. The following are certainly borrowed: V. *mesclen* N.H.G. *muschel*, *redior* = Eng. *reader*, *hering* Eng. *herring*, *hot* (caputium) = Eng. *hat*, *roche* (fannus), *streing* (fibula) = Eng. *string*,

P. *strek* (radius sanguinis), *strekis* (plagae) = *strike*, V. *strifor* (contentiosus), P. *stryff* (contentio), *strevye* (altercari) = *strive;* W. 3. *helym helm, iarll* (comes) = O.N. *iarl*, A. Sax. *ëorl*, *ysl(e)ipanu*, to draw or tie (a bow), *yswein* pl. *ysweinieit* = O. N. *swein* (Eng. *swain*), *ysmwg* (vapour) = Engl. *smoke*. On the other hand, W. 2. 3. *talu* (solvere) and the German *zahlen* have, perhaps, come from a common source.

The agreements of the Celtic with all three languages, or, at all events, with the Teutonic and Slavonian, at the same time, are certainly not exceedingly numerous, but for the most part all the more significant. Thus we again meet in Celtic with certainly a part, and very probably others, of those very words and forms which Schleicher has pointed out as exclusively common to the Teutonic and Slavonian.

WORDS AND ROOTS COMMON TO CELTIC, LITHUANIAN, SLAVONIAN, AND TEUTONIC.

aball (malus), W. 2. *aball* (mali), *aballen*, 2. 3. V. *awallen* f. malus), P. *avell* (pomum), W. 3. *awal*, pl. *au tleu aueleu* (poma), *hwylbrenni* (mali):=A. Sax. *äppel*, Frisian *appel*, O.H.G. *aphul aphol*, O. Norse *epli* n. (malum); Lith. *obelis* f. (malus), *obălas*=Lett. *ābols* (malum); Slav. *jablŭko jablŭka* (pomum), *ablanĭ abloni jablanĭ* (malus).

crocann, crocenn (receptaculum), W. 3. *crochann* (vas, olla), V. *crogen* (concha)—cf. O.H.G. *kruog* (lagena, amphora); Ch. Slav. *krŭczagŭ* (vas fictile), *krŭczĭmĭnica* a drinking house, *krŭczĭvĭnikŭ* host; Lith. *kurczamà* a drinking house (N.H.G. *krug*) — Lett. *krôgs* borrowed.—?

crauell f. W. 2. (pala fornacea), V. *grauior* (sculptor)—Goth. *graban*, Sl. *grebą* (fodio), *grobŭ* (sepulcrum), Lith. *grabas;* the root is also no doubt Gr. (γράφω), but with this signification it is, according to Schleicher, Teutonic and Slavonian.

dodálim (fundo), *fodáli* (distinguit), *fondrodil* (qui id divisit), *fodlaidi* (dividendus), *fodail fodil* (divisio)—also *dil* (gratus), *diliu, dilem; diles* (proprius, certus, fidelis)?—W. 1. *didaul* (expers)=Goth. *dailjan* (dividere), Sl. *děliti*, Lith. *dalýti*, Lett. *dallit* to share, Prus. *dellieis* imper. share with; Goth. *dails*, Lith. *dalìs* f. a share.

W. 1. *drogn* (coetus), *drog* (factionem), i.e. no doubt *drogg drong* — cf. the perhaps Gaulish, *drungus* (a troop) with its un-Latin *anlaut* [*dr*]—Goth. *driugan* to perform military service, *gadrauhts* a warrior, O.H.G. *truhtin* (dominus), *truhtinc* (paranymphus), O. Norse *drótt* f., pl. *dróttir* a troop, servants, *dróttinn* lord, *dróttning* queen; Lith. *draũgas*, *draũgalas* a companion, partner, Sl. *drugŭ* (socius, alter, amicus), Lett. *draudse* (i.e. * *draugia*) a community.

du do, K. *do dy di y*=Goth. *du*, A. Sax. *to*, O.H.G. *zŭ zĭ zuo*, Slav. *do*, Lith. *du-*. is wanting in O. Norse.

Ir. *droighean*, Welsh DRAEN has been compared by Grimm (Gesch. d. d. Spr. 1028) with Slav. *trŭnŭ*, Goth. *þaurnus;* this comparison is, however, only right if a guttural be supposed to have fallen out in the Skr. *trna*, Goth. and Slav., so that Lat. *truncus* and Gr. τέρχνος might also be connected therewith. O. Gaedh. *draigen* ("pirus") and V. *drain* (spina), pl. V. Arm. *drein*, P. *dreyn*, are found in Zeuss along with O. Gaedh. *driss* (vepres), *dristenach* (dumetum), W. 3. *dryssien* f. (frutex)—?

V. *er* (aquila)=Goth. *ara*, Lith. *eris* (Beitr. I. 234), *erélis*, Lett. *érglis*, Slav. *orlŭ*.

[*ged*], V. *guit* (auca), i.e. *guid* (anser)= N.H.G. *genter*, A.Sax. *gandra*, O.H.G. *ganzo*, Pliny *ganta;* also Lith. *gàndras* (a stork)?

mang macc (root) (already spoken of in the Zeitschr. VI. 238 in the signification *augere*, also in existence in derivatives *mar* (magnus), *macc* (filius)— the Goth. *mag* (possum)=Sl. *mogą*,

Lith. *móku moké'ti* (to be able, to understand, to count, pay), etc., are specially represented by O. Gaedh. *cumaing cumúing* (valet), *cumang* (potestas, posse), *cumacc* (potens), *cumacht cumacht(a)e* n. (potentia)=W. 3. *kyfoeth kyuoeth* (potestas), O. Gaedh. *cumachtach* (potens), comp. *cumachtchu* (potior)=W. 3. *kyuoethawc* (potens), V. *chefuidoc* ("omnipotens"). Especially the Lithuanian tenuis agrees in a wonderful manner with the Celtic forms.

menicc menic, W. 3. *mynych*, P. *menough* (frequens)=Goth. *manags*, Slav. *muogŭ* (multus); O. Gaedh. *meince* (abundantia)=Goth. *managei*, N.H.G. *menge*; *mencain* (penus).

nocht-chenn (nudus capite), P. *noyth*, Arm. *noaz* = Goth. *naqvaþs*, O. Norse *naktr (nakinn)*, O.H.G. *nachat*; Slav. *nagŭ*, Lith. *nŭgas*.—The Lat. *nudus* is a different form; it is wanting in Gr.

W. 3. *priawt*, V. *gur priot* (sponsus), Arm. *priet* (maritus)=O.H.G. *friudil fridil*, M.H.G. *vriedel* (amasius), also used for the husband)—Lith. *prételius*, Sl. *prijatelĭ* (amicus). Either *priawt* is to be compared with *brawt* (frater), therefore almost exactly= O.H.G. *friudil*, &c. (with *l* for *r*), or a participle (amatus), to which the Welsh per. pass. W. 3. *-at, -et, -it, -wyt, -awt*), and Arm. part. (*-et*) accurately agree; in the latter case the adj. *priawt* (proprius),—from whence also W. 2. *amprioduur* (non possidens),—represents the Homeric φίλος and N.H.G. "*werth*" (cf. *yny priawt person*, in (his) proper person). It is in any case one of the most interesting agreements between the Celtic, German, Slavonian, and Lithuanian.

sil (semen), W. 3. *heu* (serere), *hewyt* (satum est)—connects itself to a root form, which, according to Schleicher, is exclusively Germano-Slavonian: Goth. *saian*, Sl. *sejati*, Lith. *sè'ti*, *sëklà*, *sé'mens*. The root *rád*, no doubt general, but in certain significations only Celtic, Teutonic, Litho-Slavonian (cf. Beitr. I. 426 seq.)

snechti (nives)—the root is general (fundamental form *snigh), but the *s* has only been preserved in the northern languages: Lith. *snēgas*, Slav. *snēgŭ*, Goth. *snaivs* (=*snaigas, *snaigvas); in the Gr. ἀγάννιφος there is still a trace (=*ἀγάνιχϝος); in the Lat. *nix nivis* (=**nihvis, nigvis*) it has wholly vanished.

flaith f., gen. *flatha flatho* (imperium), *fla(i)themnacht* f. (gloria, dignitas, gradus), *flaithemnas* (gloria), W. 3. *gwlat* (regio), pl. *gwladoed gwledyd*, V. *gulat* (patria), P. *gwlas* (terra)—fundamental form *vlati with the same transposition of the medial to the tenuis as in *ithim* (edo)—V. *vuludoc* (dives), W. 1. *guletic* (potens), 3. *gwledic* (imperans, princeps)= Goth. *valdan*, Sl. *vladiti vlasti vladą* (imperare), Lith. *valdaú valdýti*, Lett. *waldit* (N.H.G. *walten*, to govern).

W. 3. *gwerth* (pretium), *gwerthawr* (pretiosus), P. *gwerthe* (vendere), *gorthye* (venerari)—Goth. *vairþs*, Lith. *vèrtas*, Pruss. *werts* (the latter was perhaps borrowed, as the Polish *wart* certainly was?).

§. 6. *Glossarial affinities of the Celtic and Teutonic.*

The correspondences with the Teutonic are most numerous; some of them are no doubt the result of borrowing, while in the case of others, the relation is not clear; many, however, give no occasion for such a supposition. Compare for instance:

WORDS AND ROOTS COMMON TO CELTIC AND TEUTONIC.

agathar (timet), *aichthi* (timendus)= Goth. *óg, ôgan*.
aithirge ithirge (poenitentia), *aidrech* (poenitens), *taidirge* i. e. *do-aithirge* (misericordia), P. *eddrek, edrege*, *poenitentia*=Goth. *idreiga*.

arbae orpe n.=Goth. *arbi*; *orpam* m., pl. *horpamin*=Goth. *arbja, comarpe* =*gaarbja*; *comarbus* (coohereditas); *nomerpimm* (trado me, confido), *nobirpaid* (tradite vos, confidite), *nachiberpidsi* (ne conf.), *roerbad* (com-

missum est) pl. *roairptha*; *innarbar* (abigitur, removetur), *arenindarbe* (ut abigat), *nachimrindarpai-se* (quod non me repulit), *arnachitrindarpither* (ne sis exherculatus) represents exactly N.G.H. *enterben*.
baga (contentiones), *bagim* (glorior), *bágul* (praeda)—O.H.G. *bágan biag* (contendere, objurgare), *bágén* (contendere), *bága* f. (contentio), O. Norse *baga* (obstare, resistere), *baeyjask* (vexare, molestare), *bági* m. (difficultas), *bágr* (molestus).
biáil biail buáil,W. 1. *bahell*, 2. *buyall* (securis), 1. *laubael* (handbill)=O.H.G. *bihal pihal bigil pigil*, M.H.G. *bil*—still unexplained in both languages.
bolg bolc (uter), Gaul. *bulga*=Goth. *balgs*, O. H. G. *palc*, O. Norse *belgr* (follis, uter).
borg=Goth. *baurgs* (see supra).
(?) V. *boch*=O.H.G. *boch poch*, O. Norse *bokki*, A. Sax. *bucca*—cf. O. Gaedh. *cuilennbocc* ("cynyps")— borrowed from the German, according to Grimm.
W. 3. *bwa* (arcus)—O. Gaedh. *fidbocc* (arcus ligneus)=O. Norse *bogi*, A. Sax. *boga*, O.H.G. *bogo poco*.
W. 3. *burd bord* m., pl. *byrdeu* (mensa) =Goth. *baurd* a board, *fótubaurd* a footstool, O. Norse *borð* n. a board, table, ship, O. H. G. *bort borti borto* m. (ora, navis, mensa).
W. 3. *blodeu*, V. *blodon* (flos)=O.H.G. *bluot* f, M.H.G. *bluot* m. f., pl. *blüete*. —the Lat. *flos* has a different suffix.
bróen (pluvia)=Goth. *rign*. The root also in βρέχω, Lat. *rigo*, the special word-formation only recurring in the Teutonic.
buáid f. (victoria, bradium), *buide boide*, Z. 611 gratiae), *buidech* (gratus, contentus), *ho-buidnib* (copiis); W. 1. 3. Arm. *bud* (bradium, victoria, fortuna), W. 1. *budicaul*, 3. *budugawl* (victoriosus, felix), W. 1. *bodin* (turma), pl. *bodiniou*, 3. *bydin* f. — the root is the same as in Goth. *anabiudan*, *faurbiudan* (jubere, mandare), the fundamental signification was probably to announce=Skr. *bódhayâmi* (denuntiare); cf. N. H. G. *aufgebot* with *bodin*.—The signification is different in Slavo-Lithuanian.
(?) W. *bad* m., pl. 3. *badeu* (scaphae)— cf. O. Gaedh. *bádud* (naufragium)= boot, not High German, O. Norse *bátr*, A. Sax. *bát*—borrowed from the Celtic, according to Grimm.

cath, K. *cat* (pugna)—Gaul. *Caturiges*, *Catuslogi*—O.H.G. *hadu* (only in names), A. Sax. *heaðo*, M.H.G., N.H.G. *hader*.
(?) W. 1. *carr*, 2. *car*, Gaul. *carrus* (Caesar). — O.H.G. *karra garra charra* f., O. Norse *kerra* (appears to have come into German through borrowing).
W. 3. *craff* (firmus), P. *cryff*, *cref* (fortis, gravis), Arm. *cref creff* (firmus, tenax), *criff* (fortis), *craf* (avarus), W. 3. *kyngryfet* (aqua fortis), *crajfu* (fortiter incedere), *creffit* (ars) —cf. O.H.G. *chraft* (not in Tatian), A. Sax. *craft*, O. Norse *kreftr*, and *kramph*.—?
cruim (curvus)=O.H.G. *chrump*, A. Sax. *crumb* (remoter and doubtful Lat. *curvus*, Lith. *kreívas*, Slov. *krivŭ*).
W. 2. *cussan*, V. *cussin* (osculum)—O. Norse, A. Sax. *coss*, O.H.G. *chus*.
dorche f. pl. (tenebrae)=A. Sax. *deorc*, Eng. *dark*, O.H.G. *tarch*, O. Norse *döckr* (obscurus).
dún (arx), W. 2. 3. *din* (castellum)= O. Norse, O. Sax. A. Sax. *tún*, O.H.G. *zún*, Engl. *town* (on the names of places see Beitr. II., part 1).
gabul (furca, patibulum) = O.H.G. *gabala*.
gaide (pilo praeditus), Gaul. *Gaesati*, *gaesum*=O.H.G. *gêr*, A. Sax. *gár*.
gell (pignus)=Goth. *gild* (tributum)? (see *giall*).
V. *ghel* (sanguisuga)=O.H.G. *egala*, *ecala*.
W. 3. *gerthi* (virga), V. *garthou* (stimulus) may, no doubt, be compared with the O.H.G. *gartja* (switch), but the Goth. *gazds*=O.H.G. *gart*, N.H.G. *gerte* (goad, switch, whip), points to a borrowing into Celtic from the Teutonic.
giall (obses) (*gell* (pignus) Z. 64, see supra), V. *guistel* (obses), W. 3. *gwystyl* (obses, pignus), P. *gustle* (spondere), Arm. *goestlas* (spopondit) =O.H.G. *gisal?*
(?)*glass glas* (glaucus), Arm. *glisi* (livor, aegritudo)—O. Norse, O.H.G. *glas*, A. Sax. *gläs* (vitrum).
V. *grou* (arena) — O. Norse *griot* (lapides, saxa), A. Sax. *gréot* (scobs), O.H.G. *grioz* (glarea).
(V. *hos* (ocrea), W. 3. *hos(s)an*, pl. *hossaneu* (braccae)=O.H.G. *hosa* (caliga), A. Sax. *hos* (calcaneum), *hosa* (caligae). Evidently borrowed, but by whom?

(W. 2. *hucc* (sus), V. *hoch* (porcus)=
Engl. *hog*; the latter appears to have
been borrowed from the Celtic (*h*=*s*,
therefore related to *sus*). According
to Grimm, it was the Celtic which
borrowed from the German, N.H.G.
haksch (verres)—?)

iarn (gen. *híairn*. Inc. Sg.), W. 3. *heyrn*,
V. *hoirn* (O. Arm. *haiarn*-, *hoiarn*-)=
Goth. *eisarn*, O.H.G. *isarn*, O. Norse
isarn iarn.

[*eo*], V. *hiuen* (taxus)=O.H.G. *iwa* f.;
A. Sax. *iv*, O. Norse *ŷr* m. (cf. Zacher
das Goth. Alph. p. 10. *seq*.)

[*lár*], W. 1. *laur*, 3. *llawr* (solum), V.
lor, P. *ler lear* (pavimentum, solum)
—with the dropping of *p*=*flur*,
M.H.G. *vluor*? (Grimm 307 also
compares A. Sax. *flór*, Engl. *floor*).

V. Arm. *lagat*, P. *lagas*, W. 3. *llygat*
(oculus)—A. Sax. *lócian*, O.H.G.
luogén, N.H.G. *lugen*—Skr. root *lax*?

land: dat. *isind*- *ithlaind* (in area), W.
3. *lann* (area, ecclesia), O. Arm. *lann*,
Ital. Fr. Provençal *landa*, *lande*=
Goth. *land*.

V. *loven* (pediculus)=O.H.G. A. Sax.
O.N. *lús* (?)

leim (saltus), W. 1. *lammam* (salio),
lemenic (salax), W. 3. *llemhidyd* (sal-
tator)=M.H.G. *limpfen* to limp (*lam*
N.H.G. *lahm*, Engl. *lame*)? Thence
also W. *llamp*=Goth *lamb* (the hop-
ping)?

loathar (pellis)=O.H.G. *ledar*, O.N.
ledr; A. Sax. *léðer* (funis)?—The
meaning would answer, yet the
Gaedh *oa* and the O.H.G. *ë* differ.

marc, K. *march* (Gaul. acc. μάρκαν)=
O.H.G. *marach*, f. *meriha*, M.H.G.
march (*marc*).

mí- (is wanting as a prefix in Kymric)
=Goth. *missa*, N.H.G. *mis*-. To this
is to be added the comp. *messu* (pejor); further W. 3. *gormes* f., pl.
gormesseu gormessoed (miseria, afflic-
tio, infortunium).

mong, W. *mwng*, pl. W. 1. *mogou*
(read *moggou* i.e. *mongou*)=*mähne*,
O.H.G. *mana*, once *manha*, M.H.G.
man (?).

mucc, W. 3. *moch* (sus), according to
Grimm. N.H.G. *mucke* (?).

W. 3. *ychen* pl., O. Arm. *ohen*=Goth.
auhsans (the Latin *vacca* deviates).

ós, *úas*, *uch*, Corn. *ugh*, Arm. *us* (supra),
gen. *úasal*, K. *uchell* (altus)—cf.
Gaul. *Uxellodunum*, Brit. οὔξελλον,
οῦξελλα—Goth. *auhuma*, *auhumists*
(supremus). The Picenian *Auximum*

has a different meaning (Zeitschr
III. 248).

labar, Kymr. *lavar* (loqui), O. Gaedh.
amlabar, V. *aflauar* (mutus), *mab
aflauar* (infans)=N.H.G. *plappern*
(*blappen*, *blappern*)?—Bopp compares Skr. *lap*, the *l* appears however
to be old.

rún, K. *rin*=Goth. *runa*, O. H. G. *rún*
(mysterium).

sam (*sol*), W. 1. *ham*, 2, 3. V. *haf*, Arm.
haff (aestas)—O. N., O. H. G. *sumar*,
A. Sax. *sumor sumer*.—Also Goth.
sunna, *sunnô*, A. Sax., O. N. *sunna*,
O.H.G. *sunna sumna*? Pictet and Leo
Meyer (Zeitschr. IV.) have explained
differently.

scoloca (servi [scholastici?]), *banscala*
(servae)—Goth. *skalks*?

seol sóol (velum, carbasus), W. 1. *huil*,
V. *guil* (velum)=O. N. *segl*, O. H. G.
segal, A. Sax. *sëgel*.

sét (via), dat. *séit*, pl. *seúit seuit*; *sétche*
(uxor), dat. *seitchi* (properly a female
fellow-traveller, *Gefährtin*; a word
from the nomadic time?); W. 1. *hint*,
Arm. *hent* (via), thence V. *camhinsic*
(injustus), *eunhinsic* (justus)=Goth.
sinþs; O. H. G. *sind* m.

slíci m. pl. (ostreae), Sg. *slice* (lanx)=
O. H. G. *snecco* (limax), A. Sax. *snegel* (limax, cochlea, testudo), O. N.
snigil (limax), more especially M.N.L.
slecke (limax).

snáthe m. (filum), dat. *snáthiu*; V. *snod*
(vitta), V. W. 3. *snoden* (filum), W.
3. *ysnoden* (vitta)——cf. O. N. *snara*
(laqueus), O. H. G. *snuor* f. (filum)
from the same root.

[such and] W. 1. *suh* (vomer) according
to Haupt in Z.=O.H.G. *sech*(?).

tré, *tri*, Kym. *trui*=Goth. þairh (Beitr.
I. 312).

uile, K. *oll*=Goth. *alls*.

(*h*)*uathath* (*h*)*uathad húathad hothad*
(singularis, singularitas), gen. *uathid
hodid*, dat. *óthud uathuth*, acc. *hua-
thuth*; *úaithed* (singularis, solus, solitarius); f. acc. pl. *huathati* (singu-
lares), dat. pl. *uathataib* (*t*=*thth*);
óthatnat (pauculus)—of one stem with
óa (minor) from Skr. *ava*; but also
comparable with Goth. *auþeis* (de-
sertus) N.H.G. *öde*=Skr. *avatya*.
[? Lat. *pau*-cus?].

fén (plaustrum), Brit. Belg. *covinus*=
O. N. *vagn*, O.H.G. *wagan*, A. Sax.
vägen. (The Greek and Slavonian
have different suffixes).

fiadnisse (testimonium)=O.H.G. *giwiz-*

nesi f., *giwiznes* n., A Sax. *gewitnesse*, *gevitnes*, Engl. *witness*. *fid* n., K. *guid*, Gaul. *vidu-*=O. N. *viðr* m., O. Sax. *vidu*, A. Sax. *vudu*, O.H.G. *witu* n. (Beitr. I., 160), with an equal change of meaning, thence, for example, V. *colviden* (corylus), with the singulative suffix.

folcaim folcaimm (humecto, lavo), W 2. 3. *golchi*, Arm. *gnelchi*, P. *golhy* (lavare)—A. Sax. *volcen*, O. Sax. *wolcan*, O.H.G. *wolchan* (nubes) as moist or moistening? W. 3. *gwyllt*, V. *guill*, P. *gwyls*=Goth. *vilþeis*.

§. 7. *Glossarial affinities of the Celtic and Lito-Slavonian.*

The exclusive agreements between the Celtic and the Lito-Slavonian are very much less numerous. To these belong, for example:—

WORDS AND ROOTS COMMON TO CELTIC, LITHUANIAN, AND SLAVONIAN.

Gaedh. K. *bran* (corvus)=Slav. *vrană*, Lith. *várnas* (corvus), *várna* (cornix).
W. 3. Arm. *gallaf*, P. *gallof* (possum. potero)=Lith *galiù galė́ti*.
Gaedh. *nem*, K. *nef*, Sl. *nebo* n., Lett. *debbes* f. with the signification heaven (contrary to Lat., Gr., Lith., and Germ.).
caire f. (accusatio, nota, culpa), *cairigud* m. (reprehensio), [W. 1. *cared*, gl. nequitiae,] W. 3. *keryd* m. (reprehensio)—Ch. Slav. *karati* (rixari), Lith. *koravóti* (punire).
Gaedh. *cruim* in the form=Lith. *kirmis* (the Lat., Gr., and Germ. have lost the *k*).

W. Arm. *merch* (filia, puella), V. *moroin*, W. 3. *morwyn* (puella) [O. Ir. *morn*] perhaps=Lith. *mergà*, *mergéle̊*?
W. 1. 2. *melin*, 3 *mclyn* (flavus, livídus), f. 1. *melen*, pl. 1. *milinon*, 3. *melynyou*, V. *milin* (fulvus, flavus)=Lith. *mé̊lynas* blue? according to Diefenbach (Beitr. I. 483) from M. Lat. *melinus* = μήλινος, in this case, however, we ought to expect Kymr. *mailin*, *moilin*.
(?) *glún*, W. 3. Arm. *glin* m. (genu)—perhaps=Sl. *koléno* (genu), Lith. *kulnìs*, heel, *kelýs* knee? (*g* instead of *k* in *gabor, gabunm* also?)

Finally, the Celtic also is of course not wanting in words which heretofore have not been found in any primitively related tongues, or, at least, in any European language. Of the first kind is, for example, *tene*, K. *tan*, in contradistinction to the Skr. *agni*, Lat. *ignis*, Lith. *ugnìs*, Sl. *ognĭ*, as well as to the Greek πῦρ, Umbr. *pir*, O.H.G. *fiur*: among the special agreements with the Sanskrit, the similar nomenclature of the points of the compass (Z. 67. 566) is particularly remarkable.

All these glossarial agreements and deviations would of course, taken by themselves, prove very little, as we find even between the most nearly related idioms, striking differences, such as between Slav. and Lith. in the case of the name of God, between Lat. and Umbr. in the appellation of fire. Where, however, the same or nearly related words recur in great numbers, there we have at least every inducement to further investigate whether special agreements may not be found in the grammar also, and in this expectation we are rarely disappointed. Among the words and forms quoted in the preceding pages (and I believe I have been perfectly impartial in their selection), there recur exclusively about fifty undoubtedly in the Teutonic tongues, not quite forty certainly in the Latin; if to these we add about twenty which certainly recur in Latin and Teutonic, about a dozen in Latin and Greek, at least as many in Teutonic and Lito-Slavonian, it follows that the degree of relationship between the Celtic and Teutonic on the one hand, and the Celtic and the Latin on the other, is pretty nearly the same, with however some preponderance to the side of the Teutonic, which is still further somewhat strengthened by the few Teutonic-Greek agreements. The Lithuanian and Slavonian on the one hand, and the Greek on the other, are decidedly further removed as regards glossarial resemblances, being as compared with each other about equal. With the Celtic they are chiefly connected by the Teutonic and the Italic tongues. The Celtic prepositions also show that a similar proportion is to be expected in the grammar; among them, for instance, *ad* is again found in Teutonic and Latin only, *di* and *tar* only in Latin, *ire* only in Teutonic, and *du* in Teutonic and Slavonian.[89] The prefixes *du-* and *su-*, which otherwise are everywhere wanting, lead nearer to the Greek, while the privative *an-* is again found in Greek, Teutonic, and Latin (the Sl. Lith. *u-* in, for example, *ùbagas*, *ubogŭ*, appears to correspond rather to the Skr. *ava-*).

§. 8. *Phonological affinities;—Vocalismus.*

In Phonology, the principles according to which we might judge of an earlier or a later separation of tongues, are as yet by no means finally established, and agreements between unrelated languages, and differences between the nearest related ones here present themselves often so strikingly, that we should avoid deciding about their relationships according to such data. Thus, for example, the treatment of the mutes in O. Gaedh. agrees in the most wonderful way with that in the Hebrew (מֶלֶךְ, בִּלְתִּי, דָּבָר, דְּבַר, even יְחִי instead of יִחְיֶה), while the Polish wholly departs from the Slavonian rules (as in *wilk* = Lith. *vilkas*, in opposition to O. Slav. *vlŭkŭ*). I think that a geography of sounds is chiefly wanting to arrive at a conclusion as to how far the phonetic laws of languages are affected by physical, genealogical, or social influences;[90] in this the vocalismus

---

[89] [*Du* occurs in composition in O. Lat.: in-*du*-perator, in-*du*-pedio.]

[90] [I am glad to find that so competent a philologist as Ebel has come upon this idea of a geography of sounds, which, so far as I am aware, I was the first to put forward, though crudely, in Vol. II. of the *Atlantis*. If such a man as Dr. Ebel were to turn his attention to this subject, the foundation of an important branch of science might be laid. Brücke's attempt to classify all the articulate sounds which could possibly be produced by the tongue (*Grundzüge der Physiologie und Systematik der Sprachlaute*. Wien, 1856), affords a basis to begin upon, for if we

as well as the consonantismus, and the relations of both to one another, should be taken into account. The above-mentioned phonetic similarity of the Gaedhelic and Hebrew, for instance, appears to be due to similar physical conditions; the sporadically occurring one of the Polish with the Lithuanian to social (historical) circumstances. The agreement already pointed out by Lottner of the Goth. *mikils* with the Gr. and Lat. μέγας *magnus*, in contrast to the Skr. *mahat*, appears to point to a closer relationship between the European tongues; so in like manner the Goth. *daur* with Gr. and Lat. θύρα, *fores*, in contrast to Skr. *dvâra*. One of the most important points in connection with, and most conclusive evidence of, earlier or later separation of the individual languages, namely, the elementary developement of the vocalismus, can be followed out with clearness unfortunately only in a single language, the Gothic. The Gothic triad of the short vowels a, i, u (as in Skr. and O. Persian), speaks unanswerably for a proportionably early separation of the Teutonic from the other European tongues, at a time when none of the then united languages had developed an $\breve{e}$ and $\breve{o}$; in like manner the Lithuanian must have separated from the Slavonian before the latter had developed an $\breve{o}$; the Lithuanian from the Lettish before the long $\hat{a}$ was changed into $\hat{o}$. The Latin and Greek, on the other hand, admit of the assumption of $\breve{e}$ and $\breve{o}$ before their separation. The sign no doubt only, and not the sound of o, was wanting to the older Umbrian and the Oscan. The Latin and Greek afford a marked contrast to the Teutonic in the circumstance, that perhaps everywhere in them, certainly at least as the rule, the $\breve{a}$ has been changed into i, only through e; in the Latin also through o into u; in Teutonic, on the other hand, it is the reverse, a being changed into e through i, and into o through u. The Celtic takes in this respect so far a middle place, inasmuch as a direct passage of a into o (and e) cannot be denied already in Gaulish nominatives like Σεγομαρος, and accusatives as νεμητον, as also in the (primitively long) Old Gaedhelic genitive endings -*o* (I. 177, 180); it places itself, however, by the side of the Teutonic by the circumstance that in both living branches u has passed into o, i into e (not o, e into u, i), and just as in Teutonic partly by breaking (*fer*: *firas=O.H.G *wolf*: Goth. *vulfs*), partly by simple weakening (Arm. *ed*: Welsh and Cornish *yd*=O.N. *son*: Goth. *sunus*; compare also Slav. *snocha*, *denĭ* for older *snŭcha dĭnĭ*), and the u and i appear here also for Sanskrit a, without the middle stages

---

knew all possible sounds, and could classify them, we would merely have to determine in what part of the world each sound occurred. I hope to return to this subject at another time.—W.K.S.]

o and *e*, as in Teutonic and Slavonian: *cóic*, Kym. *pimp*=Goth. *fimf*=Skr. *panca*; Gaul. *dula* (πεμπέδουλα probably Graecised) =Skr. *dala; duine* Kymr. *dyn, den* (homo), perhaps from a root *dan*=ϑαν in ϑνητός? Decide, therefore, as we may regarding the interesting agreement spoken of in Bcitr. I. 163, of the Celtic and Teutonic in breaking and umlaut, whether we recognize herein with Lottner (Zeitschr. VII. 27. cf. Schleicher KSl. Formenlehre p. 11) a certain family likeness, or in consequence of its later origin, leave it with Schleicher (Bcitr. I. 442) unnoticed, the direct passage of *a* into *o* and *e* (*ocht, ech*=*octo, equus*) should not, at all events, be looked upon as a proof of a closer relationship to the Latin, especially as it also occurs in Slavonian, the *o* of which nevertheless was evidently originated only after its separation from the Lithuanian. Vowel-changes analogous to those in Teutonic and Slavonian are besides also found in the Celtic roots: *guidimm* (precor), where *ui* is umlaut from *u*, along with *ro-gád* (rogavi), *foddáli* (distinguit), along with *fo-ro-dil* (divisit), *lánad*, along with *linad* (complere), *bráth*, along with *breth* (judicium). I will not, however, lay much stress upon all these agreements, in consequence of the uncertainty which still generally prevails in such questions. But in the diphthongal system the Celtic comes decidedly nearest to the Teutonic, and at least much nearer to the Lito-Slavonian than to the Latin or Greek. The Teutonic starts from four diphthongs: *ai, ei, au, iu*, and after all the changes has returned in New High German to four: *ai, ei, au, eu*. The Celtic most distinctly leads back to four diphthongs: *ai, oi, au, iu*. The Lito-Slavonian appears also to have had only four diphthongs before it divided, to which the Slav. *ě, i, va, u*, and the Lith. *ai, ei*, and *ě* (both=Prus. *ei*) *au, ŭ*, point back; the Lith. *ui* and Slav. *y* appear to be of later origin. In the Latin and Greek, on the contrary, six diphthongs evidently lie at the base of their system: *ai, ei, oi, au, eu, ou*. An interesting analogy, although of later origin, occurs between Gaedh. *ia, ua*, along with *ê, ô*, O.H.G. *ia, ua* (*ie, uo*), along with Goth. *ê, ô* (Grimm. Gesch. d. d. Spr. 844), and Lith. *ě, ŭ*, Slav. *ě, va* for the guna diphthongs; on the other hand the Kym. *û* =Gaedh. *oi* (*oe*) agrees with the Lat. *û* for the older *oi* (*oe*).

§ 9. *Phonological affinities;—Consonantismus.*

In its consonantismus the Celtic connects itself with the Lithuanian and Slavonian in this, that in its older phonetic stage it had no aspirate. The Kymric *ch* is throughout only a sharpening of the spirant *h* for *s*, as in Slavonian, and of similar origin, only that it has not attained the extension of the Slavonic *ch*; the Gaedhelic *f* is a hardening of the initial *v*, the Kymric *f*

(f) is nowhere, as Zeuss thought, a primitive aspirate, but has arisen from *s* or belongs to loan-words (see Beiträge, II. 82), only the Gaulish f is still obscure. In this respect the Celtic stands in marked contrast to the Greek, with its three aspirates, somewhat less so to the Latin, which to be sure has no aspirates, but whose spirants f and h rest upon old aspirates. It deviates from the Teutonic inasmuch as the latter has preserved dialectically to the present day an aspirate *th*, and has also *ch* in the Frankish, but it agrees with it therein that, in both languages the aspirates which do occur are all hysterogens, and rest upon older tenues. Gaedhelic and Teutonic exhibit some agreement in this also, though it is of later origin, that the secondary aspirates have also frequently changed themselves into medials (or medial-aspirates). The change of the old aspirates into medials is common to all European languages, in the Greek occasionally, chiefly after nasals; in the Latin pretty regularly in inlaut; in the others almost without exception; here the Celtic and Teutonic agree best, because sibilants often take the place of old aspirates in the Slavonian and Lithuanian. The Celtic exhibits a remarkable approach to the Teutonic in the occasionally occurring hardening of the medials, as for instance in the root *gen*, where even the Gaulish affords the combinations *Oppianicnos, Toutissicnos*,[91] in *tenge* (along with Goth. *tuggó*, therefore, for **denge*), in inlaut in *ithim, ith, cumacc* along with *cumang* (here likewise in accord Lith. *móku*, as opposed to Slav. *mogą*), *rofetar* (scio) along with Goth. *vait* = Skr. *véda*. This looks almost like a beginning of the German provection of sounds; but on the other hand medials occur instead of tenues in *gabor*, Kymr. *gavar* = Lat. *caper capra*, Teut. **hafar*, in Gaedh. *gabáil* = Cym. *cavael*, Lat. *capere*, Teut. *hafjan*, in Gaul. *ande-*, Gaedh. *ind-* compared with Gr. ἀντί, Goth. *and-*, with which the Lith. *gélbèti* = Goth. *hilpan* agrees. The Gaedhelic thickening of the *n* [rather *nn*] into *nd* in certain positions, Z. 54, is decidedly of later origin; it has peculiar analogy to the Goth. *hunds*, N.H.G. *jemand*, O.H.G. *phant* (= Fr. *pan*). Considering the ignorance which for the moment exists, as to how far phonetic relations may be taken as a measure of relationship, I have meanwhile thought it would be useful to also bring forward such agreements as are of demonstrably later origin, or which might appear in the present discussion of inconsiderable importance.

§. 10. *Affinities of word-formation.*

In word-formation, the suffix *-tion* appears to be exclusively

---

[91] See Pictet's recently published Essai sur quelques inscriptions en langue Gauloise.

Italo-Celtic (the contraction to -*tin* only in Oscan, Umbrian, and Celtic), not much exclusively northern can be opposed to it; the use of -*li* as an infinitive suffix is akin no doubt to the Slavonian -*lŭ* in the participle; it is confined, however, to the single *gabáil* and its compounds. Other suffixes are generally, or pretty generally diffused, such as -*iá* in the feminine abstracts in *e*, -*ti* in the infinitives,[92] the latter seldomest in Latin. The following seem to have been borrowed: -*aire* -*ire* = Goth. -*areis*, Slav. -*arĭ*, Lith. -*orius* (from the Latin -*arius*, which appears to have arisen from *-*asius*); and -*dóit* = W. 2. -*taut* -*daut*, 3. -*dawt*, Arm. *dêt* (from Lat. *tas*), both chiefly in loan-words (likewise the Kymr. -*es* of the fem. = Romance *issa* from the Greek -ισσα, and -*uis* m. = Romance -*ésis* from the Latin -*ensis*). The suffix-combination *-*antat*, [rather *-*antát*] in O. Gaedh. -*atu*, -*etu* (Z. 272) is quite peculiar to the Celtic. The Celtic word-formation, however, so far as it is known to us, bears a modern character like that of the Romance; such a heaping-up of suffixes, as is the rule in the known Celtic languages, is a very rare occurrence in the Latin especially. The use of the suffixes has especially much more widely extended itself in composition; while, for instance, an ἄοπλος ἄνοπλος sufficed for a Greek, and an *inermus*, at most changed into *inermis* (instead of **inermius?*) for a Roman, the O. Irish, like the Kymric, could scarcely attain in the Greek way (λόγος, ἄλογος, ἀλογία) to an *amlabar* (mutus) = V. *aflauar*, or W. 2. *anuab* (ἄτεκνος), but mostly had recourse to suffixes: *cretem, ancretem, ancretmech* (= belief, unbelief, unbelieving). In general *k* especially has attained a much wider extension than in the Classic languages: already in the Gaedhelic -*ach* plays as a determinative suffix a much more important part than in the Latin (*senex*) and Greek (γυναικός), and numerous forms such as *apstallac*(*h*)*t*, *brithemnac*(*h*)*t* may be opposed to the single *senectus;* but in the Welsh participles in -*etic* the -*ic* places itself completely by the side of the Slav. *sladŭkŭ*, etc. The Celtic agrees with the Teutonic, especially in the derivation of the verbs in -*aigimm* and -*igur;* while *cumachtagimm*, *cumachtaigim* still connects itself with *cumachtach*, like the N.H.G. *bemächtige* with *mächtig; asmecnugur* (eradico), *nomisligur* (humilio me) go quite as far beyond the limits as the N.H.G. *peinige, reinige* (In Graff. IV. 3, there are only three such verbs without adjectives: *bimunigôn, chruzigôn, tiligôn*).

§. 11. *Affinities of declension.*

As regards the declension, the circumstance which I have

---

[92] See *ante*, pp. 60, 61.

already touched upon in the introduction, namely, that the so-called Pelasgic tongues only have feminine *a*-stems (-ος, -*as*), appears to me of importance; the Celtic here agrees with the northern languages. Masculine *a*-stems, which, beside the Latin and Greek, occur also in the Slavonian and Lithuanian, appear to be just as foreign to the Celtic as to the Teutonic: compare, however, Stokes.[93] The Celtic has just as few feminine *u*-stems as the Lithuanian,[94] and at bottom also the Slavonian, whose -*y* (*ŭĭ*) is transformed into -*ŭvĭ*, -*vi* and -*va* (Schleicher K. Slav. Formenlehre, 214). On the other hand, it approaches to the Classic languages at least nearer than the Teutonic and Lito-Slavonian in this respect, that it has preserved pure more consonantal stems; it, however, again separates itself from them by the treatment of *s*-stems, and lastly the passage of vocalic stems into consonantal ones seems to be found in Europe exclusively in the Classic languages. The preservation of the ablative, if it were established, would certainly speak strongly for the connection of the Celtic with the Latin; that has, however, as yet by no means been done, and least of all by forms like *innurid*,[95] whose *d* could not possibly represent a primitive final ablative -*d* or -*t*. (In the opposite case the construction of prepositions with the dative would bring the Celtic close to Teutonic). I cannot lay the same weight as Schleicher does upon the preservation of the *b* in the dative plural; the absence of any contraction in this case rather indeed places the Celtic nearest to Teutonic. But then it approaches the Greek and Latin by the total want of the peculiar pronominal declension, which no doubt, on the other hand, has left evident traces in the Umbrian PUSME and *esme, esmei*. The agreement between the genitive singular and nominative plural of the masculine *a*-stems in Old Gaedhelic and Latin, appeared to me from the very first extremely remarkable; the deviation of the Oscan and Umbrian from the Latin in both cases on the one hand, and the reappearance of the fundamental form -*ai* in the nominative plural of the Lithuanian and Slavonian, as also the Greek, had, however, hindered me from drawing further conclusions from it, especially as I could never thoroughly convince myself of the correctness of Rosen's interpretation of the Latin genitive -*î* adopted by Bopp. The communication of the old locative forms by Stokes[96] now to be sure throws a new light upon this genitive also, and makes me more favourable to Bopp's view. To draw further conclusions from so wonderfully exclusive an agreement as that which the Latin exhibits to the

---

[93] Beitr. I. 464.
[95] Beitr. I. 454.
[94] See *ante*, p. 58.
[96] Beitr. I. 334.

Celtic, in opposition to its nearest relatives, remains, however, always attended with uncertainty, because the other agreements in the case-forms (dat. *-iu -u*, voc. *-ĕ*, acc. pl. *-ûs*) recur everywhere except in Teutonic. In the consonantal declension the gen. sing. *-as*, nom. pl. *-is* or *-es*, by the side of the Greek -ος, -ες (Old Lat. gen. *-os -us*), and in opposition to the Gothic *-is*, *-as*, bring the Celtic phonetically close to the "Pelasgic"; but similar points of contact are also found between very remotely related tongues.

§. 12. *Affinities of Gradation.*

In the gradation or comparison, the Greek isolates itself from the analogy of the other languages by its superlative suffix -τατος (simple -τος, and ατος is also, except in numerals, foreign to the others), the Latin by its *-issimus* ($=is+timus$); the Celtic *-am*, *-em* (**-amas*, **imas*) likewise occur only sporadically elsewhere (in prepositional derivatives), its *-imem* nowhere. The Sanskrit, Greek, and Teutonic *-ista*, is wanting in the Latin and Celtic, and every proper superlative suffix in the Lithuanian and Slavonian (except remains like Lith. *pìrmas* = Goth. *fruma*). The superlative forms in the Gaedhelic particle-composition *iarm-*, *remi-*, *tairm-*, *tremi-*, correspond to the Lithuanian *pirm*, Goth. *fram* (both used as prepositions and prefixes); *com-* before (vowels and) aspirated consonants, Z. 842, is no doubt a form of the same kind. I have already[97] mentioned a very significant analogy between the Celtic, Teutonic, and Slavonian, and attempted to explain the Celtic forms,—the double formation of the comparative in Old Gaedhelic *-a* and *-iu* (*-u*), Goth. *-iza* and *öza*, Slav. *-ii* (*-ĭszi*) and *-ĕi:* a similar relationship appears to exist in the Lithuanian between the comparative (*-ésnis*, adv. *-jaŭs*) and the superlative (*-jáusias*, adv. *jáusei*).

§. 13. *Affinities of the Pronouns.*

The Celtic differs from all its relatives in the pronoun in the giving up of the nominative singular of the first and second person; for *mé, me* (cf. Fr. *moi*) is either originally the accusative, or formed from the stem of the oblique cases, and *tú, tu,* appears aspirated as a true vocative only in the combination *athusu* (*o tu*), otherwise it resists aspiration, and has accordingly been explained by Stokes as the accusative. But the pronoun of the third person exhibits in the noun *é, sí, ed*, whose feminine we again find in the Kymr. *hi*, an extremely striking similarity with the Teutonic; this exactly resembles the Gothic *is, si, ita*, and the retention of *d* in primary auslaut even appears to indicate a

---

[97] See *ante*, p. 94.

form *ita*. The accusative feminine -*se* (as the *t* instead of *d* in *inte, intesi,* shows) and the accusative plural -*su, -siu,* (cf. *intiu* and the almost constant double *r* in *airriu, erriu, erru,* and constantly in *etarru* and *forru*) correspond to the Old High German *sia* and *sie, sio, siu;* perhaps indeed the Old Latin forms like *sum, sos,* may likewise be here compared, but not in the nom. sing. fem. We only find in the Sanskrit forms corresponding to the genitive *ái, á* pl. *añ;*[98] so likewise to the dative plural -*aib, -ib*=**abis* [rather -*abo*] (compare *dóib, doib, doaibsem* along with 2. *dúib, duibsi, foraib, forib,* along with 2. *foirib fuirib, indib* is, on the contrary, common to 2. and 3). The pronoun *ta,* the use of which in its isolated form is foreign to the Latin, otherwise preserved everywhere, appears to be preserved in the dative *uad, ood,* f. *uadi,* plur. *uadib, uaidib,* the *d* of which cannot be easily explained otherwise, so likewise in *indid*. The pronoun *ana,* which is foreign to the Classic languages, and on the other hand is preserved pure in the Lithuanian *ans,* Slavonic *onŭ,* in the Gothic *jains* with a (hardly merely phonetic) addition, is evidently again found in the Celtic article, although it appears there are in the Gaedhelic forms with a prefixed *s* also (from *sa* ?)

§. 14. *Affinities of Conjugation.*

But, most remarkable of all is the position of the Celtic with respect to all the cognate languages in the conjugation. Very peculiar combinations and new formations have occurred here, to such an extent that, for instance, the old ending of the first person singular present -*û* (=Lat. -*o,* Gr. ω, Lith. -*u,* Goth. -*a,* O.H.G. -*u,* Slav. -*ą* for primitive -**ami*) has been preserved pure only in extremely few Old Irish forms: *bíu* (sum), *táu* (sum), *dogníu* (facio), *déccu* (video), *tiagu* (venio), *tucu, tuccu* (intelligo), *roiccu* (indigeo), *togu* (eligo), and is to be recognized in some others, at least by the umlaut, *e. g. forchun* (praecipio). Again, striking agreements with the Latin occur in the formation of the tenses and the passive. Notwithstanding these circumstances, a wonderful analogy with the Teutonic and Slavonian is found to exist, which points to a most special connection of these languages, the result either of long continued unity, or of a very special relationship of the mind of the peoples. The Old Gaedhelic paradigm completely connects itself with the Lithuanian in this respect, that the present and the praeterite have quite the same endings, not even deviating in the singular, as in the Greek; compare, for instance—

---

[98] See *ante*, p. 73.

Pres.	Praet.	i.e.
gniu	ro-gnius	-sû
gní	ro-gnis	-sî
gní	ro-gni	-*sati(?)
gniam	ro-gensam	-*samas
gniith	ro-gensith	-*satis(?)
gniat	ro-gensat	-*santi

The Kymric -*st* of the second person singular praet. has been looked upon as the more primitive form, and compared with the Latin -*isti*, although in the Celtic there is nothing in the plural analogous to Lat. -*istis* (Lottner, Zeitschr. VII. 41) ; that this explanation does not strictly apply, but rather that the Kym. -*t*, as Pictet[99] had already surmised, is, as in many other verbal forms, a relic of the pronoun (*e.g.* O. Ir. *carim, cairim*), is shown by the corresponding O. Ir. deponential form: *ru-cestaigser* (disputasti), which has no -*t*, while the third person *rolabrastar* (locutus est) has preserved the -*t (th)*, which has frequently disappeared in the present, and always in the præ- terite. This seeming agreement may, however, be accidental, even unreal. The Kymric agrees more closely and certainly with the Slavonian, as Schleicher[100] remarked, in the combination of the roots *bhû*+*dhâ*; W. 3. *bydaf*=Ch. Slav. *bądą*; but in a more general manner there may be also compared the Ch. Slav. *idą* (eo) *jadą* (ascendo), Goth. *iddja* (ivi) and the -*da* in German weak præterites, -*da*- in the Lithuanian imperfect and present participle. This composition with ·*dhâ* extends farthest in Slavonian *idą*, and next to it in Welsh *bydaf*, *bydwn*, *byd;* even W. 3. *oedwn* (eram), the *d* of which is wanting in the present *wyf*, also appears to explain itself in the same way, and perhaps even the *awd* in the 3rd per. sing. praet. (Z. 504, frequentissima et omnibus verbis communis terminatio, ita ut in hodierna, lingua eadem (scripta -*odd*) sola pro hac persona in usu sit), though -*awt* in the passive, no doubt, also appears by the side of it. It is particularly remarkable that this -*d* likewise passes over into the root composition peculiar to Kymric (especially Welsh) so that for example in *gwybydy* (scis) three roots occur fused together, *gwyd*+*bu*+*da*, and in *gwnathoed* (fecerat), even as many as four, *gwyn*+*ath*+*oe*+*da*. All these agreements in particulars appear insignificant, however, compared to a pervading analogy in the Slavonian, Teutonic, and both branches of the Celtic, which has forced itself from the beginning, on me at least, as one of the strongest proofs of the correlation of these languages.

As is well known, the Slavonian dialects mark the distinction between the imperfect and perfect, continuous and momentary action, which the Greek, Latin, and Romance languages express

---

[99] De l'affinité, etc. 150.   [100] Beitr. I. 505.

by special tense-forms, by separate verbs, the composition with prepositions playing therein a great part. Thus, for instance, almost the whole of stem verbs are imperfect in the Polish, but become perfect by composition. What appears strangest to a foreigner is, that the present is wanting in perfect verbs, because the form of the present has assumed a future signification; but we again find the same phenomenon, because it is founded in the idea of the verb, in the Greek εἶμι, whose present has future, whose moods and imperfect, have aoristic signification. That this phenomenon does not, as it at first seems, stand isolated without any analogy in other languages, was shown by Grimm in his introduction to the translation of Wuk's Servian Grammar (1. *seq.*) and he expressly pointed to a similar distinction in German ("*starb*" and "*verstarb*", "*ich reise*" and "*ich verreise morgen*"), and also indicated that a still more accurate agreement with the Slavonic might be found in Old German.[101] Schleicher[102] has worked this out farther and more accurately, in the first instance only in relation to the future in the Gothic and Slavonian, glancing however at other forms which characterize the Gothic compositum as verbum perfectum. An extremely interesting point with regard to this has been overlooked, namely, the translation of the Greek part. aor. by the part. praes. of compound verbs: *usstandands* ἀναστάς Math. c. ix. v. 9; *gastandands* στάς Mark, c. x. v. 49; *gahausjands* ἀκούσας c. x. v. 41. 47; *ushlaupands* ἀναπηδήσας, *afvairpands* ἀποβαλών v 50, *andhafjands* ἀποκριθείς, v. 51, *andbindandans* λύσαντες, c. xi. v. 2, *gataujandan* κατεργασάμενον I. Corinth. c. v, v. 3; *samaþ gagaggandam izvis* συναχθέντων ὑμῶν, c. v. v. 4 (where Massmann, altogether wrongly, and entirely misunderstanding this peculiarity, prints, contrary to the manuscript, *gaggandam*). The whole power to alter the sense here resides in the particle, which, when no other is present, is *ga-*. In New High German, such distinctions as also occur in the passage of Tatian, already quoted by Grimm: *thaz siu bâri, inti gibar* (ut pareret, et peperit) have for the most part been obliterated, but sometimes petrified also: thus in the *ge-* of the part. praes., the prototype of which may likewise be found in Gothic, *e. g. fulan gabundanana* πῶλον δεδεμένον, Mark, c. xi. v. 2. 4.

What herein especially separates the Teutonic and Slavonian from other tongues which have something analogous, is the great force of the particle in composition, and we meet with a perfectly

---

[101] The verbs with a double theme in Greek and Sanskrit offer a somewhat analogous phenomenon, *e.g.*, λαμβάνω imperfect, ἔλαβον perfect; compare also the future use of the conj. λάβω in Homer.
[102] Zeitschr. IV. 187 *seq.*

analogous order of things in the Celtic languages also. In the old languages, wherever another particle (O. Gaedh. *ni*, W. 2. *ed*, 3. *yd*) has not effected its suppression, we also always find the idea of the perfect denoted by a particle, and as in Teutonic by *ga*-, by a special one: *ru*- (*ro*, *ra*, W. 2. P. *re*, W. 3. *ry*, Arm. *ra*), wherein I have already (*infra*, p. 163, with Stokes's concurrence, Beitr. I. 459) conjecturally traced the Sanskrit *pra*. This particle denotes exactly, as in Gothic and Slavonian, the perfect as well as the future, and, just as in German, its use in the modern language is limited and fixed for certain cases. The Celtic deviates in its grammatical form from the Teutonic in this, that its *ru*- remains before or (like the Greek augment) after other prepositions: *ni roimdibed* (non est circumcisus), *im-meruidbed* (circumcisus est), while the German *ge*- does not enter into true composition. The reason of this after-position of the *ru*- in Old Irish is obviously this, that here, as in the oldest Greek and Sanskrit, the prepositions remain in perpetual *tmesis* (sit venia verbo!) as the treatment of the so-called infixed pronouns shows: *imm-um-ru-idbed* (circumcisus sum properly: me circumcisum est); forms like *asrobrad* (dictum est) therefore agree perfectly with German ones, such as *ausgesprochen* (in separable composition). The Kymric, which does not actually affix its pronouns after other prepositions, also does not put the *ru*- in the middle, but the Cornish and Armoric deviate therein from the Welsh, that the two former put the pronouns also before *ru*-, the latter allows them to follow.

At the other side of the Channel we find this particle—Firstly before the præteritum along with the usual sign of the tense: O. Ir. *rorélus* (manifestavi), W. 1. *ro-gulipias* ("olivavit"), 2. *re-briuasei* (vulneraverit), P. *re-werthys* (vendidi), *re-wresse* (fecerat), so also in the passive before the original participle, in order to denote the perfect: O. Gaedh. *ro-noibad* (sanctificatus est), P. *re thyskas* (instituti sunt), W. 3. *ry echewit* (relicti sunt).

Secondly, before the present and the future (like Gothic *ga*- before the present participle), which are thereby changed into the perfect future exactum: O. Gaedh. *ro-comalnither* (completum est), *ro-ainmnichte* (denominatum sit), *arnachit-r-indar-pither* (ne sis exheredatus), *ro-beimmis* (fuissemus), *ra-n-glana* (emundaverit se); the treatment of the infinitive in Welsh is extremely interesting in this respect: 2. *e-re kafael* (se invenisse, properly: suum invenisse), 3. *ry-gaffel* (accepisse), which accurately corresponds to that of the participle in Gothic.

Thirdly, before present forms, especially the conjunctive and secondary present, which acquire thereby a future signification, as *robia*, *robbia*, *ropia* (crit), or, what is analogous to it, conjunctive signification (cf. Gr. ὅπως ποιήσει, also μὴ λάβῃς, along with μὴ λάμβανε, like Latin ne dixeris), therefore *coro- corro- conro-* (ut), *e.g. conrochra* (ut amet), *conrogbaid* (ut sumatis), *conrobam* (ut simus). We only find the second and third methods in Armoric, but here the custom of the language has gradually decided for the use in the conjunctive, which connects itself more especially with the third way. The Gothic also shows all three uses.

The Gaedhelic has only so far passed beyond the limits of the Slavonian and German as to have also given a particle to the tenses of incomplete action, *nu-, no-* (explained by Stokes as the Skr. *anú*, Beitr. I. 470), only in simple verbs however, mostly also only to the secondary tenses, seldom to the primary present, and future. I will not even venture to make a surmise as to what the Kymric *yd* (W. 2. *ed*, P. *y*, Arm. *ez*), which occurs before all tense-forms, signifies, and what may be its origin;[103] the Gaedhelic *du (do),* which we find instead of the *ru (ro),* does not differ, probably, from the preposition *du; mu (mo)* instead of *nu (no)* is obscure to me.

The use of the particle before the future and for the future, was perhaps much more extensive in Celtic in ancient times, and has thus probably in part become the cause why the future has disappeared, in Gaedhelic in so many instances, in Kymric almost wholly; at all events, the Celtic is in most beautiful harmony with the Slavonian, and above all with the Gothic, as regards its use of the verbal particles.

At least equally significant analogies of the Celtic to the Teutonic (and in a secondary degree to the Lito-Slavonian) as to the Italic (and further on to the Greek) have then everywhere presented themselves; a kind of middle position will accordingly scarcely be denied to it. It appears, however, as if the phenomena which it has in common with the Teutonic were precisely those which chiefly indicate the intellectual life, the internal character of the language. In this category I include, besides the great extension of the composition with independent words, as well as with suffixes, the twofold formation of the degrees of comparison, and the importance of the verbal particles.

In conclusion, it may be mentioned that a comparative syntax might bring to light many peculiar points of contact between the Celtic and Teutonic, such as the use of the infinitive with *do,* the government of the accusative by *cen* (sine); and that in general, the Celtic, so far as it is known to us, bears in its syntax so decidedly modern a stamp that, to me at least, it is very diffi-

---

[103] [The Gaulish *ate-?*]

cult to imagine its connection with the Latin to be so intimate as Schleicher does. In this respect, the Latin evidently bears the most antique stamp, the Greek a much more modern one (for instance, by the freedom in the use of the infinitive and by the use of the article); again, the Lithuanian and Slavonian a much more antique one than the Teutonic; but the most modern of all is the Celtic; so that many things in the Romance languages appear to rest upon Celtic peculiarity. Of this, perhaps, another time.

ON PHONOLOGY IN IRISH.

§. 1. *Necessity of establishing an organic Orthography; and great importance of a comparison of the Modern Irish forms for the purpose.*

SCHLEICHER has justly remarked, that an organic orthography is, above all things, necessary to enable us to get a right knowledge of the Old Irish language. This aim will, no doubt, be only to some extent satisfactorily attained when more extensive and more connected linguistic monuments shall be in our hands than we have at our service on the Continent, and when the editors will strive to attain a greater literal accuracy in their publication, than unfortunately appears to have been hitherto mostly done. Take a few examples in order to show how little, on the whole, one can trust to the literal accuracy of citations:—Zeuss quotes the same word from the same place three times differently spelled, 263 *béisti*, 1009 *bessti*, 1059 *béssti;* O'Donovan gives the following from Cormac's Glossary in two different ways, 292 *tibradaibh*, 360 *tipradaibh*, so likewise 151 *carput*, 252 *carbat*, as dative singular. Fortunately we see, at least in the first case (although we may remain in doubt as to the reading of the codex), by the Middle Irish *ocht m-biasta*, and *na n-ocht m-biast* (Visio Adamnani in O'Donovan 440, 441), as well as from W. 3. *bwystuil*, that the *é* is long, and consequently that *bessti* is wrong, and in both the other examples the *tiprait* of the Leabhar Breac (O'D. 249) and *carpat* in Cormac's Glossary (O'D. 3), as also the Latin loan-word *carpentum*, prove that the true O. Ir. form required two tenues *p* and *t*, which sunk to mediæ only in Middle and Modern Irish,—*tobar* (Keating in O'D. 394) and *carbad*. In *tipra* (or *tipru?*), gen. *tiprat*, an *nt*-stem (Stokes Beitr. I. 457), the *p* appears, however, to have arisen from *b*, by means of the hardening action of an original preceding mute, as in *idpart*, *aedparthi*, and in the examples in Zeuss 80, consequently *ti-* instead of *tid-* as *taith-*, *taid-* (Z. 852) derived from *doaith*,[104]—Cf. *tid-barid* (offerte) Z. 253.

But we have not everywhere at our disposal similar sources

---

[104] So likewise probably in *timne n.* (mandatum, præceptum) from *do- aith-mne*

from which to obtain aid in determining the true old form, and where a new and unknown word presents itself to us, we are at present almost helpless. The necessity is then the more pressing for Celtologists to use every available means for fixing the phonetic laws, and establishing an organic orthography. For this purpose the most important of all is the comparison of the Middle and Modern Irish forms, where this is possible; the comparison of the scanty remains of the Gaulish language, which are almost confined to proper names, and the Kymric dialects, are only of secondary importance, and last in order is that of the other Aryan languages.

The Modern Irish is often so strangely disfigured, even in comparison with the Old Irish, and from want of literary cultivation has (like vulgar languages generally) become so very irregular that a direct comparison of its words and forms with those of Sanskrit and the kindred languages would be very daring, and hazardous, in a still higher degree, for instance, than if we were to directly compare the New High German with the Sanskrit. Most of the errors in the first comparative investigation of the Celtic by Pictet and Bopp were due to this cause, and it was only by the publication of old Irish forms in Zeuss' *Grammatica Celtica* that a firm ground was gained and a solid foundation laid for Celtic philology; everything correct that had been found before that time, we must consider as the especially lucky result of a wonderful divinatory faculty.[105] Who could, for instance, recognize the root *gab* (capere) in the imperatives *fagh* (find) *fág* (leave), *tóg* (raise), the first of which has even a present *faghaim*, without such forms as the infinitives *d'fagbháil*, *d'fágbháil*, *do thógbháil*, which have still preserved the ending consonants. The O. Ir. forms *fagebtis* (haberent, caperent)—together with *fogbaidetu* (usura)—, *foácbat* (gl. deponant, *i. e.* relinquant) Z. 1072, *foracab* (reliquit), *fotrácbussa* (reliqui te), *fácab* (he left) Tir. in O'D. 437, lastly *cotaucbat* Z. 1072, and *cotaocbat* (attollunt se, surgunt) supply the explanation, and the Middle Irish *faghbait, faghbat* (they obtain, find) O'D. 241, *foghébha* (thou wilt get) 242, and, on the other hand, *fagbas*, *fagbus* (he leaves), 155, *tógbhaidh* (raise), 180, show the pas-

---

(root *man*). Cf. *taithminedar, taidminedar, taidmenader* (significat, memorat) in Z. and Mid. Ir. *timnais* (he bids), in O'D. 155; *damnae* (Tirechan in O'D. 436) appears=*do-mne*.

[105] Unfortunately M. Pictet has again lately (Beiträge, II. 84 sq.) trodden the same dangerous path. I cannot, according to what has been said above, recognize as conclusive, nor yet disprove, the examples which are there to prove the passage of *p* into *f*, so long as the corresponding older forms shall not have been pointed out, and only regret that so highly deserving a scholar does not determine to forsake a way which, I am firmly convinced, is an erroneous one.

sage. The first form contains consequently, one preposition *fo-*, after which the media was aspirated, the other several prepositions *fo- ad-* and *do- fo- od*, whilst *d* dropped, after it had changed the following media into tenuis, which however again sunk to a media in Middle Irish; the *gh* in *fagh* is, according to this, mere root anlaut, the *g* in *fág* and *tóg*, in which the fusion of several prepositions is also indicated by the length, is the softening of the *c* which has arisen from *dg*. The form *gheibhim* (I find), given as a parallel form to *faghaim*, shows by the aspirated anlaut, which clearly distinguishes it from *gabhaim* (I take), O. Ir. *gabimm-se* (accipio, sumo), the loss of a preposition ending with a vowel, perhaps *fo-*, for *do-* in *an-dorogbid* (gl. donantes), in Z. 1042, produces a different meaning; on the other hand, in *bheirim* (I give), parallel form of *tabhraim*, likewise plainly distinguished from *beirim* (I bear), by the anlaut, *do-* appears to have fallen off, for already O. Ir. *dobiur* along with *tabur*, i. e., *do- fo- bur* (*do*) exists. In *deirim* (I say), also, just as in the above-mentioned forms, a *bh* has been dropped, which is still retained in the perfect *dubhras* (Keating—*dubhart*), and is confirmed by the O. Ir. *do-m-ber-som* (quae dicit ille); the imperative *abair* (Mid. Ir. still *apair* O'D. 239), and the so-called conjuctive *go-n-abraim*, on the other hand, contain the same root *ber*[106] combined with another preposition (*aith-* Z. 80) cf. *epiur epur* (dico), *apir* (dicis) *atbeir adbeir epeir epir* (dicit), also *dianaiper* (de quo dicit), Z. 1068, *dian-eprem* (de quo dicimus), and many other forms in Z. to which *nadipru, nadipro* (who would not speak), Tir. in O'D. 436, instead of *nad-idbru*, appear also to connect themselves. Less striking disfigurations, but still sufficiently great to warn us of the necessity of extreme caution and moderation in the use of Modern Irish, are, for example, the softening of tenues to mediae almost everywhere in the inlaut, but even in the anlaut in *gá* (what), *gibé* (whoever), *gach* (each, every), *gan* (without), *go* (to, with), and *go* (that), with the part. verb. *gur*, instead of *cia* (quid?), *cip é, cib é* (quicunque), *cach* (omnis), *cen* (sine), *co* (ad, cum), *co* (donec, ut) and *coro;* the loss of the initial *f* in *ri* (with), and *ar* (upon), for *fri* (πρός) and *for* (super)[107], which is probably only a continuation and repetition of an older phonetic process, so that a change into

---

[106] Cf. Skr. *brú*, Zend *mrú*, Gr. ϝερ and ϝρε (ἐρέω, ῥήτωρ), Lat. *ver-bum*, Goth. *vaur-d*.
[107] In the Modern Irish *ar*, the two prepositions *ar* and *for* are so mixed up that it is difficult in each particular case to determine which of them we have to deal with; the forms with suffixed pronouns undoubtedly contain *for*, and not *ar* : *orm, ort, air, uirre* or *uirri, orrainn, orraibh, orra,* or *ortha,* as evidently results from a comparison of the Old Irish—*form* (more correctly *formm*), *fort, foir, fair, fuiri, furnn* (Z. 1005) *fornn forrn, foirib fuirib furib, forru* (c. d. *foraib forib*), on the

f immediately preceded the frequent loss of the *p*, thus for example *patar* may have first changed into *fatar*, and then into *athir*; loss of a vowel in *dá* ("of which", also "which" and "if") for *dian* (from *do-an*, cf. Z. 892), the auslaut of which may still be recognized in the eclipse following; consonantal metathesis in *béarla*, *beurla* for *bélre* (lingua, sermo), for which *bérli* is once found in Z. 9, in *baistim* for *baitsimm* (baptizo), *éistim* for *éitsimm* (ausculto), *easbog* (Mid. Irish *easpog*) for *epscop*, Cornish, *escop* (episcopus).

However necessary in such cases we may find the Old Irish in the elucidation of the Modern Irish forms, and however clearly we may thereby discern the error into which the direct comparison of the latter with those of the other languages might lead us, the comparison of the newer forms is not less instructive and important for correctly understanding the older ones, nay, is often indispensably necessary, and a closer attention to those forms would have saved Zeuss from many errors. As sufficient preliminary investigations have not yet been made to render it possible to give a systematic representation of Irish phonology, I shall only touch in the following pages upon a few points to which my studies have led me.

§. 2. *Vocalismus*.

The most difficult part of the Irish phonetic system to bring to a fixed standard, is the Irish vocalismus, because three kinds of *e* and *o* appear to exist, which do not always admit of being distinguished with certainty, and further, because even the question of the priority of *a* or *o*, *a* or *e*, *u* or *o*, *i* or *e* in individual cases is often beset with insuperable difficulties (at least for the present). In order to indicate graphically the threefold genesis of the *e* and *o* without the use of new type, I propose, firstly, to leave the *e* and *o*, which have arisen directly from *a* without the action of another vowel, unmarked, equally whether they sounded *e* and *o* in Gaulish, or came into existence later by the simple weakening of *a* (perhaps in the auslaut from *ê* and *ô?*); secondly, to mark the umlaut caused by *i* and *u* with the sign of shortness, by which we gain at once a sign for original and secondary *i* and *u*, for *ai* and *au*[108] diphthongal and such as arises from umlaut; and lastly, to denote the breaking by *a*, especially

---

one hand, and *áirium*, *erut-su*, *airi* (the feminine does not occur), *erunn*, *áirib airiuib-si*, *airriu erriu erru* on the other. For the only deviating form O'Donovan adduces Middle Irish *forraind*, with which *orrainn* accurately agrees.

[108] Perhaps the most convenient way would be just to write this umlaut everywhere *aĭ*, *aŭ*. This mode of marking appears to me to be very convenient for Zend also, in order to distinguish the *ĭ* and *ŭ* in *gaĭri*, *taŭruna*, from the original in *gâus*.

weakenings from *i* and *u* by *ĕ* and *ŏ*, the former to be understood completely in the sense of the M. H. G. *ĕ*, the latter, however, in the opposite sense of *ŏ* in O. Norse.

Examples: 1. O. Celtic *e* in *ech* (equus), Gaul. *epo-*, W. 3. *ebawl*, V. *ebol* (pullus); *breth* (judicium), Gaul. *vergo-bretus; nert* (virtus), Gaul. *Nerto-marus, Esu-nertus*, W. C. *nerth*, Arm. *nerz; nemed i. e. nemedh* (sacellum), Gaul. νεμητον *i. e.* νεμετον, *Vernemetis*, W. 2. *neuat*, 3. *neuad* (aula); O. Celtic *o* in *orcaid* (occidit), *orcas* (qui occidit), *i. e. org-*, Gaul. *Orgeto-rix*, W. 1. *orgiat* (caesor); *ocht* (octo), Gaul. *Octo-durus*, W. 2. *uith*, 3. *wyth;*—2, umlaut by *i*—*aĭth-, aĭd-, ĕd-, ĭth-, ĭd-*, Gaul. *ate-*, Kymr. *at-, et-* (perhaps also W. 2 *ed-, e-*, 3. *yd-, y-*, P. *y-*, Arm. *ez-, e-*, the verbal particle, = Skr. *ati ?*); *aĭr-, ĕr-, ĭr-*, Gaul. *are-*, Kymr *ar-; ĕrbaĭd* (committit), *ĕrbĭd* (tradite), root *arb*; umlaut by *u*— *rolaŭmur, rolŏmor* (audeo)—more frequently *aŭ* (*oŭ*) and *aŭ*— *baĭll, boĭll, baŭll, baŭllu, bŭllu*; 3. breaking of *i*—*ĕtha, bĕtha, ĕtal, cĕnn, tuisĕl*; breaking of *u*—*mŏga, lŏth* (lutum), *crŏchad;* simple weakening perhaps in *fĕlsub, crŏch, dŏmun* (Gaul. *dumno-*)? In order to distinguish *ia = é* and *ua = ó* from contracted *ia* and *ua*, I mark the former with the grave accent on *a*—e. g., *biad*, (victus, esca) from *bivatha* (βίοτος), hence gen. *biith biid*, Mod. Ir. *bídh*, on the other hand, *dià* (deus), from *déva*, gen. *déĭ, dé*, so also *uàthath, uàthad* (singularis) = *óthad*.

Even though it be established that the *a* in Mid. Irish *mara* (maris), *maĭnistrech* (monasterii) is corrupted from the *o* of O. Irish *mora, monĭstre* (monasteriorum), and the same observation very probably applies to the Mid. and Mod. Ir. *a* of many endings (*e. g.*, part. pass. in *-ta*, O. Ir. *te*) as compared with O. Ir. *e*, we cannot thence by any means conclude that this is everywhere the case; thus, for instance, that in the gen. sing. *bĕtho* (mundi), we have an older form than *bĕtha*[109], in *aecaĭllse*, an older form than *aecolsa* (ecclesiae). The Mod. Ir. affords us little help in this investigation, because the uncertainty of the O. Ir. orthography (which, for example, leaves the umlaut of the *a* by *i* at one time unmarked, and at other times writes it *ai, oi, ui, e, i*, and even *ae* and *ói*) is not only in great part retained here (leaving out of consideration the action of the well known rule —*caol le caol, leathan le leathan*—a rule which, however, in its turn acts disturbingly), but also by arbitrarily confounding the simple vowels, has reached so great an extension that almost any short vowel may stand for every other. Thus *a* is found for *u* in *chugam* for *cuccumm* (ad me) in the acc. pl. *chuca* for *cuccu* (ad eos) as in Middle Irish already; *a* for *i* especially before *n* (ana-

---

[109] Although Mr. Stokes, in his valuable Irish Glosses, p. 159, appeals for it to the ogamic gen. *Atilogdo* or *Apilogdo*.

logous to the French pronunciation of *en* = Lat. *in*, in *dans* = de intus, *sanglier* = singularis even written), in the article *an* = *ind*, *ant* = *int*[110], in the preposition *a(n)* = *iṅ*, in the interrogative particle *an(n)* = *in*, while the prefix *in-* or *ion-* has preserved the *i* of the old *ind-* in *colann* (a body) = *colinn* (caro); even *u* for *i* in the preposition *um* = *imm* (also with suffixes *umam*, etc.); *o* for *e* in *romam*, etc., *roimpe* = *remi*. In spite of this confusion in the elements, which for the eye is considerably increased by the well known rule according to which *féar* is written for *fér* (gramen), *fear* for *für* (vir), *feárr* for *ferr* (melior), even *neoch*, *noch* for *nech* (qui, properly aliquis), the Modern Irish comes to our aid even in the vocalismus, whenever we have to do with the explanation and origin of true or apparent diphthongs. The O. Ir. *ai* has, for example, a threefold meaning, as a true diphthong, as umlaut from *á*, and as umlaut from *a;* the usual mode of marking these in MSS. is not sufficient to properly separate these three sounds according to their different origin, the diphthong appearing at one time with, and at another without, an accent, being consequently not sufficiently distinguished from either the short or the long umlaut. (In the marking of the umlaut by *aĭ* and *áĭ* above proposed, the accent for the diphthong *ai* may be dispensed with). The parallel forms also (*oi*, *aë*, *oë*, for the diphthong, *ĕ*, *ĭ* for the umlaut *aĭ*, *á* without umlaut for *áĭ*) do not give full security, for *ae* is sometimes found for *ĕ*, namely in anlauts and auslauts, and *ái* and *oi* sometimes for the umlaut *aĭ*, especially before liquids (Zeuss, 32). But if we compare Mod. Irish, the diphthong *ai*, *aë* appears transformed into *ao* (or its umlaut *aoi*): *caora* = *caira* (ovis), *caoin* = *cáin* (bonus), *gaoth* (already Mid. Ir.) = *gáith gáid* (ventus), *maoin* (wealth) = O. Ir. pl. *maini* (opes, pretiosa, dona), *saobh* (bad, evil) = *sáib*, *sáeb*, *sóib soeb* (falsus), *saoghal* (world) = *saigul*, *maor* (steward) = Mid. Ir. *maer;* the umlauts, on the other hand, have remained unchanged, *maith* (bonus), *ainm* = *aĭnmm* (nomen), *aimsear* = *aĭmsër* (tempus), *cailleach* (a hag) = *caĭllĕch* (anus, monacha), *gabháil* = *gabáĭl* (sumptio), except that, as already in O. Irish, *oi* frequently occurs for *aĭ*, and seldomer *ei*—*coill* (wood) = *caĭll* (silva), *cloinne* = *claĭnne* (prolis), *anoir* = *anaĭr* (easterly), *eile oile* = *aĭle* (alius). The Modern Irish does not suffice, however, to distinguish *ai* and *oi*, for it expresses both by *ao* (*aoi*) e. g., *aon* (unus) = *oën oin*, *caol* = *cóil* (macer), *coaga* = *cóica* (quinquaginta) —*cúig* = *cóïc* (quinque), is remarkable. The Kymric dialects which have retained the *ai*, *aë*, as for instance the Welsh, but change *oi*, *oë* into *u* (with few, perhaps, apparent exceptions),

---

[110] The explanation of the newer form which I have attempted at p. 88, is incorrect, because this phonetic peculiarity of the Modern Irish had escaped me.

e. g., ûn = Irish *oën*, may be here appealed to. Umlaut *aŭ* and diphthong *au* (*áu*, *ŏu*, *áŏ*, *ó*) appear to be less sharply distinguished, as the former is replaced by *u* or *o*, and the latter by *ó* or *ú*, which is sometimes shortened, or its length is not marked, cf. *auë* (nepos) and *o ua*, *augtortás* (auctoritas), and *ughdar*, pronounced *údar* (auctor); the inorganic *aŭ* instead of *aĭ* in *aŭd*-, *aŭr·* (Z. 7. 8) does not occur at all in Modern Irish.

§. 3. *Consonantismus—Aspiration of Mediæ after Vowels.*

The comparison of the newer forms yields us much more important service in the consonants. Thus, for instance, at p. 119, a form *se* (already proposed by Stokes, Beiträge I. 450) for the acc. fem. *siu* for the acc. pl. was deduced from *intë* (in eam), *intiu* (in eos), *aĭrriu* (propter eos); *ĕtarru* (inter eos), *forru* (super eos), and the Modern Irish which has only preserved the dative after *di* and *do* (*díobh*, *dóibh*), but otherwise puts the accusative everywhere, offers proofs in abundance which confirm this conclusion. The *s* of *se* and *siu*, *su* is preserved in *tháirse*, *tháirsi* (over her) and *thársa* (over them); it has changed into *t* after *s* in the secondary form *thársta* and in *aiste*, *-ti* (out of her), *asta* (out of them), likewise in *uaiste*, *-ti* (above her), *uasta* (above them), in which consequently *s* or.*st* is to be considered as originally *ss* (the original auslaut of *tar(s)* is perhaps still to be recognized in the *rr* of *thorrainn*, *thorraibh*, -*orrainn*, *orraibh* from *for* occur also, however, and the O. Ir. *torunn* has single *r*); *th* for *s* after vocalic auslaut in *fúithe*, *-thi* (under her) and *fútha* (under them), *uaithe*, *-thi* (from her), and *uatha* (from them), *tríthe*, *thi* (through her) and *tríotha* (through them), similarly after *r* in the secondary form *ortha; rr* for *rs* in *uirre*, -*ri* (on her), *orra* (on them), *eatorra* (between them) where at the same time the depressed tenuis in *eidir* is preserved; original tenuis preserved by *s* in *aice*, *-i* (with her) and *aca* (with them), *chuice*, *-i* (unto her), and *chuca* (unto them), while *aige* (with him) and *chuige* (unto him), prove vocal anlaut by the media; tenuis after nasals derived from an original media in *uimpe*, *-i* (about her), *umpa* about them, from a secondary one (?) in *innte*, *-i* (in her), *ionnta* (in them), directly intercalated in *roimpe*, *-i* (before her) and *rompa* (before them), on the other hand *roime* (before him). All these examples are in the highest degree important and interesting by the constancy with which the *s*, which has elsewhere generally disappeared, makes its influence still left in the latest language period, and most strikingly of all in *roimpe* (for *roĭmsi* the *p* as in Lat. *dempsi*, *demptum*) along with *roime* with aspirated *m*.

But we especially want very often the Modern Irish to determine whether tenuis or media is to be read aspirated or not. As is well known, the oldest documents do not always very accurately mark the aspiration even in tenues, still less in the case of *f* and *s*, and not at all as a rule in the case of mediæ and *m*, or at most mark the unaspirated pronunciation by duplication, and in the MSS. of Zeuss, wherever the aspiration is indicated, the aspirated tenuis is found for the media. Thence arises a double ambiguity, inasmuch as we may fluctuate equally between *d* and *dh* as between *dh* and *th;* but this ambiguity is still further increased by the circumstance that tenuis not only occurs for double media, but also inversely media here and there for pure tenuis. As the Middle Irish MSS. also do not always accurately mark the aspiration of the media, it is often only the Modern Irish which can here help us, for the latter, in spite of the above mentioned corruption, has, by completely dropping aspirated consonants, and a wide spread lowering of pure as well as aspirated tenues, fortunately maintained accurately, on the whole, the limits between aspiration and pure pronunciation, with the exception of some verbal forms before which particles have dropped, and some particles whose anlaut is aspirated as, *cheana* (already), *bheos, fós* (yet) for *cene* (jam), *beos* (adhuc), *co* and *tar* in the formulae *chugam, thorm* (cf. above.)

The simple *m* which in O. Irish is not protected by consonants, becomes always aspirated in Modern Irish; *dŏmaĭn in *fudumaĭn, fudŏmaĭn* (profundus) becomes *doĭmin* (although the second vowel was probably intercalated here merely to ease the pronunciation on the dropping of the O. Irish ending), and this *ṁ* has likewise (even in Middle Irish) frequently taken the place of an original *bh* as in *naoṁ* instead of *noib* (sanctus), *neam-, neim-* instead of *neb-* (negative prefix), *claidheṁ* instead of *claĭdeb* (gladius), *fealsaṁ* instead of *felsub*, which has in consequence followed the false analogy of *brithëm*. We may, therefore, with perfect security deduce from *m* in inlaut in Modern Irish, *m̄* or *mm* (*mb*) in Old Irish, which to be sure we are not as yet always able to explain; thus *anam* points back to *animm* (anima) Z. 1059, *ainm* to *ainm̄* (nomen), *uaim* to *uaimm* (a me), etc., as *im, uim, um,* does to *imm* (*imb*)[111] while *dom* has become *daṁ* (to me), *rem roiṁ* (before).

An original media after vowels is always aspirated in Modern

---

[111] As in *imm* from *mb*, so may the *m̄ = m* in *Cormac* (for ogamic *Corpimaquas*, where the vowel dropped should produce aspiration) have been assimilated from *pm*, in *ammi* (sumus) from *sm;* in *animm, ainm̄, uaimm* it is just as unsatisfactorily explained as in 1 sg. and pl. of the verb; and singularly enough the Kymric shows just here a softening, V. *enef* Arm. *enef, eneff,* (anima), W. 3. *enw.* P. (*h*)*anow*, Arm. *hanu* (nomen), W. 3. *ohonaf, ahanaff* (a me, de me), just as *in*

Irish, adharc, brágha, buidhe, croidhe, a n-deaghaidh, foghlaim, adhradh, gen. adhartha; therefore, no doubt, to be thus represented in Old Irish: adarc (cornu), brág̊e (cervix), buĭdë (flavus), crĭdé (cor), indegaĭd-n̊ (post), foglaĭm (comprehensio), adrad (adoratio). The change between aspirated tenues and mediæ also points in the same direction; the final med. asp. is a softening from ten. asp. in adrad (probably also in indegaĭd) as frequently happens, cf. cailleach, Old Ir. caĭllĭch, gen. caillighe. After consonants the mediæ in Modern Irish also remain without aspiration, except where a vowel has dropped out, árd, fearg, bolg, borb, O. Ir.—ardd (altus), ferc for fergg (ira), bolc = bŏlgg (bulga), borp, i.e. börb (stultus); Stokes (Beiträge II. 102) has, therefore, rightly looked upon such forms as dealbh, marbh, tarbh, where the mediæ appear aspirated after liquids, as proving bh = v.[112]

On the other hand, the mediæ are often assimilated after liquids, especially after m and n [as partly already in O. Irish, uall (superbia), gen. uaĭlbe], thus in agallam = acaldam, accaldam, acaltam, i. e., accalddam (allocutio), iomad Corm. Glos. (many) = imbed (copia, ops), ionam = indiumm (in me), binn (melodious) = bind, clann = cland (proles), cunradh, Mid. Ir. cundradh (a covenant), O. Ir. cundrad (merx), connarcas (I saw), for cond. (root darc in δέρκω, etc.), coinneal (a candle), cf. caĭndlóĭr (candelarius), even Middle Irish bennacht, bennachadh = bendacht, bendachad (benedictio) likewise mallacht = maldacht (maledictio).

The so-called eclipse also depends upon the assimilation, so far as it affects mediæ, inasmuch as na-m-ball (membrorum) is pronounced nammall. I suspect, therefore, that in O. Irish also the dot over n̊ and m̅ before mediæ had more to do with the media than with the nasal, and consequently that rad ndé is to be pronounced rad né (notwithstanding the apparently contradictory mode of writing frecdairc, dofoirde), because nasals otherwise regularly drop out before tenues, but not before mediæ, or rather remain when tenuis becomes media, as in ind- (Gaul. ande-), ingor (Lat. ancora). Another assimilation according to which codhladh (sleep), céadna (the same), colna (of the flesh), are pronounced colladh, céana, colla, is not indicated in writing.

§ 4. *Consonantismus—Aspiration of Tenues after Vowels.*

The original tenues (and the hard spirants s, f) like the mediæ, are always aspirated in true Celtic words after vowels, if

---

1 sg. -af, while although an Arm. dif, diff corresponds to the Irish dom, dam, we have on the other hand W. 3. im, ym, P. thym. From this it appears that the mm in these cases is exactly comparable with the nn of the article, and was perhaps produced under the influence of the original accent.

[112] Derbh (certus) along with dearbh is very curious, so likewise is easbha (defect), pl. gen. easbhadh, cf. acc. tesbaĭd (defectum), dat. tesbaĭth.

a vowel or liquid follows, but not before mutes, except in the combination *ct*, which is sometimes written *cht*, also, as it appears, not before (dropped) *v;* and in this the Modern Irish has altered nothing, except that it has logically carried out the *cht;* with oscillation in Old Irish of aspirated tenues to mediæ, especially in *th*, less so in *ch*, in which latter in Modern Irish it has much more extensively spread. After consonants (as before mutes) tenuis remains without aspiration, also after those which have dropped out, hence *t, c,* instead of *nt, nc* (likewise *f, s,* instead of *nf, ns); but* Modern Irish has here frequently lowered the tenuis to media, both original and secondary.

The old Irish has changed organic mediæ into tenues in two ways: 1. before dropped vowels, by which the media has to a certain extent passed into auslaut, and thus become hardened to tenuis, for example in *tăirci* (efficit) from *do-ăirci*, in the compound prefixes *int-* from *in-do-, tair-* from *do-air- (d'air-) taïth-* from *do-aïth-, tes-* from *do-es-, tiar-* from *do-iar-, timm-* from *do-imm-, tin-* from *do-in-, tind-* from *do-ind-*, the same with the dropping of an *f* in *tú-, tó-* from *do-fu-, do-fo-*, in *tor-, tór- (tuar-, tur-, ter-)* from *do-for*, with the dropping of an *s* in *intsamail, intsliächt,* in the article *int-* from *ind-s-*, and in the abovementioned prepositions with suffixed pronouns; 2. by the collision of two mutes, in which the first, if it was a media, became on that account hardened, and then induced the hardening of the second, just as if it was an original tenuis or aspirate, *atomaĭg* from *ad-dom̄-aĭg, cotóndelcfam* from *cot-doñ-delcfam (cot-* according to Stokes, Beiträge II. 106 = Welsh *cant-), frĭtammiurat* from *frĭth-damm-iurat*, and others given by Zeuss, 336, *ĕdpart, ĭdpart* from *aĭth-bart*, but has then generally been dropped, or more correctly has assimilated itself (for gemination often remains unexpressed in O. Irish, and in the case of consonants capable of aspiration, always in Modern Irish, only *ll, nn, rr* are written), thus in *acaldam accaldam* (allocutio) from *ad-galdam*[113] (pronounced *atgaldam, atcaldam), ĕpĭl* (perit) along with *atbaĭl* Z. 1012 (pronounced *atpaĭl)* from *aith-baĭl, ĕcne* (cognita) along with *aĭdgne aĭth-gne, frecre* (responsum) from *frĭth-g(a)re, conucbad* (ut attolleret) from *conuad-gabad, doopĭr* (privat, aufert) from *do-od-bĭr*.

In the first case the Modern Irish preserves the tenuis which is thus produced, *e.g.* in *tim-*, in the article *ant* and in the above examples of prepositions with pronouns; in the second it allows

---

[113] Cf. *adgládur* (προσαγορεύω), *adgládathar* (appellatur); so also *comalnad* (impletio) along with *lán* (plenus). The abovementioned hardening is also, no doubt, the reason for the mode of writing *gg, dd, bb,* for *c, t, p*.

the same tenuis (the second mute) to again sink to a media, but does not aspirate it, e. g., *iodhbairt* (an offering) = *idpaĭrt*, *agallaim* (a dialogue) = *acaldam*, *ei-blim* (I die), likewise *ĕplĭmm, *eagna* (wisdom) = *ĕcne* (sapientia), *admuim* (I confess) cf. *ataĭmĕt* (profitentur) from *ad-daĭmĕt;* both united show themselves in the abovementioned *tógbhaim*, where the *t* of *tócbaĭmm* from *do-fo-od-g*) has remained, but the *c* has sunk to *g*. It has likewise changed the original tenues, to which (*n*)*t* and *t*(*v*) consequently belong, everywhere into mediæ after vowels: *codladh* (sleep) = *cotlad* (somnus) dat. *cotlŭd*, Z., 822, *fad* = *fŏt* (longitudo), *céad* = *cét* (centum), *céadna* (the same) = *cétnë* (primus), *creidim* = *cretim* (credo), sometimes even geminated ones as, for instance, *clog* = *clocc* (clocca), *beag* (little) = *becc bec* (parvus, paucum), along with these there are however *mac* = *macc* (filius), *cnoc* (a hill) = *cnocc* (gibber, ulcus), also *cruit* (a harp) = *crot*, i. e., *crott* (crotta), *breac* (a trout), gen. *bric*, which points to *brecc (cf. N.H.G. *bricke); trócaĭrë* (misericordia) from *tróg-caĭrë* (amor miseri) also remains unchanged. Fluctuations occur here after consonants; after *s* generally softening; less frequently and more properly in Gaelic after *ch* (after *gh*,—*ughdar*, O. Irish *augtortás);* after *l* and *r* the tenuis is preserved—*olc*, *marc*, *neart*, *falt*, *corp;* but *p* often passes into *b* after *l*[114] [*Alpa*, gen. *Alpan* Cormac's Gloss. in O'Don. 3. 354 (Scotland), acc. *Alpaĭ-n* (Alpes) Z. 616, from which *cenalpande* (cisalpinus), therefore properly "highland", has become *Alba*, already Middle Irish gen. *Alban* in O'Don. 83, dat. *Albain* 251], less frequently after *r* (yet *carbad* = *carpat),* *t* remains also after *n* in *muintir*, *muintear*, but *c* passes into *g*— *rángas* (I reached), *thángas* (I came), in Middle Irish still *ráncatar* (they reached), O'Don. 246, *táncamar* (we have come), 252.

It is evident that the so-called eclipse of the tenuis, and of *f*, which sinks to *bh* under similar conditions, (strictly speaking no eclipse can be spoken of in the case of *s*, as the *t* before it belongs to the article, otherwise we would be obliged to consider the *p* of *umpa* to belong to the eclipse) also depends upon this sinking to mediæ, and has properly nothing whatever to do with the nasal, which is generally dropped before it. Just as in the middle the tenuis has changed into a media indifferently, whether a nasal has fallen out before it or not, as *cét*, *ĕtar* become *céad*, *eidir*, exactly as *bec* becomes *beag*, the former is, however, accidentally the more frequent, so in the anlaut, under certain conditions, every tenuis not protected by consonants also passes into a media, and it is a simple accident that in most cases a nasal originally preceded, and that consequently, as a rule, the funda-

---

[114] Probably the *bh* in *dearbh*, *easbha* may be thence explained; see note 112, p. 142.

mentally different eclipses of the tenues and mediæ go hand in hand; that this is not a necessary condition is shown by the eclipse after *éa-*, *éi-* (O. Ir. *é-* along with *es-*, like Lat. *e* along with *ex*), which only occurs with tenues, *éagcóir* (injustice) = *écóir* (incongruus), *éadtrom* (light) = *étrum̃* (levis), not with mediæ, *eadoim̃in* (shallow), because no nasal is present.

From what has been said above, we may consequently conclude with perfect safety that Modern Irish tenuis corresponds to O. Irish tenuis, Modern Irish dura to O. Irish dura, on the other hand aspirates to aspirates with exceptions, Modern Irish mediæ to Old Irish mediæ only if aspirated, or in the combinations *rd*, *lg*, *rg* (*ld* and *nd* have been assimilated to *ll*, *nn*), while after vowels, *s* and *ch* every pure media points to an old tenuis, after *l* and *r* at least *b* is of uncertain origin. We may therefore infer from *árd ardd* (sublimis)—written *ardd*, *art*, *ard*, from *fearg fergg*—written *ferc*, from *bolg bolgg*—also written *bolc*, likewise from *agallam̃ accalddam*—written *acaldam* and *acaltam*, from *binn bindd;* on the other hand *borb* would not lead with certainty to *börbb*, if we did not find *burbë* written along with *burpë*. The circumstance that dura point back to dura will, however, be of especial use to us in the case of dentals, for the purpose of getting rid of some errors into which Zeuss has fallen in several passages of his grammar, in consequence of having neglected the newer forms.

§. 5. *Consonantismus—Cases which afford occasion for Aspiration after a preserved or lost Vowel:* (I.) *in Inlaut;* (II.) *in Anlaut;* (III.) *in Syntax.*

As is well known, the same laws which govern aspirations after vowels, apply in general to those cases also where vowels had originally existed, but dropped out, so that we may infer from the appearance of aspiration the former presence of a vowel in inlaut as in anlaut; if, therefore, for example, *s* before mutes, (according to O'Don., also before *m*, cf. *fosmachtu*, Z. 666, consequently before consonants capable of aspiration generally) be not infected by preceding vowels, as the mode of writing *tesst* shows, a *doinscann-som*, *intinnscana* (incipit) from *do-ind'-sc.*, *in-do-ind'-sc.*, will stand opposed perfectly according to rule to the *intsamuil*, *intsliŭcht* from *ind's*. The aspiration rule is, however, subject to so many exceptions in this case, inasmuch as it also depends upon the nature of the preceding consonants, that in the uncertainty of the ancient orthography we can only attain safe results by a comparison of all individual cases with constant reference to Modern Irish.

Such cases as afford occasion for aspiration by a preserved or lost vowel, belong essentially to three categories:

(I.) *In Inlaut.* In the inlaut of a word before, and in the derivative or flexional endings, especially in the word-forming suffixes *-ath, -ëth, -uth, -id, -ach, -ëch, -ĭthë (-ĭdë)*, and before the *-t (th, d)* of different conjugational endings. In all these cases occasion also often occurs for the dropping of a vowel in inflexion and derivation, and Zeuss (page 84, with which the examples 762 *seq.* may be compared) has correctly remarked that "the *t* of the ending is not aspirated after *l, n, s*, and that a *tt* (or *t*) arises from *t-t, th-t*".

The following examples are from the conjugation: *con-festa* (ut scias), *marufeste marrufeste* (si sciretis), *condigénte* (faceretis), *nígette* (Z. 264, "non faceretis"?) *conrochretesi* (concredcretis), *connáruchretesi* (ne credereltis)—with *t* for *tt*—along with *niscartha* (non abesses), *nongabthe* (q. sumebatis), fut. secund. *folnibthe* Z. 454; deponentials—*rofestar* (scit) *nifìastar* (nescit), *miàstar* (judicat) and the preterites in *-astar, -istir, -ëstar;* passive forms—*arna furastar* (ne fuscetur), *samaltir* (comparatur), *adcomaltar* (conjungitur), *donelltar* (q. declinatur), *maniréltar* (nisi manifestatur), *frisdúntar* (obstruitur), *asagnintar* (significatur), *gentar, do-géntar* (fit, fiet), *nomglantar* („emungor") *non-líntarni* (implemur), *nonnertarni* (q. confortamur) for *tt*, *con-intorgáitar* (ut non circumveniamur) and *honuntogaitarni* (ex quo fraudamur), *sluíntir* (significatur) with *t* for *dt*, on the other hand *derbthair, scríbthar ôinaĭchthir, caĭrĭgthir, lobrĭgthir, suĭdigthir, intoĭchther, indtuĭgther, arosaĭlcther, a-carthar, itarscarthar, anasberthar, asrirther, fristacuĭrther, berthir* (differently *nomthachtar* („angor") and *génthir*, Z. 470!); preterites— *dorónta* (facta sunt), *asrulenta* (inquinata sunt) along with *dorurgabtha* (prolata sunt); secondary tenses — *nolíntae* (solebat repleri), *conulíntae* (ut compleretur) along with *arna eperthe, doberrthe, roberrthe, nocrochthe, na ructhae;* past participles— *accomallte acomoltae* (conjunctus), *comchlante* (conseminatus) with *t* for *dt*, *remfoiti* (praemissi) so also *dlútai* acc. pl. (fixa) 1015 for *th't., forbanda* (secta) 845 with *d* after *n*. On the other hand, *remeperthe, sulbaĭrichthe, aĭdchuĭmthe, loĭscthe, aŭrgabtha,* (*timmorte* is curious with the *c* dropped as in the preterite *dobimchomartt,*further *imdíbthe* (circumcisus)and *foĭrcthe* (eruditus)[115] where, after the loss of the *n* of *ben-* and *can-*, we should expect uninfected *t, forngarti* (jussi) appears like *timmorte* to be formed without a copulative vowel); future participle—*eclustai, sastai, imcasti, aĭrillti, dénti, forcanti, cocarti,* for *cocartti* (emendandum), in opposition to *eperthi, imcabthi,* (*aichti* is curious!). The whole of the examples, with the exception of the evidently

---

[115] *Imdíbthe* and *foĭrcthe* may be compared with Sanskrit and Greek forms, such as *hata*, φατός, from *han*, φεν.

corrupt *génthir*, confirms throughout the observation of Zeuss; the omission of the aspiration takes place only after *l*, *n*, *s*, *d*, *t*, *th*, in opposition with *crochthe*, among others, except in the case of *nomthacthar* and *aichti* (*timmorte* and *foriigarti* may be explained in this way, that these verbs go in accordance with series III. of Zeuss); it is therefore singular that O'Donovan, in the rule for the Modern Irish passive and participles, puts tenuis after all aspirates *ch*, *gh*, *th*, *dh* (others do not here occur), except in the verbs in *-ighim*, as well as after *l*, *ll*, *n*, *nn*, *s*, while, on the other hand, he puts the aspirate after *d* and *t*. He at the same time admits, however, that the sound remains the same after *d* and *t*, whether we write *t* or *th*. This rule also receives no confirmation otherwise, inasmuch as *t* is everywhere found in derivation and flexion both in Old and Modern Irish after *l*, *n*, *s*, *t*, *d*, *th*, *dh* (only with softening in *d* after *n*, seldomer after *l*), on the other hand *th* appears equally constant after *ch*, *gh*, as after all other mutes.

The suffix *-tu* masc., *-atu*, *-itu* (cf. Beitr. II. 81), seldomer *-ti*, especially affords us examples from the declension, as it is usually affixed without a copulative (hence *tabaĭrt*, *epert*): gen. *pectha pectho*, nom. plur. *pecthi*, *pecthe*, *pectha*, gen. *pecthe*, dat. *pecthib*, acc. *pecthu* (*pectha* Z. 1003) from *peccad* (i.e. *peccáth*), gen. *cröchtho* from *cröchad*, *ëtarscartha* from *ëtarscarad*, *cúrsagtha* from *cúrsagad*, *dánĭgthëa* from *dánĭgŭd*, *foilsĭchtho indjoĭlsĭgthe* from *foĭlsĭgŭd*, *incholnĭchtho incholnĭgthëa* from *incholnĭgŭd*, *intsechtaĭgtha* (read *intś.*) from *sechtaĭgŭd*, *sulbaĭrĭchthe* Z. 618 from *sulbaĭrĭgŭd*; gen. *iarfaĭchthëo iarfaĭgtho*, dat. pl. *iarfaĭgthib* Z. 1070 from *iarfaĭgĭd*, *iarfĭgĭd* f., dat. pl., *debthib* from *debuĭth;* on the other hand, gen. *rélto* from *rélath*, *rélad* (manifestatio), *indaërchoĭltëa* from *ërchoĭliñd* (definitio), *césta césto* from *césath césad* (passio), *nerta* from *nertad* (exhortatio), *taĭrmchrutto* from **taĭrmchruthad* (transformatio), gen. *dag-imráta*, *drog-imráto* (it is to be read thus), nom. pl. *imbráti imráti*, acc. *imrátiŭ*, (Z. 1068), from *imbrádud imrádud* (cogitatio).[116] Here also *t* remains after *l*, *n*, *s*, and dental mutes, but is aspirated after all other consonants, and the Modern Irish confirms this by the plurals *sgéalta*, *seólta*, *ceólta*, *néalta*, *bailte*, *coillte*, *aitheanta*, *léinte*, *teinnte*, *linnte*, *cluainte*, *móinte*, *táinte*, *cointe*, *bróinte*, and the genitives *ionganta*, *tionnsganta*, *cosanta*, *déanta* from *sgéal* (a story), *seól* (a sail), *ceól* (music), *néal* (a cloud), *baile* (a town), *coill* (a wood), *aithne* (a commandment), *léine* (a shirt), *teinne* (fire), *linn* (a pool), *cluain* (a meadow), *móin* (a bog), *táin* (a flock), *cu* (a greyhound), *bró* (a quern), *iongnadh* (wonder),

---

[116] Zeuss, 851, erroneously assumes a nominative *dagimrat*. Stokes (Beiträge I. 450) also is in error respecting *taĭrmchrutto* (*crochta* appears to be careless writing).

tionnsgnadh (beginning), *cosnadh* (defence), *déanadh* (doing), in opposition to the plurals *múrtha, cogtha, toirthe, teangtha,* the genitives *daórtha, adhartha, cunnartha* from *múr* (a wall), *cogadh* (war), *toradh* (fruit), *teanga* (a tongue), *daóradh* (condemning), *adhradh* (adoration), *cunnradh* (a covenant), in which it makes no difference whether the suffix *-at* is originally word-forming as in *teinne,* or determinative as in *cu.*

Derivatives in *-te* (i. e. *-tia* or *-taja*) after *s, l, n,* in which, however, *d* appears generally after *l* and always after *n* (evidently pure *d* and not *dh*), see in Zeuss 763 seq.; whether, however, *místae* (menstruus), *conde* (caninus), *anmande* (animalis), *talmande* (terrestris), *eiscsende* („intensivus"), *cenalpande, aniendae,* which are evidently derived from consonantal stems, have actually lost a vowel before the suffix, remains doubtful; the *d* is to be read aspirated after *r* and other consonants as after vowels, *bithgairddi* (perpetuo breves), has been wrongly explained, like *cethargarait,* it belongs to an *i-* stem, and is to be further carried back to an *nt-* stem. To the examples for *tt, t* from *t't, d't, th't, am-brotte* (momentaneum), *gutte gutae* (vocalis) — from which *angutas* 750 (vocalitatem suam) —, *aicnete* (naturalis), *scote scotae* („violarium") from *scoth* (a flower), are evidently to be added *uàthate* (singularis) from *uàthath,* from which acc. pl. fem. *huàthati,* dat. pl. *uàthatai͏̈b,* and *slabratae* (the gloss catinensis being erroneous) from *slabrad* (catena), which Zeuss, 769, erroneously places under *-ant,* so also, most probably, *dúnattae* (castrensis) from **dúnad,* cf. *a ríghdúinte* (their royal forts), Cormac's Glossary in O'Don. 233, *arsate* (antiquarius), cf. *arsid* (a genitive as it appears) Zeuss, 581, plur. *túati* (gentiles) 1043, from *tuàth* (populus), perhaps also *tecnate* (domesticus); in the consonantel stems with the nom. *-atu, -etu* we may assume **-ntat,* but they could also have arisen from **-tvat* (cf. Skr. *-tva* n., Lith. *-tuva* m., Slav. *-stvo* n., but especially Lat. *-tút* f. in juventus, virtus, servitus, senectus), which is sufficient reason for their retaining the tenuis *-t*[117] as in the pronouns of the second person. Mod. Irish examples: *saoghalta* (worldly), *gallda* (exotic), *fíreanta* (righteous), *grianda* (sunny), *banda* (feminine), also with assimilation *daonna* (human) = *dóinde;* on the other hand, *mórdha* (majestic), *feardha* (masculine), *órdha* (golden).

Derivation with various suffixes: *écintëch* (infinitus), from *cinniŭd* (definitio) *huàtigitir* (rarescunt), from *uàthad, boltigetar* (olent), from *bolad, muntĭth* (institutor), from *munŭd; ingrentĭd* (persecutor), *líntĭdi* (fartores), *i͏̀rchoi͏̆ltĭth* (maledicus), from *i͏̀rchollŭd—esartaĭd* (caesor) is remarkable, exactly like *timmorte!—*

---

[117] *Nebmarbtu, -tath* are at all events correct forms, and unjustly doubted by Zeuss, 763.

muntar (familia) is also, no doubt, to be placed under this category, and not to be compared with Gaulish κομοντόριος; *centat* (capitulum), from *cenn*, *sráthatath*, read *-tat* (aculeus), from *sráthaih*; on the other hand, *epertith*, *berrthaïd*, *doïlbthïd*, *debthach*, and *dephthigim*, *tirthat*, from *tir*, etc.—Compare the Modern Irish infinitive, *do chantain*, but *d'fearthain*.—In *dĭltŭth*, for example, the stem-vowel has been ejected, and because *l* precedes, we do not on this account know whether a mere vowel, or *n*, or a dental mute dropped with it.

(II.) *In Anlaut*. In the anlaut of the second member of a compound, whether the first member be a noun, a numeral, or a particle, the second a noun or a verb. Neither here nor in the syntax has Zeuss brought together the exceptions to the aspiration rule; but we may assume *a priori*, that the well ascertained law, according to which the dentals are not aspirated after *l*, *n*, *s*, *t*, *d*, *th*, *dh*, has in the main come into play also in composition and syntax, because it has a pure phonetic reason in the homorgancity of these consonants. Grimm (Geschichte der deutschen Sprache, 375) observes about Modern Irish "the linguals *t* and *d* suffer, however, no aspiration after liquids, but remain unchanged"; but this is taken at once in too wide and too narrow a sense, for *m* and *r* do not hinder the aspiration,[118] and the mutes hinder it as well as *n*; what he further says, "I find also *mactire*, son of the land, as the poets call the wolf, not *macthire*", may be very simply explained in this way, that this is not true composition, but merely juxta-position of the substantive with the governed genitive (= *maqvas tírais*), where there exists no reason for aspiration. According to O'Donovan, 336 *seq.*, aspiration does not occur (except in the case of *s* with a mute following, to which, according to p. 54, we must also add *m*) with *d*, *t* after *n*, *d*, *t*; finally, in some cases not specially stated; *l*, *s* and the aspirated *th*, *dh* are not there mentioned, but it is scarcely to be doubted that they exert the same influence on *d*, *t* following, as we even find *dall-ciach* (a blinding fog) given without aspiration, so likewise *aththaoiseach* (a deposed chieftain), and *aithdheanam* (remaking); but, however, *aithtéidhte* (re-heated), *athdóidhte* (reburnt). Now, if even the Mod. Irish, in which aspiration is so widely spread, that it has come in after every particle in composition, with few exceptions[119] (*éa-* or *éi-*, *eas-*, *con-*, or *coin-*) has, nevertheless,

---

[118] Compare *imdhíden* (shelter, defence), *urdhairc eardhairc* (illustrious, renowned).

[119] The eclipse after *di* is perfectly enigmatical in *diombuidheach* (unthankful), *diombuan* (perishable), analogous to *diomolaim* (I dispraise) on the other hand, with aspiration, *díomór* (very great), *dicheannaim* (I behead), *díothoghluidhe* (impregnable).

preserved in the above position the *d* and *l* pure; with much greater certainty may we look for the same thing in Old Irish, where the original limits of aspiration are exceeded only in very few instances (in *du-* and *mí-* for **dus-* and **mis-*). Accordingly, we find *s* preserved before mutes in *banscala* (servae), *cáinscél* (bonus nuntius), *drogscéla* (malos nuntios), *soscéle* (evangelium), *athscribend* (rescriptum), *incomscribṅdaīth* (syngraphum), *doscéulaim* (experior), *doinscannsom* (incipit), after the verbal participle in *roscarsam* (recessimus); *t* after *n* in—*bantĕrismīd* (obstetrix), *griĕntaīrissĕm* (solstituim), *medóntaīrismīd* (mediastinus)—compare Mid. Ir. *baintigerna* (domina), in Stokes' Irish Glosses,—*fíntan* (vinetum), *cáintetst* (bonum testimonium), *cáintoīmtiu* (bona cogitatio), *cáintöl* (bona voluntas), *caintaīdlĕch* (satisfactio), *sentinni* pl. (anus), *intonnaīgīm* (inundo), *intursitīb* (irriguis), *tintūth* (interpretatio), *fointreb* (supellex);[120] after *l* in *ind-idultaīgae* (fani), *iltoīmddĕn* (*dd=t*, multarum opinionum), after *s* in *rostán* (rosarium), after *t* in *rechttāīrcīd* (legislator), after *th* in *frithtasgat* (adversantur), *frithtaīdechtae* (contradictionis), for which *fritt-*, *frit-* is also written; we have, consequently, to consider *d* after *n* in *bandálem* (hospita), *bandea* (dea), *bandechuīn* (diaconissae), *bandachlach* (leno)—cf. Mid. Ir. *baindea* in Stokes' Op. cit.—*cáinduthracht* (bona voluntas), *sendūīne* (vetus homo), and after *l* in *ildáni* (multae artes), as *dura*, a hardening to *t* occurs after *t, th, d* (see *supra*), *biddixnugud, i.e., bithd.,* however occurs, Zeuss, 781. For some other exceptions, such as the above mentioned *atbaīl* for *athbaīl*, *idpart* for *idhbhart*, where the hardening comes into play, at the same time (leaving out of consideration faulty spelling), I have not been able as yet to find any fixed rule; only we must not take for an exception what is not one, as for instance the name *Dúnpeleder*, Zeuss, 821, in which the *p* has remained pure, because this is no more a case of true composition than the above *mactire*, or the family names with O and Mac, which for the same reason are not aspirated, *e. g.*, *O'Briain* (gen. *I Bhriain*, dat. *d'Ua Bhriain*, acc. *ar O'Mbriain*, according to O'Molloy, in O'Donovan, 369).

(III.) *In Syntax.* In Syntax, the Modern Irish should be used only with the greatest caution for determining the laws of anlaut (which were not very clearly or completely developed by Zeuss), because it has here given way still more to the tendency to use this, originally a purely mechanical phonetic change, as a dyna-

---

[120] Zeuss indeed assumes (195,848), after *in-* also in composition unchanged anlaut, as, however, the *n* does not drop out anywhere, we must presuppose a fundamental form, like Greek ἐνί, consequently aspiration which is supported by *inchosc* (significatio), etc.

mic agent, a tendency that was already visible in the particle composition, and arbitrary rules of scribes and grammarians, who, as a rule, had no idea of the nature of aspiration and eclipse, have had their share in still further disturbing and confusing the original rule; nevertheless it may be here also of real service to us, if we consider perfectly unbiassed each grammatical form as that which it is, and not what it pretends to be, and bestow the necessary attention on the actual or apparent exceptions.

The phonetic changes are dependent in Syntax on two conditions: not merely on the nature of the sounds which come together, but also on the greater or lesser logical correlation of the words, a condition which did not at all come into consideration as an independent one in inlaut and composition; as in French, the pronunciation of the final consonant of the first word, even if it be capable of becoming sonant, does not take place between every two words, so in Irish, also, the auslaut does not exert in every position its influence upon the following anlaut. The closest combination is formed by the substantive with the preceding article and pronominal genitive, the preposition with its case, the verb with particles and pronouns, which, in writing, are either enclitic or proclitic; the substantive is less closely connected with a succeeding adjective (as a rule, a preceding one enters into composition) still less with a dependent genitive, the connection of the verb with a substantive, as subject or object, is the loosest. Next to this, the very unequal action of the auslaut is of importance: original *s-* auslaut does not apparently lose its protecting action in any position in Old Irish, upon succeeding initial consonants; final *n* also occurs often, where the combination is by no means so particularly close, as in *guidimse dià nĕrutsu;* there are even phenomena which appear to point to an $ν\ ἐφελκυστικόν$ (cf. p. 90); on the other hand, the aspiration required by vocalic auslaut often does not occur even in the anlaut of the adjective, still more frequently in that of a dependent genitive. Many instances of omission are, of course, only a consequence of careless and imperfect writing, as, for instance, *s* and *f* often appear without a dot; but others are due to perfectly determinate phonetic laws, especially to the two frequently mentioned above; this is especially seen after the article, by comparing the older and newer form.

(1.) The article originally ended in *s* in the nom. sing. masc., gen. sing., and nom. plur. fem., dat. and acc. plur. of all genders (the neuter appears to have early passed over into feminine in the plural); in *n* in the nom. sing. neut., the acc. sing. and gen. plur. of all genders; in vowels in the gen. sing. masc. and neut., nom. plur. masc., dat. sing. and nom., and acc. dual of all genders; according to this we have to expect in the acc. sing. (and nom. plur. neut.) and gen. plur. *n* (*m*) before vowels and mediæ, assimilation before liquids, and pure anlaut in the case of tenuis, *s* and *f;* in the gen. sing. masc., neut., nom. plur. masc. and dat. sing. aspiration, which is not written for mediæ, and in other instances pure anlaut of the following substantive or adjective. Most examples, also, agree with these observations, leaving out of consideration neglected aspiration, especially of *s* and *f*, which, however, in the case of *s* is generally made observable by a preceding *t* for *d;* gen. *inspirto, intesa,* etc., should not, however, be reckoned among negligences of writing, they are to be looked upon rather as actual exceptions, according to determinate laws. The *s,* in *inspirto,* cannot be aspirated on account of the following mute, hence the article is not written here either *int-* or *ind-,* because the *t* is hardened out of *d* or intercalated only before *s* (for which of the two explanations is the correct one, remains for the present still doubtful, as even in Modern Irish, *roimpe,* from *roĭm' si* also appears along with *uimpe,* from *uĭmb' si*) ; on this account *insenduine* does not get a *t* in the nom., but it does in the gen. *intsenduini,* inaccurately written *indsenduini,* and the pronouns *sa* (*so, se*) and *sin,* which are not aspirated, no doubt, because a double consonant originally existed in anlaut, form everywhere with the article *inso insin* (Zeuss, 275, 353, *seq.*). That the dental has also been preserved pure in *intesa* by the preceding sound (*n* or *d*), consequently that an aspirate is not to be pronounced here any more than in *induini,* and that Zeuss, 231, 232, 236, with all the observations appertaining thereto, is decidedly in error, is shown, besides, by the constancy in the examples (nom. fem. *indtogas,* gen. masc. neut. *intaĭrmchrutto, intesa, intaĭdlich,* dat. *ontechtaĭriu, dontorŭd, isintuisiulsin, óntrédiu, dindtrediu, iarsintaĭrgiriu, hisintórunt, hontecnatatu, dintecnatatu, issintodochidiu, isintuaĭchli,* nom. masc. pl. *intuisil*), also by the Modern Irish, which has maintained the same rule.

The laws of anlaut after the article look, to be sure, on first sight, and as represented by the grammarians, wonderful enough ; that the nom. fem. and gen. masc. cause aspiration, and the gen. pl. eclipse agrees with the old rule; but that eclipse should occur in the dat. sing. after all prepositions, except *do* in West Munster, as O'Donovan gives at p. 63,—and except *do* and *de,* as is stated at p. 393,—that *s* suffers the so-called eclipse only after *do, de, is* with the article, consequently aspiration with an intercalated *t* before it, p. 70,—that *t* and *d,* as a rule, suffer in the singular as little eclipse as aspiration, while in the genitive plural, on the other hand, they are regularly eclipsed,—appears enigmatical, and the contradictory rules of the grammarians respecting the anlaut of adjectives (p. 110–117), appear to make the matter completely inexplicable. But if we examine this phenomenon closer, and compare the use of the prepositions and the examples from Keating (p. 394, *seq.*), light will be thrown upon this peculiarity, in which the confusion of speech among the people, and the foolish caprice of grammarians, have gone hand in hand, and immediately the exceptions become satisfactorily explicable. At p. 78 *seq.* (*ante*) attention has been before directed to the confusion in the case-endings, which had partially begun already in Old Irish, and which has been carried to an extreme in the Middle and Modern Irish; we can now complete and correct what has been there said. In the first place, almost every distinction between nom. and acc. has disappeared, in the singular, the nominative form, in the plural at one time the latter, at another time the former, has alone been preserved, and even where in an isolated instance both forms occur, they appear to be promiscuously used; the accusative form has very early replaced the nominative in the plural of the article; in the singular, on the other hand, the nominative has replaced the accusative, of which the Middle Irish already affords examples (cf. *der* in the Allemannian dialect of German). The syntactical peculiarity of the Old Irish of putting the accusative in many instances in place of the nominative, especially in the passive, and the complete similarity of both cases in the plural, which often originally existed or arose at an early period, as well as the slight difference in the singular masculine, which completely disappeared before tenuis, and *s*, *f*, facilitated this intermixture; in addition to this, in the article, both were from the beginning alike in the feminine plural; and in the noun, the accusative and vocative plural were the same, the latter being the only true accusative form, which is still preserved, and which may also be recognized as such by the unaltered anlaut of a following adjective. The confusion has gone so far in the spoken language, that this form occurs for the dative in the plural even after prepositions, one says, indeed, *do na fearaibh* (to the men), but also *do na capuil* (to the horses), O'Donovan, 83 *seq.* $= \pi\rho\grave{o}\varsigma \, \tau o\grave{v}\varsigma \, (\tau o\tilde{\iota}\varsigma) \, \mathring{\iota}\pi\pi o\iota$; O'Donovan directs the supposed accusative to be put after *gan* (without), and *idir* (between), in the singular, in reality, therefore, the nominative. The true accusative form is to be found, on the other hand, in the so-called dative singular, for *o'nm-bárd* is as little a true dative as the French *au poète* (= ad illum poetam). Even in Old Irish the dative distinguished itself from the accusative in the vowel only in the *a*- (*ia*-) and *u*-stems, which were capable of an *u* umlaut, and this distinction must have ceased in Modern

Irish with the loss of this umlaut; all feminine and consonantal stems formed both cases alike, from the beginning with *i*-umlaut; there only remained, consequently, the difference of the auslaut towards the anlauts following. But we have already seen in the case of the pronominal suffixes, that the dative has only maintained itself after *de* and *do* in *díobh* and *dóibh;* on the other hand, the accusative has come in after all other prepositions, as the peculiar phonetic phenomena in *aca*, etc., show; consequently in that which the grammarians call the dative singular, a true dative is only to be recognized after *de* and *do;* after other prepositions, on the other hand, the accusative; and we should not wonder that in Keating, and in the North Munster dialect, the article gives rise to aspiration only in these cases (both prepositions, except in the County of Kilkenny, sound alike *do*), while everywhere else it produces eclipse. Here, also, then, similarity of form has gone hand in hand with syntactical corruption; the Modern Irish is surpassed in the latter respect by the Modern Greek, which has wholly lost the dative, and even combines ἀπό and μέ (μετά) with the accusative. The occurrence of the dative after all prepositions (even *gan* and *idir*) in the plural of substantives, is, no doubt, due to an effort to gain a prominent distinction, which was not given here by the form of the article (*na* without change of sound). Hence there have been preserved pure in the written language, the dative plural, only that already in the earliest times the article had begun to become truncated to *na*, the genitive singular and plural, and the nominative singular, in all instances; the dative singular, on the other hand, only after *de, do*, the accusative singular after the other prepositions (*gan* and *idir* excepted), never as objective case, the nominative and accusative plural only where they have sounded alike as in the vocalic feminine stems, otherwise they are always confounded. If we now study the treatment of the anlaut after the article, everything may be satisfactorily explained conformably to the old rule, *e. g.*:—

m. n.	*an t éan*	*an fear*	*an sruth*	from	*int-*
g.	*an éin*	*an fir*	*an t-srotha*	,,	*ind-*
d.	*do'n éin*	*do'n fear*	*do'n t-sruth*	,,	*dond-*
(a)	*ó'n éin*	*ó'n bh-fear*	*ó'n sruth*	,,	*inn-*
f. sg n.	*an uair*	*an chlann*	*an t-súil*	,,	*ind-*
g.	*na h-uaire*	*na chloinne*	*na súla*	,,	*na-*
d.	*do'n uair*	*do'n chloinn*	*do'n t-suil*	,,	*dond-*
(a)	*ó'n uair*	*ó'n g-cloinn*	*ó'n súl*	,,	*inn-*
pl. n.	*na h-uaire*	*na clanna*	*na súile*	,,	*na-*
d.	*na n-uar*	*na g-clann*	*na súl*	,,	*nan-*
g.	*do-na-h-uaraibh*	*ó na clannaibh*	*do na súilibh*	,,	*nab-*

When, therefore, *s* suffers the so-called eclipse after *is* (*in*) as in Keating—*is in t-saoghal* (in the world), the dative form is there exceptionally preserved, while '*san seanchus* (in the history) contains the usual accusative form; it is perfectly according to rule that *t* and *d* should remain pure after *do'n* (*de'n, isin*) for they are withdrawn by the *n* from the aspiration which should occur here; after other prepositions the strict rule requires, however, eclipse as well as in the genitive plural. But even the most abnormal modes of treatment of anlauts (as in Kilkenny and Tipperary, where *b*, *f*, *g*, suffer eclipse, *c* and *p* aspiration after all prepositions, and *s* is eclipsed, that is, aspirated by *t*; a real dative is preserved here, as the aspiration of the *c*, *p*, *s* shows, but *b* and *g* are assimilated with the nasal to *m* and *ng*, the softening of the *f* to *bh* is curious) agree, however, in this, that *t* and *d*, after the article, are nowhere aspirated; proof enough that in the Old Irish, also, we have to deal with a distinct law, and not with a negligence of writing. If individual writers have also changed the anlaut of substantives without the article, *e. g.*, have eclipsed in the genitive plural, it is because they have totally misapprehended the cause of the phenomena, it is, therefore, wholly unjustifiable.

That the adjective after the article is subject to the same laws of anlaut as the noun substantive, may be concluded *a priori;* but in general the case occurs very seldom, as the adjective comes mostly after the substantive, in the opposite case composition takes place, although they are sometimes separately written, as in *arnóib briathraib*, Zeuss, 926 (read *arnsibbriathraib*, as the absence of the ending requires). In Modern Irish such combinations are, to be sure, mostly written separate, but the adjective remains unchanged, and the anlaut of the substantive is aspirated (except in instances like *seanduine*) so that the composition is readily recognizable (O'Donovan, 347, 349).—Besides the pronouns *cach, cech, nach, alaile*, and the cardinal numerals which regularly precede (*indula* appears to be compound, the ordinary numerals besides *cétne* and *tánaise* always precede the substantive) *sain* occurs now and again inflected before the substantive (*saini persin* in the nom. fem. plur., but *hipersonaib sainib*), mostly, however, compounded; *uile* fluctuates, *cétne*, also, mostly precedes, but sometimes comes after the substantive; *aile* and *tánaise* are, on the other hand, always placed after it.

(2.) The same influence of the auslaut on the following anlaut occurs, of course, between adjective (adjectival numeral and pronoun) and substantive, whenever the adjective has attributive value, whether it goes before or after; the examples in Zeuss are, however, few, as the aspiration is never noticed in the case of *b, d, g*, *m*, and very irregularly in the case of *s* and *f*, and for the reasons above given must often be suppressed in the case of *t* (*d*). Examples for the aspiration of the adjective: in the nom. fem., *mo thol cholnĭde, cach thúare;* in the gen. neut., *indfolaĭd chétnai;* in the dat. neut. *isindanmatm̄ chétnĭdiu, hi togarmĭm frecndaĭrc;*[121] in the dat. fem., *diṅgutai thóĭsiy, iar rĭagoĭl chenélaĭg, for lắm chli;* in dual fem., *díguttai fodlaĭdi.* The aspiration is suppressed according to determinate rules in: gen. masc., *inchruĭnn toĭrthich, toĭrthig;* in the dat. neut, *fardiŭll tan.* (*tánaĭsiu*); in the dat. fem., *do persĭn tanaĭsi, hí persĭn tánaĭsi, isindepistil tŏĭsich;* from negligence in the dat., *huàndlŭĭthi seím*, etc. Examples of the transvected nasal are given at p. 90. That the principle has not lost its force, we see in the Modern Irish, where we again find in the adjective placed after the substantive aspiration and eclipse, under the same conditions (and also the same confusion in the dat. sing.) as in the case of the substantives; aspiration occurs in the voc. sing., only after consonants in the nom. plur., not after vowels, *na fir thréana*, but *treasa móra*, because in the former -*i* was the original auslaut, and in the latter *s;* in like manner, the voc. plur. preserves the original anlaut—*á feara tréana*.

Examples for the aspiration of the substantive: in the gen. masc., *alaĭli thríum* (I have not as yet found nom. fem. sing.); in the dat. masc., *re cach thuisiul, ónach fochun ailiu, isinóinchorp, in óen sosŭth sill-*, 1017, neut., *icachthir*, fem., *ón chetni phersĭn;* in the nom. plur., (*inchamthuisil* appears to be a compound), *itchethir chét;* the aspiration is prevented in the dative (f.) *ondóentóisrinn;* left out from negligence in *con alaĭliu fogoir, ó óin sil., don chétni persin, hi cétni persin, in óen sill.,* 1017, and remarkably enough in almost all cases which I have yet found, after *cach*—gen., *caĭch cenéuĭl*, dat., *do cech cenélu, do cach ceneoll, do cach cenéolu, ocech cenélu, hi cach ceniul, do cach ceniul, do cach cathrur, do cach corp, hi cech caingním, icach sens* (does a similar euphonic law rule here, except in the last instance, as in the case of *t* after dentals? *Nephpiandatu* may be regular). The curious *cachnóen chrann,* 999 (the subject in the acc. like *cech consaĭn,* 1017), may be explained as composition, as in the nom., *óenchoĭmdiu, oinchorp,* 587, acc. *in óenchorp,* 580, *tri óen pheccad* (on the other hand *cach óen creitfess,* gen. fem., *inna oena méĭte*), and is therefore to be read, *cach-n óenchrann; aon* is always to be looked upon as in composition with its substantive in Modern Irish, for it

---

[121] These two formulæ show that of the two attempted explanations given in Beiträge, I., 451 (Stokes' "Observations on the Irish Declension") only the second is possible: *anm̄anbi, anm̄ambi, anm̄ammi, anm̄aĭmm*.

aspirates the anlaut of the substantive, *e.g.*, *aon chluas* (one ear), f., *aon chraun* masc. If the masc. follows *dá* (which in Mod. Irish has also replaced the fem. *dí*), in the same form as in the nom. sing., the fem. in the same form as in the dative singular, but both being aspirated, *dá chrann, da chluais,* and that the adjective in the plural occurs with aspiration, we have an exact correspondence with the little we know of the dual in Old Irish (see p. 86 *seq.*), and even the *n* of the old neutral form *dan*, is still to be recognized in the eclipse in *dá d-trian* (two thirds); O'Molloy had also suspected relics of the dual in it, and O'Donovan's argument against this view, as well as in respect of the form after *céad, míle* and the decades, is only in part true; that is, the apparent similarity of form which as a rule occurs between the nom. sing. and plur. of both genders, and between the nom. sing. and dual masc., has gradually led to the use of the nom. sing. after these numerals even where the gen. pl. (or nom. dual masc.) had preserved the original difference. The occurrence of eclipse after *seacht, ocht, noí, deich,* is easily explained, and was already founded in the Old Irish by the *n* after these words. The explanation is more difficult of the pure anlaut after *cuíg* and *míle,* where we should, certainly, have expected primitive vocalic auslaut; in the former, according to the analogy of πέμπε, *quinque,* in the latter, in consequence of the Old Irish *dí míli*, which points to a feminine; the consonantal auslaut which we must assume in *céad* (perhaps already O. Ir. masc., compare the above *cethirchét*) and *sé* (for *ses=sex*), as in the plural forms, *trí* and *ceithre,* is easily understood; we have *nt*-stems in *fiche,* and the remaining names of the decades, whose nom. sing. are pronounced *fichë, tricha triocha,* gen., *fichët fichead, *trichat triochad,* and nom. plur. (like the dat. and acc. sing.) **fichit fichid, trichit trochaid,* etc.[122]

(3.) The combination between the substantive and a succeeding genitive is much weaker. Examples of the nasal preserved in the accusative, (*frislond nilfolad,* 1029), nominative neuter (*torbe nimdibi*), and the genitive plural, are numerous enough (compare On the so-called prosthetic *n*, p. 90); but, as has been already above remarked, no very particularly close combination is necessary for this; on the other hand, aspiration occurs rather seldom. The nom. fem., *trebaire chollno, toll chollno, ciàll chésto, ciàll chésta* (the neut., *aīnm thriuīn* is singular, beside the *aīnm̄-n* of the examples in p. 91), dat., *hitosūg suīn,* 1011, *do immfolung fuīl,* 1016, *in óen sosuth sill.,* 1017, *do thaídbse superlaīt, ó thoīl*

---

[122] The doubt expressed at p. 433, vol. I., of the Beiträge is removed by this; *fichë, tricha,* for primitive *vicint, *tricant,* now approach much closer to the Sanskrit *trimçat,* and are a mean between the latter and the Latin *viginti, triginta*; in meaning they express the Greek εἰκάς, τριακάς.

cholno, do láni chétbutho, are opposed, for example, in great number, besides the regular *ond áes tuáithe, dothabaĭrt toĭrse*, by the nom. fem., *bandea cruĭthnechta, bandea tenëd, hirës creĭtme, ciáll cech muĭd* (*tír taĭrngĭri* may, like *tír-n-erend*, depend upon a change of gender); by the gen., *eĭsseĭrgi cr.*, the dat., *do hícc cáĭch, illestur ferce, fomám pectho, a raĭnn pectha, di rect pectho, do dechrugud persĭne, isóiri ceneóĭl, hi claar crúdi, di muntir cessaĭr, do cach ceneólu serbe, oc ascnam tíre taĭrngĭri, hi foĭsĭte césto*, so that it would appear the fluctuation could scarcely have been here confined merely to writing. According to O'Donovan, 368, *seq.*, aspiration in Modern Irish, also, is generally only usual in proper names, although Keating used it also in other cases; but it has here inorganically extended itself to cases like *Airdeasbog Chaisil* (the Archbishop of Cashel), and consequently is used as a purely dynamic agent; on the other hand, the above mentioned exception, which the family names with *O* and *Mac* make, rests fully upon the Old Irish anlaut laws.

(4.) The pronouns stand in such intimate combination, as well with the substantive as with the verb, that many depend upon both parts of speech, not merely as enclitic or proclitic, but even penetrate between the preposition (verbal particle) and the verb. Thus the anlaut of the noun is under the influence of the so-called possessive pronouns, *i.e.*, the genitive of the personal pronouns, whether the latter appear in their complete form (absoluta of Zeuss), or in a shortened form (infixa of Zeuss); *mo, do*, 3. masc. *á* end in vowels, 3. fem. *á.*, originally in *s*, the plurals, *aṅ, farṅ* or *barṅ, i.e., bharṅ* and *aṅ*, in nasals, hence:—*mothol, mochland, imchuĭmriŭg, domthoschid; thúal=dofual, itchóimthecht* (inaccurately, *dosennáthar, itsenmáthĭr, cutseítchi*); *achésta* (inaccurately *apectha*); *aggním; arnét, arndiis, armbrethre, arloure-ni, arsóire-ni; farnintliucht, farcliu, forserce; ananman, ambës, accursagad*. This influence is even now still felt in:—*mo súil, m'fuil, do chos; a cheann; a ceann, a h-inghean; ár g-cinn; bhar g-cosa; a g-cinn*. The anlaut of the verb is dependent upon the preceding personal pronoun (infixa of Zeuss), but the decision as to their original auslaut is rendered more difficult by the contradictory ways in which they are written, and also by the circumstance that Modern Irish has not this kind of combination. Vocalic auslaut appears to be certain in 1. and 2. sing.—*ni m charatsa, nomthachtar, nimtha, nímptha, fomchridichfider-sa, nudamchrocha, cofordumthésĭd-se, fritumthĭagar, fordomchomaĭther, rotchechladar*; we find, however, *condumfel, aromfoimfea, immumforling, fomfĭrfidersa, romsóirsa, coatomsnassar; rodchúrsach*, to be sure, is found in 3. sing.; but, on the other hand, we have *immidforling, cenodfil, rondpromsom* (with rel. *n.*), *n-* and *s*-, appear never to aspirate—*ronsóir, nistabur*, there is, however, *nonchretid-si* (ut in cum credatis); we read in 1. plur., *fonsegar, nunsluīnfem-ni, nonsóirfëa, ronsóirni cininfīl, ronfitūd-ni, ninfortéit-ni* (*conintorgáitar, honuntogaitarni, nintá* are indifferent in consequence of the *n-t*), in 2. plur. *atobcí, nobcarad, fordubcechna, forndobcanar, rondobcarsam-ni, robcar-si, nondubcairim-se, robclandad, nibtá, dobtromma, atobsegatsi, cotobsechfīder, nondobsommīgëtar, nobsóirfa-si, nachibfēl, condibfēl, manudubfēl, robfothīgëd,* and yet *nidan chumachtīg* and *atdubelliub* (i. e., *atdudfelliub*) appear to point to aspiration; in 3. plur. *da-*, as well as *sn-*, seem to be without aspirating power—*nodascara, rondasaibset, nondasoirfëa, nosīguid-som, dosīmbera, nisfitir, nosmoidet, nisfitemmar, rospredach, roscomal.* The combination between the verb and relative pronoun is equally close—*an* (*anasbiursa, arrocar, acarthar, apredchimme*) and *no* (*nocretim, nopredchim-se*, correctly or negligently written?); it is curious that in Modern Irish the nom. *a* aspirates and eclipses only after prepositions, or as absolute neuter (what, all that).

Enclitic pronouns and pronominal adverbs are, for their part, in respect to the anlaut, under the influence of the preceding word, the suffixed pronoun *sa* (*se, so, su*), even in respect to the vowel. We must, consequently, conclude from the circumstances that the *s* remains uninfected, that an original double consonant existed in anlaut, not only for *som* (*sem*) as Stokes has correctly remarked (Beiträge, I. 469), but also for *su, sa, so* (*se, siu, sin*), especially as *intíthall*, with aspiration, stands opposed to *intísin*, and *messe, tussu* are found, whilst with the article we have, as was mentioned above, not *intso* or *indso*, but *inse, insin;* only it remains doubtful whether all these pronouns belong to the same stem (say *sva-n*), or whether the *-sa* after pronouns is to be separated from the (as it appears) adverbial *-sa, -sin*, after substantives. Simple anlaut, on the other hand, is betrayed by the dative *siu*, and the compound pronouns *síde* (*saĭde*, nom. plur *saĭdai*, Z., 9), *sodaĭn* by the aspiration in *desiu*, Z., 595, and *ósuidi*, dat. fem., *olsuĭde*, am. *sodaĭn, arsodaĭn, olsodaĭn, olsodĭn, fosodĭn*.

(5.) I have nothing to add to what Zeuss has said on the treatment of the anlaut after prepositions and other particles; that the *s* after *ren, con, in, iarn, for, tri* (and in part also after *la, a, fri*) belongs to the article, is now, I believe, generally admitted. I know no explanation for the hardening of mediæ in the verb substantive (also *ni ténat*, Z., 585, for *ni dénat*) after *ro* and *ní*, which, nevertheless, otherwise produce aspiration; *trithemel, trichretim,* along with *tresinfuil,* among others, is equally striking. The *dús* (*dúus*) before *in-* in the indirect interrogative is, no doubt, contracted from *do-fius, du-fius* (ad sciendum). Compare English *to wit.*

(6.) The action of the verbs on the object as regards anlaut must have been already in Old Irish very weak. Zeuss gives only two examples, and O'Donovan has nothing about it in Modern Irish; on the other hand, the aspiration of the anlaut after *ba, budh* is given by him, also, as a rule, while in the documents in Zeuss, more examples without aspiration after the root *bâ* may be found than with it.

§. 6. *Loss of P in Celtic.*

One of the most interesting phonetic peculiarities of Gaedhelic is a certain aversion to *p*, which is manifested in different ways.

Firstly, the Gaedhelic, as was long since remarked, has very frequently preserved the guttural where other languages, especially the Greek and the Kymric, have allowed the labial to replace it: thus, in accordance with the Latin, as opposed to the Greek and the Italic dialects, in the interrogative pronoun and all derivatives, Ir. *cách* = Kymr. *paup*, quivis, Gaedh. *nach nech* = Kymr. *nep* aliquis; in the numerals Gaedh. *cethir* = Kymr. *petguar* four, and Gaedh. *coíc* = Kymr. *pimp* five; further, for example, in Gaedh. *macc* = Kymr. *map* filius, Gaedh. *cland* = Kymr. *plant* proles, Gaedh. *crann* = Kymr. *pren* arbor, Gaedh. *cren* = Kymr. *prenu* emere, Gaedh. *ech* = Kymr. *ep equus (Gaul. *epo-*, Welsh *ebawl* a foal), Gaedh. *sech* praeter = Kymr. *hep* sine, also, no doubt, Gaedh. *cenn* = Kymr. *penn* caput, although Pictet (Beiträge 86) considers *penn* = *pinda* older. Compare, also, Gaedh. *sechim* sequor, *sechitir* sequuntur, in opposition to which the defective Welsh *heb* inquit may be equated with the Greek ἔννεπε.

Secondly, even *c* or *ch* has sometimes replaced primitive *p*[123] even in loan-words, as *caisc* (pascha), *corcur* (purpura);[124] the circumstance is somewhat different with *cuingeis*, which, like O.H.G. *fimfchusti* is only half borrowing, half imitation of pentecost; I cannot, however, look upon *fescor* or *fescar* vesper, as borrowed, for the Welsh *ucher*, as opposed to Corn. *gwesper*, Arm. *gousper*, likewise betrays a guttural (*ch* = *sc*) like Lith. *vakaras*, Slav. *večerŭ*. *Cht* is found for *pt* (as in Low German, *nichte* for *nifte*) in *secht* septem, *sechtmaine* septimana, *necht* neptis.

But in anlaut an aversion to *p* shows itself in an especial

---

[123] To this category I also reckon the first guttural in *cóic*, as in Lat. *quinque* and *coquo*, which I attribute to assimilation (as in part the second labial in πέμπε and πέπων).

[124] Pott, Hallesche Literarische Zeitung, 1844, S. 289, Anmerkung.

manner, not only in inconvenient combinations like *ps*, where, for instance, Gaedh. *salm* agrees with O.H.G. *salmo* for *psalmo*, but in the most convenient *pl* and *pr*, nay even before vowels, and not merely in Gaedhelic only, where perhaps the majority of cases of *p*- anlaut is due to borrowing (as in German, cf. *peccad* peccatum, *persan* persona, *precept* praeceptum, *amprom* improbus, *prím* primus, for the true Celtic *cétne*), but frequently also in Kymric, which is otherwise, however, as little averse to *p* as, perhaps, the Greek. It especially strikes one that, at first sight, we cannot discover, in both branches of the Celtic family, a single one of the many prepositions in Sanskrit and the other cognate languages with *p*- anlaut (*pará, pari, pra, prati*, and their relatives). Pictet and Bopp have assumed that the *p* in these words has passed either into *b* or *f*, and very little of importance can be objected against the examples of the *b* for *p* in Pictet (De l'affinité, etc., p. 49), isolated examples also occur in all languages of an irregular change between tenues and mediæ, in Celtic, for example— Gaedh. *gabar*, Kymr. *gafar* = Lat. *caper*, O. Norse *hafr*, A. Sax. *häfer*; Gaedh. *gabál* = Kymr. *kafael*, Lat. *capere*, Goth. *hafjan*, conversely, Gaedh. *tenge* = Goth. *tuggó*; Gaedh. *ithim* = Skr. *admi*, Lat. *edo*, Goth. *ita*; but the pretended change of *p* into *f* is therefore the more doubtful. Scarcely one of the examples quoted has direct evidence in its favour, but certainly the parallel Kymric, *gu, gw*, does not admit of the assumption of the direct passage of *p* into *f*, at most, of one through the mediation of *v*, from which the Gaedhelic *f*, and the Kymric *gu*, were then evolved according to their special phonetic laws. So, for example, Gaedh. *frith*, Kymr. *gurth*, certainly admit of being connected with the Sanskrit *prati* by a Celtic fundamental form *vrith, *verth (= *vrati, *varti), by which the aspirates would be developed in both languages perfectly according to rule, in the Gaedhelic between the vowels, in the Kymric in the position *rt*. The end vowel in isolated use must then, however, have dropped off very early, as the Gaedhelic has there only the form *fri*, which does not infect the following consonants; for the *o* before the article belongs as little to the preposition *an* in this case as in *ré, iar, in, tri*. But the transformation of the Sanskrit *pra* to Gaedh. *for*, Kymr. *guor*, appears altogether improbable to me; for the Celtic preposition (with which the intensive *guor-*, Gaul. *ver-* appears to be identical) is obviously related to Gaedh. *fo*, Kymr. *guo*, in form and meaning exactly like *super* to *sub*, ὑπέρ to ὑπό, Goth. *ufar* to *uf* (which also agree in the double construction), therefore, also, as Skr. *upari* to *upa*. Only a doubt can, therefore, exist as to whether the Celtic had perhaps (like the Slavonian in *na* = ἀνά and *po* = *upa*) dropped the initial vowel, and then changed *p* into *v*, or whether it had softened and suppressed the *p* after the *u*, so that the fundamental forms **va* and **vari* from *u(p)a* and *u(p)ari*, common to the Gaedhelic and Kymric, had developed themselves; the latter is my subjective conviction. If the *i*, dropped in *for, guor*, no longer exerts, almost anywhere,[125] an action upon the following consonant, it shows that the Celtic agrees with the Latin, Greek, and Gothic in the early rejection of that vowel; but perhaps a trace of the *i* may be recognized (as in O. Norse *yfir* in opposition to Gothic *ufar*) in the Gaulish intensive prefix *ver-*, the *e* of which may have arisen either directly, or through the intermediate stage of *i* from *a* by the influence of *i* in auslaut.

The Sanskrit *pra* and *pari* are rather to be found in a fourth class, among words which have wholly lost the *p* in anlaut, as in the Gaedhelic *iasg* = Kymr. *pisc, pysg* piscis, *athir* pater, which includes in both languages the root Skr. *par (pr̂)*, which always appears here, as in German, Greek, and Latin, with *l* for *r*. To this category belong, with a preceding liquid, Gaedh. *lín* = Kymr. *laun* (Welsh *llawn*, Corn. *len leun*, Arm. *leun*) plenus, *líne* plenitudo, *lanad* and *línad* implere, *rolín* implevit, Welsh *llewni* implere, *lloneit* plenitudo (quantum implet); with a preceding vowel, Gaedh. *comalnad* impletio, *comalnadar* implet, *comalnamar* implemus, *comallnithe* impletus. From the same root descends further **paru* much = Skr. *puru*, Gr. πολύ, Goth. *filu*, which the Gaedh. *il* (for *pil*) very accurately represents, whence *ilar* multitudo, *ilde*, pluralis; the Gaedh. comparative *lia* agrees with the Greek πλείων, Lat. *plus;* compare further Welsh *liaus, lliaws, laws*, multus, multitudo = Corn. *luas, leas*, W. *llawer* = Corn. *llewer* multus, Gaedh. *laur, lour* = Corn. *loar* sufficiens, satis and *loure* sufficientia, W. *lluossyd* multitudo.

Similarly Gaedh. *lethan*, Kymr. *litan, llydan* broad, Welsh *lledann* to spread out (*llet*) *lled* and *llyd* latitudo, connect themselves with Skr. *prthu* for *prathu*, Gr. πλατύς; the Kymric adjectives in *-lit, -llyd*, fem. *-lled* with the meaning " full of something", if they are really compound, belong in their second part either to the root in question, or to the preceding one.

I now likewise recognize the Skr. *pra* in the prefix *ro*, which appears in inseparable combination as an intensive particle, and in separable combination, as nota praeteriti especially; to the

---

[125] We find, nevertheless, in O. Ir., the secondary forms *forchanim forchun* praecipio, *forchain* praecipit, *fortheit* adjuvat, *forchongrim* mando jubeo, *forchongair* mandat, along with *forcanim* (*forcetal* doctrina), *forteit, forcongrim forcongur, forcongair*, in Modern Irish, *foircheann* for the old *forcenn* finis ; the rarer form *foir-* owes its *i*, no doubt, to the influence of the vowel of the following syllable (as in *foirbthe* for *forbuide*). Zeuss, p. 212, also mentions eclipse in Kymric along with aspiration, which likewise proves vocalic genesis.

same stem belong Gaedh. *ré, rén, rémi* (superlative form as primum?) and Kymr. *rac* (=Skr. *prâc?*) I suspect the Skr. *pari* [but compare the next section] in the Gaul. *are*, whose fundamental form appears to be *ari; compare Gaedh. *ar, air, er, ir,* Kymr. *ar, er, yr*, which may be very well compared with the Gr. περί, in the meaning generally, and in the shades of meaning which it expresses; thus the intensive *er* agrees with the Gr. πέρι, περ, Lat. *per* in *permagnus*. If a separation could be carried out between *ar* and *air*, I would prefer comparing *ar* with the Gr. παρά; Caesar's *Armorica* might then be justified as παραλιά; *Aremorica* (περιθαλάσσιος) may, however, be also explained. The Corn. and Arm. *war* contains, perhaps, an indication of the lost labial; the form *am-* also, which the primitive *an* assumes in Gaedh. *amires* (unbelief), *amiressach* (unbelieving), may owe its origin to the subsequently dropped *p* of *ir-es*.

Finally, the Gaedh. *ire* ulterior (erroneously described by Zeuss as a comparative, for *ireiu* is the comparative), may be referred to the stem Skr. *para*, and compared with its nearest akin the Greek περαῖος.

§. 7. *Loss of P in Celtic, continued.*

Since the preceding was written, I have found an interesting example of the loss of *p* in anlaut in *én* (avis) = *ethn, V. *hethen* (volatile), W. 1, *aetinet* plur., (volucres),—with the derivatives V. *idne* (auceps), *ydnic* (pullus), the compositum, W. 1, *etncoilhaam* (augoror),—and the related words, W. 3, *adaned*, plur., (pennae), W. 1, *atar*, 2, 3, *adar*, (coll. aves), sing. W. 1, *eterinn* masc., 2, 3, *ederyn* (avis, volucris), evidently from the root *pat* (πέτομαι),— compare Skr., *patatra*, *patra*, A. Sax. *feđer*, O.H.G. *fëdara*, Gr. πτερόν, and Lat. *penna*, from *petna. Pictet (Beiträge, II. 90), like Pott (Etymologische Forschungen, I. 2te Aufl., 699 *seq*.), equates Gaul. *are-*, with the Vedic *ârâ;* I cannot, however, convince myself that this, in descent as in meaning, still very ambiguous word has been preserved as a preposition in European languages,[126] and therefore, I still assume the loss of a *p* in this preposition; but I entirely give up the equation with *pari*, περί, to which I was even then persuaded with difficulty by the form *air-*. Many prepositions appear in Old Irish just as in Lithuanian (Schleicher's Lit. Gram., p. 133), in a double, nay, even in a treble form, a circumstance which I did not formerly observe, the shortest mostly occurring in independent use, the stronger in com-

---

[126] Also I do not see why (notwithstanding Pott's energetic protest against it) Lat. *ad* and *ar*, which only appear before labials, could not have coexisted during a long period as dialectically different forms, just as well as N.H.G. *sanft* and *sacht*, as the transition of *d* into *r* is proved by *meridies*.

position, and before pronominal suffixes, with which the peculiar intercalated syllables in Kymric may be compared. Examples: *iṅ* (*ingiŭn, itossŭch*) *in'* (*inchosc*) *ind'* (*indiumm*), *coṅ c. d.* (*condiuiti, coséitchi*) *com'* (*comchésad*) rarely *coṅ* (*cosmil*), *cos* (?) *c. a.* (*có osnada*) *cuc'* (*cucci*), *reṅ* (*renatrite, recach*) *rem'* (*remib*) *remi* (*remiepur, remthechtas*), *iarṅ* (*iarmbaïthiŭs, iar timnu*) *iarma* (*iarmafoich, iarm(s)uidigthe*) once *iarṅ* (*iarfaïgĭd*); *as* (*abás, asind-*) *ass* (*ĕsib*) *as* (*asoirc*), *tars* (*tar crích, tarsin-*, 3. *taraïs*) *tarmi* (*taïrmthecht*), *trīs* (*trithemel?* *tresin-*, 3. *triit*) *tremi* (*tremdírgedar*), *fris* (*fricach, frissin-*, 3. *friss*) *frith'* (*frithcheist*) seldomer *fris* (*frisbiur*); *ó* (*hóthoïl*) *uad* (*uadfialichthi*); even *forthéit* along with *fortéit* points to *for'*. Thus *ar'* (*archiŭnn, archĕnn*) also represents undoubtedly a fundamental *ara (therefore, perhaps, *para), *aïr'* (*aïrchinn*) and *aïri* (*aïriumm*) on the other hand, very probably a strengthened form *aré from **(p)arai*, and Ausonius' measurement *Arémŏrĭcae* need not be at all looked upon as forced by the hexameter; hence **ara=ar'* is to παρά as **aré=aïr'* is to παραί=Lith. *prë* (*pry-, pri-*)=Slav. *pri*, and Gaul. *arémoricos* would be *παραιθαλάσσιος, as the modern Breton *arvorek* παραθαλάσσιος. But the fundamental meaning of *ar-* appears to be N. H. G. *vor* [Engl. *fore*] (*pro* and *prae*) from which *fūr*, with all its shades of meaning, was developed, which the English *for* and French *pour* might denote: *archiunn* (*vor dem angesicht, before* the face), *archĕnn* (*vor das angesicht*), *arse* (*pour cela, for* that), *arnaïb uïlib cumactib* (*prae omnibus potestatibus*), *aïri* (therefore, c'est pourquoi), *doaŭrchanim* (portendo), *argur* (Goth *faurbiuda*, N.H.G. *verbiete*), *araṅ* (*pour que*); even the conjunction *ar* is to be found in the English *for;* again *anaïr* is properly N.H.G. *von vorn* [Engl. *from before*], *aïrthĕr*=παροίτερος (πρότερος), O.H.G. *fordoro*, *aïre* and *aïrĕch* represent the Skr. *púrva* and the N.H.G. *vorig*. Now how does all this agree with *parâ*, which the Gr. παρά is supposed to represent? At the risk of being considered a very great heretic in etymology, I answer, certainly not with Skr. *parâ* to which Greek and Latin forms in ε and *e* correspond (παρά either not at all, or only in certain combinations), and which is itself only weakened from *apará; but no doubt with the *parâ of the primitive Indo-European language, which appears again in Skr. *purâ*, but is preserved in Gr. παρά, as is *paras, Skr. *puras*, in the Gr. πάρος; for notwithstanding the Gothic *faura*, the Sanskrit *purâ* has no more preserved the primitive vowel than *puras*, because Goth. *faur* may be equated with it, hence not only Zend *paoŭrva*, but also Old Persian *paruva* represent Skr. *pûrva*, and the Goth. *fairnja* (*fairneis*) with the more modern derivative, represents the Skr. *purâna*, all being relatives of the Lat. *prae, pro, por·*, the Gr. παρά, παραί, πρό, the Lith. *pra, prë*, Slav. *pra, pro, pri*, as well as of the O. Ir. *ar* and *aĭr*, and as *vor* ethically modifies its meaning to *für*, so it also weakens itself in meaning to *an* (compare *praebere*=παρέχειν). I have already spoken above of Modern Irish *ar*, to which the supposition of Pictet respecting Old Irish *for* applies.

APPENDIX.

APPENDIX.

I.—ZEUSS ON THE INFLEXIONS OF NOUNS IN IRISH.

[The following pages contain a translation of the part of the second chapter of the *Grammatica Celtica* of Zeuss, concerning the inflexions of the noun, to which reference is so frequently made in the Celtic studies of Dr. Ebel. One of the most remarkable features of Zeuss' work is the large number of examples taken from MSS. which he has brought forward as the basis upon which his grammatical canons are founded. Thus the examples given in the part of the chapter here translated fill considerably more than thirty pages. All these examples not being necessary for the purposes for which this translation was made, only a small selection of them has accordingly been given.

(A) *Declension.*

In the Old Irish language, the nouns of which have preserved a great variety of forms—in this respect far surpassing the Welsh even of the same period—we find two orders of declension, of which the first, on account of the prevalence of vowels in the inflections, may be called the "vocalic", and the second, for a similar reason, the "consonantal order". To the former belong the adjectives, which do not, as in other languages such as the German and Sclavonic, possess peculiar forms of their own; substantives alone are found in the latter, though in less number than in the first. In both orders the flexional vowels are either exterior, applied to the end of the word, or interior, placed immediately before the final consonant, whether it be a radical or derivative one. There are, moreover, some anomalous nouns differing from the usual forms of declension, and exhibiting others peculiar to themselves.

FIRST ORDER.

Substantives and adjectives of the masculine and neuter genders agree in their declensions. Those of the feminine gender have forms of their own. I shall give first a table of all the forms of declension, which I call series, with a paradigm of each; and then substantives and adjectives from the codices confirming the forms of all the series here exhibited, or even such as present any slight varieties.

DECLENSION OF NOUNS *Masculine and Neuter.*

Paradigms: I.—*Céle* (a companion). It has not appeared so necessary to give an example of a derivative of this first series, such as *echire* (a horseman, a muleteer?), *tectire* (an envoy), as of the following, on account of the internal vowels inflected: II. *ball* (a member), primitive, *tuisel* (a case), derivative example. III. *bith* (the world), primitive, *dílgud* (forgiveness), derivative.

The neuter differs so far only from the masculine, that the accusative and vocative are formed like the nominative; and, in the plural number, the same three cases take peculiar inflexions, different from the masculine, as will be rendered evident by the examples which follow:—

		I. Series.	II. Series.		III. Series.	
Sing.	Nom.	céle	ball	tuisel	bith	dílgud
	Gen.	céli	baill	tuisil	betho	dílgotho
	Dat.	céliu	baull	tuisiul	biuth	dílgud
Sing.	Acc.	céle	ball	tuisel	bith	dílgud
	Voc.	céli	baill	tuisil	bith	dílgud
Plur.	Nom.	céli	baill	tuisil	betha	dílgotha
	Gen.	céle	ball	tuisel	bithe	dílguthe
	Dat.	célib	ballib	tuislib	bithib	dílguthib
	Acc.	céliu	baullu	tuisliu	bithu	dílguthu
	Voc.	céliu	baullu	tuisliu	bithu	dílguthu

DECLENSION OF NOUNS—*Feminine*.

Paradigms: IV.—*tuare* (food). V. *rann* (a part), primitive, *bríathar* (a word), derivative.

		IV. Series.	V. Series.	
Sing.	Nom.	tuare	rann	briathar
	Gen.	tuare	rainne	bréthre
	Dat.	tuari	rainn	bréthir
	Acc.	tuari	rainn	bréthir
	Voc.	tuare	rann	briathar
Plur.	Nom.	tuari	ranna	briathra
	Gen.	tuare	rann	briathar
	Dat.	tuarib	rannib	briathrib
	Acc.	tuari	ranna	briathra
	Voc.	tuari	ranna	briathra

I. SERIES.—Of nouns externally inflected, and ending in -*e*, which in the different cases becomes -*i*, -*iu*, -*ib*. Neuter nouns in the nom. acc. and voc. plural vary from -*e* to -*i*.

SINGULAR.

NOMINATIVE.—Substantive Masculine—*céle* (a companion, husband), Wb. Sg.; *duine* (a man), Wb.; *dalte* (a disciple), etc.

Subs. Neut. (I give examples only of such as are met with the article), *anesseírge* (the resurrection), Wb. 30ᵇ; *atréde* (trinitas), *acetharde* (four), Wb. *cumachtae* (power), Sg. 6ᵃ.

Adjectives. Masculine. *céetne fer* (first man), Wb. 7ᵇ; *intathir nemde* (the Heavenly Father), Wb. 4ᵇ; derivative adj. in *de, te, the,* are of frequent occurrence.

Adjectives. Neut. *anuile* (all), *anuilese* (all this), Wb. 16ᵇ; *ni nuae ńdo anatrabsin* (this possession is not new to him), Ml. 17ᵇ.

GENITIVE.—Subst. Masc. *corp induini* (the man's body), Wb. 12ᵃ.

Subst. Neut. *claar cridi* (table of the heart), Wb. 15ᵃ; *comalnad soscéli* (fulfilment of the Gospel).

Adj. Mas. *comalnad indhuili recto* (fulfilment of all the law), Wb. 20ᵃ.

Adj. Neut. *áinsid cetni diil* (accusative of the first declension), Sg. 91ᵇ.

DATIVE.— *-u* occurs frequently instead of *-iu*.

Subst. Masc. *do duiniu* (to the man), Ml. 20ᵈ; *donduini* (to the man), Wb. 4ᵇ.

Subst. Neut. *dondédiusin* (to these two), Wb. 9ᶜ; *hi farcridiu* (in your heart), Wb. 5ᵈ; *In esseirgu, in heseirgiu* (in resurrection), Wb. 4ᵇ 13ᵇ; *iarnesseirgiu* (after resurrection), Wb. 3ᶜ.

Adj. Masc. *donchoimdid nemdu* (to the Heavenly Lord), Wb. 27ᶜ.

Adj. Neut. *far cétnu diull* (in the first declension), Sg. 90ᵇ.

ACCUSATIVE.—Subst. Masc. *imfolngi induine firian, imfolngi induine slán* (facit hominem justum, salvum), Wb. 4ᵈ.

Subst. Neut. *ní dilgaid anancride* (you forgive not the spite), Wb. 9ᶜ; *predchimmi soscéle* (we preach the Gospel), Wb. 14ᶜ.

Adj. Masc. *lasinnathir nemde* (with the Heavenly Father), Wb. 19ᵈ.

Adj. Neut. *cen imdibe stóride* (without bodily circumcision), Wb. 2ᵈ.

VOCATIVE.—Subst. and Adj. Mas. *a iudidi* (O Jew!), Wb. 1ᵈ; *a már thormachtai* (gl. macte, magis aucte) Sg. 76ᵃ.

PLURAL.

NOMINATIVE.—Subst. Masc. *comarpi* (co-heirs), Wb. 19ᶜ.

Subst. Neut. *-e* in Nom. and Acc., *ataat ilchenéle* (there are many kinds), Wb. 12ᵈ.

Adj. Masc. *dé nemdai* (heavenly gods), Sg. 39ᵃ.

Adj. neut., *na accobra colnidi* (the carnal desires), Wb. 20ᶜ.

GENITIVE.—*buáid innam miled talmande* (victory of the worldly soldiers), Wb. 11ᵃ.

DATIVE.—*donab huilib doinib* (to all men), Sg. 189ᵇ.

ACCUSATIVE.—Subs. Masc. *friarceiliu* (against our companions; *i. e.* against others), Wb. 33ᵇ; *eter dóini* (amongst men), Wb. 28ᵇ.

Subst. Neut. same as Nom.; *ruchualatar ilbélre* (they heard many tongues), Wb. 12ᵈ.

Adj. Masc. *farnuili baullu* (all your limbs), Wb. 3ᵇ.

Adj. Neut. *na huli dorigniussa* (all that I have done), Wb. 24ᵇ.

VOCATIVE.—No instances occur for this series in the MSS. Elsewhere, however, the Voc. plural agrees with the Acc.; and here it may be fixed for the masc. *-iu*, and for the neut. *-e, -i*.

II. SERIES.—Internal inflection, whereby in several cases, especially the Gen. Dat. sing. and Nom. plural, the signs of the cases—*i* and *u*—either accompany or suppress the final radical or derivative vowel. The vowels which are most frequently so affected are *a* and *e*. *A* in those cases either becomes *ai* (*oi, ui*) and *au*, or disappearing leaves the *i* and *u*. But *e* with *i* and *u* becomes *i* and *iu*. The vowels *o, ó, á*, of more rare occurrence, and sometimes *a* in position, never admit of *u* by their side, but with *i* they become *oi* (*ui*) *ói, ái; é*, for which *éu* is sometimes found, with *i* becomes *eíui, íui, éoi;* with *u iu; ói* and *ái* are nowhere changed. Substantives and adjectives neuter take *a* in the nom. acc. voc. plural.

SINGULAR.

NOMINATIVE.—Subs. Masc. *inball* (the limb), Wb. 12ᵇ; *inmacc* (the son), Wb. Sg. *infer* (the man), passim.

Subst. Neut. *anaccobor* (the will, desire), Wb. 3ᵈ; *anderbad* (the certainty), Sg. 90ᵃ.
Adj. Masc. *inspirut nóib* (the Holy Ghost), Wb. 4ᵃ; derivatives in *ach*, *ech* are very frequent.
Adj. Neut. *atir romanach* (the Roman land).
GENITIVE.—Subs. Masc. *ainm thríuin* (a hero's name), Sg. 96ᵃ; *di muntir Cessair* (of the family of Cæsar), Wb. 24ᵇ.
Subst. Neut. *imchloud diill* (change of declension), Sg. 31ᵇ; *recht naicnid* (law of nature), Sg. 217ᵇ.
Adj. Masc. *isinanmim inspiruto nóib* (in the name of the Holy Ghost), Wb. 9ᶜ.
Adj. Neut. *asainreth indanma dilis* (that is peculiar to a proper name).
DATIVE.—Subs. Masc. *dondaum* (to the ox), Wb. 10ᵈ; *dofiur, donfiur, do óen fiur* (to the man, to one man), Wb. 10ᵇ, 11ᶜ, 21ᵃ.
Subst. Neut. *far cétnu diull* (in the first declension; *diall*), Sg. 90ᵇ.
Adj. Masc. *on spirut nóib* (from the Holy Ghost), Wb. 14ᶜ. Adjectives in *ach* are not changed : *donbráthir hiressach* (to the faithful brother), Wb. 10ᵇ.
Adj. Neut. *ar anmmaimm dilius* (for a proper name), Sg. 27ᵃ.
ACCUSATIVE.—Subst. and Adj. Masc. *ar óen fer* (for one man), Wb. 4ᵇ.
Subst. and Adj. Neut. *ataidlech* (the satisfaction), Ml. 23ᵃ; *cen sáithur* (without labour), Wb. 27ᵇ.
VOCATIVE.—*á fir* (oh man!), Wb. 10ᵃ.

PLURAL.

NOMINATIVE.—Subst. Mas. *adimmaicc* (you are sons), Wb. 9ᵃ. *Itcorp inboillsin* (these limbs are a body), Wb. 3ᵇ.
é is changed, as in gen. sing. : *asberat mo beiúil* (my lips say), Wb. 12ᵈ.
Adj. Masc. *sláin* (saved, *slán*), Wb. 28ᵇ; *adib iressich* (you are faithful), Wb. 12ᵈ.
Subst. and Adj. Neut. differ by the termination *a : atercitla* (their prophecies ; *tercital*) Ml. 19ᵇ.
Adj. Neut. *cecha dethidnea domundi* (all worldly cares), Wb. 3ᵈ.
Final *i* is also met, especially in derivatives : *itsaini inna rinn* (there are different stars), Ml.; *isli* (gl. sunk, stars) Cr. 18ᵇ; *isli doibsom infechtsa innahi ruptar ardda dunnai* (those [stars] are now low for them, which were high for us), Cr. 18ᵇ.
GENITIVE.—Subst. Masc. *irchre flatho román* (the decline of the Roman Empire), Wb. 26ᵃ. *Riagoil sengrec* ([the] rule of the old Greeks), Sg. 1ᵃ.
Subst. Neut. : *airitiu na forcetalsin* (the reception of these doctrines), Wb. 16ᵃ.
Adj. Masc. *esseirge innanuile marb* (the resurrection of all the dead), Wb. 13ᵈ; *indocbál inna nóib innim* (the glory of the saints in Heaven), Wb. 13ᶜ.
Adj. Neut. *foragab duaid inna anman adiecta cen tabairt anman trenfriu* (David assigned to them nouns adjective, without the addition of appellatives), Ml. 30ᵃ.
DATIVE.—*Donaib ballaib ailib* (to the other members), Wb. 12ᵇ.
ACCUSATIVE.—Subst. Masc. *farnuili baullu* (all your members), Wb. 3ᵇ.
Adj. Masc. *la marbu* (with the dead), Wb. 25ᵇ.
Subst. and Adj. Neut., same as in the nom. *fodaimimse imnetha* (I suffer tribulations), Wb. 23ᵇ.
VOCATIVE.—Subst. and Adj. Masc. *a Rómanu* (oh Romans!), Sig. 41ᵇ; *a Galatu burpu* (oh foolish Galatians), Wb. 19ᵇ; *a Judeu et geinti hireschu* (oh Jews and faithful Gentiles), Wb. 3ᵃ.
Adj. Neut. *inna anman adiecta* (the nouns adjective), Ml. 30ᵃ.

III. SERIES.—Of nouns externally inflected, except the dat. sing., in which the internal *u* occasionally appears. Endings peculiar to this series, besides the *u* just mentioned, *ib* dat. plural, and *u* acc. and voc. plural, are : -*o* gen. sing. for which *a* is of frequent, and *e* of rare occurrence ; -*a* nom. pl., for which -*e* and -*i* are also met with ; -*e* gen. pl. : neuter substantives do not take an ending in those cases of the plural which differ from the masculine, but present their naked form. I have met with no adjectives of this series, unless it happens that *tualang*, pl. *tuailnge* (gnari)[127], be one, Wb. 17^b.

SINGULAR.

NOMINATIVE.—Sub. Masc. *bith* (the world); *mug* (a slave), Wb. And derivatives in *as, chas, ad, id, thid, ud, igud.*
Subst. Neut. *atir* (the Earth), Sg. 33^a.
GENITIVE.—Masc., *imnetha inbetho* (tribulations of the world), Wb. 14^b; *mórad daggnimo* (magnifying of a good deed), Wb. 6^a.
Neut., *ainm renda* (name of a constellation), Sg. 73^a.
DATIVE.—Masc., *isinbiuthso* (in this world), Wb. 12^d; *do mórad dǽ* (to the magnifying of God), Wb. 15^c.
Neut., *di thír* (of the Earth), Wb. 9^b.
ACCUSATIVE.—Masc., *tri óen pheccad* (through one sin), Wb. 3^a.
Neut., *crenas tíir* (who purchases land), Wb. 29^d.
VOCATIVE.—I do not know an example of the vocative of this series.

PLURAL.

NOMINATIVE.—Masc. *adib mogæ* (you are slaves), *mogi sidi uili* (these are all slaves), Wb. 3^b. 7^d. The ending *i* is only found in sub. masc. in *-id, -thid : foglimthidi* (disciples) 13^a.
Neut., *itsaini inna rinn* (there are different stars), Ml.
GENITIVE.—*lóg apecthe* (the reward of their sins), Wb. 1^c.
DATIVE.—*diamogaib* (to his slaves), Wb. 22^d.
ACCUSATIVE.—Mas., *na dánu diadi* (the divine gifts), Wb. 28^c.
Neut., *inna mind* (gl. insignia, celebramus nostræ redemtionis), Cr. 41^c.
VOCATIVE.—Does not occur; by analogy, *bithu, gnimu*, etc.

IV. SERIES.—Of nouns fem. externally inflected, ending in *-e* and *-i*, and, therefore, corresponding to mas. and neut. nouns of the first series in *-e, -i,* and *-u*.

SINGULAR.

NOMINATIVE.—Masc.: *láne, lanæ* (fulness), Wb. 26^d, 27^a; *fírinne*, (truth) Wb. 2^d.
Adj. *fírinne rectide* (righteousness of the law) Wb. 24^a.
GENITIVE.—*Maicc soilse* (sons of light), Wb. 25^c.
Adj. *hi foirciunn na cetnae rainne* (at the end of the first part), Sg. 18^b.
DATIVE.—Subst. *co failti* (with joy), Wb. 24^b.
Adj. *icomairbirt núidi* (in understanding the [New Testament]), Wb. 3^c.
ACCUSATIVE.—Subst.: *cen fírinni* (without truth), Wb. 2^a.
Adj. *tresinfuil spirtaldi* (through the spiritual blood), Wb. 20^d.

PLURAL.

NOMINATIVE.—Subst. *cit sochudi* (though there be many), Wb. 4^d.
Adj. *inna ranna aili* (the other parts), Sg. 22^a.
GENITIVE.—Subst. *do airbirt biuth inna túaresin* (to enjoy this food), Wb. 10^c.
Adj. *etarcne narúun diade* (knowledge of the divine mysteries), Wb. 26^c.
DATIVE.—*Ibartolaib* [*Inbartolaib?*] *marbdib* (in your mortal wills), Wb. 3^b
ACCUSATIVE.—Subst. *inna lobri* (the infirmities), Wb. 6^c.
Adj. *adciamni na rúna diadi* (we perceive the divine mysteries), Wb. 12^c.

V. SERIES.—Of nouns fem. inflected both externally and internally, and corresponding at once to Series II. and III. mas. and neut. Special vowel endings are: *-e* in gen. sing., *-a* in nom. and acc. pl.; besides internal *-i* in dat. and acc. sing., if the last syllable admit of the insertion.

---

[127] [Tualaing properly means able, competent.]

SINGULAR.

NOMINATIVE.—Subst. (of frequent occurrence in the codices): *ess, iress* (faith), *nem* (Heaven), *lám* (the hand), etc.

Adj. also numerous : *serc mór* (great love).

GENITIVE.—Subst. *tuag nime* (rainbow), Sg., 107ᵇ.

Adj., *airde serce móre insin* (this is a sign of great love), Wb. 24ᶜ.

Instead of *-e*, the regular case-ending, *-o* and *-a* occur (or *vice versa -e* for *-o*, *-a* in Series III. mas. and neut.), whether by affinity or dialectical variety; *luct inna œcolsa* (those who are of the church), Wb. 12ᵇ.

DATIVE.—Subst., *isindinducbáilsin* (in this glory), Wb. 4ᶜ; *isinbliadinsin* (in this year), Cr. 32ᵇ.

Adj., *o laim deiss* (on the right hand), Sg. 17ᵇ.

ACCUSATIVE.—Subst., *tri hiris* (through faith), Wb. 2ᶜ; *pridchossa hiris* (I preached the faith), Wb. 7ᵇ, *fri toil dé* (against the will of God), Wb. 4ᶜ; *fri etáil* (against Italy), Wb. 6ᵈ.

Adj., *isarnach nindocbáil móir* (it is for every great glory), Wb. 23ᵇ.

VOCATIVE.—*A nóib ingen* (oh holy virgin! gl. marg.), Sg. 112ᵃ.

PLURAL.

NOMINATIVE.—Subst., *láma et cossa* (hands and feet), Wb. 12ᵇ; *na bretha* (the judgments), Wb. 17ᵇ, *inna ranna* (the parts), Sg. 22ᵃ, 26ᵇ; *na briathrasa* (these words), Wb. 28ᶜ. *-e* and *-i* also occur in many, as the result of assimilation: *octṅdelbæ andsom* (gl. sunt formæ octo), Sg. 166ᵃ; *na litre* (the letters), Sg. 10ᵃ; *inbértar epistli uáin* (shall the letters be sent from us ?), Wb. 15ᵃ; *athissi* (gl. conflictiones ; sing. nom. *aithiss*, Wb. 13ᵇ, compos. ut *iress* ?) Wb. 29ᵇ; *teora bliadni* (three years), Cr. 32ᵇ.

Adj. in *-a*: *béisti olca* (evil monsters, or reptiles), Wb. 31ᵇ. Adj. in *-i*: *itnephchumscaichti na teora litreso* (these three letters are unchangeable), Sg. 10ᵃ.

GENITIVE.—Subst., *etarcne naruun* (knowledge of the mysteries), Wb. 26ᶜ.

Adj., *inna teora liter* (of the three letters) Sg.

DATIVE.—*Hó lámaib* (from hands), Wb. 9ᵃ; *donaib teoraib personaib uathataib* (of the three persons singular), Sg. 186ᵃ.

ACCUSATIVE.—Subst., *adciamni na rúna* (we perceive the mysteries), Wb. 12ᶜ; *fri tola inbetho* (against worldly desires) Wb. 29ᵃ.

Adj., *nigette* [*nigente?*] *na brithemnachta becca* (you would not form slight judgments), Wb. 9ᶜ.

Subst. and Adj. in *-i*: *acosmiligm̃er déli ecsamli* (we compare things dissimilar) Sg. 211ᵃ.

VOCATIVE.—*ni riccim forless a chossa* (I require not your aid, oh feet!), Wb. 12ᵃ.

SECOND ORDER.

Nouns of this class end for the most part in consonants, or rather have in some cases consonantal endings which, being originally, no doubt, derivative, show traces of an internal derivative inflection, with the mutable vowels *a, e,* and *i* preceding the final consonant. The final consonants are the liquids *m, n, r,* and the mutes *d, ch,* which with the internal vowels form a series of terminations—*ir, ar, ir; in, an, in; id, ad, id,* etc. The one series of the substantives in *-m* and *-im,* which I place first, developes certain special forms. If *e* appears instead of *a,* two divisions arise : (a) *an, in, ad, id;* (b) *en, in, ed, id.* Which discrepancy of vowels can scarcely be ascribed to assimilation, in the face of such forms as *senman, menman, foirbthetad, orpamin,* and others.

Examples of the liquid series (I.) (II.) (III.): *ainm* (a name), *béim* (a stroke), *menme* (the mind), *dítu dítiu* (a roof), *athir* (a father).

Examples of the mute series (IV.) (V.) *druid* (a Druid), *cathir* (a town).

Zeuss on the Inflexions of Nouns.

		I. Series.		II. Series.		III. Series.
		a.	b.	a.	b.	
Sing.	Nom.	ainm	béim	menme	dítiu	athir
	Gen.	anma	béme	menman	díten	athar
	Dat.	anmim	bémim	menmin	dítin	athir
	Acc.	ainm	béim	menmin	dítin	athir
Plur.	Nom.	anman	bémen	menmin	dítiu	athir
	Gen.	anman	bémen	menman	díten	athre
	Dat.	anmanib	bémnib	menmanib	dítnib	athrib
	Acc.	anman	bémen	menmana	dítne	athru

		IV. Series.		V. Series.
Sing.	Nom.	druid	fili	cathir
	Gen.	druad	filed	cathrach
	Dat.	druid	filid	cathir
	Acc.	druid	filid	cathrich
Plur.	Nom.	druid	filid	cathrich
	Gen.	druad	filed	cathrach
	Dat.	druidib	filidib	cathrichib
	Acc.	druida	fileda	cathracha

I. Series consists of some substantives in *im*, *m*, taking in the gen. sing. *-a* or *-e;* in the dat. *-im*, with duplicated *m;* and in the plural either *an* or *en*, these two endings forming two distinct classes. In the first (a), the noun *ainm*, of constant occurrence, is proved to be of the neut. gender, from the passage (Sg. 56^b): *asṅdirruidig. anainmsin*[128] (this noun is derived). Of the same gender, no doubt, are all other nouns of this form. Of the second class (b) but few examples occur, and these not uniform. There is no instance of a vocative in this or any of the other series.

SINGULAR.

Nom.—(a) *ainm*, *ainmm* (a name), Wb. Sg. passim.
(b) *béim* (a blow), *ingreim* (persecution), Wb. 18^d.
Gen.—(a) *indanma dilis* (of the proper name), Sg. 26^b; (b) no example found in the codices.
Dat. (a) *isinanmim inchoimded ihu. cr.* (in the name of the Lord Jesus Christ), Wb. 9^c.
(b) *ocmingraimmaimse* (at my persecution), Ml. 33^a.
Acc.—(a) *cen ainm* (without a name), Sg. 211^a.
(b) *ní agathar áingreim* (his persecution is not dreaded), Wb. 1^a.

PLURAL.

Nom.—(a) *asbertar ananman* (their names are mentioned), Wb. 28^a.
(b) *bémen dígle* (strokes of revenge), Wb. 17^d.
Gen.=(a) *diall nanmann* (declension of nouns), Sg. 27^a.
(b) *foditiu nan ingremmen* (endurance of the persecutions), Wb. 23^c.
Dat.—(a), *inanmanaib lait.* (in Latin names), Sg. 6^a; (b) no example known; *bémnib* in the table is, therefore, hypothetical.
Acc.—(a) *tre anman* (by nouns), Sg. 29^a.

II. Series.—Consists of nouns taking in the oblique cases *an*, *in*, and *in*, *en*, whence two divisions. To the first belong derivatives in *-min*, *-man*, *-mn* (which is reduced, however, in the nominative to *-me*, or *·m*

---

[128] [Uncontracted form *asṅdirruidigthe anainmsin*.]

only), to the second belong derivative nouns in *-in* which in the same manner in the nom. becomes *-iu*, *-u*. In the oblique cases singular, likewise, especially the dative, other curtailed forms are found by the side of the fuller. These fuller forms of derivatives appear in the case of secondary derivatives: *menmnihi* (gl. dissensiones, from the sing. *menmniche; menme*), Wb. 18[a]; *brithemnacht, brithemnact* (judgeship), Wb. 6[b]; *brithemandu* (gl. judiciali, from the nom. *brithemande—brithem*), Ml. 26[c]; *anmande* (pertaining to the soul—*anim*), Wb. 13[d]; *talmande* (pertaining to the earth—*talam*), Wb. 3[d]; *noidenacht* (infancy—*noidiu*, an infant), Wb. 24[d]; *caintoimtenach* (well-thinking—*toimtiu*), Ml. 31[b]; *ermitnech* (gl. reverens—*ermitiu*), Ml. 32[b]. For the vowels *a*, *e*, I add *brátharde*, brotherly, from *bráthir*.

To the second division (b) of this series belong numerous feminine nouns in *tu*, derived from verbs (*tu* for *tiu*, not to be confounded with masculines in *-tu*, gen. *-tad*, of the fourth series, and derived from adjectives). There are other feminines of the second class in *-tiu*, and in *siu*, derived also from verbs. In the first division are met both masculines, as, *brithem*, and feminines, as, *talam*, *anim*.

SINGULAR.

Nom.—(a) *isbeo indanim* (the soul is living) Wb. 4[a].
(b) *toimtiu* (supposition), Wb. 23[a].
Gen.—(a) *rosc fornanme* (eye of your soul), Wb. 21[a].
(b) *dliged remcaissen, dliged remdeicsen*, (law of Providence), Ml. 19[d], 27[d].
Dat.—(a) *inim et talam, inim et italam* (in Heaven and Earth), Wb. 21[a].
(b) *oc tuiste dúile* (at the creation of the elements, *i.e.*, of the world), Wb. 5[c].
Acc.—(a) *accobor lammenmuin* (desire in the mind), Wb. 3[d].
(b) *nertid arfrescsinni* (he strengthens our hope), Wb. 5[d].
The final *iu*, *u* of the nom. seems to have disappeared from some nouns in *t*, as, *fortacht* (help) Ml. 1[a]; *bendacht* (benediction), Sg.

PLURAL.

Nom.—(a) *matuhé ata horpamin* (if these be heirs), Wb. 2[c].
(b) *derbaisndisin* (the very pronunciations), Sg. 3[b].
Gen.—(a) *do icc anman sochuide* (for the salvation of many souls), Wb. 24[d].
(b) *dedliguth innan iltoimddensin* (in right of these many opinions), Sg. 26[b].
Dat.—(a) *diarnanmanaib* (for our souls), Wb. 24[d].
(b) *huafoisitnib* (from confessions), Sg. 33[a].
Acc.—(a) *aforcital iccas corpu et anmana* (the doctrine which heals bodies and souls), Wb. 30[d].
(b) *for genitne* (by genitives), Sg. 45[a].

III. Series.—Of nouns of relationship, mas. and fem. in *-ir*, there is but one class, as *e* never occurs for *a* in the interior.

SINGULAR.

Nom.—*Athir* (father), *máthir* (mother), *bráthir* (brother), Wb. Sg. passim.
Gen.—*Bráthir athar* (gl. father's brother), Sg. 56[a].
Dat.—*Dondathir* (to the father), Wb. 13[b].
Acc.—*Lasinnathir nemde* (with the Heavenly Father), Wb. 19[d].

PLURAL.

Nom.—No instances in the codices, *athir* by analogy.
Gen.—*Maic indegaid anathre* (sons after their fathers), Wb. 30[b].
Dat.—*Uambraithrib* (from their brothers), Wb. 33[d].
Acc.—Does not occur. I supply mas. *athru, bráthru*—fem. *máthra*.

IV. SERIES.—Of derivatives in -*id*, forming in the oblique cases by the variation of the internal vowels two divisions (*a*) *ad, id;* (*b*) *ed, id.* To the first belong very frequent nouns in -*u*, shortened from -*id*, as above, -*u*, -*iu*, from -*in*. The ending *id*, has been preserved only in the word *druid*, in the others becoming -*e*, as: *tenge* (a tongue), *ume* (brass). The terminations of the second class have also become in the nom. -*iu*, -*i*, or -*e*. The full form of the derivatives here also, as in the second series, is apparent from nouns and adj. of secondary derivation: *filedacht* (poetry; *fili*, gen. *filed*), Sg. 213[a]; *óigedacht* (hospitality, *ogi*) Wb. 26[b]; to which I add, *Tenedon* (*tene, tened*), a Gaulish topographical name. Further *traigthech* (gl. pedester; *traigid*, Wb.) Sg. 38[b], 50[b].

The nouns of both divisions are masculine.

SINGULAR.

NOM.—(*a*). Abstract Nouns in *u* from adjectives are very frequent. The ending is either -*u* simple, or the fuller -*atu*, -*etu*.

Adj. of different form taking -*u*: *artu* (height), = *arddu, ardu* (from *art, ardd, ard*); *domnu* (depth, from *domun*) Incant. Sg. So also -*atu*, -*etu*: *dánatu* daring) Sg. 90[a].

Adj. in -*ide*, -*de*, -*te*, taking -*u*: *óentu* (unity, adj. *óente, óende*, Wb. 7[c]); *corpdu* (corporality, adj., *corpde*), Wb. So also, -*atu*, -*etu*: *fliuchaidatu* (humidity, adj., *fliuchaide*), Cr. 18[c]; *fóirbthetu* (firmness), Wb. passim.

(*b*) *cóindiu* (Lord), Wb.; *tene* (fire), Sg., 69[b].

GEN.—(*a*) *tech nebmarbtath* (house of immortality), Wb. 15[c].

(*b*) *bandea tened* (goddess of fire, Vesta), Sg. 53[a].

DAT.—(*a*) *ondnephpiandatu* (from the impunity), Ml. 28[a].

(*b*) *do filid* (to a poet), Sg., 14[a].

ACC.—(*a*) *cen torbatid* (without utility), Wb. 12[d].

(*b*) *lassincoimdid* (with the Lord), Wb. 25[b].

PLURAL.

NOM.—(*a*) *dorigénsat druid* (druids made), Wb. 26[a].

(*b*) *intan labratar indfilid* (when the poets speak), Sg. 162[a].

GEN.—(*a*) from the Irish Annals: *Muiredac na tengad* (Muiredach [professor] of the languages) Tigern. ap. O'Con. 2, 275.

(*b*) *dolbud filed* (poetic fiction), Sg. 71[b].

DAT.—*secndapthib* (to the agents), W[b]. 19[d].

ACC.—(*a*) *lasna filedasin* (with these poets), Sg. 63[b].

V. SERIES.—Of certain feminine nouns in -*r*, to which are added the suffixes -*ach*, -*ich*, -*ig*. The cases, though not all, of the noun *cathir* (a town), are met with in the codices, and the same declension is followed by *nathir* (a serpent) with the article in Sg.: *indnathirsin* (gl. natrix, *i. e.* serpens hic) 69[a]. and doubtlessly by others in *ir*. Vestiges of this formation appear to have been preserved in the modern Irish: *caora* (a sheep, old form: *cáir, cáer?*) Gen. *caorach*, pl. nom. *caoirigh*. gen. *caorach*, dat. *caorchaibh*, voc. (acc.) *caorcha*. It is certainly preserved in some others in *ir*, as: *láir* (Old Irish *láir*, a mare, Sg. 49[b]=*lá-ir*), *lasair* (a flame), gen. *lárach, lasrach*, pl. *láracha, lasracha*. Here, also, the derivative *ch*, appears in the adj. *cáirchuide*, Sg. 37 (ovine); compare the Gaulish name *Caeracates* in *Tacitus*, and perhaps also *Caracalla*, the name of a Gaulish robe, (for *caeracalla?*), it is wanting, however, in *trechatharde* (gl. tripolites), Sg. 38[b].

SINGULAR.

Nom.—*Cr. dim* [*din*] *issi inchathir* (therefore Christ himself is the city), Wb. 21ᶜ.
Gen.—*aitribtheid inna cathrach asb. tibur* (gl. *Tiburs:* an inhabitant of the town which is called Tibur), Sg. 124ᵇ.
Dat.—One would expect -*ich*, -*ig*, by analogy, but the contracted form of the nom. obtains in Wb. 13ᵇ. : *robói issinchaithir* (he was in the city).
Acc.—*Romuil doforsat incathraig* (Romulus founded the city), Sg. 31ᵇ.

PLURAL.

Nom.—*ilchathraig* (many cities), Sg. 13ᵃ.
The other cases must be supplied : Gen. *cathrach.* Dat. *cathrichib* (or *cathrib?*) Acc. and Voc. *cathracha.*

The Dual Number.

After the twofold formation of the Irish declension, we may here add a few words concerning this number, on account of the small number of examples furnished by the codices for all the series given above. It does not, of itself, denote two persons or things, as for instance in Greek, but constructed with the numerals *dá, di, dib,* it presents in the language of our codices mixed sing. and pl. forms, relics no doubt of more ancient forms peculiar to this number.

The only form of the article in any case or gender, is, *in* before *d,* the initial letter of the numeral, which in one of the following examples is written *dd,* hard.

We shall give, first, paradigms of the series of the *first order,* and then such examples as occur in the codices. The forms enclosed in brackets are hypothetical, or formed by analogy.

MASC. AND NEUT.

	I. *Series.*	II. *Series.*	III. *Series.*
Nom.	céle (i ?)	ball	bith
Gen.	céli	(baill)[129]	betho
Dat.	célib	(ballib)	bithib
Acc.	céle	ball	bith

FEMININE.

	IV. *Series.*	V. *Series.*
Nom.	tuari	rainn
Gen.	tuare	rann
Dat.	tuarib	rannib
Acc.	tuari	rainn

I. SERIES.

Nom.—The Nom. Masc. appears to occur in the adj. *dadruith ægeptacdi* (two Egyptian Druids) Wb. 30ᶜ.
Neut. *indagné* (the two forms), Sg. 168ᵃ.
Gen. and Dat.—Gen. and dat. are not met.

---

[129] [xxxv. Rectè *ball,* which aspirates,* must, therefore, have had a vocalic auslaut (-*ó* -*au?*) and so cannot possibly be (as Ebel supposes, On Decl. in Irish, §. 10 On the Celtic Dual, p. 85) identical with the gen. plur.]

* We say (*e.g.*), *athair an dá macfhionn* (father of the two fair sons), *cailleach an dá adharc fhionn* (hag of the two white horns).

Acc.—Masc. or Neut.: *dobir dasale. dabir imduda are* (ἅπαξ λεγόμενα) Incant. Sg.[130]

II. SERIES.

Nom.—Masc.: *da mod*, (two moods) Sg. 138ᵇ.
Neut.: *comescatur da cenel indib*(gl. two genders are mixed up in them), Sg. 61ᵃ.
Gen.—Of the gen. no instances.
Dat.—Neut.: *frisgair intestiminse dondib dligedib remeperthib* (this testament answers to the two previous laws), Sg. 193ᵇ.
Acc.—*imbir indamér* (ply the two fingers), Incant. Sg.

III. SERIES.

Nom.—*biet da atarcud and* (there will be two relations there), Sg. 198ᵇ.
Gen.—*Cechtar da lino* (either of the two parts), Sg. 162ᵇ.
Dat.—*Coms. ó dib nógaib* (composed of two parts), Sg. 98ᵃ.
Acc.—*Andiall foadanóg* (the declension in both its parts), 98ᵃ. Sg.
Neut.: *indá érrend* (gl. stigmata, porto), Wb. 20ᵈ.

IV. SERIES.

Nom.—*It digutai bíte indeog.* (there are two vowels in a diphthong), Sg. 18ᵃ.
Gen.—*Fogor dagutæ indeog.* (the sound of two vowels in a diphthong), Sg. 18ᵃ.
Dat.—Evidently *do dib guttib*.[131]
Acc.— Adj. in Sg. 74ᵇ, *indi rainn iṅgraidi* (into two intelligible parts).

V. SERIES.

Nom.—*Di húair* (two hours), Cr. 31ᵇ.
Gen.—*Cechtar indarann* (either of the two parts), Sg. 74ᵇ.
Dat.—*Ní chen dliged anephdiall ó dib rannaib* (gl. alteruter, alterutrius non absque ratione non declinatur; i. e. non declinatur e duabus partibus), Sg. 75ᵃ.
Acc.—*Coitchenaso etir di árim* (common to two numbers*)*, Sg. 72ᵃ.

Duals of the second order are very rare. The following are instances:—

Tuicsom inda nainmso (he understands these two names), Wb. 21ᵈ; *da druith ægeptacdi* (two Ægyptian Druids), Wb. 30ᶜ.

Anomalous Substantives.

Which do not follow a fixed rule and form like all those above enumerated, but have peculiar and shifting forms of their own. Of this kind are: *dia* (God), *dia* (a day), *duine* (a man), *ben* (a woman), *ríg* (a king), *lá* (a day).

I. *Dia* (God): sing. gen. *etargne ṅdæ* (knowledge of God), Wb. 21ᵃ; dat. *ó dia* (from God); acc. *fri dia* (with God), Wb. 20ᵈ; voc. *a dáe* (oh God). Wb. 5ᵇ; plur. nom. *dé nemdai són* (Heavenly Gods), Sg. 39ᵃ; dat. *do déib* (to the Gods), Sg. 39ᵇ; acc. *tarsna deo* (by the Gods), Sg. 217ᵇ; Fem. sing. *dea,*—in composition *bandea* (goddess), Sg. 60ᵃ; plur. *bándǽ* (goddesses), Sg. 53ᵇ.
II. *Dia* (day): *cach dia* (daily), Wb. 18ᶜ; *indiu, hindiu* (to day), Wb.; *fride, fridei* (by day); *dia brátha* (in the day of judgment), Wb. 23ᶜ.
III. *Duine* (man)—the radical *ui* becomes *ói* in the plur.; sing. gen. *corp duini* (a man's body), Wb. 12ᵃ; dat. *donduini* (to the man), Wb. 4ᵇ; acc. *imfolngi induine slán* (he saves man), Wb. 4ᵈ; voc. *a duini* (O man), Wb. 1ᶜ; plur. nom. *indóini*

---

[130] [xxxvi. *Da sale* is *salivam tuam (da* for *du, do); im du da are,* "around thy two temples"; *are* (tempus capitis) gen. *arach,* is a c-stem. These examples are, therefore, improper.]
[131] [xxxvii. Rather *do dib ṅguttib,* where *dib n*=the Sansk. dwâbhyâm, Greek δυοῖν (from δυοφιν).]

bí (the living men), Sg. 39ª ; gen. *icc incheneli dóine* (the salvation of the race of men), Wb. 26ᵈ; acc. *coræ fri dia et dóini* (peace towards God and men), Wb. 20ᵈ.

IV. *Ben* (woman)—interchanges with the forms *ban, mná: iccfe inmnái* (thou wilt heal the woman), Wb. 10ª.

V. *Ríg* (king): sing. gen. *itaig ríg* (in the king's house), Wb. 23ᵇ; dat. *ainm̄ diaríg* (gl. Lar rex Vejentorum, *i. e.*, the name of their king), Sg. 64ª; plur. gen. *hi lebraib ríg* (in the books of kings), Ml. 30ᵇ ; acc. *conroibtis ocdenum rectche la riga* (gl. volentes esse legis doctores, *i. e.*, to the kings),Wb. 28ª.

VI. *Lá*(day) is inflected from the forms *lú, lae,* and *laithe, lathe* (neuter). Sing. n. *alaithe*, Ml. 21ᶜ ; gen. *ammi maicc lai* (we are the sons of day), Wb. 25ᶜ ; dat. *illau báiss* (in the day of death), Wb. 29ᶜ; acc. *fri laa brátha* (to doomsday), Wb. 29ª; plur. gen. *ar lín laithe* (in the number of days), Ml. 17ᵈ.

(B) *Diminutives.*

Common to both subst. and adj., like the declension of the first order. The instances that occur, especially in codex Sg., present the following terminations, *-án, -én*, and *-that*, which are more usual in the mas. and neut., and *-éne, -ne, -nat, -net* in the fem.

Masc. and neut. AN in substantives: *duinán* (a mannikin), Sg. 47ᵇ; *táidán* from *táid* (a thief), 47ᵇ. In adjectives *becán* (gl. paullulus), Sg. 48ª; *trogán* (gl. misellus), 48ª.

Numerous old proper names have the same ending: *Tresan, Gibrian, Veran, Abran, Petran* (vita S. Tresani, Boll., Febr. 2, 53).

EN: *duinén* (mannikin), Sg. 45ª.

THAT: *sráthathat* (a sting), Sg. 47ª; *centat* (gl. capitulum), 47ª. CHAT, NAT, NET, are less frequent: *duinenet* (a mannikin), 45ᵇ.

Fem. ENE: *laréne* (from *láir*, a mare), Sg. 49ᵇ.

NAT in subst.: *siurnat* (gl. sororcula), Sg. 46ᵇ ; *talamnat* (gl. terrula), 48ª.

NET, NIT: *fochricnet* (gl. mercedula), Sg. 47ª; *tonnait* (gl. cuticula), 46ᵇ.

(C) *Degrees of Comparison.*

Comparative and superlative. The forms of the first, in the old language, are the more copious, these are either regular or irregular.

COMPARATIVE.

Of this there are two forms, *-ithir, -iu, -u*,—the first of which may be compared with the Greek ὅτερος, and the second with the old Latin *-ios, -ius*, the *s* of which passed into *r*. Inflections are not found.

Ithir I have only met in one codex Wb., and in one passage 27ᵈ : *islerithir*.

Iu and *u* are used indifferently, though the former is more usual in monosyllables, the latter in polysyllables. The particle *de* is often met after the comparative, corresponding seemingly to the Latin *eo*.

Iu: *níbia di mútaib bes huilliu inoensill*. (there cannot be more of mutes in one syllable), Sg. 7ª ; *lériu* (more industrious), 41ª ; *semiu* (more slender), 14ᵇ ; *goiriu* (more pious), 40ᵇ.

U: *oillu oldate cóiccet fer* (more than fifty men), Wb. 18ᵈ; *isassu, ba assu* (easier), Wb. 15ᶜ; *ata lobru* (that are weaker), Wb. 12ᵇ ; *gliccu* (wiser), Wb. 26ᵈ ; *istairismechu infer* (the man is firmer), Wb. 28ᵇ. There are some anomalous comparatives either in *a*, which sometimes becomes *o*, or with peculiar forms of their own. Of the former the principal are:—*máa, máo, móa, móo* (greater), *messa* (worse), *nessa* (nearer), *tressa* (stronger). Besides *óa* (less), *lía* (more), *ire* (ulterior), *ferr* (better).

Máa from adj. *már* (great), for which *mór* also occurs. From the form *már* are produced *máa, má, máo : asmáa alailiu* (greater than another), Wb. 12ª. From *mór* are made *móa, móo, mó : móa léu sercc atuile* (greater with them is the love of their own will), Wb. 30ᶜ; *fresciu fogchricce asmóo* (hope of the reward, which is greater), Wb. 10ᶜ.

Messa (worse): *fodaimid nech asmessa dúib* (endure one who is worse to you), Wb. 17ᵇ; *creitmechsin asmessa ancreitmech* (this believer is worse than an infidel), Wb. 28ᵈ.

Nessa (nearer): *isnesa do geintib* (he is nearer to the Gentiles), Wb. 2ᵇ; *innahi ata nessa* (those which are nearer), Cr. 44ᵃ.

Tressa (stronger): *combad tressa de hiress apstal do fulung* (that the faith of the Apostles might be stronger to endure), Wb. 25ᵃ; *ishé dim [din?] ambés adi inti diib bes tresa orcaid alaile* (it is their habit that the stronger kill the weaker) Ml. 19ᵈ.

The three following comparatives, on account of the verbs accompanying them regularly in the sing., appear to have been originally substantives, with a comparative signification. They also sometimes act as adverbs in their naked form.

Oa (less): *acoic indid oa q. xxx* (the five in it less than thirty) Cr., 33ᵇ.

Lia (more, a greater number): *nabad lia diis no thriur dam* (let there be not more than two or three) Wb. 13ᵃ; *itlia sillaba o illitrib* (there are more syllables of many letters), Sg. 71ᵃ.

Ire (ulterior): *aither. ní ashire oldáta m. ocus aui* (patronymics no further than sons and grandchildren), Sg. 30ᵇ.

Ferr (better): *ni ferr nech alailiu and* (no one better than another there), Wb. 2ᵃ; *nipat ferr de* (they are not better of it), Wb. 12ᵈ.

In the majority of the foregoing examples, the particle *as*, preceding the comparative, is evidently the verb subst. 3 pers. sing. in dependent position. It is often, however, a different word, increasing the sense of the gradation, *ex. gr.* the comparative: *ni asse acleith rafitir aslia* (it cannot be easily concealed, many know it), Wb. 23ᶜ, or of the superlative: *asmaam*. The meaning of comparative is still further increased by its repetition with the intervening formula *ass: corrop moo assa moo et corrop ferr assa ferr donimdigidesseirc [donimdigid desseirc] dé et comnessim* (so that it may be better and better, you increase your love of God and [your] neighbour), Wb. 23ᵇ; *ferr asaferr* (better and better), Wb. 15ᶜ.

SUPERLATIVE.

There are two endings, *-em* and *-am*, the former of adjectives which form their comparatives in *-iu -u*, the latter of anomalous adjectives ending in *a* in the comparative. Internal inflexion occurs in the forms ending in *am*.

Em: faillsem (most clear, lucid, from *follus*, open, clear), Cr. 40ᵃ; *tóisigem* (the first; in the verse: primus de Danaum magna comitante caterva), Sg. 42ᵃ.

The following are instances of the fuller form, *-imem, -ibem, -bem* after a double consonant or diphthong radical: *huaislimem* (the highest), Ml. 28ᵈ; *itdoini saibibem dogniat inso* (they are most false men who do this,—from *saib* false, or properly delusive), Ml. 3ᵃ.

Am: oam (the least), Wb. 13ᵇ; *asmaam rosechestar arsidetaid* (it is he has reached as great an age as possible), Sg. 208ᵇ, *ata nessam* (the nearest) Incant. Sg. *comnesnam* (the neighbour [lit. " nearest]), Ml. 36ᵃ. Gen.: *desserc dé et comnessim* (love of God and (our) neighbour), Wb. 23ᵇ. Dat.: *ho chomnesam* (from a neighbour), Ml. 36ᵃ. Acc.: *galar bess fairechomnessam* (the disease which is over on his neighbour), Cod. Camar.; *athis forachomnesam* (reproach against his neighbour), Ml. 36ᵃ.

II.—THE CELTIC MSS. UPON WHICH ZEUSS' GRAMMATICA CELTICA WAS FOUNDED; AND TABLE OF THE ABBREVIATIONS USED IN REFERRING TO THEM.

The following list of MSS. used by Zeuss in his *Grammatica Celtica*, and of the abbreviations he uses in referring to them, may be found useful to those who may not have that work:—

Irish MSS.

1. Codex Prisciani Sancti Galli (No. 904). A copy of Priscian preserved at St. Gall, and thickly interspersed with marginal and interlinear glosses. Zeuss denotes this MS. by Sg.

2. Codex Paulinus Bibliothecae nunc Universitatis Wirziburgensis—marked M. th. f. 12. An MS. containing the epistles of St. Paul, formerly belonging to the cathedral church of Würzburg, but now to the university. Zeuss refers this MS. to the eighth century; although smaller than the St. Gall MS., it exhibits the same copiousness of glosses, if not greater, as they accompany the text after the manner of a continuous commentary, less by single words (like the St. Gall MS.) than explaining the context of St. Paul by Irish sentences. Zeuss denotes this MS. by Wb.

3. Codex Mediolanensis bibliothecae Ambrosianae (marked C., 301, and denoted by Zeuss, Ml.), an MS. of St. Jerome's commentary on the Psalms, containing a mass of glosses, not less than the MSS. above mentioned. Zeuss agrees with Muratori and Peyron, that these commentaries were written by St. Columbanus, the founder of Bobbio, from whence the MS. was transferred in 1606. by Cardinal F. Borromeo, when he established the Ambrosian Library. Zeuss had only time to copy a small part of the glosses of this MS.

4. Codex bibliothecae Carlisruhensis (No. 83, denoted by Zeuss, Cr.), an MS. formerly belonging to the monastery of Reichenau, containing " Computus de signis XII. et intervallorum; Beda de ratione temporum". The text of Bede is interspersed with Irish glosses.

5. Codex Prisciani bibliothecae Carlisruhensis, No. 223, denoted by Zeuss, Pr. Cr., a MS. of Priscian, also formerly belonging to Reichenau. It contains much fewer glosses than the St. Gall one, with which it agrees in part, and in part differs.

6. Codex Sancti Galli (No. 1395), containing a collection of fragments from ancient MSS., made by Ildefonso von Arx, chief librarian. Folio 419, vol. II., has Irish formulæ of incantation, hence Zeuss denotes it by Incant. Sg.

7. Codex Civitatis Camaracensis (No. 619) an MS. belonging to the City of Cambray, containing the canons of an Irish Council held in 684; in one place in the middle of the book is preserved a fragment of an Irish sermon on self-denial intermixed with Latin sentences. The book was compiled for Alberic, Bishop of Cambray from 763 to about 790.

Welsh MSS.

1. The vellum MSS. in the Bodleian Library at Oxford,—Auct. F. 4-32, described by Wanley, in his catalogue of Anglo-Saxon MSS. 2, 63. The parts which supplied material to Zeuss being: *a*, a part of the grammar of Eutychius,

with interlined Welsh glosses, from p. 2^b to 9^a; b, the exordium of Ovid's Art of Love, p. 37^a to 45^b, also containing interlined Welsh glosses. These glosses he believes to have been written in the eighth or ninth century. c, The alphabet of Nemnivus, giving the forms of the letters and their Welsh names; d, some accounts of weights and measures in Welsh, intermixed with Latin, at p. 22^b to 23^a.

2. A later vellum MSS. (Bodl. 572), containing theological tracts, and in the middle, from p. 41^b to 47^b, a list of Latin words with Welsh ones, which are written either over the Latin, or in the same line, with the sign .i. (*id est*), according to the custom of glossographers.

3. The MS. of the Church of Lichfield (formerly of that of Llandaff), containing the Gospels, in various parts of which (*e.g.* p. 9^b 10^b, 71^a, 109^b), donations made to the Church of Llandaff at very ancient periods, not later than the glosses of the first Oxford MS., are noted in Latin, but with Welsh names, and even sentences, which Wanley has already published (p. 289).

4. The Luxemburg Folio, a single leaf with Welsh glosses of the ninth century, which Mone found in the town library of Luxemburg, pasted to the cover of another MS.

The glosses of these four MSS. have been published by Zeuss in the appendix to the *Grammatica Celtica*.

5. *Liber Landavensis*, or book of Llandaff, compiled from more ancient documents about the year 1132. It contains many descriptions of boundaries of land, and also privileges of the bishopric, written in Welsh. It has also scattered through it Welsh proper names, especially of men and localities. This book was published in 1840 under the title, "The Liber Landavensis, *Llyfr Teilo*, or the Ancient Register of the Cathedral Church of Landaff", from MSS. in the Libraries of Hengwrt and of Jesus College, Oxford, with an English translation and explanatory notes by the Rev. W. J. Rees, published by the Welsh MSS. Society, Llandovery, 1840.

6. *Codex legum Venedotianus*, or the Venedotian MS. of laws. This MS., which belongs to the Hengwrt collection, is considered to have been compiled in the twelfth century. The latest edition of these laws, the first collection of which is attributed to Hywel Dda (Howel the Good), who died A.D. 950, was published by the Record Commission, under the title "Ancient Laws and Institutes of Wales"; comprising laws supposed to be enacted by Howel the Good, modified by subsequent regulations under the native princes prior to the conquest by Edward the First: and anomalous laws, consisting principally of institutions which by the statute of Ruddlan were admitted to continue in force. With an English translation of the Welsh text, 1841.

7. The Red Book of Hergest (*Llyfr coch o Hergest*), now in the Library of Jesus College, Oxford. It is the chief of all the MSS., preserving the middle forms between the old and the living languages. Turner determined this MS. to be of the fourteenth century. The principal narratives relating to the history of Arthur and his Knights of the Round Table, which it contains, were published in three volumes, under the title of "The Mabinogion, from the *Llyfr coch o Hergest*, and other Welsh MSS., with an English translation and notes, by Lady Charlotte Guest". London, 1849.

Cornish MSS.

1. The vellum MS. marked Vesp. A. 14, in the Cotton collection in the British Museum. It is the most ancient monument which is known to exist of the Cornish language, and dates most probably from the twelfth century. It has been transcribed by Zeuss himself, and printed entire in the *Grammatica Celtica*, vol. II. 1100. It is also printed, more correctly, and arranged alphabetically, by Mr. Edwin Norris, in the second volume of his Cornish Drama.

2. A Cornish poem on the passion of Christ, of which four copies are extant, Of these, one is in the British Museum, and two are in the Bodleian Library. Both Cornish text, and an English version made in 1682, were published in London in 1826, under the title "Mount Calvary, or the history of the passion, death, and resurrection of our Lord and Saviour Jesus Christ", written in Cornish

(as it may be conjectured) some centuries past, interpreted into the English tongue in the year 1682, by John Keigwin, Gent., edited by Davies Gilbert. Mr. Whitley Stokes has recently published in the *Transactions of the Philological Society of London* (1862) a new and corrected edition of this poem, with a translation, which is a great boon, as the former edition was almost worthless.

Armoric MSS.

1. The Chartularies of the monasteries of Rhedon or Roton and Landevin. The former probably began at the end of the tenth or beginning of the eleventh century, and ended in 1162; and the second in the beginning of the eleventh century. Those which have been printed will be found in Courson's *Histoire des peuples Bretons dans la Gaule et dans les îles Britanniques*, Paris 1846, and Dom Morice's *Mémoires pour servir de preuves à l'histoire ecclésiastique et civile de Bretagne*.

2. The life of St. Nonna, or Nonita, a dramatic poem preserved in a paper MS., which was found by Marzinus, notary to the Bishop of Quimper, on his pastoral circuit, and presented by him to the editor. This MS., which Zeuss thinks belongs to the fourteenth century, has been published under the title: *Buhez Santez Nonn, ou vie de Sainte Nonne, et de son fils Saint Dévy* (David) *Mystère composé en langue bretonne anterieurement au 12ᵐᵉ Siecle, publié d'apres un manuscrit unique, avec une introduction par l'Abbé Sionnet et accompagné d'une traduction littérale de M. Legonidec et d'un facsimile du manuscrit*, Paris, 1837.

Abbreviations used in Dr. Ebel's Celtic Studies.

Irish words. All the Celtic words not specially distinguished by letters, whether quoted by Dr. Ebel or added to his lists, are Old Irish, and are taken from the Irish MSS. in the foregoing list. As the language of all of them is of about the same age—the eighth or beginning of the ninth century,—Ebel has not thought it necessary to indicate the particular MS. from which the word is borrowed.

Welsh words. Words taken from the Welsh MSS. 1, 2, 3, and 4 in the foregoing list, are indicated by W. 1; those from 5 and 6, by W. 2; and those from 7, by W. 3.

Cornish words. Words taken from the Cornish MS. 1 are indicated by V; those from MS. 2, by P.

Armoric words. All words taken from the Armoric MSS. 1 and 2 in the foregoing list, are indicated by the abbreviation Arm.

The other abbreviations used by Dr. Ebel are:

A.S.=Anglo-Saxon
Ch. Sl.=Church Slavonic
Corn.=Cornish
Fr.=French
Gaedh.=Gaedhelic
Gaul.=Gaulish
Goth.=Gothic
Gr.=Greek
Incant. Sg. refers to the Irish MS. No. 6
K.=Kymric
Lat.=Latin
Lett.=Lettish
Lith.=Lithuanian
Med. Lat.=Mediæval Latin.
M.H.G.=Middle High German

M. Ir.=Middle Irish
N.H.G.=New or Modern High German
O.H.G.=Old High German
O. Ir.=Old Irish
O.N.=Old Norse
O.S.=Old Saxon
Osc.=Oscan
Pruss.=Prussian
Sab.=Sabine
Slav. and Sl.=Slavonian
Skr.=Sanskrit
Umbr.=Umbrian
Z. refers to Zeuss' Grammatica Celtica; the numbers to the pages.

An * prefixed to a word indicates, as mentioned at Note 37, p. 60, that the word is hypothetical. The mark ꝛ, used at p. 79 to indicate the degeneration of the case endings, is only an arbitrary sign.

INDICES VERBORUM TO POSITION OF THE CELTIC.

[The figures after the words, except where there is a special reference to a note, indicate the page; the italic letters after the figures refer to the columns,—*a* indicating the first or left hand column, and *b* the second or right hand column; where these letters are not found, the word occurs in the general text.

All the old Celtic and old Irish words which have been explained or analysed by Mr. Stokes in his *Irish Glosses*, are indicated by the letters St.; the numbers which follow those letters without the letter *p*, refer to the numbers in his commentary on that work; where the letter *p* precedes the figures, the latter refer to the page of that work.

The letters *C*, *l*, *w*, after a word, indicate that it is also to be found in the list of Latin loan words given at p. xx. of Mr. Stokes' edition of Cormac's Glossary, published by Messrs. Williams & Norgate, London, 1862. Whenever the word is spelled differently in Cormac from what it is in Zeuss, the word as spelled by the former is given in brackets.]

INDO-EUROPEAN, OR PRIMITIVE ARYAN.

akva, 113
agni, 119
antar, 108*b*
ava, 118*b*
avatya, 118*b*
as (*root*), 112
aina, 113
ghaima, 112
tautâ, 113
daiva, 113
dacru, 113
dant, 113

daru, 112
diva, 113
dus, 108*b*
dhâ (*root*), 112, 128
nava, 111*b*
navya, 111*b*
nâu, 108*b*
panca (pancan), 122
pra, 130
bhû (*root*), 112, 128
râd (?) (*root*), 110*b*
vaskara, 112

vid (*root*), 112
vidhavâ, 113
visha, 108*b*
vîra, 113
sak (*root*), 113
sâna, 113
sarpa, 109*a*
sâuala [?], 113
su-, 109*b*
sru (*root*), 112
svastar, 113

SOUTH ARYAN.

Sanskrit.

agni, 119
anu, 131
antar, 108*b*
anda, *note* 88, *p.* 112
ava, 118*b*, 120
as (*root*), 112
âyus, 109*a*
âvja, 113
jan (*root*), 110*b*
jnâ (*root*), 110*b*
tamas, 113
trna, 115*a*
dala, 122
dus-, 108*b*

drç (*root*), 113*a*
druh (*root*), 114*b*
dvâra, 121
dhâ (*root*), 112, 128
nava, 111*b*
navya, 111*b*
nâu, 108*b*
panca (pancan), 122
pibámi (*Ved.*) 108*b*
pra, 130
bôdhayâmi, 117*a*
bhû (*root*), 112, 128
mahat, 121
lax (*root*), 118*a*
lap (*root*), 118*b*
vâta, 114*b*

vid (*root*), 112
vidhavâ, 113
visha, 108*b*
vîra, 113
vrhat, *note* 82, *p.* 97
vêda, 123
çru (*root*), 112
sarpa, 109*a*
su-, 109*b*
sru (*root*), 112
srôtas, 111*b*

Old Persian.

vazarka, *note* 82, *p* 97.

NORTH-WEST ARYAN.

HELLENIC.

Greek.

ἀγάννιφος, 116*b*
* αγασνιχϝος, 116*b*
ἄγχι, 109*a*
ἄγω, 107*a*

ἄελλα, 107*b*
ἀήρ, 107*a*
αἰών, 109*a*
ἀϝέλιος, v. ἥλιος, 112*a*
ἀκούσας, 129
ἀλέω, 111*a*

ἀλλάσσω, 107*a*
ἄλλομαι, 109*a*
ἄλλος, 109*a*
αλογια, 124
αλογος, 124
ἅλς, 111*b*

14B

186 Indices Verborum to Position of the Celtic.

ἀμφι, 99a
ἀναπηδήσας, 129
ἀναστάς, 129
ἀνήρ, 108b
ἄνοπλος, 124
ἀντί, 99a, 123
ἄοπλος, 124
ἀποβαλών, 129
ἀποκριθείς, 129
ἀτεκνος, 124
-ατος, 126
αὐχμός, v. σαυχμός, 112a
αὐχμηρός, v. σαυχμός, 112a

βάνα (Boeot.), 109b
βίος, 109b
βοῦς, 108a
βραχίων, 108a
βρέχω, 117a

γένεθλον, 110b
γεννάω, 110b
γέρανος, 113a
γίγνομαι, 110b
γιγνώσκω, 110b
γράφω, 102b, 115a
γραῦς, 108b
γυναικός, 124
γυνή, 109b

δάκρυ, 110a
δαμάζω, 110a
δεδεμένον, 129
δεξιός, 110a
δέρκω, 113a
δόρξ, 108b
δόρυ, 110a
δρῦς, 110a
δυς-, 108b

εγγύς, 109a
ἰξ, 107b
ἔθος, 113b
εἶδαρ, 110b
εἶμι, 129
εἴναλος, 108b
ἰκάς, 109a
ἑκυρός, ἑκυρά, 111b
ἔλαβον, 129
ἐλάσσων, 111a
ἕλμινς, 110a
ἔνη, 112a
ἔννεπε, 112a
ἕπομαι, 112a
ἔριον, 112b
ἑρπετόν, 109a
-ες, 124

ἕςπερος, 112b
ἑταῖρος, 112a
ἔταρος, 112a
εὖ, 109b

ζόρξ, 108b
ζυγός, 111a

ἥβη, 111a
ἦθος, 113b
ἠίθεος, 112b
ἥλιος, 112a

θαν (root), 122
θεός, 110a
θνητός, 122
θύρα, 110b, 121

ἴζω, 112a
ἰός, 108b
ἵππος, 110b
-ισσα, 124

καβάλλης, 110a
κάμπτω, 110a
καρδία, 109b
κατεργασάμενον, 129
κεύθω, 110a
κνήμη, 108a
κύων, 110a

λάβω, 129
λαγχάνω, 113a
λάιγξ, 108b
λαμβάνω, 129
λείχω, 111b
λίθος, 108b
λόγος, 124
λόγχη, 108b
λύσαντες, 129

μέγας, 121
μέδομαι, 108b
μέλι, 108b
μείς, (Ion.), 111a
μέμονα, 111a
μήλινος, 119b
μίσγω, 111b
μήν, v. μείς, 111a
μήτηρ, 111a
μύλη, 111a

ναῦς, 108b
νέειν, 108b
νεφέλη, 111b
νήθειν, 108b

ὀδούς, 110a
ὀδυνήφατος, 113b

οἶκος, 112b
ὄνομα, 107a
ὅκως, 231
ὀρθός (Fορθός),107b
-ος, 124

παλάμη, 111b
πατήρ, 109b
πέλεκυς, 104b
περιδερκής, 113a
πεφήσομαι, 113b
πέφνον, 113b
πλάτος, 111a
πλατύς, 111a
πλημμυρίς, 111b
πῦρ, 119
πύργος (φοῦρκος), 113b
πῶλον, 129

ῥεω (σρέFω), 111b

σαυκός, 111b
σαυχμός, v. αυχμος, 112a
σαυσαρός, v. σαυκός, 112a
σκότος, 113b
σρέFω, v. ῥέω, 111b
στάς, 129
στρύμον (Thracian), 111b
συναχθέντων, 129
σφυρόν, 108b

ταῦρος, 109b
τανάος, 112b
τανυ-, 112b
-τατος, 126
τέγος, 112b
τέρετρον, 109b
τέρχνος, 115b
τέττα, 109b
-τος, 126
τρέχω, 113a
τρύχω, 113b

ὑμῶν ,129
ὕπνος, 111b

φαλλός, 107b
φεν, 113b
φιλος, 116a
φόνος, 113b
φρητήρ, 109b

χαίνω, 113b
χειμών, 110b
χιών, 110b

ὠλένη, 110b
ᾠόν, 112b

Latin Index. 187

ITALIC AND ROMANCE.

Latin.

abbas, 99a
abecedarium, 99a
abstinentia, 99a
accentus, 99a
accidens, 99a
accommodatio, 106a
aceo, 99a
acer, 99a
acetum, 99a
actualis, 99a
acuenda esset, 99a
acutus, 99a
ad-, 113a
adigit, 107a
adjectivum, 99a
ador, 108b
adorare, 99a
adoratio, 99a
adulterium, 99a
adversarius, 99a
aër, 107a
aetas, 108b
aevum, 109a
agnus, 109b, 111b
ago, 107a
alius, 109a
ala, 113a
alo, 113b
altare, 99a
altum, 99a
amnis, 107b
anachoreta, 99a
ancora, 99a
angelus, 99a, 114
angor, 109a
angustia, 109a
angustus, 109a
anima, 107a
animal, 99a
apostolus, 99a, 114
appetere, 104b
applicare, 99a
arare, 109b
aratrum, 99a
archiepiscopus, 102a
arduus, 107b
argentum, 99a
-arius, 124
arma, 99b
armilla, 99b
ars, 99b
articulus, 99b
artus, 107a
arvum, 107a
asinus, 99b

atomum, 99b
auctoritas, 99b
augusti, 99a
aura, 107a
aurum, 99b
avignus, v. agnus, 109b
axilla, 113a

baculum, 99b
badius, 108a
balbus, 99b
baptista, 99b
baptizo, 99b
baptisma, 99b
barba, 99b
barca, 99b
basilica, 100a
basium, 100a
battuere, 100a
beatus, 100a
benedico, 100a
benedictio, 100a
benedictus, 100a
bestia, 100a
betula, betulla, 108a
blasphemare, 100a
bibo, 108b
bos, 108a
brachium, 100a, 108a
brassica, 100a
brevis, 100a
broccus, brocchus, 100a
bulla, 100a
buxus, 100a

caballus, 110a
cadere, 108a
caecus, 113b
calamus, 100a
callidus, 100a
calix, 100a
camisia, 100a
cancella, 100a
cancellarius, 100a
cancer, 100a
candela, 100a
candelarius, 100a
candelabrum, 100a
cano, 108a
candidus, 108a
canis, 110a
canon, 100a
capellanus, 100a
caper, 114a, 123
capere, 123
capio, 114a
capistrum, 100a

capitulus, 100a
capra, 114a, 123
captus, 100a
caput, 100a
carbunculus, 100a
carcer, 100a
caritas, 100a
car(o)enum, car(o)enaria, 100a
carpentum, 100b
carus, 108a
cascus, 100b
castellum, 100b
castra, 103a
castrum (for cad-trum v. note 85), 108a
castus, 100b
castitas, 100b
catena, 100b
cathedra, 100b
catholicus, 100b
caucus, 100b
caules, 100b
causa, 100b
cedere, 100a, 108a
cedria, 100b
cella, 100b
celo, 114b
census, 100b
cera, 100b
cervus, 108a
cervical, 100b
cervisia, 100b
character, 100b
chorda, 100b
christianus, 100b
chrisma, 100b
cilicium, 100b
circare, 100b
circinus, 100b
circulus, 100b
circumflexus, 100b
civitas, 100b
clarus, 100b
classis, 100b
claustrum, 100b
clavi, 108a
clericus, 100b
clima, 100b
coccus, 100b
coloni, 100b
columba, 100b
columella, 100b
columna, 100b
*cominitiare, 101a
commatres, 101a
commixtio, 111b

commodum, 101a
communio, 101a
compar, 101a
comparativus, 101a
compatres, 101a
concedere, 101a
confessio, 101a
confligere, 101a
confortare, 101a
consecratio, 101a
consilium, 101a
consimilis, 109a
consona, 101a
conventus, 101a
coquina, 101a
coquus, 101a
cor, 109b
cornu, 114a
corona, 101a
coronatus, 101a
corpus, 108a
corrigia, 101a
corylus, 101a
coryletum, 101a
costa, 108a
coxa v. costa, 108a
craticula, 101a
creator, 101a
creatura, 101a
credo, 108a
credulus, 101a
crepusculum, 101a
creta, 101a
cribrum, 101a, 108a
crispus, 113b
crudelis, 101a
crux, 101a
crystallus, 101a
cucullus, 101a
culcita, 101b
cultellus, 101b
culter, 101b
culus, 108a
cuprum, 101b
curvus, 117b
cutis, 110a
cymbalum, 101b
cypressus, 101b

dacrima, v. lacrima, 110 a
daemon, 101b
damnare, 101b
damnatus, 101b
daurus, v. laurus, 110a
de, 103b
debilis, 101b
decedere, 101b
decima, 101b
defendere, 101b
denarius, 101b

dens, 110a
deprecatio, 101b
descendere, 101b
desiderabat, 101b
despectus, 101b
deus, 110a
dexter, 110a
diabolus, 101b
diaconus, 101b
diaconissae, pl., 101b
dictator, 101b
dies, 110a
dies jovis, 101b
dies solis, 101b
digamma, 101b
dignus, 101b
diluvium, 101b
dingua, v. lingua, 110a, 114b
discere, 101b
discipulus, 101b
discretus, 101b
discus, 101b
divinator, 101b
doctus, 101b
dolor, 101b
dominica, 101b
domo, 110a
draco, 101b
drungus, 115a
du. note 89, p. 120
dubitare, 101b
dubius, 101b
dubitantia, 101b
durus, 101b

ecclesia, 101b
edit, 110b
eleemosyna, 101b
elephantus, 102a
emendare, 102a
emineo, 108b
-ensis, 124
episcopus, 102a
epistola, 102a
equus, 110b, 122
eremita, 102a
esculus, 102a
esox, 102a
etymologia, 102a
ex, 107b
excommunicatus, 102a
evangelium, 102a

faba, 102a
facies, 102a
fagus, 102a
faginus, 102a
falco, 102a
fallere, 102a

favere, 102a
femininum, 102a
fenestra, 102a
ferre, 109b
fibula, 102a
ficus, 102a
ficulnus, 102a
fides, 102a
figura, 102a
finis, 102a
firmamentum, 102a
flagellum, 102a
flamma, 102a
flecto, 102a
flos, 117a
foeniculum, 102a
fores, 110b, 121
forma, 102a
fossa, 102b
fragrare, 102b
frater, 109b
frenum, 102b
fructus, 102b
fugere, 102b
fuga, 102b
fulgur, 102b
funis, 102b
fur, 102b
furca, 102b
furnus, 102b
fustis, 102b

geminantur, 102b
gentes, 102b
gentilis, 102b
gentilitatis, 102b
genitivus, 102b
gens, 102b
gerundium, 102b
gigno, 110b
gladius, 108a
glossa, 102b
gradale, 102b
gradus, 102b
gratia (gratias agimus), 102b
gravari, 102b
gravis, 102b
grus, 113a

habilis, 102b
haeresis, 102b
haeretici, pl. 102b
hastula, 102b
hiare, 113b
hiems, 110b
historia, 102b
honor, 102b
hora, 102b
hospes, 102b

humilis, 102b
humilitas, 102b
hymnus, 102b

idolum, 102b
idus, 102b
ignis, 119
imago, 102b
impedicare, 102b
imperator, 102b
imperium, 102b
improbitas, 105a
improbus, 105a
incensum, 103a
indupedio, *note* 89, p. 120
induperator. *note* 89, p. 120
inermis (*inermius), 124
infamis, 103a
infernum, 103a
infinitivus, 103a
initium, 103a
insece, 112a
instrumentum, 103a
insula, 108b
inter, 108b
interjectio, 103a
interrare, 103a
-issimus, 126
-isti, 128
-istis, 128

jejunium, 103a
judex, 103a
jugum, 111a
jusculum, 103a
justitia, 103a
juvenis, 111a
juvencus, 111a

kalendar, 103a

labes, 108b
labo, 108b
labor, 108b
lac, 108b
lacrima, *v.* dacrima, 110a
laicus, 103a
lana, 112b
lancea, 108b
lapis, 108b
latex, 103a
latro, 103a
latus, 111a
laurus, *v.* daurus, 110a
lector, 103a
lectus, 103a
legalitas, 103a
legere, 103a
legio, 103a
leo, 103a

levis, 111a
liber, 103a
ligo, 103a
lilium, 103a
lingo, 111a
lingua, *v.* dingua, 110a, 114b
linquit, 108b
linum, 103a
liquida, 103a
littera, 103a
liveo, 114a
lividus, 114a
livor, 114a
loculus, 103a
locus, 103a
locusta, 103a
longa, 103a
longa (*navis*), 103a
lorica, 103a
lucerna, 103a
lunaris, 103a
lutum, 108b

magister, 103a
magnus, 121
major, 103a
maledicis, 103a
maledictio, 103a
maledictus, 103a
malitia. 103a
malva, 103a
mancus, 103b
manere, 103b
manna. 103b
mantellum, 103b
manus, 103b
mare, 111b
margaritae, 103b
martulus (martellus), 103b
martyrium, 103b
masculinum, 103b
mater, 111a
matutinus, 108b
medicus, 103b
medicina, 103b
meditor, 108b
medius, medium, 111a
mel, 108b
membra, 103b
memini, 111a
memoria, 103b, 111a
mendicus, 103b
mensa, 103b
mensis, 111b
mensura, 103b
meretrix, 103b
metrum, 103b
mille. 103b
millefolium, 133b

miles, 103b
militia, 103b
ministrare, 103b
minus (minus facere), 103b
mirabile, 103b
miraculum, 103b
mirus, 103b
misceo, 111b
modus, 103b
molina, 103b
molo, 111a
monachus, 103b
monasterium, 103b
mons, 108b
moralis, 103b
mori, 111a
morticinium, 103b
mortuus, 111a
morus, 103b
mulus, 103b
mulxi, 111a
murus, 103b
muta, 103b
myrias, 103b
myrtus, 103b

nascor (gnascor), 110b
natalicia, 103b
nates, 104a
natio, 104a
natrix, 114a
navis, 103a, 108b
nebula, 111b
negotium, 104a
nepos, 114a
neptis, 114a
nere, 108b
nerio, Nero, 108b
neutrum, 104a
nidus, 114a
*nigvis, nihvis, *v.* nix, 116b
nimbus, 104a
nix, nivis, 116b
nosco (gnosco), 110b
nota, 104a
notarius, 104a
novellus, 104a
novus, 111b
nox, 111b
nudus, 116a
numerus, 104a
nuptiae, 104a
nux (cnux), 110a

obediens, 104a
oblatio, 104a
occulo, 114b
octo, 122
oenos, O. L., 111b
offerre, 104a

olea, 104a
olor, 107a
operarius, 104a
optativus, 104a
opus, 104a
oraculum, 104a
orate, 104a
oratio, 104a
ordinare, 104a
ordinatio, 104a
ordino, 104a
ordo, 104a
ostiarius, 104a
ostreum, 104a
ovum, 112b

paganus, 104a
pagus, 104a
pallium, 104a, 114b
palma, 104a, 111b
palus, 104a
panis, 104a
papa, 104a
papilio, 104a
papyrus, 104a
paradisus, 104a
parare, 104a
paries, 104a
parochia, 104a
pars, 104a
pascha, 104a
passio, 104b
patella, 104b
pater, 109b
paucus, 118b
pauper, 104b
pausa, 104b
pavo, 104b
pax, 104b
peccatum, 104b
pedester, 104b
pelliceus, 104b
pensus, 104b
pentecoste, 104b
penultima, 104b
peregrinus, 104b
perfectus, 104b
pergaminum, 104b
persona, 104b
petere, 104b
phiala, 104b
philosophus, 104b
philosophia, 104b
pinnaculum, 104b
pinus, 104b
piper, 104b
pirus, 104b
piscis, 104b, 114a
piscator, 104b
pistor, 101a

pistrinum, 101a
plaga, 104b
plangere, 104b
plenus, 104b, 111a
plebs, 104b
plicare, 104b
pluma, 104b
poena, 104b
poenitere, 104b
poenitentia, 104b
pondo, 105a
pons, 105a
populus, 105a
porcellus, 105a
porcus, 105a
porta, portus, 105a
portare, 105a
positivus, 105a
postilena, 105a
postis, 105a
praebendarius, 105a
praeceptum, 105a
praedico, 105a
praelatus, 105a
praeservare, 105a
praestare, 105a
prandium, 105a
presbyter, 105a
pretiare, 105a
primus, 105a
princeps, 105a
prior, 105a
probabitur, 105a
probatus, 105a
probus, 105a
prologus, 105a
pronomen, 105a
propositus, 105a
propheta, 105a
proprius, 116a
prudens, 105a
psalmus, 105a
psalterium, 105a
purgatorium, 105a
purpura, 105a
purus, 105a
puteus, 105a

quadragesima, 105a
quaerere, 108b
quaestio, 105a
quinquagesima, 105a
quiritare, 102b

rastrum, 105a
rectus, 114b
reddere, 105b
regnare, 105b
regula, 105b
reliquiae, 105b

remus, 105b
rete, 105b
rex, 105b, 114a
rigo, 117a
rogavi, 122
rosa, 105b
rosetum, 105b
rota, 111b
ruber, 111b
ruta, 105b

sabbatum, 105b
saccus, 105b
sacerdos, 105b
sacrificium, 105b
sacrilegium, 105b
saeculum, 105b
sagita, 108b
sagum, 109a
sal, 111b
salicastrum, 105b
salio, 109a
saliva, 105b
salix, 109a
saltus, 105b
salutare, 105b
salvare, 105b
sanctus, 105b
scabellum, 105b
scala, 105b
scandere, 105b
schola, 105b
scholasticus, 105b
sciens, 105b
scribere, 105b
scrinium, 105b
scripulus, 105b
scutella, 105b
scutum, 109a
sēbum, 105b
securus, 105b
secus, 109a
sedeo, 112a
senator, 105b
senex, 112a, 124
senior, 105b
sensus, 105b
sepelire, 105b
sepultura, 105b
septimana, 105b
septuaginta, 106a
sequor, 112a
sermonarius, 106a
serpens, 109a
serus, 106a
sextarius, 106a
siccus, 111b
signum, 106a
similis, 109a
situla, 106a

Latin Index.

socer, 111b
socrus, 111b
sól, 112a
solarium, 106a
solitarius, 106a
somniari, 106a
somnus, 111b
sophista, 106a
soror, 112a
sors, 106a
-sos, 127
spatium, 106a
sperare, 106a
spina, 106a
spiraculum, 106a
spiritus, 106a
spoliare, 106a
spongia, 106a
sponsa, 106a
stabulum, 106a
stagnum, 106a
stannum, 106a
status, 106a
stimulus, 106a
stlocus (O. L.), 103a
stola, 106a
stragulum, 106a
strata, 106a
strigilis, 106a
-sum, 127
superlativus, 106a
sus, 118a
syllaba, 106a
synodus, 106a

tabellarius, 106a
taberna, 106a
tabes, 106a
tacere, 114b
talentum, 106a
tardare, 106a
-tas, 124
taurus, 109b
tellus, 106a
temere, 112b
tempero, 106b
templum, 106b
temptare, 106b
tendere, 106b
tenebrae, 112b
tenuis, 112b
terebra, 109b
terminus, 106b
terra, 109b
tertia, 106b
testis, 106b
testimonium, 106b
theca, 106b
theoria, 106b
thesis, 106b

thronus, 106b
thus, 106b
Titan, 106b
titulus, 106b
torques, 106b
torrens, 111b
torta, 106b
totus, 106b
tractus, 106b
traditio, 106b
trans, 109b
tribunus, 106b
trinitas, 106b
tripus, 106b
tristis, 106b
tructa, 106b
truncus, 106b, 115b
trux, 114b
tuba, 106b
tugurium, 112b
tunica, 106b
turba, 106b
turris, 106b
tympanum, 106b

ulna, 110b
ultima, 106b
uncia, 106b
únctare, 106b
unguere, 106b
unicornis, 106b
unus, 111b
ursus, 106b

vacca, 118a
vagina, 106b
vates, 109b
velum, 106b
venenum, 106b
ventus, 114b
vermis, 110a
versatile, 106b
veru, 107b
versus, 106b
verus, 106b
vesper, 112b
vetus, 107a
vicus, 112b
vidua, 107a, 112b
vigil, 107a
villani, 107a
vinea, 107a
vinum, 107a
viperae, 107b
vir, 112b
viridis, 109b
virus, 108b
virtus, 107b
visio, 107b
vita, 109b

vitium, 107b
vivus, 109b
vocula, 107b

Mediæval Latin.

baro, 100a
brace, 100a

caldaria, 100a
cattus, 100b
clocca, 100b
cloccarium, 100b
companium, 101a
conucula, 101a

follis, 102a
fontana, 102a
foresta, 102a
forestis, 102a

gridare, 102b

hanapus, 102b

melinus, 119b
mirare, 103b
multo, 103b

padulis, 104a

sappetus, 105b
sicera, 106a
solta, 106a
stratura, 106a

torneamentum, 106b

Picenian.

Auximum, 118a

Sabine.

ausum, 99b
nerio, 108b

Oscan

ner, 108b
nesimo, 114a
teerùm, 109b
túvtú, 112b

Umbrian.

berus, 107b
berva, 107b
esme, 125
esmei, 125
nesimo, 114a

ner, 108*b*
pir, 119
pusme, 125
toto, 112*b*
trûf, 109*b*

Romance.

-êsis, 124
finisco, 102*a*
-issa, 124
pêso, 104*b*
putana, 105*a*
rendere, 105*b*
stendardo, 106*a*

Italian.

landa, 118*a*
veltro, 107, 118*a*

Provençal.

landa, 118*a*

French.

bai, 108*a*
blâmer, 100*a*
broche, 100*a*

charité, 100*a*
chérir, 108*a*
commencer 101*a*

empêcher, 102*b*
encens, 103*a*
estaminet, 106*a*
estonner, étonner, 102*a*

foudre, 102*b*

haster, hâter, 102*b*

lande, 118*a*

merveille, 103*b*
mesfaire, méfaire, 103*b*
moi, 126

TEUTONIC.

Gothic.

ada (*Kr. Goth.*) *note* 88,
   page 112
* *ADDIA* (*Prim.*), *note*
  88, *page* 112
afvairpands, 129
aggilus, 114
ains, 111*b*
aivs, 109*a*
alan, 113*b*
aleina, 110*b*
alis, 109*a*
alja-, 109*a*
aljan, 113*b*
alls, 118*b*
anabiudan, 117*a*
and-, 123
andbindandans, 129
anhafjands, 129
apaustaulus, 114
ara, 115*b*
arbi, 116*b*
arbja, 116*b*
-areis, 124
at-, 113*a*
auhsans, 118*a*
auhuma, 118*a*
auhumists, 118*a*
auþeis, 118*b*

balgs, 117*a*

banja, 113*b*
baurd, 117*a*
baurgs, 113*b*, 117*a*
braids, 111*a*
brôþar, 109*b*

dailjan, 115*a*
dails, 115*a*
daur, 110*b*, 121
daurô, 110*b*
driugan, 115*b*
du, 115*b*

eisarn, 118*a*

fadar, 109*b*
faurbiudan, 117*a*
fimf, 122
fisks, 114*a*
fôtubaurd, 117*a*
fram, 126
fruma, 126
fulan, 129
fulls (*i.e.* fulns), 111*a*
fulljan, 111*a*

ga-, 130
gaarbja, 116*b*
gabundanana, 129
gadrauhts, 115*b*
gagaggandam, 129
gahausjands, 129
gastandands, 129

pan, 123
parfait, 104*b*
paroi, 104*a*
pavillon, 104*a*
petit, 104*b*
pommaille, 105*a*
prison, 105*a*

rame, 105*b*
recommendare, 105*b*

sauver, 105*b*
sou, 106*a*
songer, 106*a*
sorte, 106*a*
soutenir, 106*a*

talent, 106*a*
tonneau, 106*b*
trahison, 106*b*
tribunal, 106*b*

vice, 107*b*

gataujandan, 129
gazds, 117*b*
gild, 117*b*
graban, 115*a*

hafja, 114*a*
haihs, 113*b*
hairto, 109*b*
haurn, 114*a*
hilpan, 123
huljan, 114*b*
hunds, 110*a*, 123

iddja, 128
idreiga, 116*a*
is, 126
ita, 126
-iza, 126
izvis, 129

jains, 127
juggs, 111*a*
juhiza, 111*a*
juk, 111*a*

kan, 110*b*
kuni, 110*b*

laigô, 111*a*
lamb, 118*a*
land, 118*a*
leihts, 111*a*

Old High German Index.

mag, 115*b*
manags, 116*a*
managei, 116a
man, 111*a*
mêna, 111*b*
mênôþs, 111*b*
mês, 103*b*
mikils, 121
missa, 118*a*

nadr, 114*a*
namô, 109*a*
naqvaþs, 116*a*
nêhv, 114*a*

ôg, 116*a*
ôgan, 116*a*
-oza, 126

qvêns, 109*b*
qvinô, 109*b*
qvius, 109*b*

raihts, 114*b*
reiks, 114*a*
rign, 117*a*
runa, 118*b*

saian, 116*b*
salt, 111*b*
salta, 109*a*
sakan, 112*a*
samaþ, 129
sauil, 112*a*
si, 126
sidus, 113*b*
sineigs, 112*a*
sinista, 112*a*
sinþs, 118*b*
sitan, 112*a*
skadus, 113*b*
skalks, 118*b*
* snaigas, * snaigvas v.
snaivs, 116*b*
snaivs, 116*b*
sokjan, 112*a*
stiur, 109*b*
sunna, 118*b*
sunnô, 118*b*
sunus, 121
svaihra, 111*b*
svaihrô, 111*b*
svistar, 108*a*, 112*a*

tagr, 110*a*
taihsvs, 110*a*
tamjan, 110*a*
timan, 110*a*
triu, 110*a*
tuggô, 114*b*, 123

tunþus, 110*a*

þahan, 114*b*
þairh, 118*b*
þaurnus, 115*b*
þiuda, 112*b*
þragja, 113*a*

ushlaupands, 129
usstandands, 129

vair, 112*b*
vairþs, 116*b*
vait, 123
valdan, 116*b*
vaurms, 110*a*
veihs, vêhs, 112*b*
viduvô, 112*b*
vilþeis, 119*b*
vinds, 114*b*
vulfs, 121
vulla, 112*b*

Old Teutonic.

* hafar, 123
hafjan, 123

Old High German.

ahsala, 113*a*
ali-, 109*a*
angi, 109*a*
angil, v. engil, 114
aphul, aphol, 115*a*

bâga, 117*a*
bâgan, v. biag, 117*a*
bâgên, 117*a*
bana, *f.*, 113*b*
bano, *m.*, 113*b*
banôn, 113*b*
bart, 99*b*
biag, v. bâgan, 117*a*
bigil, v. bihal, pigil, 117*a*
bihal, v. pîhal, 117*a*
bimunigôn, 124
biseh, 111*b*
bisihan, 111*b*
blat, v. plat, 111*a*
bluot, 117*a*
boch, v. poch, 117*a*
bogo, v. poco, 117*a*
bort, 117*a*
borti, 117*a*
borto, 117*a*

charra, v. karra, garra, 117*b*
chona, 109*b*

chraft, 117*b*
chranuh, 113*a*
chrump, 117*b*
chruzigôn, 124
chuo, 109*b*
chus, 117*b*

dach, 112*b*
demar, 112*b*
dunni, 112*b*

ecala, 117*b*
egala, 117*b*
ei, 112*b*, *note* 88, *p.* 112
elithiotic, 109*a*
engil, v. angil, 114
êwa, 109*a*

fiur, 119
folma, 111*b*
friudil, fridil, 116*a*

gabala, 117*b*
galingan, 113*a*
ganzo, 115*b*
garra, v. karra, 117*b*
gart, 117*b*
gartja, 117*b*
gêr, 117*b*
ginên, 113*b*
ginôn, v. ginên, 113*b*
gisal, 117*b*
giwiznes (*neut.*), 119*a*
giwiznesi (*fem.*), 118*b*
glas, 117*b*
grioz, 117*b*

hadu, 117*b*
helan, 114*b*
heli, 114*b*
hiruz, 108*a*
hnot, 110*a*
hosa, 117*b*
hulla, 114*b*
hut, 110*a*
hutta, 110*a*

îsarn, 118*a*
îwa, 118*a*

karra, v. garra, chirra, 117*b*
kramph, 117*b*
kruog, 115*a*
krûs, 113*b*

ledar, 118*a*
luogên, 118*a*
lûs, 118*a*

mana (manha), 111
marach, 118*a*

meriha, *f. v.* marach, 118*b*
mias, 103*b*
miscjan, 111*b*
muotar, 111*a*

nachat, 116*a*
natra, natara, 114*a*
nefo, 114*a*
nest, 114*a*
nibul, 111*b*
nift, 114*a*
niftila, 114*a*

palc, 117*a*
phant, 123
pigil, *v.* bigil, 117*a*
pîhal, *v.* bihal, 117*a*
plat, *v.* blat, 111*a*
plî, 114*a*
plîwes, 114*a*
poch, *v.* boch, 117*a*
poco, *v.* bogo, 117*a*
postul, 114

rad, 111*b*
reht, 114*b*
rîchi, 114*a*
rûn, 118*b*

sagên, 112*a*
sech, 118*b*
segal, 118*b*
sia, 127
sie, 127
sind, 118*b*
siniscalc, 112*a*
sio, 127
siu, 127
snecco, 118*b*
snuor, 118*b*
stroum, 111*b*
sumar, 118*b*
sumna, 118*b*
sunna, 118*b*

tarch, 117*b*
tiligôn, 124
triugan, 114*b*
truhtin, 115*b*
truhtinc, 115*b*

wagan, 118*b*
wër, 112*b*
wëralt, 112*b*
witu, 119*a*
wolchan, 119*b*
wolf, 121

za, zi, zuo, 115*b*
zand, zan, 110*a*

zi, *v.* za, 115*b*
zoraht, *v.* zhort, 113*a*
zorht, 113*a*
zorft, *v.* zohrt, 113*a*
zûn, 117*b*
zuo, *v.* za, 115*b*

Middle High German.

bîl, 117*a*
bluot, *pl.* blüete, 117*a*
hader, 117*b*
limpfen, 118*a*
man, 118*a*
march (marc), 118*a*
vluor, 118*a*
vriedel, 116*a*

New High German.

aufgebot, 117*a*
ausgesprochen, 130

bemächtige, 124
blappen, blappern, *v.* plappern, 118*b*

enge, 109*a*
enterben, 117*a*

gefährtin, 118*b*
genter, 115*b*
gerte, 117*b*

hader, 117*b*
haksch, 118*a*
hülle, 114*b*

jemand, 123

kind, 110*b*
krug, 115*a*

lahm, 118*a*
lugen, 118*a*

machtig, 124
maulthier, 100*a*
menge, 116*a*
mis-, 118*a*
mucke, 118*a*
muschel, 114

öde, 118*b*

peinige, 124
plappern, *v.* blappern, 118*b*

reinige, 124

walten, 116*b*

werth, 116*a*
windbeutel, 102*a*

zahlen, 115

Old Saxon.

ehu, 110*b*
reht, 114*b*
tûn, 117*b*
vidu, 119*a*
wolcan, 119*b*

Frisian.

appel, 115*a*

Low German.

kaute, kute, 105*a*

Middle Dutch.

slecke, 118*b*

Anglo-Saxon.

ägg, *note* 88, *p.* 112
äppel, 115*a*
bât, 117*a*
boga, 117*a*
bucca, 117*a*
coss, 117*b*
craft, 117*b*
crumb, 117*b*
dëorc, 117*b*
ëorl, 115
flôr, 118*a*
folma, 111*b*
gandra, 115*b*
gâr, 117*b*
gevitnesse, 119*a*
gevitnes, 119*a*
gläs, 117*b*
grëot, 117*b*
häfer, 114*a*
heaðo, 117*b*
hos, 117*b*
hosa, 117*b*
iv, 118*a*
lëðer, 118*a*

Old Slavonic Index. 195

lôcian, 118a
lûs, 118a

nest, 114a
nefa, 114a
nift, 114a

sëgel, 118b
snegel, 118b
sumor, sumer, 118b
sunna, 118b

to, 115b
tûn, 117b

vägen, 118b
volcen, 119b
vudu, 119a

English.

dark, 117b

flat, *note* 87, *p.* 111
floor, 118a

hat, 114
herring, 114
hog, 118a

lame, 118a

nut, 110a

reader, 114

smoke, 115
strike, 115
string, 114

strive, 115
swain, 115

town, 117b

witness, 119a

Old Norse.

ala, 113b

baegjask, 117a
baga, 117a
bâgi, 117a
bâgr, 117a
bana, 113b
bani, 113b
bâtr, 117a
belgr, 117a
bogi, 117a
bokki, 117a
borð, 117a

coss (koss), 117b

döckr, 117b
drôtt, *pl.* drôttir, 115b
drôttin, 115b
drôttning, 115b

egg, *note* 88, *p.* 112
epli, 115a

flatr, *note* 87, *p.* 111

glas, 117b
griot, 117b

hafr, 114a
heill, *note* 84, *p.* 108

iarl, 115
iarn, *v.* isarn, 118a
iôr, 110b
isarn, 118a

kerra, 117b
kreftr, 117b

ledr, 118a
lûs, 118a

naktr (nakinn), 116a
nift, 114a

segl, 118b
snigil, 118b
snara, 118b
son (sonr), 121
sumar, 118b
sunna, 118b
svefn, 111b
svein, 115

tīvar, 110b
tönn, 110a
tûn, 117b

þak, 112b
þior, 109b

vagn, 118b
viðr, 118a

ŷr, 118a

WINDIC OR LITO-SLAVONIAN.

A. Slavonic.

Old Slavonic.

ablanĭ, ablonĭ, *v.* jablanĭ, 115a
agne, *v.* jagne, 111b
agnica, *Ch. Sl.*, 111b
agnĭcĭ, *v.* jagnĭcĭ, 111b
aice, *v.* jaice, 112b
anĭgelŭ, *Ch. Sl.*, 114
apostolŭ, *Ch. Sl.*, 114
-arĭ, 124
ązŭ, 109a
ąza, 109a

bądą, 128
brada, 99b
bratrŭ, 109b

bratŭ, 109b

czrĭvĭ, 110a
czrŭmĭnŭ, 110a
czrŭvĭ, 110a

dělĭti, 115a
denĭ, *v.* dĭnĭ, 121
desĭnŭ, 110a
dĭnĭ, 110a, 121
do-, 115b
drěvo, 110a
drugŭ, 115b
drŭva, 110a
dvĭrĭ, *pl.* 110b

* geravjas, *v.* żeravlĭ, 113a

gnězdo, 114a
gołąbĭ, 100b
govędo, 109b
grebą, 115a
grobŭ, 115a

idą, 128
igo (jĭgo), 111a
imę, 109a

jablanĭ, 115a
jabłŭko, jabluka, 115a
jadą, 128
jagnę, *v.* agnę, 111b
jagnĭcĭ, *v.* agnĭcĭ, 111b
jaice, *v.* aice, 112b
jązą, 109a

196   *Indices Verborum to Position of the Celtic.*

jęza, 109a
junŭ, 111a

karatí, 119aa
kobyla, 110a
kobylica, 110a
kolěno, 119b
konĭ, 110a
krivŭ, 117b
krŭczagŭ, 115a
krŭczĭmĭnica, 115a
krŭczĭvĭnikŭ, 115a

lĭgŭkŭ, 111a
lizą, 111a

mogą, 115b, 123
mati, 111a
měsęcĭ, 111b
měsiti, 111b
mnogŭ, 116a

nagŭ, 116a
nebo, 119a

ognĭ, 119
onŭ, 127
orĭlŭ, 115b

Lithuanian.

àngëlas, 114
àuksztas, 109a
anksztá, 109a
ans, 127
apàsztalas, 114
aszarà, 110a
àszva, 110b
ąt-, 113a
àuksas, 99b

barzdà, 99b
bròlis, 109b

da-, 115b
dalìs, 115a
dalýti, 115a
dantìs, 110a
deni, 121;
děná, 110a
derva, 110a
deszìné, 110a
děvas, 110a
dìnĭ
draúgalas, 115b
draúgas, 115b
dùrys, 110b

pamętĭ, 111a
plŭnŭ, 111a
prijatelĭ, 116a

sladŭkŭ, *note* 82, *p.* 97, 124
sejati, 116b
sěsti, 112a
sestra, 112a
sladŭkŭ, *note* 82, *p.* 97, 124
slŭnĭce, 112a
sněgŭ, 116b
snocha *v.* snŭcha, 121
snŭcha, 121
sobaka, 110a
solĭ, 111b
srŭdĭce, 109b
struja, 111b
struga, *v.* struja, 111b
suchŭ, *Ch. Sl.*, 112a
suka, 110a
sŭnŭ, 111b
svekrŭ, 111b
svekrŭvĭ, 111b
svekry, *v.* svekrŭ, 111b

tĭma, 112b
tĭnĭkŭ, 112b
trŭnŭ, 115b
turŭ, 109b

B. Lettic.

erélis, 115b
eris, 115b
-ésnis, 126

galé ti, 119a
galiù, 119a
gàndras, 115b
gélbėti, 123
gervė, 113a
gìmti, 110b
grabas, 115a
gývas, 109b

ìnkaras, 99a

jáunas, 111a
-jaŭs, 126
-jáusei, 126
-jáusias, 126
jungas, 111a

kàmpas, 110a
karczamà, 115a
kelýs, 119b
kìrmėlė, 110a
kìrminas, 110a
kìrmis, 110a, 119a
koravóti, 119a

vązŭ, 109a
veczerŭ, 112b
vĭdova, 112b
vĭsĭ, 112b
vladą, 116b
vladiti, 116b
vlasti, 116b
vlŭkŭ, 120
vlŭna, 112b
vranŭ, 119a

żena, 109b
żentĭ, 110b
żeravlĭ, 113a
żima, 110b
żivŭ, 109b
znają, 110b

Polish.

jaje, 112b

wart, 116b
wilk, 120

Servian.

junak, 111a

kreívas, 117b
kuìnas, 110a
kulnìs, 119b
kumélė, 110a
kumelùkas, 110a
kùmpas, 110a

laiżau, 111a
lengvas, 111a

maiszýti, 111b
mélynas, 119b
mėnes, *v.* mėnù, 111b
mėnŭ, 111b
mergà, 119b
mergėlė, 119b
mokéti, 116a
móku, 116a, 123
moté, 111a

nugas, 116a

obelìs, 115a
óbŭlas, 115a
-orius, 124

pìlnas, 111a
pirm, 126
pìrmas, 126

Old Irish Index.

platùs, 111a
prételius, 116a
ratns, 111b
sakaú, 112a
saldùs, *note* 82, p. 97
sápnas, 111b
sáulė, 112a
saúsas, 112a
séklà, 116b
sekù, 112a
sémens, 116b
sénas, 112a
sònis, 112a
sesti, 112a
sesu, 112a
sẻti, 116b
snégas, 116b
snocha, 121
snūcha, 121
sraúmė, 111b
stógas, 112b
szu, 110a

szirdis, 109b

tamsù, 112b
tauta, 112b

ugnis, 119

vákaras, 112b
valdaú, 116b
valdýti, 116b
várna, 119a
várnas, 119a
vėnas, 111b
vertas, 116b
vüse′ti, 112b
vesz-pats, 112b
vilkas, 120
vilna, 112b
výras, 112b

žėmà, 110b
žináu, 110b

Lettish.

abols, 115a
dallit, 115a
debbes, 119a
d⁻ws, 110a
draudse (* draugia), 115b
ėrglis, 115b
gόws, 109b
krôgs, 115a
sapnis, 111b
tauta, 112b
waldit, 116b
wėns, 111b
wirs, 112b

Old Prussian.

nins, 111b
dellieis, 115a
emnes, 109a
* ganna, 109b
tauta, 112b
werts, 116b
widdewû, 112b

CELTIC.

Old Celtic.

ad-, 113a
ande-, 99a, 123 (St. 734)
Argento-ratum, 99b (St. 607)
Arduenna, 107b
ate, *note* 103, p. 113

bulga, 117a (St. 217)

Camba, 110a
Cambodunum, 110a. (St. p. 150)
carrus, 117b
cataracton, *note* 85, p. 108
* catarax, *note* 85, p. 108
Caturiges, 117b
Catu-slôgi,'117b(St. 1003)
Cebenna, 107b
covinus, (*Brit.*, *Belg.*) 118b
Crixus, 113b

dan (*root*), 122
drungus, 115a
dula, 122 (*see* πεμπέδουλα; St. 765)

Gaesati, 117b (St., Gaisatî, 216)
gaesum, 117b

Κάρνον τὴν σάλπιγγα, 113b
Κάρνυξ, 114a

λαγκία, 108b
Lutetia, Luteva, 108b

μαρκαν, *acc.*, 118a
Μορικάμβη, 110a

νεμητον, *acc.*, 121 (St. 423)

ούξελλον, ουξελλα (*Brit.*), 118a (*v.* St. 13)
Oppianicnos, 123

πεμπέδουλα, see dula, 122 (St. 765)

Σεγομαρος, 121 (St. 423, p. 156)
Seno-magus, 112a

tarvos, 109b (St. p. 159)
Toutissicnos, 123

Uxellodunum, 118a (St. 13)

vertragus, 107, 113a (St. 74)

vidu, 119a (St. 46)

Old Irish.

ab, 99a (*C. l. w.*)
aball, 115a (St. 555)
abstanit, 99a
accidit, *v.* aiccidit, 99a
accus, *v.* ocus, 109a
achtail, 99a (*C. l. w.*)
áctegim, 99a
acuit, 99a
accus, *v.* ocus, ocuis, 109a
achtail, 99a (*C. l. w.*)
áctegim, 99a
acuit, 99a
acus, *v*, ocus, ocuis, 109a
ad-, 113a, 120
adaltras, 99a (St. 882)
adgénsa, 110b
adgeuín, 110b
adiect, adiecht, 99a
admuinur, 111a
adrad, 99a (*C. l. w.*)
adras, 99a
adrorsat, 99a
adsaitis, 112a
aeclis, *dat. abl.; v. gen.*, ecolso, ecilse; 101b
aér, *v.* áiar, 107a
ag (*root*), 107a
agathar, 116a

198 *Indices Verborum to Position of the Celtic.*

áiar, v. aér, 117a
-aib, v. -ib, 127
aibgiter, 99a (C. l. w.)
aiccent, aiccend, dat. aicciund, 99a
aiccidit, v. accidit, 99a
aicher, 99a (C. l. w.)
aichthi, 116a
aidrech, 116a
aile, 109a, 113 (St. 158)
ailigim, 107a
aine, 103a (C. l. w.)
aingel (angel), 99a, 114 (C. l. w.)
aimm, 107a, 109a (St. 991)
airdircc, v. erdirc, irdircc, 113a
-aire, v. -ire, 124
airccal, 104a
airget, v. argat, 99a
airlech, 103a
airriu, 127
áis (óis), gen. álsa, aisso (óissa, óesa), 109a (St. 735, 812)
aith (*ati-), 113a (St. 155)
aithgne, 110b
aithirge, v. ithirge, 116a
al, (root) 113a
almsan, acc. almsin, 101b (C. l. w.)
alt, 107a
altóir, 99a
altram, 113a
-am, 126
amail, amal, 109a
amlabar, 118b, 124 (St. 1133)
amprom, amprome, 105a
ana, 127
ancretem, 124
ancretmech, 124
angel (aingel), 99a, 114
anim, 107a, 109
apstal, 99a, 114 (C. l. w.)
apstallacht, 124
ar (root), 109b
arafulsam, 113a
arathar, 99a
arbae, v. orpe, 116b (St. 752, p. 168)
ardd, 107b
arenindarbe, 117a (St. 752)
argat, v. airget, 99a
arm, arma, v. dat. ísindairm, 99b
arnachitrindarpither, 117a, 130

art, 99b (C. l. w.)
articol, gen. sing., nom. pl., articuil, dat. artucol, 99b
arva (arba), 107a
as (a, es), 107b
asan, 99b
asdul, 102b (astol, C. l. w.)
asil, 113a
asmecnugur, 124
asrobrad, 130
atbela, 113b
athir, 109b, 113 (St. 13, 1046)
athusu, 126
atom, 99b
atomaig, 107a
-atu, v. -etu, 124
augtortás, 99b (St. 1107)
augaist, 99b (C. l. w.)

bachall, 99b (C. l. w.)
bádud, 117a
baga, 117a
bagim, 117a
bágul, 117a
baislic, 100a (C. l w.)
baitsim, acc. baithis, dat. bathius, 99b
bal (root), 113b
balb, 99b (C. l. w.)
ball, 107b (St. 638)
ban, v. ben (root), 113a
ban (mulier), v. ben, 109b (St. 21)
bandechuin (pl.), 101b
banscala, 118b
bar, v. ber (root), 109b
barc, 99b (C. l. w.)
bás, 113b
bathach, 113b (St. p. 163)
bauptaist, 99b (C. l. w.)
béisti, f. pl., 100a (C. l. w.)
bémen (pl.), 113b
ben, v. ban (root), 113a
ben (mulier), v. ban, 109b
bendachae, 100a
bendacht, 100a (C. l. w.)
béo, v. biu, 109b
beod, 113b
beogidir, 109b
beothu, bethu, 109b
ber, v. bar (root), 109b
berach, 107b
bethe, 108a
bethu, beothu, 109b
biad, 109b (St. 477)
biáil, biail, buáil, 117a
birdae, 107b

biu, v. béo, 109b
bíu, 127
bóchaill, 108a (St. 583)
boide, v. buide, 117a
bolg, bolc, 117a (St. 217)
boll, 100a (St. 159; C l. w.)
borg (borcc), 113b, 117a
borggde, v. borg, 113b
bou, 108a, 109b
bracc, 100a (C. l. w)
braich, 100a (C. l. w.)
braisech, 100a
bran, 119a
bráth, 122 (St. 336)
breth, 122 (St. 336)
bráthair, bráthir, 109b (St. 1047)
breib, 100b
brithemnacht, 124 (St. 336)
bróen, 117a
buáid, 117a
buáil, v. biáil, biail, 117a
buide, v. boide, adj. 108a, (St. 803), subst. 117a
buidech, 117a
buidnib, 117a

caech, 113b
cacht, 100a (C. l. w.)
cailech, 100a
caille, 104a, 114b (C. l. w.)
caimse, 100a (caimmse, C. l. w.)
caindlóir, 100a (St. 44)
caingel, 100a
caiptel, 100a (C. l. w.)
caire, 119a
cairigud, 119a
caisc, 104a (C. l. w.)
cáise, 100b (C. l. w.)
caisel, 100b (C. l. w.)
calann, 103a (C. l w.)
callaid, 100a (C. l. w.)
camm, 109b
cammaib, dat. pl., v. camm, 109b
cammderc, 109b
camthuisil, 109b
can (root), 108a
canóin (acc.), 100a (C. l. w.)
car (root), 108a
carachtar, 100b
carcar, gen. pl. carcre, dat. carcáir, 100a
carim, cairim, 128
carmocol, 100a

Old Irish Index.

carpat, 100*b* (*C. l. w.*)
cast, 100*b*
castoit, 100*b* (*C. l. w.*)
cath, 117*b*
cathir, cathair, 108*a* (St. 13)
cathlac, 100*b* (*C. l. w.*)
cathrach, *gen. v.* cathir, *note* 85, *p.* 108
caut, 100*a*
cedir, 100*b*
céir, 100*b* (*C. l. w.*)
ceirbsire, 100*b*
ceist, 105*a* (cest, *C. l w.*)
cél, 108*a*
cell, 100*b* (cel, *C. l. w.*)
cen, 131
cenaélugud, 110*b*
cenél, 110*b* (St. 676)
cenélach, 110*b*
cenélae, 110*b*
cercenn, 100*b* (*C. l. w.*)
cérchaill, 100*b* (*C. l. w.*)
cercol (*acc.*), 100*b*
cetlaid, 108*a* (St. 3)
cilic, 100*b*
cimbal, 101*b*
cingcidis, 104*b*
cingices, 105*a* (cingciges, *C. l. w.*)
circumflex, 100*b*
ciuil (*gen.*), 108*a*
cís, 100*b* (*C. l. w.*)
* cladibas, 108*a*
claideb, 108*a*
clais, 100*b*
clechir, 100*b*
clechti, 100*b*
clérech, 100*b* (*C. l. w.*)
climata (*pl.*), 100*b* (*C. l. w.*)
clocc, 100*b*
clochmuer, 100*b*
clói, 108*a*
clúm, 104*b* (*C. l. w.*)
cnám, 108*a* (St. 269)
cnu, 110*a*
cochull, 101*a* (*C. l. w.*)
coibse, 101*a* (*C. l. w.*)
coic, 101*a*, 122 (St. 776; *C. l. w.*)
cóis (*dat.*), 100*b* (St. 434, *acc. sing.*)
coisecrad, 101*a* (St. 880)
colcaid, 101*b* (*C. l. w.*)
coll, 101*a*
colomna (*nom. pl.*), 100*b* (*C. l. w.*)
colum, 100*b*
columnat, 100*b*

com-, 126
comacus, 109*a*
comadas, 101*a*
comadasogod, 101*a*
comaicsiu, 109*a*
comalnadar, 111*a*
comarbus, 116*b*
comarpe, 116*b*
commescatar, 111*b*
companacht, 101*a*
comparit, *pl.* -iti, *gen.* -ite, 101*a*
conflechtaigthi, 101*a*
congnam, 110*b*
conoscaigesiu, 111*b*
conrobam, 131
conrochra, 131
conrogbaid, 131
conroscaigissiu, 111*b*
conson, *gen.* consine, 101*a*
corcur, 105*a*
corgais, 105*a*
coro-, corro-, conro-, 131
corp, 108*a* (*C. l. w.*)
cos, 108*a*
cosmail, cosmuil, cosmil,
  * consamali, 109*a*
credal, 101*a*
crepscuil, 101*a* (*C. l. w*)
cresen, 100*b* (*C. l. w.*)
cretem, 124
cretes, crettes, creites, *pl.*
cretite, *v.* cretim, 108*a*
cretim, 108*a*
criad, 101*a*
criathar, 108*a* (St. 700; *C. l. w.*)
crichaib, 113*b*
cride, 109*b* (St. 1102)
crismal, 100*b*
crocann, crocenn (*leg.* croccan), 115*a* (St. 56)
croch, 101*a*
cruim, 110*a*, 117*b*, 119*a*
cruimther, 105*a* (*C. l. w.*)
cú, 110*a*
cuach, 100*b* (*C. l. w.*)
cuicenn, 101*a* (cucenn, *C. l w.*)
cuigel, 101*a*
cuilennbocc, 117*a* (St. 498)
cuimlengaithi, 113*a* (St gl. N°. 45, *p.* 147)
cuisil, 101*a* (*C. l. w.*)
cúl, 108*a* (*C. l. w.*)
cumacc, 109*a*, 116*a*, 123
cumacht, 109*a*, 116*a*
cumachtach, 116*a*, 124
cumacht(a)e, 116*a*

cumachtagimm, cumachtaigim, 124
cumachtchu, *comp. v.* cumachtach, 116*a*
cumaing, 116*a*
cuman (*v.* ni cuman lim), 111*a* (St. 111)
cumang, 109*a*, 116*a*, 123
cummasc, *gen.* cummisc 111*b*
cumsciget, 111*b*
cumúing. *v.* cumaing, 116*a*
cupris, 101*b*
cusecar, 101*a*
cute, 105*a*

dairde, daurde, 110*a* (St. 554)
dam (*root*), 110*a*
damilsi, 111*a*
dark (*root*), 113*a*
daur, 110*a* (St. 554)
daurauch, 110*a* (St. 554)
daurde, dairde, 110*a* (St. 554)
déccu, 127
demne, *gen. pl. v.* demuin, 101*b*
demuin, *v.* demne, (*gen.*), 101*b* (*C. l. w.*, deman)
* denge, *v.* tenge, 123
dénim, 112 (St. 899)
dér, 110*a*
derucc, 110*a* (St. 554)
derwen, 110*a*
descipul, 101*b* (deiscipuil, *n. pl.*, *C. l. w.*)
dess, 110*a* (*leg.* des, St. 386)
dét, 110*a*
di, 108*b*, 120
dia (dies), 110*a* (St. *p.* 163; dia, *C. l. w.*)
dia (Deus), 110*a* (St. 81
diabul, 101*b*
diblide, 101*b*
dictatóir, 101*b*
digaim, 101*b*
dil, diliu, dílem, 115*a* (St. 1120)
díles, 115*a*
dilui, 101*b*, 115*a*
dinair, 101*b*
diprecoit, 101*b* (*C. l. w.*)
discreit, 101*b* (*C. l. w.*)
do, du, 115*b*, 131 (St. 570)
do-, *v.* du-, 108*b* (St. 85)
doaibsem, 127
doaithirge, *v.* taidirge, 116*a*

15

doaurchanaim, 108a (St., doaurchanim, 704, 837)
dodálim, 115a
doforsat, 112a
dofuibnimm, 113a
dogéntar, 110b
dogniu, 110b, 127 (St. 908)
dóib, doib, 127
doiseich, 112a
-dóit, 124
domnach, 101b (C. l. w.)
doménarsa, 111a
domoiniur, 111a
domuinursa, 111a
do-omalgg, v. omalg, 111a
dorche, f. pl., 117b (St. 331)
dorósat, 112a
dorus, 110b
dosaig, 112a
doseich, 112a
drac, 101b (C. l. w.)
draigen, 115b (St. 559)
driss, 115b (St. 587)
dristenach, 115b (St. 587)
droch, drog, 114b
drochgním, 114b
drochgnimu, acc. pl., 114b
drog, droch, 114b
droighean, 115b
du, do, 115b, 120, 131 (St. 570)
du-, v. do-, 108b, 120, 131 (St. 85)
dúib, 127
duibsi, 127
duine, 122 (St. 89)
dún, 117b (St. 674)
dúr, 101b

é, v. sí, ed
ech, 110b, 122 (St. 17)
ecolso, ecilse, gen., v. aeclis, 101b
ed, v. é, sí, 126
-em, 126
emnatar, 102b (St. 1010)
eo, 118a
epil, 113b
epistil, 102a (C. l. w.)
epscop, 102a (St. 982 ; C. l. w.)
erdaircigidir, 113a
erdarcai, pl. v. airdircc, 113a
erdirc, v. airdircc, irdircc, 113a
erriu, erru, 127
escalchaill, 102a (St. 115)
estar, 110b

etar, etir, v. itir, 108b
etardibe, 113b
etargeiuin, 110b
etargne, etarcne, 110b
etarru, 127
ethemlagas, 102a
etirdibnet, 113a
-etu, v. -atu, 124

fagde, 102a
faigen, 106b
fáith, 109b (St. 2)
fedb, 107a, 112b
fellsube, 104b
felsub, 104b (St. p. 159)
femin, 102a (femen, C. l. w.)
fén, 118b
fer, 112b, 121
fers, gen. fersa, ferso, 106b
ferte, nom. pl., v. ferto, 107b
ferto, ferte, gen, 107b (C. l. w.)
fescor, 112b (St. 224 ; C. l. w.)
fetarlaice, fetarlice, fetarlicce, 107a
fí, 108b
fiadnisse, 118b (St. 959)
fíal, 106b
fiar, v. sethar, 112a
fích, 112b
ficuldae, 102a
fid, 119a
fidbocc, 117a
figil, 107a (C. l. w.)
fimf, 122
fín, fínn, 107a (C. l. w.)
fíne, 107a (C. l. w.)
fír, 106b
* firas, 121
firaib, forib, 127
firtu, acc., v. ferto, 107b
fis, 107b (C. l. w.)
flaith, gen. flatha, flatho, 116b
fla(i)themnacht, 116b
flaithemnas, 116b
flur, 118a
focul, 107b (C. l. w.)
fodail, fodil, 115a
fodaimimse, 110a
fodáli, 115a, 122
fodlaidi, 115a
fognám, 110b (St. 815)
fogní, 110b
foircthe, 108a
folcaim, folcaimm, 119b (St. 1045)

fondrodil, 115a
foraib, foirib, forib, 127
forcanim, forchanim, 108a
forchun, 108a, 127
forcital, forcetal, 108a (St. 837)
forcitl(a)id, forcetlaid, 108a (St. 837)
forlán, 111a
forlongis, 103a
forodil, 122
forru, 127
fuirib, v. foraib, 127
fulang, 113a

gab (root), 114a
gabáil, 123
gabor, 114a, 119b, 123 (St. 372)
gabimm, 119b
gabul, 117b (St. 135)
gaide, 117b (St. 216)
gaimred, 110b
géd, 115b
gein, gen. geine, 110b
geinddae, 110b
geinti, v. genti, 102b
geinti, pl., 102b (géinte, C. l. w.)
geintlecte, gen. fem., v. gentlide, 102b
geintlide, 102b
gell, 117b
gen (root Skr. jan), 110b
gen (root Skr. jnā), 110b
gen, dat. giun, 113b
genitiu, 102b
genti, v. geinti, 102b
gentlide, 102b
gentar, genthir, 110b
gerind, 102b
giall, 117b (St. 216)
glass, glas, 117b (St., note, p. 91)
gluais, 102b
glún, 119b
gné, 110b
gnethid, 110b
gním, 110b (St. 908)
gniu, 128
grád, gen. gráid, 102b (C. l. w.)
graif, 102b
grazacham, 102b (C. l. w.)
guidimm, 122 (St. 870)

heritic, pl., 102b
híairn, gen. v. iarn, 118a
ho buidnib, 117a
hodid, gen. v. uathid, 118b

Old Irish Index.

(h)omaldóit, v. umaldóit, 102b
horpamin, (pl.) v. orpam, 116b
hothad, v. (h) uathath, etc. 118b
húathad, v. (h)uathath, etc.), 118b
huathath acc., v. (h)uathath, etc. 118b
huathati, fem. acc. pl., v. úaithed, 118b
(h) umaldóit, v. umaldóit, 102b

iach, 102a (St. 216)
iarm-, 126
iarn, v. gen. híairn, 118a (St. 608, 812)
-ib, v. -aib, 127
ibim, 108b
id, 102b
ídol, 102b (C. l. w.)
ifurnn, gen. ifirnn, 103a (iffearn, iffern, St. 519)
il, v. lia, 111a (il, St. 13)
imb-, 99a
imdibe, 113b
imdibenar, 113a
immefolngai, immefolngai, immolúgai, 113a
immeforling, imforling, 113a
-imem, 126
immeruidbed, 113b, 130
immumruidbed, 130
immolúgai (see immefolngai, etc.), 113a
ind-, 99a, 123 (St. 734)
indatbendachub, 100a, v. bendacht
ind-figor, 102a
indib, 127
indid, 127
indlach, 113a
indluug, 113a
infinit, 103a
ingor, 99a (St. 68)
inis, gen. inse, 108b
init, 103a
innarbar, 117a
innerese (acc.), 102b
innoc(h)t, 111b
innurid, 125
inobar, v. saibes, 104a
inrolég, 103a
insádaim, 112a
insce, 112a
inte, 127
interiecht, 103a

intesi, 127
intiu, 127
-ire, v. -aire, 124
irgnae, 110b
ísind-airmim, dat. v. arm, 99b
isind-ithlaind dat., v. land, 118a
itargninim, 110b
ith, gen. etha, 108b, 123 (St. 1037)
ithim, 108b, 110b, 116b, 123 (St. 40)
ithirge, v. aithirge, 116a
itir, v. etir, etar, 108b
iúgsuide, 103a

labar, 118b
lacht, 108b
laech, 103a (C. l. w.)
lagait, 111a
laigiu, lugu, 111a (St. 923)
láine v. láne, 111a
lán, 111a (St. 13)
láne v. láine, 111a
lánad, 122
land, dat. isind-ithlaind, 118a (St. 132)
lang (root), 113a
lanmair, 111a
lar, 118a
lebor, v. libur, 103a (libar, St. 371 ; C. l. w.)
lechdach, 103a (St. 1071)
lecht, 103a (C. l. w.)
led, leth, 111a
legend, 103a (St. 853)
legtoir, 103a
* léic, 108b
léicci, 108b
léim, 118a
leth, led, 111a (St. p. 156)
lethan, 111a (St. 13, 925)
lethscripul, 105b
lí, 114a
lia, v. il, 111a
líac, 108b (liacc, St. 133, 573, p. 156)
libur, v. lebor, 103a
lígim, 111a
lim (ne cuman lim), 111a
lín, 103a (St. 863 ; C. l. w.)
línad, 111a, 122
línmaire, 111a
liter, 103a (letir, C. l. w.)
loathar, 118a
lobur, 108b
loc, 103a

loing, 103a
loingtech, 113a
long, 103a (St. 574 ; C. l. w.)
loth, gen. loithe, 108b
lúacharnn, 103a
lugimem, 111a (St. 923)
lugu (see laigiu), 111a
lúirech, 103a (St. 154)
lunáir, 103a

macc, v. mang (root), 115b
macc (filius), 115b
máer (v. mór-máer), 103a (C. l. w.)
magistir, nom. pl., magistru, acc. pl., 103a (St. 365)
mainn, 103b
maldachæ, 103a
maldacht, 103a (St. 915)
maledic, 103a
malg (root), 111a
man, 103b
man (root), 111a
manach, 103b (C. l. w.)
mang (root, v. macc), 115b
mar (root), 111a
mar, 115b (múr, St. 663)
marb, 111a (St. p. 159)
marc, 118a
martre, fem. pl. martri, 103b (St. 738 ; C. l. w.)
masc (root), v. misc, 111b
mascul, 103b
matal, 103b
máthir, 111a
matin, 108b (C. l. w.)
mé, me, 126
mebuir, 103b
medón, 111a
meince, 116a
meirddrech, 103b
melim, 111a
membur (pl.), 103b
mencain, 116a
menicc, menic, 116a
mertrech, 103b (C. l. w.)
messa, v. mi-, 118a (St. 1117)
metair, metir (gen.), 103b (metuir, C. l. w.)
mí, 111b (St. 1117)
mí-, 118a
mías, 103b (C. l. w.)
midiur-sa, 108b
mil, 108b
mil, 103b
míle (fem.), 103b

15 B

mindchichthiu, 103*b*
mindchigitir, 103*b*
mindechu, 103*b*
mirt-chaill, 103*b* (St. 115)
misc (*root*), *v.* masc, 111*b*
mistae, 111*b* (St. 1051)
mo-, mu-, 131
mod, *v.* muid, mud, 103*b*
molt, 103*b*
mong, 118*a*
monistre (*gen. pl.*), 103*b*
mór *v.* máer, 103*a* (St. 663)
moralus (*dat.*), 103*b*
mori, 111*a*
moru, 119*b* (móru, St. 1020)
mu-, mo-, 131
mucc, 118*a* (St. 1029)
mud, *dat., v.* mod, 103*b*
muid, *gen., v.* mod, 103*b*
muin-torc, 106*b* (St. 744)
muir, 111*b* (St. 860)
muirtchenn, 103*b* (*C. l. w.*)
mulenn, 103*b* (St. 701; muilenn, *C. l. w.*)
múlu (*acc. pl.*), 103*b* (St. 295)
múr, 103*b* (*C. l. w.*)
mút, 103*b*

nachiberpidsi, 116*b*
nachimrindarpai-se, 117*a*
nát, 104*a*
nathir, 114*a* (St. 88)
naue (*gen.*), noe, 108*b*
nebthóbe, *v.* nephthóbe, 113*b* (St. 987)
necht, 114*a* (St. 224)
nem, 119*a* (St. 812)
nephthóbe *v.* nebthóbe, 113*b*
nert, 108*b*
nessa, nesam, 114*a* (St 1117)
neutor, 104*a* (neutur, *C. l. w.*)
neutrálde, 104*a*
ni-, 111*a*, 130
niae, 114*a*
nicumanlim *v.* ni, cuman, lim, 111*a*
nicumscaichti, 111*b*
nid, 114*a*
nimb, 104*a* (*C. l. w.*)
niroimdibed, *v.* roimdibed, 130
níule *v.* níulu, 113
níulu, *dat.* (in niulu) 111*b*

noacuitigfide *v.* acuit, 99*a*
nobbendachat, 100*a*
nobirpaid, 116*b*
nocht-chenn, 116*a*
noct, 111*b*
nogigned, 110*b*
nometargnigedar, 110*b*
nomerpimm, 116*b*
nomisligur, 124
not, nota, 104*a*
notail, 113*a*
notaire, notire, 104*a*
notlaic, 103*b* (*C. l. w.*)
nu-, no-, 131
nú (nua), nue, nuae, núide, 111*b* (St. 21, 803)

óa, 118*b* (St. 758)
obar, 104*a*
oblann, 104*a*
ocht, 122
ochte, octe, 109*a*
óclachdi, 110*b* (St. 758)
ócmil, 111*a* (St. 758)
ocus *v.* accus, 109*a*
ocus, ocuis (*et*) *v.* acus, 109*a*
og, 112*b* (St. 955)
óin, óen, 111*b*
oipred, 104*a* (St. 889)
oipretho, *gen., v.* oipred, 104*a*
óir, *gen., v.* ór, 99*b*
oirclech, 104*a*
óis, *v.* áis, 109*a* (St. 812)
oissa, oessa, *gen., v.* áis, óis, 109*a*
oistreoir, 104*a*
olachaill, 104*a*
olachrann, 104*a*
(h)omaldóit, *v.* (h)umaldóit, 102*b*
omalgg, (*v.* do omalgg), 111*a*
onóir, 102*b*
ood, *v.* uad, 127
optait, optit, 104*a*
orait, 104*a* (oróit, *C. l. w.*)
ord (ordd, ort, urt), 104*a* (St. 943; *C. l. w.*)
orpam, *v. pl.* hórpamin, 116*b*
orpe, *v.* arpae, 116*b*
orthain, *acc. sing.*, 104*a* (*C. l. w.*)
ort, *v.* ord, 104*a*
ós, *v.* úas, uch, 118*a*
othatnat, 118*b*

óthud, *dat., v.* uathuth, 118*b*

pagan, 104*a*
páin, 104*a* (*C. l. w.*)
paiper, 104*a*
pairche, 104*a* (*C. l. w.*)
pairt, 104*a* (*C. l. w.*)
pais, 104*b* (*C. l. w.*)
papa, 104*a*
partus, 104*a*
peccad, 104*b* (*C. l. w.*)
pellec, 104*b*
pén, *v.* pían, 104*b*
peneult, 104*b*
pennit, 104*b* (pennait, *C. l. w.*)
persan, 104*b* (St. 87)
pían, *v.* pén, 104*b*
piss, 104*b* (*C. l. w.*)
plag, 104*b*
popul, 105*a*
port, 105*a* (St. 676, 725; *C. l. w.*)
posit, 105*a*
predach, 105*a*
predchim, 105*a*
precept, 105*a* (*C. l. w.*)
preceptóir, 105*a*
predag, 105*a*
prelait, 105*a*
prím, 105*a* (*C. l. w.*)
proind, 105*a* (*C. l. w.*)
prolach, 105*a*
promfidir, 105*a*
pronomen, 105*a*
propost, 105*a* (*C. l. w.*)
pupall, 104*a*
púr, 105*a* (*C. l. w.*)
purgatoir, 105*a*

ra-, *v.* ru-, ro-, 130, 131
rád, 116*b*
rám, 105*b*
ranglana, 130
rastal, 105*a*
rect, recht, 114*b*
reilic, 105*b* (relic, *C. l. w.*)
remi-, 126
rí, 114*a*
riagul, riagol, 105*b* (St. 61)
ribar, 101*a* (*C. l. w.*)
ríg, *gen., v.* rí, 114*a* (St. 1036)
ro-, *v.* ra-, ru-, 130, 131
roainmnichte, 130
roairptha, *pl. v.* roerbad, 117*a*

Old Irish Index.   203

robeimmis, 130
robia, robbia, ropia, 130
rochumscigther, 111*b*
rocomalnither, 130
roerbad, 116*b*
rofetar 123
rogád, 122
rogen(a)ir, 110*b*
roiccu, 127
roimdibed, 130
rolín, 111*a*
rolabrastar, 128
rommunus, rommúnus, 111*a*
rondpromson, 105*a*
ronoíbad, 130
ropia, *v.* robia, 130
rorélus, 130
roschaill, 105*b*
rostae, 105*b*
rostán, 105*b*
roth, 111*b*
ru-, *v.* ra-, ro-, 130, 131
rucestaigser, 128
rún, 118*b*

sabaltair, 105*b* (*C. l. w.*)
saboit, 105*b* (*C. l. w.*)
sacardd, 105*b* (sacart, *C. l. w.*)
sacc, 105*b*
sacorbaic, sacarbaic, 105*b* (*C. l. w.*)
sad (*root*), 112*a*
sái, 109*a*
saibes (saibes inobar), *v.* inobar, 104*a*
saichdetu, 112*a*
saiged, 112*a*
saiges, 112*a*
saiget, 108*b* (St. 214)
saigid, saiged, 112*a*
saigim, 112*a*
saigul, 105*b* (St. *p.* 146)
saile, 105*b* (St. 651; *C. l. w.*)
sailestar, 105*b* (soilestar, *C. l. w.*)
* saillim, 109*a*
sailm, *pl.*, *v.* salm, 105*a*
sak (*root*—to say), 112*a*
sak (*root*—to follow), 112*a*
salann, 111*b* (St. 977)
salm, 105*a* (*C. l. w.*)
salmu, *acc.*, *v.* salm, 105*a*
salt, 105*b* (*C. l. w.*)
saltair, 105*a*
saltir, *dat.*, *v.* saltair, 105*a*
salto, *gen.*, *v.* salt, 105*b*

saltrach, *gen.*, *v.* saltair, 105*a*
sam, 118*b*
samail, samal, * samali, * samali, 109*a*
sancht, 105*b* (St. *p.* 161; *C. l. w.*)
sapati, *pl.*, *v.* saboit, 105*b*
scath, 113*b*
sciath, 109*a*
scipar, 104*b*
scol, 105*b* (St. 338)
scoloca, 118*b*
scríbend, 105*b* (St. 853)
scrín, 105*b* (*C. l. w.*)
scule, *gen.*, *v.* scol, 105*b*
sech, 109*a*
sechem, 112*a*
sechimtid, 112*a*
sechtmaine, 105*b*
seib, 102*a* (*C. l. w.*; St. 109)
seinser, 105*b* (seindser, *C. l. w.*)
séit, *dat.*, *v.* sét, 118*b*
séitchi, *dat.*, *v.* sétche, 118*b*
sén, 106*a* (*C. l. w.*)
sen, 112*a* (St. 735)
senatóir, 105*b*
sens, 105*b*
seol, sóol, 118*b*
septien, 106*a*
sét, 118*b* (St. 470, 1073)
sétche, 118*b*
sethar, siur (siar, fiar), 108*a*, 112*a*
seúit, seuit, *pl.*, *v.* sét, 118*b*
sí, *v.* é, ed, 126
síansib, *dat. pl. v.* sens, 105*b*
siar, *v.* sethar, 112*a*
síd, 113*b*
síl, 116*b*
sillab, 106*a*
siur, *v.* sethar, 112*a* (St. 216)
slechtaim, 102*a*
slice, 118*b*
slici, *pl.* 118*b*
snáthe, 118*b* (St. 817)
snathiu, *dat.*, *v.* snáthe, 118*b*
snechti, 116*b*
soillse, 112*a*
sóol, *v.* seol, 118*b*
sosad, sossad, 112*a*
spíracul, 106*a* (*C. l. w.*)
spirut, 106*a* (*C. l. w.*)

spongc, 106*a* (*C. l. w.*)
srathar, 106*a* (St. 262)
srían, 102*b* (St. 109, 1039)
srogell, 102*a*
sruth, 111*b* (St. 999)
stán, 106*a*
su-, 109*b*, 120
suan, 111*b*
such, 118*b*
suide, 112*a* (St. 812)
suidiguth, suidigud, 112*a*
suist, 102*b* (sust, *C. l. w.*)
superlait, superlit, *pl.* superlati, 106*a*
surnn, 102*b*

ta, 127
tablaire, 106*a*
taidirge, *v.* doaithirge, 116*a*
taig, *dat.*, *v.* teg, 112*a*
taigae (idultaigae, *gen.*, *v.* teg) 112*a*
* taigi, *v.* teg, 112*a*
tairm-, 126
talland, 106*a*
tám, 106*a* (*C. l. w.*)
tana, 112*b* (St. 1017)
tar, 109*b*, 120
tarb, 109*b*
táu, 127
tech, *v.* teg, 112*a* (St. 569)
teg, *v.* tech, 112*a*
teirt, 106*b* (*C. l. w.*)
teis, 106*b*
tellrach, *gen.*, *v.* telluir, 106*a*
telluir, 106*a* (tellur, *C. l. w.*)
temel, 112*b*
tempul, 106*b*
tene, 119
tengad, *pl.*, *v.* tenge, 114*b*
tenge, *gen. sing.*, 114*b*, 123
teoir, 106*b* (St. 744; *C. l. w.*)
tercital, 108*a*
tesc, 101*b*
test, 106*b* (teíst, *C. l. w.*)
testimin, 106*b* (testimon, testimoin, *C. l. w.*)
tíach, 106*b* (St. 41, 371)
tiagu, 127
tigerne, *dat.* tigerni, 112*b*
timpan, 106*b*
tir, 109*b* (St. 703)
titlu, *acc. pl.*, *v.* titul, 106*b*
titul, titol, 106*b*
tobe, 113*b*

togu, 127
tort, 106*b* (*C. l. w.*)
tot-mael, 106*b*
tracht, 106*b*
trag (*root*), 113*a* (St. 74)
traig, 113*a* (St. 74)
tré, tri, 118*b*, 120
trebun-ṡuide, 106*b*
tremi-, 126
tri, *v.* tré, 118*b*
trindoit, 106*b*
tú, tu, 126
túath, 112*b* (St. 423)
tucu, tuccu, 127 (St. p. 165)
tuib, *gen.*, 106*b*
tuinech, 106*b* (*C. l. w.*)
tuir, 106*b*
tus-lestar, 106*b* (St. 1134)

uad, ood, 127
uadi (*fem.*), 127
uadib, uaidib, *dat.*, *v.* uad, 127
úaithed, 118*b*
uan, 109*b*
uar, 102*b*
úas, *v.* ós, 118*a*
uathataib, *dat. pl.*, *v.* úaithed, 118*b*
uathath, uathad, *v.* (h)uathath, 118*b*
uathid (hodid), *gen.*, *v.* (h)nathath, 118*b*
uathuth, *dat.*, *v.* óthud, 118*b*
uch, *v.* ós, *and* úas, 118*a*
uile, 118*b*
uilt, *acc.*, *v.* ult, 106*b*
ult, 106*b*
umal, 102*b*
(h)umaldóit, *v.* humaldóit 102*b*
ungae, unga, 106*b*
úrde, 109*b*
urt, *v.* ord, 104*a*

*vlati, 116*b*

Middle Irish.

aibherseóir, 99*a* (St. 517)

banprioir, 105*a* (St. 23)
biait, 100*a*

cabellanacht, 100*a* (cabillanacht, St. 172)
command, 101*a*
coróin, 101*a* (St. 75)

crisdal, 101

fairche, 104*a* (*C. l. w.*)
fersaid, 106*b* (St. 568)
firmamint, 102*a* (St. 749)

gredáil, 102*b* (St. 854)

instrumint, 103*a*

orc (?), 105*a* (*C. l. w.*)

proisté, 100*a* (St. 852)
pústa, 106*a*

sdair, 102*b* (St. 84)
senadh, 106*a* (St. 551; senod, *C. l. w.*)
sinistir, 102*a*
sitheal, 106*a* (St. 241; sithil, *C. l. w.*)
soifist, 106*a* (St. 842)
soiler, 106*a* (St. 740)
spín, 106*a*
stanamhail, 106*a* (St. 610)

taibherne, 106*a* (St. 169)
tital, 106*b* (*C. l. w.*)

Modern Irish.

astaig, 112*b*
meilg, 111*a*
pit, 104*b*

Welsh.

aball, 115*a*
aballen, 115*a*
abbadeu, *pl.* 99*a*
abl, 102*b*
acen, 99*a*
agos, 109*a*
alarch, 107*a*
all, *v.* allt, 99*a*
alldut, *v. pl.* alltudion, 109*a*
allor, 99*a*
allt, alt, all, 99*a*
alltudion, *pl.*, *v.* alldut, 109*a*
amherawdyr, 102*b*
amherodracth, 102*b*
amherodres, 102*b*
ampriodaur, 116*a*
angor, 99*a*
aniueil, *v. pl.* anyueilyeit, 99*a*
aniueileit, anniuieleit, *v.* anyueilyeit, 99*a*

anniueileit, *v.* aniueileit, anuab, 124
anyueilyeit, *pl. v.* aniueil, aradr, 99*a*
araut, 104*a*
archescyb, *pl.*, 102*a*
arfeu, *v.* arueu, 99*b*
ariant, *v.* aryant, 99*a*
armel, 99*b*
arueu, *v.* arfeu, 99*b*
aryant, *v.* ariant, 99*b*
assen, 99*b*
aual, *pl.* aualeu, aueleu, 115*a*
auon. 107*b*
auonyd, 107*b*
-awd, -awt, 128
awel, 107*b*
awr, 102*b*
awst, 99*b*
awyr, 107*a*

bad, *pl.* badeu, 117*a*
bagl, 99*b*
bahell, *v.* buyall, 117*a*
baraf, baryf, 99*b*
barg, 99*b*
barwn, 100*a*
baryf, *v.* baraf, 99*b*
bathor, 100*a*
bedeu, 108*a*
bedyd, 99*b*
bendicetic, 100*a*
bendith, 100*a*
bereu, 107*b*
blodeu, 117*b*
bodin, *pl.* bodiniou, 117*a*
bord, *v.* bwrd, 117*a*
boutig, 108*a*
brag, 100*a*
braut, brawt, 109*b*, 116*a*
breich, 100*a*, 108*a*
brodyr, *pl. v.* braut, 109*b*
buch, 108*a*
bud, 117*b*
budicaul, 117*a*
budugawl, 117*a*
buyall, *v.* bahall, 117*a*
bwa, 117*a*
hwl, 100*a*
bwrd, *v.* bord, 117*a*
bwystuil, 100*a*
byd, 128
bydaf, 112, 128
bydin, 117*a*
bydwn, 128
byleynyeyt, *pl.* 107*a*
byrdeu, *pl. v.* bwrd, 117*a*
byw, 109*b*
bywyt, 109*b*

Welsh Index. 205

cadeir, 100*b*
cadwyn, 100*b*
caeth, 100*a*
calamennou, 100*a*
callaur, 100*a*
cam, 110*a*
cancher, 100*a*
cann, 108*a*
cannwyl, 100*a*
car, *v.* carr, 117*b*
carbwncl, 100*a*
cardotta, 100*a*
cared, 119*a*
carr, *v.* car, 117*b*
carrei, *v.* corruui, 101*a*
cath, 100*b*
cawg, 100*b*
caws, 100*b*
celeel, 101*b*
cenitol, 110*b*
cenitolaidou, 110*b*
cepister, *v.* kebyster, 100*a*
ceroenhou, 100*b*
cestill, cestyll, 100*b*
chwaer, chwioryd, *pl.*, *v.* chwior, 112*a*
chwior, 108*a*, 112*a*
circhinn, 100*b*
cledif, cledyf, 108*a*
cloeu, *pl.*, 108*a*
coc, 101*a*
coch, *pl.* cochyon, 100*b*
cogail, 101*a*
coll, 101*a*
colenn, 101*a*
coronawc, 101*a*
corruui, *v.* carrei, 101*a*
craff, 117*b*
craffu, 117*b*
crauell, 115*a*
creaticaul, 101
crefft, 117*b*
cret, 108*a*
criched, 113*b*
crochann, 115*a*
cristawn, 100*b*
cruitr, 108*a*
crych, 113*b*
cudyaw, 110*a*
cultel, 101*b*
cultir, 101*b*
cussan, 117*b*
cwlltor, 101*b*
cwydaw, 108*a*
cylleil, *pl.* cylleill, *v.* kylleil, 101*b*
cymhar, 101*a*
cymsc, 111*b*
cymun, 101*a*
cyson, 101*a*

dacrlon, 110*a*
dagreu, *pl.* 110*a*
danned, *pl.* 110*a*
dar, *v. pl.* deri, 110*a*
datkanu, 108*a*
-daut, dawt, *v.* -taut, 124
decum, degum, 101*b*
dehou, deheu, 110*a*
derwen, 110*a*
desko, 101*b*
di, 108*b*
didaul, 115*a*
diffenu, 101*b*
diffrwyth, 102*b*
dihu, *v.* diu (*dies*), 110*a*
din, 117*b*
discl, 101*b*
disgynnu, 101*b*
dispeilaw, 106*a*
diu (*dies*), *v.* dihu, dyw, dyd, 110*a*
diu (*Deus*), *v.* dyhu, dyu, dyuu, duw, duhu, duo, 110*a*
doeth, 101*b*
doethou, 101*b*
doguomisuram, 103*b*
dolur, 101*b*
dor, *pl.* dorcu, 110*b*
doythion, doeth, 101*b*
draen, 115*b*
dreic, *pl.* dreigeu, 101*b*
drog, 115*a*
drogn, 115*a*
dros, *v.* trus, 109*b*
drus, 110*b*
drwc, 114*b*
drws, 110*b*
drycket, 114*b*
dryssien, 115*b*
duhu, *v.* diu, 110*a*
duo, *v.* diu, 110*a*
dur, 101*b*
duw, *v.* diu, 110*a*
duyuaul, 110*a*
dyd, *v.* diu (*dies*), 110*a*
dyhu, *v.* diu (*dies*)
dyrys, 101*b*
dyscyl, disgyl, 101*b*
dyu, dyuu, *v.* diu, 110*a*
dyw, *v.* diu (*Deus*), 110*a*

eccluis, 101*b*
ed, *v.* yd, 121, 130, 131
eglwys, 101*b*
egr, 99*a*
egwyddor, 99*a*
ehawc, 102*a*
elestr, 105*b*

eliffeint, 102*a*
elin, 110*b*, 113
emendassant, 102*a*
enw, 107*a*
epscip, *pl. v.* escyb, 102*a*
erckafael, 130
erw, 107*a*
escolectaut, 105
escoleycyon, *v. pl.* yscoleigyon, 105*b*
escyb, *v.* epscip, 102*a*
eskemun, 102*a*
eskenho, eskynho, 105*b*
estauell, *v.* ystauell, 106*a*
eur, 99*b*

ffa, 102*a*
ffawyd, 102*a*
ffenigl, 102*a*
ffer, 108*b*
ffiol, 104*b*
fflam, 102*a*
ffo, 102*b*
ffol, 102*a*
fforch, 102*b*
fforest, 102*a*
ffrowyll, 102*a*
ffrwyn, 102*b*
ffurf, 102*a*
ffust, 102*b*
ffustawd, 102*b*
ffynnawn, 102*a*
fin, 102*a*
finnaun, 102*a*
fos, foss, 102*b*
fruinn, 102*b*
frut, 111*b*
fruyn, 102*b*
frwt, *v.* frut, 111*b*
fual, 102*a*
funenneu, *pl.*, 102*b*
funiou, *pl.*, 102*b*

gaem, 110*b*
gafar, 114*a*
gallaf, 119*a*
ganet, 110*b*
gauar, 114*a*
gayaf, 110*b*
gerthi, 117*b*
glin, 119*b*
gofyn, 111*a*
golchi, 119*b*
gormes, *pl.* gormesseu, gormessoed, 118*a*
gorsedua, 112*a*
gratell, 101*a*
grawys, 105*a*
gref, 102*b*
grefiat, 102*b*

griduan, 102b
gryd, 102b
grydiaw, 102b
gulan, 112b
guletic, 116b
guneyr, 110b
guodeimisauch, 110a
gwain, 106b
gweddw, 107a
gwennwyn, 106b
gwenwynic, 106b
gwerth, 116b
gwerthawr, 116b
gwerthyd, 106b
gwiberot, 107b
gwir, 106b
gwlat, pl. gwladoed, gwledyd, 116b
gwledic, 116b
gwledyd, pl., v. gwlat, 116b
gwnaf, 110b
gwr, 112b
gwrach, 108b
gwyllt, 119b
gwyrd, 109b
gwystyl, 117b

haf, 118b
haliw, 105b
ham, 118b
he-, 109b
heb, 112a
hedwch, 113b
helic, 109a
helym, helm, 115
henoid, 111b
hestaur, pl. hestoriou, 106a
hestawr, 106a
hestoriou, v. hestaur, 106a
heu, 116b
heul, 112a
hewyt, 116b
heyrn, 118a
hint, 118b
histr, 104a
hoedel, hoedyl, 108b
ho(s)an, pl. hossaneu, 117b
hucc, 118a
huil, 118b
hun, 111b
hwylbrenni, 115a
hwyr, 106a

iarll, 115
ieuhaf, 110b
ieuanc, pl. ieueinc, 110b
inis, v. ynys, 108b
iot, 110b

iou, 111a
istrat, v. strat, 106a

kaerllion, 103a
kaghellaur, kyghellaur, 100a
kalaned, pl., 100b
kanu, 108a
karchar, 100a
karw, 108a
* kassiau, v. keissaw, 108b
kauacus, 109a
kaus, 100b
kebyster, v. cepister, pl. kebystreu, kebesteryeu, 100a
keffyl, 110a
kegin, 101a
keissaw, 108b
keleuyn, 100a
kenedel, kenedl, kenedyl, 110b
kerwyn, 100b
keryd, 119a
* kessiaw, v. keissaw, 108b
keuedac, 110b
kiwtawt, 100b
kiwtawtwyr, 100b
kolouen, 100b
koveint, 101a
krissant, 101a
kuyr, kwyr, 100b
kyfagos, 109a
kyffelyp, kyffelyb, 109a
kyfoeth, kyuoeth, 116a
kyghellaur, v. kaghellaur, 100a
kylleil, pl., v. cyllell, 101b
kyngryfet, 117b
kynnhaeaf, 110b
kyrchu, 100b
kyuoeth, v. kyfoeth, 116a
kyuoethawc, 116a

laethauc, 108b
laiðver, 108b
lammain, 118a
lann, 118a
laubael, 117a
laur, v. llawr, 118a
leeces, 103a
lemenic, 118a
litan, 111a
liuou, pl., 103a
llamp, 118a
llanw, 111a
llawr, v. laur, 118a
llawn, 111a
lle, 103a

llech, 108b
llegest, 103a
llei, 111a
lleidr, lleidyr, 103a
llemhidyd, 118a
llew, 103a
lleycyon, pl., 103a
lliw, 114a
llong, pl. llongeu, 103a
lludedic, 108b
llwfr, 108b
llygat, 118a
llyghes, llynghes, 103a
llygorn, 103a
llythyren, 103a
loggeu, loggou, pl. v. llong, 103a

maer, 103a
mair, 103a
mal, 109a
manaches, 103b
maru, 111a
medeginyaethu, 103b
medhecynyaet, 103b
medic, 103b
medwl, medol, 108b
medylyaw, 108b
meitin (yr meitin), 108b
meldicetic, 108a
melen, 119b
melin, melyn, 119b
melineu, 103b
melynyon, pl., v. melen, 119b
meneich, 103b
menoent, 111a
merch, 119b
mererit, 103b
metrut, 103b
meun, 111a
milinon, pl., v. melen, pl. melynyon, 119b
milwr, 103b
mis, 111b
moch, 118a
modreped, 111a
mogau, pl. (leg. moggou), 118a
morthol, 103b
morwyn, 119b
mur, pl. muroed, 103b
mut, 103b
mwng, 118a
mwys, 103b
mynnir, 111a
mynych, mynnych, 111a, 116a
mynyd, 108b
myrd, 103b

Welsh Index. 207

myrthw, 103b
mys, v. mis, 111b
mywn, 111a

nadolic, v. nodolyc, 103b
neges, 104a
neithawr, 104a
nifer, v. niuer, 104a
nimer, 104a
niuer, v. nifer, 104a
nodolyc, v. nadolic, 103b
nouel, 104a

oedawc, v. oetawc, 108b
oedwn, 128
oen, 109b
oes, 109a
oet, 108b
oetawc, v. oedawc, 108b
ofrum, 104a
ois, 109a
oleu, 104a

padell, v. patel, 104b
palf, 104a, 113
pall, 104a
pap, pl. papeu, 104a
parchell, 105a
part, parth, pard, 104a
pasc, 104a
patel, 104b
pau, 109a
pawin, 104b
pawl, v. polyon, 104a
pebreid, v. pybreid, 104b
pebyll, 104a
pechaut, 104b
pedestyr, 104b
pelechi, 104b
penydyaw, 104b
pererin, 104b
peri, 104a
person, 104b, 116a
peth, 104b
pethedic, 104b
plumauc, 104b
plycca, 104b
poguisma, 104b
polyon, pl., v. pawl, 104a
pont, 105a
popuryes, pophuryes, 101a
porffor, 105a
porth, v. pyrth, 105a
porthant, 105a
porthes, 105a
porthi, 105a
porthmon, 105a
post, 105a
postoloin, 105a
poues, 104b

priawt, 116a
prif, 105a
prud, 105a
pryf, 110a
pull, 104a
punt, 105a
pur, 105a
purdu, 105a
purgoch, 105a
purwynn, 105a
putein, 105a
pwys, 104b, 106a
pybreid, v. pebreid, 104b
pyllawc, 104a
pyrth, pl., v. porth, 105a
pysg, 104b
pysgadwr, 104b

rascl, 105a
re-, v. ry, 130
rebriuasei, 130
rcith, reyth, reis, 114b
rhwyd, 105b
rogulipias, 130
rud, 111b
rygaffel, 130
ryt yssu, 110b
ry (ry echewit), v. re-, 130

sacth, 108b
sant, v. pl. seint, 105b
sarff, 105b
scribl, 105b
seint, pl., v. sant, 105b
snoden, 118b
stebill, pl., 106a
strat, v. istrat, ystrat, 106a
strotur, 106a
strouis, 106a
suh, 118b
sumpl, 106a
swllt, 106a
swyf, 105b
sych, 111b

taguel, v. tawel, 114b
talu, 115
tarater, taradyr, 109b
taru, 109b
-taut, v. -daut, 124
taw, 114b
tawel, v. taguel, 114b
tei, pl., v. ty, 112a
teml, 106b
temperam, 106b
teneu, 112b
testion, 106b
testu, 106b
tewi, 114b
tigern, 112b

torch, 106b
torth, 106b
tracth, 106b
tribedd, 106b
trintaut, 106b
trist, 106b
tristau, 106b
tristit, tristyt, tristwch, 106b
truch, 106b
trus. v. dros, 109b
turwf, v. twryf, 106b
twr, v. tyreu, 106b
twrncimeint, 106b
twryf, twrwf, 107b
ty, v. pl., tei, 112a
tynnu, 106b
tyreu, tyroed, pl., v. twr, 106b
tywyll, 112b

ucher, 112b
ufern, uffern, 103a
uyeu, pl., 112b

* vira, 112b

wyf, 128

y, 108b
yd, v. ed, 121, 130, 131
ychen, pl, 118a
ymun, 102b
ynyd, 103a
yny (yny priawt person), 116a
ynys, 108b
yscawl, v. pl., ysgolyon, 105b
yscolheic, v. escoleycyon, 105b
yscoleigyon, pl., v. escoleycyon, 105b
yscynnu, 105b
ysgolyon, pl., v. yscawl, 105b
ysgymunn, 102a
yskumunetic, 102a
ysl(e)ipanu, 115
ysmwg, 115
ysnoden, 118b
ysp, 102b
yspeilaw, 106a
yspcit, 106a
yspwys, 106a
ystabyl, 106a
ystauell, 106a
ystondard, 106a
ystrat, v. strat, 106a
yswein, pl. ysweinieit, 115

Kymric.

ad-, v. at-, 113a, 120
all, 109a
at-, v. ad-, 113a

bran, 119a

caer, cair, 108a
* cardaut, 100a
cat, 117b
cav (i.e. cabh), 114a
cavael, 123
ci, 110a
corf, 108a
corn, 114a

dant, 110a
do, dy, di, y, 115b, 120
dyn, den, 122

ech, 122
ep, 110b
-es, 124
esel, 113a

* garan, 113a
gavar, 123
guid, 119a
guin, 107a
* guint, 114b
gwnathœd, 128
gwybydy, 128

hep, heb, 109a
hen, 112a
hi, 126

lavar, 118b
lin, 103a

mam, 111a
march, 118a
melin, 103b
mil, 103b
moilin, v. muilin, 119b
mor, 111b
muilin, v. moilin, 119b

nef, 119a
nerth, 108a
nos, 111b

oll, 118b

pimp, 122

rin, 118b

tan, 119
tat, 109b

-taut, 100a
tir, 109b
troit, 113a
trui, 118b
tut, 112b

uchell, 118a
un, 111b

y, v. do, 115b
yd, 121, 131

Cornish.

abat, 99a
abestely, pl. v., apostol, 99a
aflauar, v. mab, 118b, 124
ail, v. eyll, el, 99a
als, 99a
altor, 99a
anauhel, 107b
ancar (ancora), 99a
ancar (anachoreta), 99a
anow, v. (h)anow, 107a
apostol, v. abestely, 99a, 114
archescop, 102a
argans, arghans, 99b
arvow, 99b
ascient, v. guan, 105b
asen, 99b
auain, 102b
auallen, 115a
auhel, 107b
auon, 107b
avel, 109a
avell, 115a

barf, baref, 99b
bat, 100a
batales, 100a
bathor, 100a
bay, 100a
bedeven, 108a
benen, benyn, pl. beneynas, 109b
benegis, 100a
benenrid, 109b
benenuat, 109b
ber, 107b
bethaff, 112
beu, 109b
bewe, 109b
bewnas, bewnans, 109b
biu, 109b
blamye, 100a
blodon, 117a
boch, 117a
bom, v. bum, 113b
box, 100a

brag, 100a
braud, v. broder, 109b
brech, 100a, 108a
broche, 100a
broder, v. braud, 109b
buch, 108a
bugel, 108a
bum, v. bom, 113b
burges, 113b

caltor, 100a
cam, 110a
camhinsic, 110a, 118b
can, 108a
cancher, 100a
cane, 108a
canores, 108a
cantuil, 100a
cantulbren, 100a
carogos, 109a
caruu, 108a
caul, 100b
caws, v. cos, 100b
ceroin, 100b
chefuidoc, 116a
cheniat, 108a
clauster, v. cloister, 100b
clear, 100b
clethe, 108a
cloch, 100b
cloireg, 100b
cloister, v. clauster, 100b
cober, 101b
coir, 100b
colom, 100b
colter, 101b
collel, 101b
colviden, 101a, 119a
comfortye, 101a
commisc, 111b
corden, v. kerdyn, 100b
cos, v. caws, 100b
cothe, 108a
creador, 101a
cref, v. cryff, 117b
croadur, 101a
crogen, 115a
croider, 108a
crois, crows, 101a
cruitr, 108a
cryff, v. cref, 117b
cugol, 101a
cuic, 113b
curun, 101a
cussin, 117b
cusul, cussyl, cusyl, cusill, 101a
cuthe, 110a

dagrow, 110a

Cornish Index. 209

dampnye, 101*b*
dampnys, 101*b*
dans, 110*a*
dar, *v.* deri, 110*a*
darat, 110*b*
deserya, 101*b*
det, 110*a*
deth, *v.* dyth, 110*a*
dethiow, *pl.*, *v.* deth, dyth, 110*a*
dew (dew sull), *v.* sull, 101*b*
dewolow, *pl.*, *v.* dywolow, 101*b*
deyow, 101*b*
diagon, 101*b*
diffenor, 101*b*
discebel, *v.* dyscyplys, dyscyblon, 101*b*
discomfortys, 101*a*
diskient, 105*b*
diskynna, 101*b*
disliu, 114*a*
doyn, 112
drain, *pl.* drein, 115*b*
dreyn, *pl. v.* drain, 115*b*
dris, drys, 109*b*
drocger, 114*b*
drocgeriit, 114*b*
drochoberor, 104*a*, 114*b*
drok, 114*b*
dug, 110*a*
dyghow, 110*a*
dyscyblon, *pl.*, *v.* discyplys
dyscyplys, *pl.*, *v.* discebel, 101*a*
dyskas, 101*b*
dysky, 101*b*
dyspyth, 101*b*
dyth, *v.* deth, 110*a*
dywalow, *pl.*, *v.* dewolow, 101*b*

eddrek, 116*a*
edrege, 116*a*
eglos, 101*b*
ehoc, 102*a*
el, *v.* ail, eyll, 99*a*
elerhc, 107*a*
elin, 110*b*
emperiz, *fem.* 102*b*
emperur, 102*b*
encois, 103*a*
enef, 107*a*
er, 115*b*
ereu, 107*a*
ermit, 102*a*
erv, 107*a*
escop, 102*a*

estren, 104*a*
eunhinsic, 118*b*
eur, *v.* owr, 99*b*
eyll, *v.* ail, el, 99*a*

fadic, 102*b*
falhun, 102*a*
fall, 102*a*
fallens, 102*a*
fellet, *v.* guin-fellet, 102*a*
fenester, 102*a*
fenochel, 102*a*
feth, *v.* fyth, 102*a*
ficbren, 102*a*
finweth, 102*a*
fiol, 104*b*
firmament, 102*a*
flair, 102*b*
flam, 102*a*
fo, 102*b*
fodic, 102*a*
fol, foll, 202*a*
forn, 102*b*
frot, 111*b*
funten, *v.* fynten, 102*a*
fur, 102*b*
furf, 102*a*
fyll, 102*a*
fynten, fynteon, *v.* funten, 102*a*
fyth, *v.* feth, 102*a*

galloff, 119*a*
garthou, 117*b*
gauar, 114*a*
geaweil, 102*a*
genys, 110*b*
ghel, 117*b*
gluan, 112*b*
golhy, 119*b*
gorthye, 116*b*
gotheff, 110*a*
gothevell, 110*a*
govynny, 111*a*
goyf, 110*b*
goyn, 106*b*
graf, *v.* gwraff, 110*b*
gras, 102*b*
grat, 102*b*
grauior, 115*a*
grevye, 102*b*
grou, 117*b*
guan (guan ascient), 105*b*
guedeu, 107*a*, 112*b*
guein, 106*b*
* guid, 115*b*
guil, 106*b*, 118*b*
guill, 119*b*
guilter, 107

guinfellet, 102*a*
guins, 114*b*
guir, *v.* gwyr, 106*b*
guirt, 109*b*
guistel, 117*b*
guit, 115*b*
gulat, 116*b*
gur, *v.* priot, 112*b*, 116*a*
gurah, 108*b*
gurthuper, 112*b*
gustle, 117*b*
gwerthe, 116*b*
gwesper, 112*b*
gwlas, 116*b*
gwraff, *v.* graf, 110*b*
gwyls, 119*b*
gwyns, 114*b*
gwyr, *v.* guir, 106*b*

haf, 118*b*
haloin, halein, 111*b*
hanaf, 102*b*
(h) anow, *v.* anow, 107*a*
heligen, 109*a*
hering, 114
heuul, *v.* houl, 112*a*
hiuen, 118*a*
hoch, 118*b*
hoirn, 118*a*
hos, 117*b*
hot, 114
houl, *v.* heuul, 112*a*
huir, *v.* piur, 112*a*
huis, 109*a*
hun, 111*b*
huuel, 102*b*
huueldot, 102*b*
hveger, 111*b*
hvigeren, 111*b*

ieu, 111*a*
incoislester, 103*a*
intre, *v.* yntre, 108*b*
iouenc, *v.* jouonc, 110*b*
iskel, 103*a*

jouonc, *v.* iouenc, 110*b*

kalagueli, 100*a*
kat, 100*b*
keghin, 101*a*
kelegel, 100*a*
kemeskis, kemyskis, 111*b*
kerdyn, *pl.* 100*b*
kigel, 101*a*
kinethel, 110*b*
kog, 101*a*
kyniaf, 110*b*

lad, 103*a*

lader, ladar; *pl.* ladron, laddron, 103*a*
lagat, 118*a*
lagas, 118*a*
lait, 108*b*
lear, *v.* ler, 118*a*
legest, 103*a*
leic, 103*a*
len, *v.* leun, 111*a*
ler, *v.* lear, 118*a*
leu, 103*a*
leun, *v.* len, 111*a*
lilie, 103*a*
litheren, 103*a*
liuer, *v.* luffrow, 103*a*
liuor, 114*a*
logel, 103*a*
lor, 118*a*
loven, 118*a*
luffrow, *pl.*, *v.* lieur, 103*a*
lugarn, 103*a*
lyw, 114*a*

mab, *v.* aflauar, 118*b*
mair, 103*a*
maister, 103*a*
malou, 103*a*
manach, 103*b*
manaes, 103*b*
mans, 103*b*
mantel, 103*b*
marth, 103*b*
medhec, 103*b*
medhecnaid, 103*b*
mel, 108*b*
menistror, 103*b*
menit, meneth, 108*b*
menough, 110*a*
meras, 103*b*
mesclen, 114
mester, *v.* maister, 103*a*
metin, 108*b*
milin, 119*b*
minfel, 103*b*
mis, 111*a*
modereb, 111*a*
mols, 103*b*
moroin, 119*b*
moyrbren, 103*b*
muis, 103*b*
mynny, 111*a*

nader, 114*a*
neid, 114*a*
nevor, 104*a*
noi, 114*a*
noit, 114*a*
noyth, 116*a*

ober, 104*a*
oberor, 104*a*
ogas, 109*a*
oin, 109*b*, 111*b*
oleu, 104*a*
oleubren, 104*a*
oliphans, 102*a*
or, 102*b*
ors, 106*b*
owr, 99*b*
oys, 109*a*

padelhoern, 104*b*
palf, 104*a*, 111*b*
parchemin, 104*b*
parth, 104*a*
paun, 104*b*
peber, 101*a*
penakyll, 104*b*
perbren, 104*b*
pesadow, *pl.*, 104*b*
pesy, 104*b*
peynys, 104*b*
pinbren, 104*b*
pirgirin, 104*b*
pisc, 104*b*, 114*a*
piscadur, 104*b*
piur, *v.* huir, 112*a*
plentye, 104*b*
plufoc, 104*b*
plui, 104*b*
pluuen, 104*b*
pobel, pobyll, *v.* popel, 105*a*
pol, 104*a*
pons, 105*a*
popei, 101*a*
popel, *v.* pobel, pobyll, 105*a*
porchel, 105*a*
porth, 105*a*
porthas, 105*a*
porthow, 105*a*
poruit, 104*a*
pow, 104*a*
powesough, 104*b*
poys, 104*b*
praysys, 105*a*
prefis, previs, 105*a*
prif, 110*a*
prins, pryns, 105*a*
princis, *pl. v.* prins, 105*a*
priot (gur priot), *v.* gur, 116*a*
profuit, 105*a*
profusy, *pl. v.* profuit, 105*a*
pronteryon, *pl. v.* prounder, 105*a*
prounder, 105*a*

redior, 114

rethyskas, 130
rewerthys, 130
rewresse, 130
roche, 114
rud, 111*b*
ruid, 105*b*
ruif, 105*b*
rute, 105*b*
ruy, 114*a*

sach, 105*b*
saw, 105*b*
sawye, 105*b*
scauel, 105*b*
scod, 113*b*
scol, 105*b*
scolheic, 105*b*
screfe, 105*b*
scriuen, 105*b*
scriuiniat, 105*b*
scriuit, 105*b*
scudel, scudell, 105*b*
seithum, 105*b*
sened, 106*a*
seth, 108*b*
settyas, 112*a*
setva, 112*a*
sibuit, 105*b*
sicer, 106*a*
skentyll, *v.* skyntyll, 105*b*
skientoc, 105*b*
skyntyll, 105*b*
snod, 118*b*
snoden, 118*b*
soler, 106*a*
sols, 106*a*
spirit, 106*a*
steuel, 106*a*
stol, 106*a*
strail, 106*a*
strailelester, 106*a*
streil, 106*a*
strek, 115
strekis, 115
strevye, 115
strifor, 115
streing, 114
stryff, 115
suif, 105*b*
sull (dew sull), 101*b*
sur, 105*b*

talgel, 100*b*
tarow, 109*b*
taw, 114*b*
tempel, 106*b*
temptye, 116*b*
tenewen, 112*b*
tensons, 106*b*
termyn, 106*b*

Armoric Index. 211

tevolgow, v. tivulgow, 312b
the, 108b
ti, 112a
tist, 106b
tistuin, 106b
tivulgow, v. tevolgow, 112b
tonnel, 106b
trait, 106b
treason, 106b
trech, 106b
trest, 106b
tribet, 106b
trud, 106b
tur, 106b
tustunny, 106b

ugh, 118a
uncorn, 106b
untye, 106b
uy, 112b

vertu, 107b
vuludoc, 116b

y-, 131
yd, 108b, 121
yffarn, yfforn, 103a
yntre, v. intre, 108b
yonk, 110b
yorch, 108b

Armoric.

ael, v. el, hel, 99a
ampeig, 102b
aneualet, 99a
apostol, 99a, 114
appetaff, 104b
applicquet, v. em, 99a
archescob, 102a
argant, 99b
aour, 99b
auber, v. ober, 104a
auel, 107b
auiel, 102a

badez, 99b
ben(n)iguet, 100a
bennoez, 100a
beo, 109b
beuaf, 109b
bezaff, 112
bizif, 112
brech, 108a
breuder, pl., 109b
bud, 117a
buez, buhez, 109b

cador, 100b
cam, 110a
christen, 100b
clezef, 108a
cloarec, 100b
coar, 100b
coffes, 101a
coma(e)zreset, 101a
comance, 101a
compizrien, 101a
concedis, 101a
coulm, 100b
craf, 117b
cref, creff, 117b
cridif, 108a
criff, 117b
crocadur, 101a
croeer, crouer, 101a
cruel, 101a
cusul, 101a
cuzet, 110a

dafnet, daffnet, 101b
daffny, 101b
decedy, 101b
derch, 113a
deiz v. diziou, 110a
despez, 101b
desquebl, 101b
-dèt, 124
di, 108b
dinoul, 101b
difen, 101b
diner, 101b
dimalicc, v. diualicc, 103a
disguiblion, 101b
disquennet, 101b
disquif, 101b
disprisonet, 105a
diualicc, v. dimalicc, 103a
diuiner, 101b
diziou, pl., v. deiz, 110a
doan, 112
doe, 110a
doen, 112
doetaf, 101b
doetanc, 101b
douet, 101b
douetaf, 101b
drein, pl., 115b
dreist, 109b

ed, 121
el, v. ael, hel, 99a
elin, 110b
em (em em appliquet) 99a
emtennet, 106b
enef, 107a
enes, 108b
enterraf, 103a

entre, 108b
esper, 106a
estonaff, 102a
euel, 109a
euffrou, pl. v. oberou, auber, 104a
ez, 131

falc'houn, 102a
fall, 102a
feunteun, feunten, pl. feuntenyon, 102a
fez, feiz, 102a
finisaf, 102a
finuez, 102a
flerius, 102b
foll, 102a
forest, 102a
fos, foss, 102b
foultr, 102b
fruez, 102b
fur, 102b

gallaf, 119a
ganet, 110b
glin, 119b
glisi, 117b
gloan, 112b
goestlas, 117b
gouaff, 110b
gousper, 112b
gouzaf, gouzaff, 110a
graf, v. groaf, 110b
grif, v. groaff, 110b
groaff, v. graf, gruif, griff, 110b
gruif, 110b
guelchi, 119b
guent, 114b
guir, 106b

haff, 118b
haiarn, v. hoiarn, 118a
hanu, 107a
hastomp, 102b
hel, v. ael, el, 99a
hent, 118b
histren, 104a
hoiarn, v. haiarn, 118a
hun, 111b

iffam, 103a
iustice, 103a

kaoter, 100a
kemmeski, 111b

lagat, 118a
lann, 118a

lealtet, 103a
lech, 103a
leiffriou, 103a
len, leun, 111a

manc, 103b
manen, 103b
martir, 103b
maru, 111a
maruaill, 103b
menaf, mennaf, v. minif, 111a
merch, 119b
mesfectouryen, 103b
mester, 103a
millic, 103a
minif, v. menaf, 111a
ministren, 103b
mir, 103b
miret, 103b
miro, 103b
musur, 103b

nation, 104a
nezaff, 103b
nifer, v. niuer, 104a
niuer, v. nifer, 104a
noaz, 116a
noter, 104a

obediant, 104a
ober, v. auber, 104a
oberau, pl. v. ober, 104a
oferen, pl. offerennou, 104a
ohen, 118a
ordren, 104a

paradis, paradoes, 104a
parfetaff, 104b
parz, v. perz, 104a
pechet, pl. pechedou, 104b
peden, pl. pedennou, 104b
penedour, 104b
peoryen, pl., 104b
perz, v. parz, 104a
peuch, 104b
pidif, pidiff, 104b
plen, 104b
pligadur, 104b
ploeys, 104b
ploi, v. plue, plueu, 104b
plue, plueu, v. ploi, 104b
poan, pl. poanyou, 104b
pomell, 105a
porz, 105a
porzit, 105a
pou, 104a
poues, 104b
prelat, 105a
preservo, 105a
prestis, 105a
prezec, 105a
priet, 116a
proffe, prouffe, 105a
psaulter, 105a

querchat, querchit, 100b

ra-, 130
recommant, 105b
reiz, v. rez, 114b
renaff, 105b
rento, 105b
reol, 105b

rez, v. reiz, 114b
roed, 105b
roen, 105b

sacrileig, 105h
saludomp, 105b
sant, 105b
sarmoner, 106a
sceurt, 106a
scler, 100b
scoet-, scoit-, 109a
sebeliaf, 105b
sent, pl. v. sant, 105b
sin, 106a
soav, 105b
soingaf, 106a
soliter, 106a
soutenet, 106a
speret, 106a
squient, 105b
stat, 106a

tardomp, 106a
tempel, 106b
teniff, 106b
test, 106b
ti, v. ty, 112a
trindet, 106b
tron, 106b
ty, v. ti, 112a

úasal, gen. v. us, 118a
urz, 104a
us, 118a

vicc, 107b

ylis, 101b

CELTIC INDEX TO PHONOLOGY IN IRISH.

Gaulish and old Celtic.

ande-, 143
are-, 139, 164
arêmoricos, 165
ate-, 139
dumno-, 139
ech, 139
epo-, 139, 161
Esu-nertus, 139
κομοντόριος, 150
νεμητον, 139
Nerto-marus, 139
Octodurus, 139
Orgetorix, 139
ver-, 162, 163
vergo-bretus, 139
Vernemetis, 139

Irish.

[The Modern Irish words are printed in Italics, the Old and Middle Irish in Roman letters.]

a, á, 159
a, 160
abair, 137
abás, 165
aca, 141, 155
acaldam, accaldam, acaltam, 143, 144, 145
acarthar, 147, 160
accomallte, acomaltae, 147
accursagad, 159
achésta, 159
ad-, 137
adarc, 143
adbeir, 137
adcomaltar, 147
adgládathar, note, 144
adgladur, note, 144
adharc, 143
adhradh, gen. adhartha, 143, 149
admuim, 145
adrad, 143
æcaillse, 139
æcolsa, 139
aedparthi, 135
áes, 159
agallam, 143, 145
aggnim, 159
aice, 141
aichti, 147, 148
aicnete, 149
aïd-, 139
aïdchuïmthe, 147
aige, 141
aïle, 140, 157
aïliu, dat. masc., 157
aïmsear, 140
aïmser, 140
aïnmm, 140, 142, note, 142, 158
aïnm, 158
aïnm, 140, 142
aïr, 139, 165, 166
air, 164
air, note, 137
aïrchinn, 165
Airdeasbog, 159
aïre, 165
aïrüch, 165
aïri, note 138, 165
áirib, note 138
aïrillti, 147
áirium, note 138
airiuibsi, note 138
aïriumm, 165
aïrriu, note 138, 141
airthër, 165
aiste, 141
aïth-, 137, 139
aithdheanam, 150
aithne, pl. aitheanta, 148
aithtadhte, 150
alaïle, 156
alaïli, gen. masc., 157
alaïliu, dat. 157
Alba, 145
Alban, gen. M.I.; dat. Albain, 145
Alpa, gen. Alpan, acc. Alpaï-n, M. I., 145
ambés, 159
ambrotte, 149
amires, 164
amiressach, 164
amprom, 162
ammi, note 142
an, 162
an, 140
a (n), 140
an (n), 140
añ, 159
anaïr, 140, 165
anam, 142
ananman, 159
anasberthar, 147
anasbiursa, 160
andeaghaidh, 143
an dorogbid, 137
angutas, 149
aniendæ, 149
animm, 142, note 142
anm̄aïmm note 157
anm̄ambi, note 157
anmammi, note 157
anm̄anbi, 157 note
anmande, 149
anoir, 140
ant, 140, 144
aon, 140, 157, 158
apair, M. I., 137
apectha, 159
Apilogdo, gen., note 139
apir, 137
apredchimme, 160
ar, 137, note 137, 166
ar, 164, 165, 166
ar', 165
arań, 165
arb (root), 139
archënn, 165
archiünn, 165
árd, 143, 146
ardd, 143, 146
argur, 165
armbrethre, 159
arloure-ni, 159
arü, 159
arna, 147
arnaïb, 165
arnét, 159
arndiis, 159
arnóib, 156
arnóibbriàthraïb, 156
aromfoimfea, 159
arosaïlcther, 147
arrocar, 160
arsate, 149
arse, 165
arsid, gen. 149
arśodaïn, 160
arsóire-ni, 159
art, v. ardd, 146
as, aś, 165
asagnintar, 147
ascnam, 159
asind-, 165
asrirther, 147
asrulenta, 147
ass, 165
asta, 141
ataïmět, 145

atbaïl, 144, 151
atbeir, 137
atdubelliub, 160
athdóidhte, 150
athir, 138, 163
athscribend, 151
aththaoiseach, 150
Atilogdo. gen, note, 139
atobcí, 160
atobsegatsi, 160
atomaïg, 144
aŭd-, 141
auë, 141
augtortás, 141, 145
aŭr-, 141
aŭrgabtha, 147

ba, 161
baile, pl. bailte, 148
baïll, 139
baindea, M. I., 151
baintigerna, M. I., 151
baistim, 138
baitsimm, 138
banda, 149
bandachlach, 151
bandálem, 151
bandea, 151, 159
bandechuïn, 151
banscala, 151
banterismïd, 151
bárd, 154
barŭ, v. farŭ, 159
baŭll, 139
baŭllu, 139
beag, 145
béarla, v. beurla, 138
bec, becc, 145.
beirim, 137
béisti, 135
bélre, 138
bendachad, 143
bendacht, 143
benachadh, M. I., 143
bennacht, M. I., 143
beos, 142
ber (root) = Skr. brû, 137
bérli, 138
berrthaïd, 150
berthir, 147
bessti, béssti, v. beïsti, 135
bëtha, 139
bëtho, gen. sing., 139
beurla, 138
bheirim, 137
bheos, 142
biad, gen. biith, biid, 139
biasta, M. I., 135
biast, M. I., 135
biddixnugud, 151

bídh, 139
bindd, bind, 143, 146
binn, 143, 146
bithgaïrddi, 149
boïll, 139
bolad, 149
bolgg, bolc, 143, 146
bolg, 143, 146
boltigetar, 149
borb, 143, 146
borp, 143
brága, 143
brágha, 143
breac, gen. bric, 145
*brecc, 145
breth, 139
briáthraib, v. arnóibbriáth-
  raïb, 156
brithëm, 142
bró. pl. bróinte, 148
buïdh, 161
brŭdë, 143
buidhe, 143
bŭllu, 139
burbë, 146
burpë, 146

cách, 137, 156, 157, 161
caïch, gen. v. cach, 157, 159
caïll, 140
cailleach, 140, 143
caillëch, gen. cailligbe,
  140, 143
cáin, 140
caïndlóïr, 143
cáinduthracht, 151
caingním, 157
cainscél, 151
caintaïdlëch, 151
cáinteïst, 151
cáintoïmtiu, 151
cáintöl, 151
caisc, 161
caira, 140
caïrïgthir, 147
caoga 140
caoin, 140
caol, 140
caora, 140
carbad, 135, 145
carbat, v. carput, 135
carpat, M. I., 135, 145
capuil, 154
carput, 135
cathrur, 157
céad, 145, 158
céadna, 143, 145
ceann, 159
cech, 156, 157, 159
ceithre, 158

cen, 137
cenalpande, 145, 149
cene, 142
cenéuïl, gen., 157
cenélu, ceneoll, cenéolu,
  ceniul, ceneóïl, dat.,
  157, 159
cënn, cenn, 139, 150, 161
cenodfil, 159
centat, 150
ceól, pl. céolta, 148
césad, césath, gen. césta,
  césto, 148, 159
cessaïr, dat., 159
cét, 145
cethargaraït, 149
cethir, 161
cethirchét, 158
cétnë, 145, 156, 162
cétni, 157
Chaisil, 159
cheana, 142
chenélaïg, 157
chésta, chésto, 158
chétbutho, dat., 159
chétni, dat. neut., 157
chétnai, gen., 157
chétnïdiu, dat., 157
chlann, decl., 155
chli, dat., 157
chluas, dat. chluais, 158
chollno, 158
cholnïde, 157
chos, 159
chrann, 157
chrann, 158
chuca, acc. pl. 139, 141
chugam, 139, 142
chuice, 141
chuige, 141
chumachtïg, 160
cia, 137
ciàll, 158, 159
cib é, cip é, 137
cinninfïl, 160
cinnïud, 149
claar, dat. 159
claïdeb, 142
claïdhem, 142
claïnne, 140
cland, 143, 161
clann, 143
clocc, 145
clog, 145
cloinne, 140
cluain, pl. cluainte, 148
cnoc, 145
cnocc, 145
co (ad, cum) 137, 142
co (donec, ut) 137

coaga, 140
coatomsnassar, 159
cocarti, 147
codhladh, codladh, 143, 145
cogadh, pl. *cogtha*, 149
cofordumthésīd-se, 159
cóīc, 140, 161, note 161
cóica, 140
cóil, 140
coill, pl. *coillte*, 140, 148
coin-, 150
coinneal, 143
colann, 140
colinn, 140
colna, 143
com', 165
comalnad, *note* 144, 163
comalnadar, 163
comalnamar, 163
comallnithe, 163
comchésad, 165
comchlante, 147
coṅ, 160, 165
con-, coin-, 150
conde, 149
condibfeīl, 160
condigénte, 147
condiuiti, 165
condumfel, 159
confesta, 147
conintorgáitar, 147, 160
connarcas, 143
connáruchretesi, 147
conrochretesi, 147
consaīn, *acc.*, 157
conucbad, 144
conulintae, 147
cóosnada, 165
corcur, 161
Cormac, note, 142
coro, 137
corp, 145, 157
Corpimaqvas, *note*, 142
coṡ, 165
cosa, pl. 159
coséitchi, 165
cosmil, 165
cosnadh, gen. *cosanta*, 148, 149
cot-, 144
cotaocbat, cotaucbat, 136
cotlad, *dat.* cotlŭd, 145
cotobsechfīder, 160
cotondelcfam, 144
crann, 161
creidim, 145
creitfess, *acc.* 157
cren, 161
cretim̄, 145

creītme, 159
crīdé, 143
crīdi, *dat.*, 159
crŏch, 139
crŏchad, *gen.* crŏchtho, 139, 148
crochtha, *note* 148
crochthe, 148
croidhe, 143
crot, 145
cruit, 145
cruīthnechta, 159
cu, pl. *cointe*, 148, 149
cuc', 165
cucci, 165
cuccu, *acc. pl.*, 139
cuccumu, 139
cúig, 140, 158
cuingeis, 161
cumactib, 165
cundrad, 143
cundradh, M. I., 143
cunradh, gen. *cunnartha*, 143, 149
cúrsagad, *gen.* cúrsagtha, 148
cutseítchi, 159

dá, 138, 158
dagimrat, *note* 148
dag- im̄ráta, drog-im̄ráto, 148
dall-ciach, 150
daṁ, 142, note 143
damnae, *note* 136
daṅ, 158
dáníg'ŭd, *gen.* dánīgthĕa, 148
daonna, 149
daóradh, gen. *daórtha*, 149
darc, (*root*) (=Gr. δέρκω), 143
de, 153, 155, 156
dealbh, 143
déanadh, gen. *déanta*, 148, 149
dearbh, note 143, note 145
debthach, 150
debuīth, *dat. pl.* debthib, 148
dechrugud, *dat.*, 159
deich, 158
deirim, 137
déntí, 147
dephthigim, 150
derbb, *note* 143
derbthaīr, 147
deṡiu, 160
d'faghbáil, d'fágbháil, 136
d'feartháin, 150

dí, 141, 158, 159
dià, *gen.* déī, dé, 139, 152
dian, 138
diannaiper, 137
dianeprem, 137
dicheannaim, note 150
diltŭth, 150
díguttai, *dat.*, 157
diṅgutai, *dat.*, 157
dintecnatatu, *dat.*, 153
dintrediu, *dat.*, 153
díobh, v. *dóibh*, 141, 155
diombuan, note, 150
diombuidheach, note, 150
diomolaim, 150
díoṁór, note, 150
díothoghluidhe, note, 150
dlútai, 147
do, 157, 158, 159
do-, 137, 159
do, 141, 153, 155, 156, 159
doaīr (d'air), 144
doaīrci, 144
doaīth, 135, 144
doaithmne, *note*, 135
doan, 138
doaŭrchanim, 165
doberrthe, 147
dobim̄chomartt, 147
dobiur, 137
dobtromma, 160
do-chantain, 150
dofius, v. du-fius, 160
dofoirde, 143
dogéntar, 147
dóibh, v. *diobh*, 141, 155
doīlbthīd, 150
doiṁin, 142
doimmfolung, 158
dóinde, 149
doinscannsom, 146, 151
dom-, 142, *note*, 143
*dömaīn, 142
dombersom, 137
domthoschid, 159
dömun, 139
don, 157
dond-, 158
donelltar, 147
dontorŭd, *dat.*, 153
doopīr, 144
dorónta, 147
dorurgabtha, 147
doscéulaim, 151
dosenmáthar, 159
dosṁbera, 160
dothabaīrt, 159
dothógbháil, 136
drogím̄ráto, 148

droġscéla, 151
du-, 151
dubhart, 137
dubhras, 137
duñus, *v.* do-ñus, 160
*dunad, 149
dúnattae, 149
Dúnpeleder, 151
dŭs, dúus, 160

é-, 146
éa, éi-, 150
eadoiṁin, 146
éadtrom, 146
éagcóir, 146
eagna, 145
éan, decl. 155
eardhairc, v. *urdhairc*, note 150
eas-, 150
easbha, gen. pl. *easbhadh*, note 143, note 145
easbog, 138
easpog, M.I., 138
eatorra, 141
ech, 139, 161
écintĕch, 149
eclustai, 147
ĕcne, 144, 145
écéĭr, 146
ŏd- 139
ĕdpart, *v.* idpart, 144
éi-,
eibliṁ, 145
eidir, 141, 145
eile, 140
eiscsende, 149!
eĭsséĭrgi, *gen.* 159
éistim, 138
éitsimm, 138
én, 164
epeir,
epert, 148
eperthe, 147
eperthi, 147
epertith, 149
ĕpĭl, 144
epir, epiur, epur, 137
*ĕplĭmm, 145
epscop, 138
ĕr-, 139, 164
ĕrbaĭd, 139
ĕrbĭd, 139
ĕrchoĭlĭud, 148
erend (tír-n-erend), 159
· erriu, erru, *note*, 138
erunn, *note* 138
erutsu, *note* 138
es-, 146

esartaĭd, 149
ĕsib, 165
ĕtal, 139
ĕtar, 145
ĕtarru, 141
ĕtarscarad, *gen.* ĕtarscartha, 148
ĕtha, 139
etruṁ, 146

fácab, 136
fad, 145
fág, 136, 137
fagbas, fagbus, 136
fagebtis, 136
fagh, 136, 137
faghaim, 136, 137
faghbáil
faghbait, faghbat, M. I., 136
faghbháil,
fair, *note*, 137
falt, 145
farcláu, 159
fardiŭll, *dat.* 157
farṅ, *v.* barṅ, 159
farnintliucht, 159
fealsaṁ
fĕar, 140
fear, 140, decl. 155
feara, voc. pl. v. *féar*, 157
fearaibh, dat. v. *féar*, 154
feardha, 149
fearg, 143, 146
feărr, 140
fealsaṁ, 142
fĕlsub, 139, 142
fĕr, 140
fĕr, 140
ferc, 143, 146
ferce, *dat.*, 159
ferr, 140
fescor, fescar, 161
fichĕ, *gen.* fichĕt, 158, *note* 158
fiche, gen. *fichead*, nom. *fichid*, 158
fíntan, 151
fir, nom. pl. v. *féar*, 157
fíreanta, 149
fo-, 137, 162
foácbat, 136
ḟochun, *dat. masc.* 157
fodlaĭdi, *dat.*, 157
fogbaidetu, 136
foghébha, 136
foghlaim, 143
foglaĭm, 143
fogoir, *dat.* 157
foĭsĭgŭd, 148

fointreb, 151
foir, *note* 137, 163
foirbthe, 163
foircheann, 163
foircthe, 147, *note* 147
foirib, *note* 137
foĭsĭte, *v.* hifoĭsĭte, *dat.* 159
folnibthe, 147
fomám, *dat.* 159
fomchridichfider-sa, 159
fomĭrfidersa, 159
fonsegar, 160
for, 137, *note* 137, 157, 160, 162, 163, 166
foracab, 136
foraib, forib, *note* 137
forbanda, 147
forcanim, 163
forcanti, 147
forcenn, 163
forcetal, 163
forchain, 163
forchanim, 163
forchongair, forcongair, 163
forchongrim, forcongrim, 163
forchun, 163
forcongur, 163
fordomchomaĭther, 159
fordubcechna, 160
form, formm, *note* 137
forndobcanar, 160
forṅgarti, 147, 148
forraind, *note* 138
forrn, fornn, *note* 137
forru, *note* 137, 141
forserce, 159
fort, *note* 137
forthéit, fortéit, 163, 165
fós, 142
fosmachtu, 146
foṡodĭn, 160
fŏt, 145
fotrácbussa, 136
frecdaĭrc, 143
frecṅdaĭrc, *dat.*, 157
frecre, 144
fri, 137, 160, 162
fricach, 165
friṡ, 165
fris, 165
frisbiur, 165
frisdúntar, 147
frislond, *acc.*, 168
friss, frissin-, 165
fristacuirther, 147
frit-, fritt-, 151
frĭtammiurat, 144

frith', 162, 165
frithaĭdechtæ, 151
frithcheist, 165
frithtasgat, 151
fritumthiàgar, 159
fudömaĭn, fudumaĭn, 142
fuĭl, *dat.*, 158
fuil, 159
fuiri, *note* 137
fuirib, *note* 137
fúithe, 141
furastar, 147
furib, *note* 137
furnn, *note* 137
fútha, 141

gú, 137
gab, (*root* "capere"), 136
gabaĭl, 140
gabar, 162
gabál, 162
gabháil, 140
gabhaim, 137
gabimn-se, 137
gach, 137
gáith, gúid, 140
gallda, 149
gan, 137, 154, 155
gaoth, 140
gentar, 147
génthir, 147, 148
gheibhim, 137
gibe, 137
go (to, with), 137
go (that), 137
go-n-aibraim, 137
grianda, 149
grièntaĭrissëm, 151
guĭdĭmse, 152
gur, 137
gutte, gutae, 149

hícc, 158
hiclaar, *v.* claar, 159
hifoĭsĭte, *v.* foĭsĭte, 159
hipersonaĭb, *v.* persin, 156
hirës, 159
hisintórunt, *dat.*, 153
hitogarmim *v.* togarmim
hitosüg, *dat.*, 158
hontecnatatu, *dat.*, 153
honuntogaitarni, 147, 160
hóthoĭl, 165
huàndlúĭthi, *dat.*, 157
huàthati, *acc. pl. fem. v.*
uathath, 149
huàtigitir, 149

iar, 157, 162

iarfaĭchthëo, iarfaĭgtho,
dat. pl., iarfaĭgthib, 148
iarfaĭgĭd, iarfĭgĭd, 148, 165
iarma, 165
iarmbaĭthiŭs, 165
iarmafoich, 165
iarm(s)uidigthe, 165
iarṁ, 160, 165
iarsintaĭrgiriu, *dat.*, 153
iartimnu, 165
iasg, 163
icachthir, *dat. neut.*, 157
id-, 139
idir, 154, 155
Idpart, *v.* ĕdpart, 144
idpart, 135, 145
idpart, 151
il, 163
ilar, 163
ildáni, 151
ilde, 163
illestur, 159
iltoĭmddën, 151
im, 142
imbed, 143
imbrádud, iṁrádud, 148
imbráti, iṁráti, *nom. pl.,*
acc. iṁrátiŭ, 148
imcabthi, 147
imcasti, 147
imchuĭmriüg, 159
imdhíden, note, 150
imdibthe, 147, *note*, 147
imm, 140, 142, *note*, 142
immfolung, *dat. v.* do im.
158
immidforling, 159
immumforling, 159
imrádud, *v.* imbradud, 148
iṁrátiŭ, *acc. v.* imbrati,
148
in', 165
iṅ, 140, 165
in, 140, 157, 160, 162
in-, 140, 160
inchamthuisil, 157
incholnĭgŭd, *gen.* incholnĭchtho, incholnĭgthëa
148
inchosc, *note*, 151, 165
inchruĭnn, *gen.*, 157
inchuĭmriüg, 159
incomscribṅdaĭth, 151
ind, 140
ind', 165
ind-, 143, 153, 155
indaërchoĭltëa, *gen. v.*
ĕrchoĭllud, 148
indala, 156

indegaĭd-ú, 143
indfoĭlsĭgthe, 148
indfolaĭd, *gen.*, 157
indidultaĭgae, 150
indiumm, 143, 165
indtogas, 153
indtuĭgther, 147
induini, 153
inghean, 159
ingiŭn, 165
ingor, 143
ingrentĭd, 149
inn-, 155
inna, 157
innte, 141
inse, 160
insenduine, *gen.* intsenduini, 153
insin, 153, 160
inso, 153
inspirto, *gen.* 153
int, 140, 144
int-, 144, 153, 155
intaĭdlich, *gen*, 153
intaĭrmchrutto, *gen.* 153
intesa, *gen.* 153
intinnscana, 146
intísiu, 160
intíthall, 160
intiu, 141
intë, 141
intoĭchther, 147
intonnaĭgĭm, 151
intsamaĭl, 144
intsamuil, 146
intsechtaĭgtha, 148
intsliŭcht, 144, 146
intuisil, *nom. masc. pl.* 153
intursitĭb, 151
iodhbairt, 145
iomad, 143
ion-, 140
ionam, 143
iongnadh, gen. *ionganta*,
148
ionnta, 141
ír-, 139, 164
ĭrchoĭltĭth, 149
ĭrcholluĭd, 149
ire, 164
ireiu, 164
is, 153, 156
isin, 156
isindanmaĭṁ, 157
isindepistil, *dat. fem.* 157
isinóinchorp, *dat. masc.*
157
isintuisiulsin, *dat.* 153
isintuaĭchli, *dat.* 153

isóiri, *dat.* 159
īssintodochidui, *dat.* 153
itarscarthar, 147
itchethir, *nom. pl.* 157
itchóimthecht, 159
īth-, 139
ithim, 162
itossŭch, 165
itsenmáthĭr, 159

la, 160
lăĭm, *dat.* 157
lán, *note* 144, 163
lanad, 163
láne, 163
láni, *dat.* 159
laur, lour, 163
lethau, 163
léine, pl. *léinte,* 141
lia, 163
línad, 163,
linn, pl. *linnte,* 148
líntĭdi, 149
lobrĭgthir, 147
loischthe, 147
lŏth, 139

mac, 145, 151, 159
macc, 145, 161
macthire, 150
mactire, 150, 151
maer. M. I., 140
maini, *pl.,* 140
maĭnistrech, M. I., 139
maith, 140
maldacht, 143
mallacht, 143
maniréltar, 147
manudubfeĭl, 160
maoin, 140
maor, 140
mara, M. I., 139
marbh, 143
marc, 145
marufeste, marrufeste, 147
medóntaĭrismid, 151
meĭte, *gen. fem.,* 157
messe, 160
mi-, 151
miàstar, 147
mĭle, 158
mĭli, 158
mĭstae, 149
mo, 157, 159
mo, 159
mochland, 159
mŏga, 139
moín, pl. *moínté,* 148
monĭstre, 139

móra, 139
mora, 157
mordha, 149
mothol, 159
muĭd, 159
muintir, muintear, 145
muntar, 150
muntir, *dat.,* 159
múntĭth, 149
múnŭd, 149
mŭr, pl. *múrtha,* 149

na, 155
nach, 156, 161
nachibfěl, 160
nadipru, nadipro, 137
na m-ball, 143
nammall, 143
naom, 142
na ructhae, *v.* ructhae
ndeaghaidh, 143
néal, pl. *néalta,* 148
neam, neim, 142
neart, 145
neb-, 142
nebmarbtu, nebmarbtath, *note* 149
nech, 140, 161
necht, 161
neim-, 142
nemed, 139
neoch, noch, 140
nephpiandatu, 157
nert, 139
nertad, *gen.* nerta, 148
něrutsu, 152
ní, 160
níbthá, 160
nidan, 160
nifiàstar, 147
nígette, 147
nilfolad, *acc.,* 158
nimcharatsa, 159
nimdibi, 158
nímptha, 159
nimtha, 159
ní, 160
ninfortéit-ni, 160
nintá, 160
niscartha, 147
nisfetemmar, 160
nísfitir, 160
nistabur, 160
niténat, 160
no, 160
nobearad, 160
nobsóirfa-si, 160
nocretim, 160
nochrochte, 147

nodascara, 160
noí, 158
noĭb, 142
nolintae, 147
nomglantar, 147
nomthachthar, 147, 148, 159
nonchretid-si, 160
nondubcairim-se, 160
nondobsommígětar, 160
nondasoirfěa, 160
nongabthe, 147
nonlíntarni, 147
nonnertarni, 147
nonsóirfěa, 160
nopredchim-se, 160
nosmoidet, 160
nosńguid-som, 160
nudamchrocba, 159
nunsluĭnfemni, 160

o, 151, 159
ó', 157, 158, 165
O'Briain, gen. I. Bhriain, *dat. d'ua Bhriain,* 151
ocht, 139, 158
ocht, 135, 139
od-, 137
óen, 157, 158
oěn, *v.* oin, 140, 141
oena, 157
óenchoĭmdiu, 157
óenchorp, 157
óenchranu, 157
oile, v. eile, 140
oin, 140
óinaĭchthir, 147
oinchorp, 157
olc, 145
olsodaĭn, olsodĭn, 160
ón, 157
ónach, 157
ond, 159
ondóentoisrinn, *dat.,* 157
ontechtaĭriu, *dat.,* 153
óntrédiu, *dat.,* 153
orcaid, 139
orcas, 139
órdha, 149
orm, note 137
orra, ortha, 137, 141
orraibh, note 137, 141
orrainn, note 137, 138, 141
ort, note 137
ortha, 141
ósuidi, *dat. fem.* olsuĭde, 160
óthad, 139
oua, *v.* us, 141

peccad, *gen.* pechtha, *decl.*
  148, 157, 159, 162
persan, 162
persĭn, 156, 157, 159
phersĭn, 157
precept, 162
prím, 162

rad ńdé, 143
raĭnn, 159
ráncatar, M. I., 145
rángas, 145
ré, 162, 164
recach, 157, 165
rechttáĭrcĭd, 151
rect, *dat.*, 159
rélath, rélad, *gen.* rélto, 148
rem, 142
rem', 165
remeperthe, 147
remfoiti, 147
remi, 140, 164, 165
remib, 165
remiepur, 165
remthechtas, 165
rén, 164
reṅ, 160, 165
renaĭrite, 165
ri, 137
riágoĭl, *dat.* 157
righdúinte, 149
ro, 160, 163
robcar-si, 160
robclandad, 160
roberrthe, 147
robfothĭgëd, 160
rodchúrsach, 159
rofestar, 147
roiṁ, 142
roiṁ'si, 153
roiṁe, 141
roimpe, 140, 141, 153
roĭmsi, 141
rolaŭmur, 139
rolín, 163
rolŏmor, 139
roṁam, 140
rompa, 141
romsóir sa, 159
rondasaibset, 160
rondobcarsam-ni, 160
rondpromsom, 159
ronfitĭd-ni, 160
ronsóir, 160
ronsóir-ni, 160
roscarsam, 151
roscomal, 160
rospredach, 160
rostán, 151

rotchechladar, 159
ructhae, 147

sa, 153, 160
sáib, sáeb, sóib, soeb, 140
saĭde, *nom. pl.* saĭdai, 160
saigul, 140
sain, *nom. pl.* saini, *dat.*
  sainib, 156
san, 156
salm, 162
samaltir, 147
saobh, 140
sacghal, 140, 156
saoghalta, 149
sastai, 147
scote, scotae, 149
scoth, 149
scríbthar, 147
*se, 141
se, 153, 160
sé, 158
seacht, 158
seanchus, 156
seanduine, 156
sech, 161
sechim, 161
sechitir, 161
secht, 161
sechtmaine, 161
sechtaĭgŭd, 148
seim, *dat.*, 157
sem, 160
sendŭĭne, 151
sens, ícach-, 157
sentinni, 151
seól, pl. seólta, 148
serbe, *dat.* 159
sgéal, pl. sgéalta, 148
side, 160
sin, 153, 160
siu, *dat.*, 160
*siu, 141
slabrad, 149
slabratae, 149
sluĭntir, 147
so, 153, 160
sodaĭn, 160
sóib, v. sáib,
som, 160
soscéle, 151
šosŭth, *dat. masc.*, 157
sráthatath, -tat, 150
sráthath, 150
sruth, decl. 155
su, 141, 160
suĭdigthir, 147
súil, decl. 155, 159
suĭn, 158
sulbaĭrĭchthe, 147, 148

sulbaĭrĭgŭd, 148
šuperlaĭt, 158

tabaĭrt, 148
tabhraim, 137
tabur, 137
taid-, 135
taidmenader, taidminedar, *note* 136
táin, pl. *táinte*, 148
taĭr-, 144
taĭrci, 144
taĭrmchruthad, gen. taĭrmchrutto, 148, *note*, 148
taĭrmthecht, 165
taĭrngirĭ, 159
taĭth-, 135, 144
taithminedar, *note*, 136
talmande, 149
túnaĭse, 156, *dat. neut.*,
  túnaĭsiu, 157, *dat. fem.*,
  tanaĭsi, 157
táncamar, 145
tar, 142
taraĭs, 165
tarbh, 143
tarcrách, 165
tarmi, 165
tar(s), 141, 165
tarsin-, 165
teanga, pl. *teangtha*, 149
tecnate, 149
teinne, pl. *teinnte*, 148, 149
ténat, 160
tenëd, 159
tenge, 162
ter-, 144
tes-, 144
tesbaĭd, *acc.*, tesbaĭth, *dat.*
  note, 143
tesst, 146
tháĭdbse, *dat.*, 158
tháirse, tháirsi, 141
thángas, 145
thársa, 141
thársta, 141
thógbháil, *v.* dothóg, 136
thoĭl, *dat.*, 158
thóĭsig, *dat.*, 157
thol, 157, 158
thorm, 142
thorrainn, dat. *thorraibh*, 141
thréana, nom. pl. 157
thríuĭn, *gen. masc.*, 157, 158
thúal, 159
thúare, 157
thuisiul, *dat. masc.*, 157

ti-, 135
tí, 141
tiar-, 144
tibradaibh, tipradaibh, 153
tid-, 135
tidbarid, 135
tim-, 144
timm-, 144
timmorte, 147, 148, 149
timnais, M. I., note, 136
timne, note 135
tin-, 144
tind-, 144
tintúth, 151
tionnsgnadh, gen. tionns
  ganta, 148, 149
tipradaibh, v. tibradaibh, 135
tiprait, M. I., 135
tipra, tipru, gen. tiprat, 135
tír, 159
tirthat, 150
tó-, 144
tobar, 135
tócbaimm, 145
tóg, 136, 137
togarmim, dat., 157
tógbhaídh, 136
tógbhaim, 145
toirthich, toirthig, gen., 157
toirse, 159
tóisich, dat. fem., 157
tol, 158
tór-, tor-, 144
toradh, pl. toirthe, 149
torbe, 158
torunn, 141
tréana, v. thréana, 157
treasa, 157
trebaire, 158
tremdírgedar, 165
tremi, 165
tresin-, 165
tresinfuil, 160
trí, 160, 162
trí, 158
trian (d-trian), 158
tricha, nom. pl. trichit, 158
trichretim, 160
triit, 165
triocha, gen. triochad, nom.
  pl. triochaid, 158
triotha, 141
tris, 165
tríthe, 141
trithemel, 160, 165
trócaire, 145

tú-, 144
tuaithe, 159
tuar-, 144
tuáti, 149
tuáth, 149
tuisel, 139
tur-, 144
tussu, 160

ua, v. oua, 141
uad, 165
uadfialichthi, 165
uailbe, v. uall
uaim, 142
uaimm, 142, note 142
uair, decl., 155
uaiste, 141
uaithe, 141
uáll, gen. uailbe, 143
uasta, 141
uatha, 141
uathaib, dat. pl. v. uáthath, 149
uathate, 149
uathath, uathad, 139, 149
ughdar, 141, 145
uile, 156
uilib, 165
uim, 142
uimb'si, 153
uimpe, 141, 153
uirre, uirri, note 137, 141
um, 140, 142
umam, 140
umpa, 141, 145
urdhairc, v. eardhairc, note 150

Welsh.

adaned (plur.), 164
adar, v. atar, 164
actinet, 164
ahanaff, v. ohonaf, note 142
atar, v. adar, 164
bwystuil, 135
cant-, 144
e-, 139
ebawl, 139, 161
ed-, 139
ederyn, v. eterinn, 164
enw, note, 142
eterinn, v. ederyn, 164
etncoilhaam, 164
heb, 161
im v. ym, note 143
laws, 163
liaus, 163

llawer, 163
llawn, 163
lled, v. llyd (llet), 163
lledanu, 163
llewni, 163
lliaws, 163
lloneit, 163
lluossyd, 163
llyd, v. lled, 163
neuat, neuad, 139,
nerth, 139
ohonaf, v. ahanaff, note 142
orgiat, 139
ucher, 161
uith, v. wyth, 139
ûn, 141
wyth, v. uith, 139
y-, 139
yd-, 139
ym-, v. im, note 143

Kymrie.

ar-, 139, 164
at-, 139
*ep, 161
er, 164
et-, 139
gafar, 162
gu, 162
guo, 162
guor, 162, 163
gurth, 162
hep, 161
kafael, 162
laun, 163
litan, 163
llydan, 163
map, 161
nep, 161
paup, 161
penn, 161
petguar, 161
pimp, 161
pisc, v. pysg, 163
plant, 161
pren, 161
prenu, 161
pysg, v. pisc
rac-, 164
yr, 164

Cornish.

ebol, 139
enef, eneff, note 142
escop, 133
gwesper, 116

(h)anow, *note* 142
hethen, 164
idne, 164
leas, 163
len, leun, 163
llewer, 163
loar, 163
loure, 163
luas, 163
nerth, 139

thym, *note* 143
war, 164
y-, 139
ydnic, 164

Armoric.

arvorek (Breton), 165
dif, diff, *note* 143

e-, 139
enef, eneff, *note* 142.
ez-, 139
gousper, 161
hanu, *note* 142
leun, 163
nerz, 139
war, 164

CORRIGENDA.

[The following have been noticed in preparing the Indices Verborum.]

Page 102 *b*, line 13 from the bottom, P. or. *should be* P. or.
,, 110 *a*, line 2 from the top, there should not be a full point after *cam.*
,, 121, line 8 from the bottom, *for the reference* (I. 177, 180) *read* (pp. 74, 77).
,, 126, line 4 from the bottom, *for* noun *é, sí, ed*, etc., *read* nom. *é*, etc.
,, 141, line 9 from the top, *for the reference*, p. 119, *read* p. 127.
,, 158, line 12 from the bottom, for *trochaid* read *triochaid*.
,, 158, line 4 from the bottom, *for* toll *read* tol.

www.ingramcontent.com/pod-product-compliance
Lightning Source LLC
Chambersburg PA
CBHW032109220426
43664CB00008B/1193